The Age
of Mass
Migration

The Age
of Mass
Migration

Causes
and Economic
Impact

TIMOTHY J. HATTON

JEFFREY G. WILLIAMSON

New York   Oxford · Oxford University Press   1998

Oxford University Press

Oxford   New York
Athens   Auckland   Bangkok   Bogota   Bombay
Buenos Aires   Calcutta   Cape Town   Dar es Salaam
Delhi   Florence   Hong Kong   Istanbul   Karachi
Kuala Lumpur   Madras   Madrid   Melbourne
Mexico City   Nairobi   Paris   Singapore
Taipei   Tokyo   Toronto   Warsaw

and associated companies in
Berlin   Ibadan

Published by Oxford University Press, Inc.
198 Madison Avenue, New York, New York 10016

Oxford is a registered trademark of Oxford University Press

Library of Congress Cataloging-in-Publication Data
Hatton, T. J.
   The age of mass migration : causes and economic impact /
   by Timothy J. Hatton and Jeffrey G. Williamson.
      p.   cm.
   Includes bibliographical references and index.
   ISBN 0-19-511651-8
1. Emigration and immigration—Economic aspects—HIstory.   2. Alien labor—History.
3 Labor market—History.   I. Williamson, Jeffrey G., 1935–   .   II. Title.
JV6217.H37   1997
331.12'791'09034—dc21   97-1305

9 8 7 6 5 4 3 2 1

Printed in the United States of America
on acid-free paper

For our wives and best friends
Alison Booth
Nancy Williamson

Acknowledgments

This book began while Hatton was a visitor at Harvard University in 1988–1989. The collaboration was launched by our research on the integration of rural-urban and regional labor markets as national economic development took place. Very early we realized that most of the same questions could be posed about the evolution of international labor markets during the age of mass migration from around 1850 to World War I. Furthermore, as contemporary debate over American immigration policy heated up in the 1990s, the global dimensions of the problem seemed to take on even more urgency. Even though much had been written on the mass migrations, we thought that a comprehensive and integrated economic account had yet to appear. In 1990, we laid out the research agenda on which this book is based. It turned out that a full understanding of the economic fundamentals driving the mass migrations and of their impact took much longer than either of us had anticipated. Whether seven years is a fair price to pay for that achievement we leave the reader to judge.

We have incurred many intellectual debts along the way. As the research grew in scope, we were joined by others in the collaboration, and they deserve a share of the credit for the outcome, especially for chapters 9 and 10. Our debt to Kevin O'Rourke is especially deep since he did the lion's share of the computable general equilibrium modeling (and estimation) that forms the heart of much of the empirical analysis underlying those two chapters. Another large piece of the empirical analysis in chapter 10 is based on a collaboration involving Alan Taylor. In addition, George Boyer was involved in the research on Ireland (chapter 9) in which he played a key role in augmenting the wage data for that country. We thank them all for stimulating and productive collaborations, and for allowing us to present the results of our joint enterprise in chapters 9 and 10. They have our affectionate thanks for valuable and constructive comments on other parts of the book as well.

We have benefited greatly from the help and advice of many colleagues and friends who have made insightful comments on our work while in progress, and who have generously shared their data and knowledge of sources. The list is long and it is invidious to single out only a few, but we must. These are Moe Abramovitz, Maria Baganha, Roy Bailey, Dudley Baines, Tommy Bengtsson, George Borjas, Albert Carreras, Barry Chiswick, Melvyn Coles, Roberto Cortés Conde, Don Devoretz, Mike Edelstein, Toni Estevadeordal, Riccardo Faini, Giovanni Federico, Richard Freeman, Betsy Field Hendrey, Francisco Galassi, Hank Gemery, Claudia Goldin, Alan Green, Chris Hanes, Jenny Hunt, Larry Katz, Kyle Kauffman, Cormac Ó Gráda, Pedro Lains, Peter Lindert, Jonas Ljungberg, Gunnar Persson, Leandro Prados, Simon Price, Jaime Reis, Blanca Sanchez-Alonso, Ken Snowden, Alessandra Venturini, Stuart Woolf, and Vera Zamagni. In addition, Williamson acknowledges the lively input received from Don Davis, David Weinstein, and graduate students in a team-taught Harvard trade seminar in the spring of 1994.

We are also grateful to the organizers and sponsors who have given us a prominent place in their conferences where we were able to present our work to critical participants who shaped our thinking. These conferences and meetings include the European Science Foundation Conferences on Migration and Development at Davos (1992), Aghia Pelagia (1994), and Mont Sainte Odile (1996); the Conference on Real Wages and Labour Market Integration at the Bellagio Rockefeller Center (1993); the 11th World Congress of Economic History at Milan (1994); the European Society for Population Economics Conferences at Budapest (1993) and Tilburg (1994); the European School of Historical Economics at Groningen (1995); and the Economic History Association annual meetings at Chicago (1995, where Williamson gave his presidential address). In addition, of course, we have received helpful comments from participants at countless university seminars in both North America and Europe. Williamson is especially anxious to thank graduate student and faculty participants in the Harvard Economic History Workshop (1990–1994, 1995–1996), the Harvard Economic History "tea" (1990–1994, 1995–1996), the Osaka Gakuin University Faculty Seminar (1994), and the European University Institute Seminar in Economic History (1994–1995).

We have been especially fortunate in receiving excellent research assistance from graduate students and research staff at Essex, Harvard, and the Australian National University (some of whom are now well established in their own academic careers). For their enthusiasm, dedication, and skill, we would like to thank Kimiko Cautero, Theo Charitidis, Bill Collins, Chris Cook, Owen Darbishire, Marco Ercolani, Asim Khwaja, Hubert Lin, Wayne Naughton, Tien Quek, Steve Saeger, and Boris Simkovich.

This book would not have been possible without generous funding received from several sources. Williamson acknowledges the National Science Foundation, which provided funding for more than six years under grants SES 90-21951, SBR 92-23002, and SBR 95-05656. For providing released time for research, Hatton acknowledges a Senior Research Fellowship H52427503194 awarded by the United Kingdom Economic and Social Research Council (1994–1995) and a Visiting Research Fellowship awarded by the Australian National University (1994).

Some of the work in this book appeared earlier. Thanks, therefore, are due to Routledge Publishers (chapters 1, 3, 10, and 11 of *Migration and the International Labor Market, 1850–1939* [London: 1994] edited by Hatton and Williamson), Springer-Verlag (chapter 1 of *Economic Aspects of International Migration* [Berlin: 1994], edited by H. Giersch), *Population and Development Review* (September 1994), *International Economic Review* (August 1996), *Journal of Economic History* (September 1993, June 1996, and March 1997), *Review of Economics and Statistics* (November 1995), *European Economic Review* (July 1995), *European Review of Economic History* (April 1997), *Scandinavian Economic History Review* (2, 1995), and the *World Bank Research Observer* (1997).

The most important is saved for the last. We would like to thank our wives, Alison Booth and Nancy Williamson, for their encouragement, patience, and tolerance while we were preoccupied—perhaps obsessed—with the research underlying this book. This one is for them.

Colchester and Cambridge   T. J. H.
September 1996   J. G. W.

Contents

The Age of Mass Migration

1

What This Book Is About

This book is about the mass migrations that took place between Europe and the New World—North and South America and Australasia—between 1850 and 1914. About 55 million Europeans sought new lives in far-away places during this period of largely unfettered migration. The movement marked a profound shift in global population and economic activity. This book tries to do more than simply describe this mass movement: it explores cause and effect. As social scientists, we search for systematic fundamentals rather than idiosyncratic details.

Interest in these past migrations has been rekindled by contemporary policy debate. The age of free mass migration ended shortly after World War I, so one could hardly expect late-twentieth-century international migrations to reach the spectacular rates recorded in the late nineteenth century. Indeed, the foreign-born share in the United States population today is only half what it was a century ago. But United States immigration has been on the rise since World War II and it now accounts for a third of population growth. Surging immigration from Mexico, Latin America, and Asia has stimulated a vast literature and intense public debate. The scholarly journals and the press in Europe are full of commentary on German migrations from east to west in the wake of the collapse of the Iron Curtain, on the African migrants flooding into southern Europe, and on the prospects for increased migration within the European Community.

In one sense the contemporary numbers are relatively small compared with the mass migrations of a century ago: after all, emigration rates of 50 per thousand per decade and immigration rates of 100 per thousand per decade are now rare, whereas they were common just prior to World War I. Furthermore, mass migrations in the 40 years prior to World War I raised the New World labor force by a third and lowered the Old World labor force by an eighth—figures that have not been exceeded even for California and Mexico over the last 40 years. In another sense, however, they are surprisingly similar. The contemporary migrations into, say, the United States have made a similar contribution to the total increase in the labor force, since natural increase is also lower than it was in the nineteenth century.

So what drives mass migration? Douglas Massey and his collaborators concluded a recent survey of the vast literature on postwar migration to the United States as follows:

> During the initial phases of emigration from any particular sending country, the effects of market penetration, network formation, and cumulative causation predominate in explaining the flows, but as migration reaches high levels and development moves societies toward urban, industrial economies, the costs and risks of movement drop to low levels, and migration is increasingly determined by wage differentials. . . . As economic growth in sending regions occurs and emigration proceeds, international wage gaps gradually close and markets for capital, credit, insurance and futures become more accessible, lowering the incentives for movement. If the sending country is ultimately integrated into the international market as a developed, urbanized economy, net migration ceases and the sending country may itself become a net importer of immigrant labor. (1994: 741)

These propositions are being applied to developing countries in the late twentieth century, but the late-nineteenth-century mass migrations offer even better evidence to test them. After all, these migrations were relatively unimpeded by the legal and bureaucratic restrictions that inhibit migration today.

Much of the current debate over international migration is motivated by precisely this issue. Should policy be more restrictive or more liberal? By what criteria should immigrants be selected? These questions have certainly been central to recent United States policy debate. While the acts of 1986 and 1990 allowed more immigration, there have been recent moves to reverse this trend. Backed by President Bill Clinton, the Commission on Immigration Reform in 1995 recomended reducing legal immigration by a third and shifting visa priorities to favor close relatives. Rising mass migration in the late nineteenth century led to a similar debate, and the Immigration Commission Report of 1911 made recommendations to restrict immigration. European policy has centered on increasing intra-European mobility while imposing common external restrictions—a moat around the European castle. In the nineteenth century, the concerns were chiefly about emigration.

Most of the historical issues raised in this book are precisely those that engage social scientists and policy makers today. Why do some countries produce more emigrants than others? Why do very poor countries send out fewer emigrants than developing, but still poor, countries? Why does the emigration rate typically rise with early industrialization? Why are emigration rates so volatile in the short run? How well do immigrant groups assimilate in host countries and what disadvantages do they suffer compared with natives? How do immigrants choose their destinations and why do they return? Are international labor markets segmented? Do immigrants rob jobs from locals? What impact do immigrants have on wage rates and living standards in the host country? Does emigration improve the lot of those left behind?

History is a good place to look for answers to these questions. Indeed, these same questions have provoked a very large historical literature, most of which has focused on the mass migrations during the century prior to World War I.

When Frank Thistlethwaite wrote his influential survey on the state of research on nineteenth-century mass migration in 1960, he observed that social scientists had done much of the early research and that historians had been slow to follow their lead. He called for more historical studies of the detailed contours and internal mechanisms of migration and migrant communities. This call has been heeded and the subsequent outpouring of historical research has greatly enriched our knowledge of the place, time, and circumstance of individual migration streams. Much of it has been written by social historians examining social networks, family ties, and cultural differentiation. The economics of the move, however, has taken a back seat to cultural, social, and even political aspects. Furthermore, microlevel research on the particular, and sometimes the peculiar, individual or group has been purchased at the cost of a weaker understanding of the economic and demographic fundamentals that more anonymously, but just as surely, drove the migrant flow. In short, it is now often difficult to see the woods for the trees. Furthermore, this new microresearch rarely compares migrants with nonmigrants or foreign-born migrants with native-born migrants. The first part of this book attempts to repair these flaws by providing new economic insights into the causes of the move and consequences of assimilation.

Thistlethwaite also observed in 1960 that

> it has been the consequences and not the causes of migration which have received most attention, and moreover, the consequences for the receiving country, not the sending country. The causes, if not exactly taken for granted, have been given more perfunctory investigation. . . . Recent American scholarship has wonderfully enriched our knowledge of immigrant adjustment but there still appears to be a salt water curtain inhibiting the understanding of European origins (1960: 19–20).

As with his call for historical studies, many scholars have taken up this injunction as well, producing an enormous body of research, not just on the European origins of migration and the factors that influenced it but on the links between experience at European origins and New World destinations. Thistlethwaite's imbalance has now been redressed, if not entirely reversed. And, again, by focusing on immigrants themselves, the literature now tends to ignore their combined impact on wages, employment, inequality, and living standards. The second half of this book concentrates on these "impact" issues.

Our approach is economic and unashamedly quantitative. We do not seek to undermine or reject the microanalysis of historians but rather to build on this by examining the causes and the consequences of mass migration at a more macro level. Only then is it possible to infer historical lessons useful for contemporary debate. This, after all, should be the principal goal of the economic historian. In the course of the research we have assembled new data that enable us to examine anew a variety of questions. We provide fresh and in some cases different answers to the questions that have long been deeply embedded in the literature. Above all, we attempt to restore to center stage the fundamental economic and demographic forces that pushed and pulled the mass migrations as well as the economic and structural changes they wrought.

This, then, is the menu we offer. Chapter 2 provides an overview pointing to the issues that have been widely debated or much neglected. Chapter 3 offers explanations for the secular trends and intercountry differences in European emigration. Chapter 4 constructs and then applies a new model to account for short-run fluctuations in emigration. Chapters 5 and 6 examine in detail the experiences of two of the most important emigrant sources: Ireland and Italy. There we explain both the annual time series and interregional variation in emigration intensity. Chapter 7 explores immigrant assimilation experience in the principal receiving labor market—the United States: how did the American melting pot work? The next three chapters rise from micro to macro: did the mass migrations have a potent impact on wages, employment, and other labor market variables? Chapter 8 makes the immigration assessment for the most important receiving country, the United States. Chapter 9 makes the emigration assessment for two important sending countries, Ireland and Sweden. Chapter 10 expands the assessment to add the effects of capital flows and trade on labor markets, and to include simultaneously all sending and receiving areas: did these open economy forces enhance or retard economic convergence between the Old World and the New? Chapter 11 explores the connection between migration and inequality within both emigrating and immigrating countries: did the mass migrations create rising inequality in the receiving countries and the opposite in the sending countries? Chapter 12 concludes.

2

The Issues

In the century following 1820, about 55 million Europeans set sail for resource-abundant and labor-scarce New World destinations. Three fifths of these migrants went to the United States. Earlier migration from resource-scarce and labor-abundant Europe had been a mere trickle. The only comparable intercontinental migration had been that of black slaves from Africa to the Americas and the Caribbean. Indeed, it was not until the 1840s that annual (free) European migration to the Americas exceeded (coerced) African migration, and it was not until the 1880s that the cumulative European migration exceeded the African (Eltis 1983: 255). Until well into the nineteenth century, the cost of the move was simply too great for many "free" migrants to afford. Indentured servitude (a temporary forfeiture of some freedom) was one way to secure a "loan" for the move under such conditions (Galenson 1984; Grubb 1994). Transportation abroad in convict chains was another. Coercion through slavery was a third. Declining costs of passage and augmented family resources for investment in the move would change these conditions throughout Europe as the century progressed.

European intercontinental emigration is plotted in figure 2.1. In the first three decades after 1846, the figures averaged about 300,000 per annum; in the next two decades the figures more than doubled; and after the turn of the century they rose to over a million per annum. The European sources also changed dramatically. In the first half of the century, the dominant emigration stream had its source in the British Isles, followed by Germany. A rising tide of Scandinavian and other northwest European emigrants joined these streams by midcentury. Southern and eastern Europeans followed suit in the 1880s. This new emigrant stream from the south and east accounted for most of the rising emigrant totals in the late nineteenth century. It came first from Italy and parts of Austria-Hungary, but after the 1890s it swelled to include Poland, Russia, Spain, and Portugal.[1]

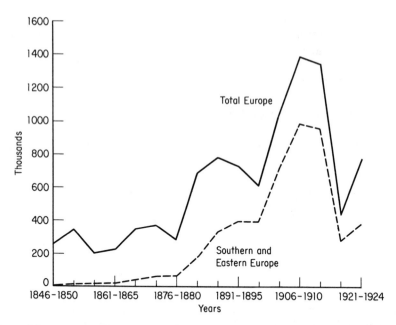

Figure 2.1 Emigration from Europe, 1846–1924 (five-year averages). *Source*: Ferenczi and Willcox (1929: 230–31)

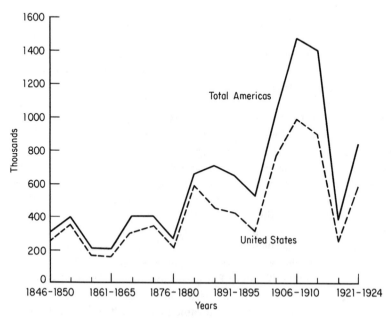

Figure 2.2 Immigration to the Americas, 1846–1924 (five-year averages). *Source*: Ferenczi and Willcox (1929: 236–37)

The overwhelming majority of the European emigrants arrived as immigrants in the Americas. Figure 2.2 plots this immigration from 1846 to the U.S. quotas in the 1920s; the pattern closely replicates the total intercontinental emigration in figure 2.1.[2] Migration to the Americas was dominated by the United States, but there were significant flows to South America after the mid-1880s, led by Argentina and Brazil, and to Canada after the turn of the century. A small but persistent stream also linked the United Kingdom to Australia, New Zealand, and South Africa.

Although they can be measured with far less precision, very important migrations also occurred within Europe. For example, the overwhelming bulk of the emigrants leaving Belgium went to neighboring France and the Netherlands. More than half of all Italian emigrants in the 1890s went to European destinations, chiefly France and Germany. Significant migrations also took place within the New World, especially those from Canada across the border to the United States. Indeed, until 1900 Canadian emigration to the United States completely offset Canadian immigration from Europe (McInnis 1994).

These statistics typically refer to gross rather than net migrations. The distinction is unimportant for most of the nineteenth century since the cost of return migration was simply too high. However, the distinction becomes increasingly important as the upward trend in gross emigration is partially offset by an even steeper rise in return migration late in the century. United States authorities estimated that between 1890 and 1914 return migration was 30 percent of the gross inflow. It varied greatly by nationality; the ratio was nearly half among Italians and Spaniards, but only about 5 percent among Russians, Irish, and Scandinavians. Similarly, the return migration rate was much higher for some New World countries than others. Between 1857 and 1924, return migration from Argentina (Italians and Spaniards) was 47 percent of the Argentine gross inflow. The high return migration rate among Italians represented a growing trend towards temporary, often seasonal, migration, so much so that eventually they would be called "birds of passage."

Since large countries can send out and receive more emigrants than small countries, we need some device to standardize migration experience. What interests us most, after all, is the number who migrate relative to those at risk. The simplest approach is to divide the migrant flow by the sending or receiving country population. Table 2.1 reports European emigration rates per decade per thousand of population.[3] They include intra-European migration where data are available. These gross rates exaggerate the net rates since they understate return migration, but they establish the orders of magnitude well enough. Rates exceeding 50 per thousand were common for Britain, Ireland, and Norway throughout the late nineteenth century, and Italy, Portugal, and Spain reached those levels at the end of the century. Sweden and Finland recorded 50 per thousand rates only in one decade (the former in the 1880s and the latter in the 1900s); none of the other European countries ever reached such high emigration rates. By comparison, 10 per thousand is high by twentieth-century standards.

Table 2.1 European Emigration Rates by Decade (per 1,000 mean population)

Country	1851–1860	1861–1870	1871–1880	1881–1890	1891–1900	1901–1910
Austria-Hungary			2.9	10.6	16.1	47.6
Belgium				8.6	3.5	6.1
British Isles	58.0	51.8	50.4	70.2	43.8	65.3
Denmark			20.6	39.4	22.3	28.2
France	1.1	1.2	1.5	3.1	1.3	1.4
Germany			14.7	28.7	10.1	4.5
Ireland			66.1	141.7	88.5	69.8
Netherlands	5.0	5.9	4.6	12.3	5.0	5.1
Norway	24.2	57.6	47.3	95.2	44.9	83.3
Sweden	4.6	30.5	23.5	70.1	41.2	42.0
Switzerland			13.0	32.0	14.1	13.9
Finland				13.2	23.2	54.5
Italy			10.5	33.6	50.2	107.7
Portugal		19.0	28.9	38.0	50.8	56.9
Spain				36.2	43.8	56.6

Source: Ferenczi and Willcox (1929: 200–01).

Table 2.2 reports some New World immigration rates. These are even larger than the Old World emigration rates, an inevitable arithmetic consequence of the fact that the sending populations were bigger than receiving populations. Every New World country but Brazil had immigration rates far in excess of 50 per thousand in the 1900s, while only half of the European countries had emigration rates above 50 per thousand, and most only barely above. The immigration rates were enormous for Argentina, and they were high everywhere shortly before World War I.

Migration rates like these imply significant economic effects on sending and receiving labor markets even if we allow for the undocumented rising rate of return migration, particularly when we recognize that migrations tended to self-select those who had most to gain from the move, namely, young adult men. Thus, the migrants had far higher labor participation rates than either the populations they left or the ones they joined. It follows that the labor migration rates were even higher than the population migration rates.

Table 2.2 New World Immigration Rates by Decade (per 1,000 mean population)

Country	1851–1860	1861–1870	1871–1880	1881–1890	1891–1900	1901–1910
Canada	99.2	83.2	54.8	78.4	48.8	167.6
United States	92.8	64.9	54.6	85.8	53.0	102.0
Cuba						118.4
Argentina	38.5	99.1	117.0	221.7	163.9	291.8
Brazil			20.4	41.1	72.3	33.8

Source: Ferenczi and Willcox (1929: 209).

Who Were the Emigrants?

Understanding the composition of the emigrant streams should help in our quest to explain late-nineteenth-century mass migrations. After all, if labor market forces in sending and receiving countries were central to the move, those who moved were likely to have been most responsive to economic incentives. Furthermore, economic explanations for the mass migrations would likely look more promising if the composition of the emigrant streams were similar across countries and cultures. If, instead, the composition of the emigrant streams varied widely across countries, culture is likely to have dominated economics. So, who were the emigrants?

The emigrants in 1900 were certainly different from those in 1800. Early-nineteenth-century migrant streams were often led by farmers and artisans from rural areas, traveling in family groups, intending to acquire land and settle permanently at the New World's frontier. In the late nineteenth century, while many still had rural roots, the emigrants *from any given country* were increasingly drawn from urban areas and nonagricultural occupations. For example, emigrants from Britain in the 1830s, a country that had then already undergone a half century of industrialization, were mainly from nonfarm occupations (Erickson 1990: 25; Cohn 1992: 385).[4] This industrialization-induced trend within emigrant countries was overwhelmed by the shift from old emigrant regions, the industrial leaders, to new emigrant regions, the industrial followers. Emigrants were also typically unskilled—no doubt partly because they were young, but also because of their limited schooling and lack of training in skilled trades. Thus, the increasing importance of less industrial eastern and southern Europe as an emigrant source served to raise those countries' proportion of rural emigrants and to lower their average skills and literacy.

By the late nineteenth century, migrants were typically young adults.[5] Only 8 percent of the immigrants entering the United States between 1868 and 1910 were over 40 years old, with another 16 percent under 15, so that young adults 15–40 accounted for an enormous 76 percent, during a period when the total United States population aged 15–40 was only about 42 percent. The mover-stayer comparison was more dramatic for the Old World: those 15–34 were only 35 percent of the Irish population but over 80 percent of the Irish emigrants. Thus, the "mass" migrants carried very high labor participation rates to the New World. The migrant flow was also dominated by men: they accounted for 64 percent of all United States immigrants between 1851 and 1910, and for more than three quarters of the emigrants from Spain and Italy.[6] Emigrants tended to be single and emigrated as individuals rather than in family groups, although a significant minority were young couples with small children. In short, the migrants carried very low dependency burdens to the New World.

This evidence also suggests that those who emigrated had more to gain from the move and were likely, therefore, to be more responsive to labor market conditions. By emigrating as young adults, they were able to reap the gains over most of their working lives. By moving as single individuals, they were able to minimize the costs of the move including earnings foregone during passage and job search.[7] Furthermore, as young adults they had the highest probability of surviving the not insignificant mortality and morbidity odds during passage.[8] And since the emigrants were typically unskilled, they also had little technology- or country-specific human capital invested and hence stood to lose few of the rents from such acquired skills (except for language). Finally, these young adults had the smallest commitment to family and assets at home.

This characterization reinforces the premise that labor market conditions at home and abroad were paramount to the migration decision and that most emigrants moved in the expectation of a more prosperous and secure life for themselves, their future children, and their future grandchildren. Many moved to escape religious or political persecution, of that there is no doubt, and others did so in convict chains (such as the early "migrants" to Australia). But most moved to escape European poverty, or at least to improve their economic status in the New World. And most moved under their own initiative without either government pressure or assistance.[9] As the technology of transport and communication improved, the costs and uncertainty of migration fell, and overseas migration came within reach of an increasing portion of the European population for whom the move offered the most gain. These forces, accompanied by European famine and revolution, gave rise to the first great surge of mass emigration in the 1840s. It was to be an important benchmark, as each subsequent surge of mass migration was to exceed the next until World War I.

The Determinants of Emigration

What determined European emigration in the late nineteenth century? What accounts for the wide differences in emigration rates from different European countries? Can the variety of European emigration rates be explained by a common economic framework, or do the explanations lie instead within each county's distinctive political, social, and cultural environment? And why do emigration rates fall in some countries yet rise in others? Above all, why did emigration rates so often *rise* from low levels as successful economic development took place at home? After all, conventional theory would suggest that successful development at home (e.g., rising wages) would make the overseas move less attractive, not more. What hypotheses can be offered for these counterintuitive events?

Various theories have been offered to explain the empirical regularities of late-nineteenth-century emigration. They draw on perspectives from economics, sociology, demography, and geography. One typology divides these theories into four broad groups (Lowell 1987: ch. 2): structural change and response, which stresses economic modernization and the demographic transition; economic, stressing the relative income incentive to migrate; innovation and diffusion, which stresses the spread of information through social networks; and rural ecology, which stresses change in the structure of landholding and in farming methods. Despite the contrary assumption often made in the literature, these "theories" are not mutually exclusive: accepting one does not necessarily imply rejecting the others.[10] While our

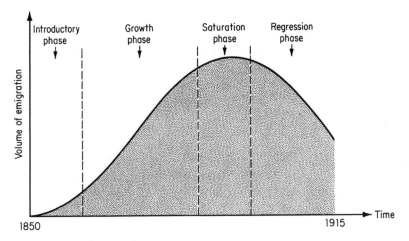

Figure 2.3 The Stylized Pattern of European Late-Nineteenth-Century Emigration. *Source*: Akerman (1976: 25)

approach is essentially economic, it does not rule out other approaches. Indeed, noneconomic hypotheses are tested in this book, and they often survive, thus broadening and enriching an otherwise narrow, economic explanation.

One important stylized fact that such theories must explain is this: during the course of modern economic growth in Europe, national emigration rates often rose steeply at first from very low levels, the rise then began to slow, emigration rates peaked, and subsequently they fell and went into permanent decline. This evolution, often seen as a multistage process, has sometimes been called the "mobility transition" (Zelinsky 1971). This pattern has emerged from studies of aggregate emigration rates for a number of countries (Akerman 1976) and of the local emigration rates within individual countries (Gould 1979). It has also been used to make predictions about the future of Mexican immigration into America (Massey 1988). This stylized fact as represented by Sweden (Akerman 1976: 25) is reproduced in figure 2.3. As we shall see in chapter 3, this mobility transition pattern can be found in the late-nineteenth-century data for a number of European countries, and we can offer an explanation for it.

In a pioneering article published almost 40 years ago, Richard Easterlin (1961) examined the relationship between European emigration and population growth. If emigration were a true vent for "surplus" population, he argued, countries with relatively high rates of natural increase should have exhibited higher emigration rates than those with low rates of natural increase. Comparing average country emigration rates from 1861 to 1910 with rates of natural increase lagged 20 years, Easterlin found a strong positive correlation. However, the comparison of trends in emigration rates across countries with the trends in natural increase yielded a much weaker relationship.

Easterlin viewed the rate of natural increase 20 years earlier as a proxy for the current rate of additions to the labor force: "Relatively high additions to the labor market would be expected, other things remaining equal, to result in labor market slack (comparatively slower growth in wages, less secure employment, etc.) and to lead to relatively higher emigration" (1961: 332). Easterlin is arguing the case for an *indirect* influence of past demographic events on present emigration through labor supply. If previous baby booms really boosted current emigration through their delayed impact on labor supply, then they would be better captured by an index of current labor market conditions, such as the real wage, which would reflect the net impact of both labor supply and demand. But was there a more *direct* effect of a previous baby boom on emigration, namely, one that raised the share of the population in the emigration-sensitive age cohort 20 years later? If so, the demographic revolution might have contributed directly to both the upswing and the downswing of the emigration cycle.

There is abundant evidence that current emigrants' cost of passage was financed by previous emigrants. This evidence takes the form of large emigrant remittances and frequent use of prepaid tickets: those traveling on prepaid tickets accounted for 30 percent of Finnish emigrants 1891–1914, for 50 percent of Swedish emigrants in the 1880s, for 40 percent of Norwegian emigrants in the 1870s, and for about 25 percent of Danish emigrants 1881–1895 (Kero 1991: 191; Hvidt 1975: 129). Such evidence clearly argues that past emigration encourages present emigration, what is sometimes called persistence or path dependence. Recognizing the links between current and past emigrant cohorts, the historical literature has termed this "chain migration" or, alternatively, the "friends and relatives effect" (Williamson 1974a; Gould 1980a: 293; Baines 1991: 33–38). The important point is that persistence is likely to matter in accounting for the variety in European emigration experience in the late nineteenth century. Historical events—like famines and revolutions—are likely to have a potent influence on emigration experience even after those events have disappeared from the memory of current generations. Low French emigration in the 1890s may have its source in the revolution-induced land reforms a century before, and high Irish emigration in the 1890s may have *its* source in the potato famine a half century before.

Assistance in the form of prepaid tickets must surely have muted the deterrent effect of the cost of passage for many emigrants. But the cost of passage *did* fall sharply in the 1860s with the shift from sail to steam on the Atlantic. As one observer puts it: "The technological revolution which followed the inception of the steamship as an ocean carrier, solved many of the problems which had previously faced the poor unfortunate emigrant. By 1870 therefore, he was able to cross the Atlantic in relative safety, at a reasonable price, in spite of the weather, in a scheduled time" (Hyde 1975: 59–60). After the 1860s, things were somewhat different. The steerage price was about £4–£6 between 1870 and 1913 and the journey time on the North Atlantic averaged about 10 days. The real price of passage exhibited little long-run trend, although it did fall as a proportion of annual earnings in origin countries. This might have added a modest upward trend to gross emigration, but it also likely boosted return migration. Changes in the cost of passage are unlikely therefore to have accounted for much of the variation in emigration flows observed after the 1860s.

Did emigration spread through Europe by some diffusion process? If so, it might help explain the late start and the sudden surge of mass migration from the countries of southern and eastern Europe. Adherants to this view often stress the social context of emigration (Zelinsky 1971: 238; Lowell 1987: 32). This view suggests that the upward trend in emigration was driven largely by noneconomic forces, but it offers few empirical predictions and says nothing about why emigration rates eventually decline.

Finally, what about the influence of industrialization and structural transformation? In many qualitative accounts of European emigration, the key factor is economic development at home, not just rising wages but the whole set of changes that accompany industrialization and changing attitudes towards emigration. As a historian of Norwegian emigration put it:

> Mass emigration occurred in the period of disruption when Norway was becoming part of the world economy, when industrialization was beginning, when new means of transport were creating a national market, when a money economy was transforming the old social order, when international competition in an age of free trade was causing Norwegian farmers to struggle for their lives and when internal migration reached unprecedented proportions, with a new social mobility being created within Norway itself. (Semmingsen 1960: 152–53)

The importance of industrialization in raising labor mobility has also recently been stressed by Massey (1988). European industrialization involved, above all, reduced attachment to the land and a rise in wage labor. The combination of more commercialized agriculture, more consolidated land holdings, diminished smallholdings, the erosion of common rights, and relatively high and rising wages in the booming cities all served to produce a rural exodus (Williamson 1990: ch. 4). The rise in overseas emigration was correlated with the growth of internal migration and can be seen as part of the same phenomenon (Baines 1985: ch. 8). Emigration of rural Europeans to New World urban jobs (or urban jobs in other European countries) is viewed by some observers as simply a rural-urban movement across international boundaries (B. Thomas 1972: chs. 7, 8).

Can We Explain Local Variations in Emigration?

One principal challenge to any theory of European emigration is whether it can explain differences in emigration rates between regions and localities within the same country. Since national emigration rates are simply an aggregation of local or regional emigration rates, a convincing theory of emigration should be able to account for some of this variation. These differences were large—often larger than between countries. For example, in 1881–1882 Italian provincial emigration rates varied between less than 0.1 per thousand for Bologna and 46.4 per thousand for Belluno, and in 1900–1901 Portuguese rates varied from 0.1 per thousand for Evora to 19.3 per thousand for Ponta Delgada in the Azores (Gould 1980b: 289). Despite such clear and obvious differences, there has been little consensus about how they should be explained (Baines 1991: 527).

Such a challenge is worth taking seriously, especially since many observers have pointed to idiosyncratic or noneconomic reasons why emigration got started earlier in some localities than others and why differences persisted in some cases but narrowed in others. Although the data are typically richer for local-level comparisons than they are for more aggregate international comparisons, few studies have used multivariate analysis to exploit these data fully, relying on partial correlations instead.[11] There is, however, a growing body of evidence that economic conditions do indeed explain variations in local emigration rates. In a recent multivariate analysis of communes in Norway and Sweden, Briant Lindsay Lowell found a strong negative effect of the local wage in Sweden on the local emigration rate, as theory would predict. He also found that emigration in both countries was associated with large landholdings and positively correlated with the proportion of landless laborers (Lowell 1987: 212–16). Other evidence suggests that the consolidation of landholding often led directly to emigration. In the East Elbian region of Germany, the midcentury rise of large estates reduced the opportunities for small-holding, converted peasants to wage laborers, and boosted emigration (Walker 1964: 64). Chapter 5 examines another case, Ireland, where the ability (or lack of it) to inherit or acquire land is often conjectured as the key to local emigration rates.

A number of studies have suggested that access to land, the availability of other rural employment opportunities, and population growth all interacted to determine emigration. In midcentury, a prominent feature associated with areas of heavy emigration in northwest Germany was a well-developed cottage linen industry. Protoindustrial areas where cottage industry was interlocked with agriculture (especially seasonally) had higher rates of natural increase than did other rural areas. They were also vulnerable to rising factory competition, and thus had increasing difficulties absorbing young workers generated by booming birthrates two decades previously. Thus, "emigration was highest where there were many agriculturists but little agriculture" (Kamphoefner 1976: 182). Similar conditions occurred somewhat later in northeast Italy, which became the earliest region of Italian mass migration (Ramella 1991). Such studies as these suggest that the possibility of temporary migration, either internal or external, as a means of acquiring land or other assets on return might influence the correlations between agricultural landholding and emigration rates—an issue we investigate in more detail for Italy in chapter 6.

What role did urbanization play? Were emigration abroad and rural-urban emigration at home substitutes? In countries with rapidly growing urban centers, migrants were drawn from the contiguous rural hinterland into urban industry, and overseas emigration was consequently lower than from more remote rural areas. Such urban influences have been identified in the Scandinavian countries, particularly around major ports (Carlsson 1976; Lowell 1987; Semmingsen 1972). It has sometimes been suggested that lack of any clear inverse relationship over time between internal (rural-urban) migration and emigration indicates that internal and external migration were not competing alternatives. But such evidence is not decisive: if urban expansion at home and abroad were positively correlated, both internal and external migration could increase, even if these destinations were viewed as substitutes by the potential rural emigrant. In fact, the link was more complex. Migrating to the city was often the first stage in migrating overseas; indeed, urban populations were more likely than rural to emigrate for a given incentive. Hence, urbanization likely had conflicting effects on emigration.

If much of the evidence points to the systemmatic influence of economic and structural characteristics of regions and localities in explaining differences in emigration intensity from time to time and place to place, what role is there for the forces of "emigration tradition" in causing persistent differences, and what role is there for "innovation and diffusion" in bringing about convergence? Persistence over time in regional emigration differentials might simply reflect the persistence of differences in the conditions that fundamentally determined emigration, although no doubt the friends and relatives effect was strong at the local level. Similarly, long-run convergence of emigration rates across localities might reflect a convergence across regions in those economic conditions that drove emigration rates. John Gould (1980b) argued that convergence in local emigration rates could be observed in a number of countries and that this evidence strongly supported the diffusion hypothesis. More recent evidence has suggested that this pattern of convergence was not universal (Baines 1991: 532). It is only possible to test this hypothesis in the negative sense that local emigration cannot be explained by observable structural variables. Such efforts have been too rarely made, and hence we devote much of chapters 5 and 6 to an examination of these issues.

Diffusion and path dependence were likely most important in the very early stages of mass emigration, especially in determining emigrant destinations. Many studies have shown that migrants from a given locality often followed a well-trodden path beaten by earlier emigrants to specific overseas locations: more than 90 percent of the emigrants to the United States from the Dutch province of Zuid Holland settled in Patterson, New Jersey; Nordeloos, Michigan; Pella, Iowa; and South Holland, Illinois (Swierenga 1991: 150). Thus, even if the intensity of emigration can be traced to economic forces in the local origin, settlement patterns in the United States were driven largely by the existence of previously established communities. Considerable evidence shows that the stock of past immigrants influenced the destinations of current immigrants from the country concerned, as the friends and relatives effect would suggest (Gallaway, Vedder and Shukla 1974; Dunlevy and Gemery 1977, 1978). Nonetheless, studies that have analyzed the intended destinations of immigrants arriving in the United States at the turn of the century show clearly that economic forces as reflected in state per capita income were also important in locational choice.

How strong was persistence in the choice of destination and why did emigrants from various European sources choose different New World destinations? How and why did these destination choices evolve over time? Chapter 6 contains a first attempt to explain destination choice using evidence from Italian provinces.

Was the International Labor Market Segmented?

Different European countries had very different late-nineteenth-century emigration histories. Some experienced declining rates while others, especially the Latin latecomers, experienced rising rates. Does this imply that different forces were at work in southern Europe? And why did emigrants from different countries chose different destinations? While the British migrated to a variety of destinations in North America and Australasia, the Germans and Scandinavians overwhelmingly chose the United States. But the major fault line was between northern and southern Europe: southern Europeans overwhelmingly emigrated to South American destinations. True, more and more southern Europeans emigrated to North America as the period evolved—a fact many American observers noted with concern. But did this changing direction of Latin emigrants reflect the growing economic attractiveness of the United States relative to South America, or did it reflect a change in the behavior of Latin emigrants themselves?

The late-nineteenth-century emigration literature has concentrated on northwest Europe to the neglect of the south and east. Of particular interest are the Latin countries—Italy, Portugal, and Spain, which were industrial latecomers and poor by western European standards. Given their poverty, why the Latin emigration delay? Since the poorest had the most to gain by the move to higher living standards, why didn't the Latins leave earlier and at higher rates than the Germans and British? Did poverty constrain their mobility? Or did agrarian peasant life in Italy and Iberia prove especially resistant to mobility until industrialization and urbanization loosened the grip of land on the peasant? Perhaps the Mediterranean family and village offered a package that made it much more difficult for young adults to leave. If so, in what way was that package any different from that of northern Europe, where emigration surged between the 1850s and the 1880s? Perhaps, instead, industrialization and rapid population growth simply came late to the Latin countries (see Molinas and Prados 1989; Federico and Toniolo 1991).

Some think that southern European and South American labor markets were highly integrated. Certainly Sir Arthur Lewis thought so. Indeed, he thought that his model of development (Lewis 1954) with immigrant-augmented elastic labor supplies applied to late-nineteenth-century Latin America (Lewis 1978). Many Latin American scholars agree. Carlos Diaz-Alejandro wrote that labor supply in Argentina before 1930 was "perfectly elastic at the going wage (plus some differential) in the industrial centers of Italy and Spain" (1970: 21–22). Nathaniel Leff believes the same was true of Brazil and that elastic labor supplies can account for stable wages in Sao Paulo and Santos from the 1880s onwards (1992: 6). If the elastic labor supply thesis is correct, nineteenth-century Latin emigration should have been far more responsive to wage gaps between home and abroad compared with those faced by early emigrants from northern Europe. Large wage gaps between Latin America and North America, gaps that persist well into the late twentieth century, could then be partially explained by those more elastic Latin labor supplies.

If Latin emigration was really more responsive to wage gaps between home and abroad, why were the wage gaps between them and the destination countries so large? Alan Taylor has argued that the Latins were in fact no more responsive to relative wage signals than were the countries of northern Europe. What differed was their destinations. Thus, British emigrants to Australia faced a wage gap just as large or larger than that faced by Italian or Spanish emigrants to Argentina (Taylor 1994: 99). Latin emigrants, effectively shut out of Australasia, were positively encouraged with government subsidies to emigrate to Argentina and Brazil. But why did the early Latin emigrants shun North America? Did this reflect language affinity and cultural preference? Did it reflect discrimination in labor markets? Or were emigrants from Italy, Portugal, and Spain ill equipped to meet the demands of the North American industrial labor markets? Whatever the nature of the barriers, the Italians (much more than the Portuguese and Spanish) began to break them; after the 1890s over half of Italian intercontinental emigrants selected the United States as their destination.

Why Were Emigration Rates so Volatile?

Recurrent waves and sharp year-to-year fluctuations in late-nineteenth-century migration were well known even to contemporary observers. And no wonder: the instability was pronounced. International migration looks like a vulnerable margin that responded to labor market conditions with a powerful multiplier. Can this instability be explained by the same economics and demography that account for long-run trends? Or is a different model required to explain fluctuations, one independent of long-run influences? Which variables ought to account for short-term fluctuations and why? Did foreign conditions matter more in determining the ebb and flow of emigration than conditions at home? These questions have been at the heart of a very old debate on the determinants of emigration flows.

The instability is illustrated in figures 2.4a and 2.4b, which display the deviations from (linear) trend in emigration rates per thousand of the population for the 12 European countries central to this book. Three features are worth noting. First, some emigration rates are much more volatile than others. Generally, those with high average rates of emigration (such as Scandinavia) exhibit greater absolute volatility than those with relatively low average rates (such as France, Belgium, and the Netherlands). Second, there are similarities in the timing of these fluctuations. The evidence shows long swings for a number of countries, with emigration rates above trend in the 1880s and 1900s and below trend in the 1870s and 1890s. Yet in many countries such long swings are notably absent. Note also the sharp year-to-year fluctuations that often halved or doubled the emigration rate in the space of a year or a few years. Particularly sharp downturns took place in 1872–1874, 1892–1893, and 1907–1908 and sharp upturns can be observed in 1878–1881, 1885–1887, and 1900–1903. Third, there are important differences between countries. While the similarities in the profiles are very strong between, say, Norway and Sweden, the correspondences between these and Ireland are weaker and between them and the Latin countries are weaker still.

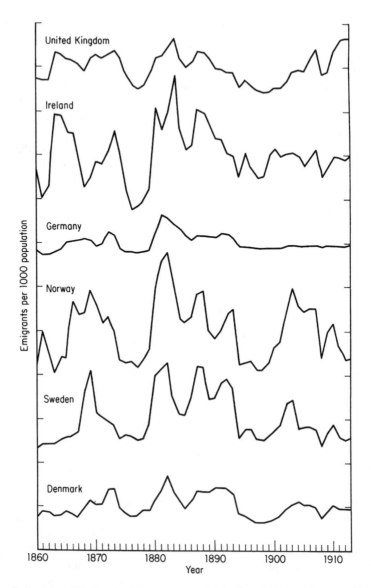

Figure 2.4a Annual Emigration Rates, 1860–1913 (absolute deviations from trend). *Source*: Derived from Ferenczi and Willcox (1929), various tables

Swings and cycles were a central focus of the pioneering emigration studies of Harry Jerome (1926), Dorothy Thomas (1941), Simon Kuznets (1952), Brinley Thomas (1954, 1972), and Richard Easterlin (1968). Jerome concluded that the timing of United States immigration was determined chiefly by the American business cycle and that conditions in the countries of origin had only a minor influ-

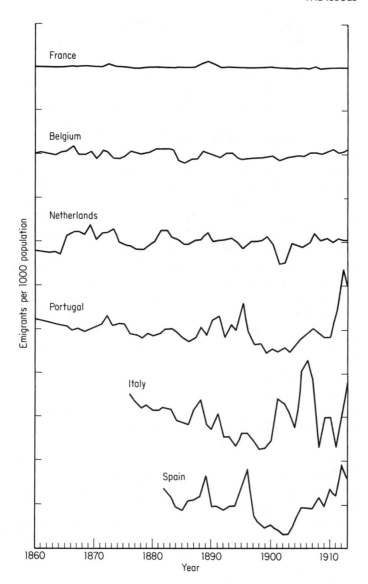

Figure 2.4b Annual Emigration Rates, 1860–1913 (absolute deviations from trend).
Source: Derived from Ferenczi and Willcox (1929), various tables

ence. He based his conclusion on the coincidence of peaks and troughs in emigration from a number of European countries and on the finding that these movements corresponded more closely with business cycles in the United States than with those in the origin countries. Easterlin argued that long swings reflected the uneven rate of development of the American economy and that immigration was an essential part of the process (1968: 31). In contrast, Dorothy Thomas argued that fluctuations in Swedish emigration were significantly and sometimes decisively influenced by harvest conditions, industrial growth, and demographic factors in Sweden (1941: 169). Also drawing on Swedish evidence, Brinley Thomas emphasized the importance of lagged natural increase in the sending countries (1972: 157).[12]

Whether low-tech description or high-tech econometrics, the literature has always been preoccupied with the relative strength of "pull" from abroad and "push" at home. Oddly enough, there has been little discussion of how these terms should be defined. Our strong preference would be to reserve them for describing underlying labor market fundamentals: the forces that served to shift labor demand and supply in the origin and destination countries (Williamson 1974a, 1974b). If they *are* defined in terms of the underlying fundamentals, they take on new meaning. Malthusian pressure at home? Capital formation abroad? Collapse in farm prices at home? Boom in export staple prices abroad? These are the fundamentals that really should matter in any push-pull debate. The discussion instead typically dwells on whether the variables representing conditions abroad have larger or more significant coefficients than those representing conditions at home. Using these criteria, the literature has reached no consensus: pull from abroad mattered in some studies (Kelley 1965; Gallaway and Vedder 1971; Richardson 1972), while push at home mattered most in others (Wilkinson 1970; Quigley 1972; Magnussen and Siqveland 1978). We believe the previous push-pull debate posed the wrong question.

Two types of variables have typically been included to represent conditions at home and abroad: prospective earnings, proxied either by GNP per capita or average wage rates, and employment opportunities, proxied by unemployment or some other cyclical variable. Allen Kelley (1965), Harry Richardson (1972), and David Pope (1981a, 1981b) all concluded that wage rates were not important in explaining fluctuations in emigration but that unemployment or activity rates were central, especially those in the receiving country. Maurice Wilkinson (1970), Thorvald Moe (1970), and John Quigley (1972) disagreed: they found highly significant coefficients on absolute or relative wage rates. As Gould (1979: 640) pointed out long ago, where adequate proxies for both wages and unemployment are included, the latter usually dominate in the regression results, hardly surprising given that cyclical conditions must have influenced the timing of the move. But does it mean that the effects of wages and demographic variables simply cannot be observed in the short run despite their apparent influence in the long run?

In the wake of Gould's (1979) critical survey of this literature, interest in it waned and many issues were left unresolved. Some historians simply rejected these time series studies as too simplistic and inconsistent with more micro evidence. Grounds for skepticism are that proxies for labor market variables are too crude, that variables rarely deal with future expected gains to migration, and that persistence induced by the friends and relatives effect is too often ignored. Perhaps the key lacuna has been the absence of a coherent theoretical framework within which the roles of different variables can be assessed and that considers emigration as a forward-looking decision. Such a model is offered in chapter 4 and then applied to the United Kingdom and the Scandinavian countries. We also ask whether our approach is applicable both to cases where emigration declined secularly (as in Ireland: chapter 5) or where it was rising sharply (as in Italy: chapter 6).

How Were Immigrants Assimilated in the New World?

Much of the literature on immigration to New World destinations has been concerned with assimilation, social as well as economic. And most of it has concentrated on the United States, which received the largest share of the immigrants. The economic debate chiefly concerns the degree to which immigrants were able to acquire the relevant skills and knowledge to compete with native-born workers on equal terms. How long did this process take? Was it complete within a single generation or did it take much longer? To what extent was assimilation retarded by discrimination and ethnic prejudice? To what extent did the concentration of immigrants in labor market niches, urban ghettos, and industrial centers inhibit or enhance the process of assimilation? Was the American melting pot myth or reality?

In his well-known book *The Uprooted*, Oscar Handlin argued that late-nineteenth-century American immigrants were poorly assimilated. He argued that they were largely from rural peasant backgrounds and were unable to adapt easily to American labor markets. They faced cultural and economic barriers that were overcome only after several generations. They crowded into ghettos—suffering poverty, squalor, and disease, segmented from the rest of society. Handlin's thesis reflects a tradition of pessimism about immigrant assimilation best represented in the *Report* of the Immigration Commission (1911), which pointed to the poor performance (relative to the native-born) of the so-called "new immigrants"—those from southern and eastern Europe who arrived in such large numbers after the mid-1880s. A new view has emerged in the last 30 years that paints a more benign picture. It argues that immigrants were able to adapt to America and that the clash of cultures was not nearly so great or as detrimental as earlier writers had suggested. By gathering in ethnic communities, immigrants could maintain some of their traditions, culture, and customs while integrating into American life (Briggs 1978; Bodnar 1985). Furthermore, immigrant communities had positive benefits. Social and kinship networks provided mutual aid, including information and access to jobs, in a more effective manner than they did for blacks moving up from the south (Bodnar et al. 1982: 82).

How was all this reflected in the economic performance of immigrants? The evidence that the foreign-born suffered greater unemployment than the native-born is weak at best. The Commissioner of Labor Survey of 1901 reported that the average unemployment rate for foreign-born household heads was 10.1 percent as compared with 8.3 percent for the native-born. Similar results have been reported from other sources, and the differences appear to be explained by the contrasts in the two groups' occupations (Keyssar 1986: 79–89). The Immigration Commission, Handlin, and others have all assembled statistics showing that immigrants in the first decade of the twentieth century earned less—often substantially less—than the native-born. Was this due to discrimination, lack of assimilation, or immigrant behavior? More recent observers have used econometric techniques to argue that these differences reflect the lower skill endowments of immigrants as demonstrated in measurable characteristics like literacy, the ability to speak English, and work experience in the United States. Such studies have generally found that the remaining earnings gap is ten percent or less and have also argued that immigrants recieved somewhat lower returns on their skills. Furthermore, they have found that earnings gaps are in part due to differences in occupational attainment and slower upward mobility. For example, Thernstrom (1973: ch. 6) found that Boston immigrants, especially the Irish and Italians, had less upward mobility than the native-born. Some groups found it difficult to break out of the manual occupations, particularly in the space of one generation.

Modern American immigrants also receive lower earnings on arrival, but they tend to catch up with, and in some cases overtake, native-born earnings as they acquire skills and experience (Chiswick 1978). True, some have argued that this impressive modern convergence overstates the true rate of convergence because immigrant quality declined between the 1950s and the 1980s, but it is *still* impressive. One might have expected to observe similar rates of catch-up and assimilation in the late nineteenth century unless labor markets operated very differently. Surprisingly, recent empirical studies suggest the contrary: immigrant age-earnings profiles were flatter than those of the native-born and immigrant earnings caught up with native earnings only at the end of the life cycle (Hanes 1996). Such results are especially puzzling since they rely on data from around 1890, when there were relatively few "new" immigrants. They suggest that the "old" immigrants who were supposed to have assimilated so well did much worse that many of the relatively disadvantaged immigrant groups in the late twentieth century. To the extent that new immigrants were present in these samples, immigrant age-earning profiles should be upward-biased, making the puzzle even greater. At stake is the relative assessment of immigrant performance in the American labor market, but the puzzle raised by comparisons with the present has scarcely been recognized, let alone resolved. Chapter 7 provides that resolution.

A related question is whether immigrant quality in the sense of labor market skills and earning power declined with the shift in immigrant origin toward southern and eastern Europe late in the nineteenth century. The Immigration Commission argued that it did, thereby providing a chief source of support for those who argued for a literacy test as a criterion for admission or, more radically, for quotas. Some observers saw the lower proportion of skilled workers among new immigrants who declared occupations and a falling share of skilled immigrants entering the American labor force as evidence of this quality decline (Jenks and Lauck 1926). Some, like Paul Douglas (1919), disagreed, although evidence of quality decline is reinforced by declining literacy rates and by an index of the (weighted) average Gross National Product (GNP) per capita of the countries of origin relative to the United States (Lindert 1978: 243). In any case, such indices have not been linked to the subsequent labor market performance of immigrants. Since immigrants often changed country and occupation at the same time, especially as young adults, it is not clear whether immigrant skill indices are a useful indicator of quality. It is even less clear *how much* such compositional shifts in immigrant characteristics on arrival contributed to lower earning power, assuming that they did at all. Chapter 7 attempts to answer these important questions by quantifying for the first time the link between immigrant entry characteristics and subsequent performance.

How Were Immigrants Absorbed in the New World?

Did immigrants time their arrival in the New World just when employment was expanding and when they were most needed? Or did immigration lead to higher unemployment? Did they relieve excess labor demand in the most rapidly growing sectors of these dynamic New World economies? Or did they flood in to lagging industries where they crowded out natives? Were their skills complementary to, or substitutes for, those of native Americans? Did they displace native Americans in the urban Northeast, thereby slowing native off-farm migration or speeding up their westward movement? Above all, did competition from immigrants drive down the wage for the native-born and previous immigrant cohorts? These questions preoccupy economists studying contemporary immigrations, but they have been surprisingly neglected in debate about late-nineteenth-century mass immigration.

Many observers from Jerome (1926) onward have noticed the procyclical movement of immigration into the United States. It is less well known that late-nineteenth-century observers also recognized the elastic response of immigration to United States business cycles, associating it with the growing share of temporary and return migration, and recognizing that these helped relieve the unemployment consequences of American business cycles. Given that the same features evidently reappeared in the European guestworker systems of France and Germany from the 1950s to the 1970s, it is surprising that the historical experience has been neglected. By the turn of the century American immigration flows sometimes varied by as much as half a million within the space of a few years, so it could have been an important margin for labor force adjustment to business cycles—perhaps *the* most important margin. Despite heightened interest in the volatility of unemployment rates,[13] very little consideration has focused on the labor force contribution of fluctuating immigration since Jerome's pioneering analysis. This major task is confronted in chapter 8.

Were immigrants and natives good substitutes in production? The little evidence we have suggests that, in fact, immigrants were close substitutes for natives at least in less-skilled occupations (McGouldrick and Tannen 1977; Foreman-Peck 1992). The finding that immigrants and natives were paid similar wages provides strong circumstantial evidence against the idea of strong segmentation between immigrants and natives in the labor market. Yet American immigrants *were* clustered in certain occupations. The Immigration Commission searched long, hard, and with some success in finding examples of industries or occupations in certain localities where jobs formerly occupied by native-born workers had been taken by immigrants. But they failed to convince their critics, like Issac Hourwich (1922: 154–59), that immigrants had genuinely displaced natives.

Perhaps examining the geographical movements of the native population in relation to the inflow of immigrants would be a more fruitful line of enquiry. Did the influx of immigrants into the American Northeast divert native migration flows? Or did immigrants simply fill the vacancies left by a westward movement initiated by the native-born? Observers such as Brinley Thomas (1972) as well as Hope Eldridge and Dorothy Thomas (1964) thought that immigrants displaced natives in the northeast—a hypothesis we subject to further scrutiny in chapter 8. If accepted, the hypothesis has important implications for the measurement of immigration's impact on both immigrant and native-born wages. Economists studying the wage effects of immigration in postwar America have often turned to the analysis of local labor markets in order to gauge the effects of immigration on native wages. They compare wage rates across localities with immigrant numbers or proportions—either in levels or changes—with results that suggest that immigration has very little impact on wage rates (Borjas 1994: 1697). But if natives responded to immigrant competition in the northeast by migrating to the west, the effects of the immigrant-augmented labor supply would have spread evenly across localities—those that received a high proportion of immigrants *and* those that did not.

The methodological difficulties of measuring the wage impact of immigration has dogged this important debate from the time of the Immigration Commission onward. Yet the issue remains important, and protagonists have not been slow to take up their positions despite such difficulties. So how can we proceed? Since the aggregate labor supply is at issue, aggregate time series offers one alternative approach. Wage adjustment or Phillips curve models suggest that excess labor supply should reduce the wage in the long run. Chapter 8 adopts this framework to evaluate the impact of immigrant labor supply in the United States.

But even this approach would fail to capture many of the indirect effects of immigration: altering prices, the structure of output, levels of international trade, and (above all) international capital flows. Computable general equilibrium (CGE) analysis provides a useful way, and perhaps the only way, of capturing the full effects of immigration. While such models have been criticized for their equilibrium assumptions, they are most likely to be appropriate for analysis over a period of 30 or 40 years when demand failure (or success) surely cannot have been a dominant factor. Yet there is a tradition dating back to Brinley Thomas (1954) suggesting that immigration generated prosperity and jobs by increasing demand and stimulating capital flows. Immigrants, it is argued, brought their jobs with them. But in the long run, only the supply side matters. Such models can take account of long-run economic adjustments that surely must have occurred in response to mass immigration, including capital inflows and industrial growth. Chapters 9 and 10 employ this approach to estimate the impact of immigration on receiving-country labor markets as well as to gauge the impact of emigration on sending-country labor markets.

Migration and the Global Economy

Is migration a good thing or a bad thing and for whom? The debate is at least as old as the Industrial Revolution, appearing first in Britain and then repeatedly among the followers. As Michael Greenwood and John McDowell (1986: 1745–47) point out, it certainly has a long history in the United States. The debate reached a crescendo in 1911 after the Immigration Commission had pondered the problem for four years. The commission concluded that it was a bad thing, contributing to low wages and poor working conditions. But what about the sending countries? The migrants and their families clearly benefited, but what about those they left behind? Did the mass migrations reduce wage and living standard gaps between poor and rich countries, raising real wages in the poor emigrating countries and lowering real wages in rich immigrating countries?

Historical correlations between rates of population increase and the real wage are unlikely to offer any clear answers to these questions. True, there is an inverse correlation for the years 1870–1913, and a good share of the population growth differentials were due to migration. Up to 1913, immigration accounted for 50 percent of Argentina's population increase, 32 percent of the United States increase, and 30 percent of Australia's increase (Taylor 1992a: table 1.1; Williamson 1974a: 248). Emigration reduced Swedish population increase by 44 percent between 1871 and 1890 (Karlstrom 1985: 155, 181).

In the absence of increasing returns, and in the presence of a given technology and at least one fixed factor, all comparative static models in the classical tradition predict that migration tends to make labor cheaper in the immigrating country and scarcer in the emigrating country. Models are one thing, however, and empirical analysis is another. The central problem facing empirical analysis is that we cannot observe the impact of immigration on the wage unless we control for the impact of other forces shifting the labor demand curve. In these circumstances it is appropriate to use CGE models that allow for the full set of interactions within the economy. A few recent efforts have used these CGEs to assess the impact of migration on sending and receiving regions. The early-nineteenth-century Irish migration to Britain offers one such example (Williamson 1990: ch. 6): Irish immigration raised the British labor force by 6 percent between 1821 and 1851, and its impact, according to a CGE model, made the British wage 4.1 percent lower in 1851 than it would have been in the absence of immigration. The impact of immigration on late-nineteenth-century U.S. labor markets was larger: an early CGE application estimated that immigration from 1870 to 1913 reduced the wage in 1910 by 9.9 percent (Williamson 1974a). Sweden presents an emigration example. In the early 1880s, Knut Wicksell argued that emigration would solve the pauper problem that blighted labor-abundant and land-scarce Swedish agriculture. The challenge Wicksell threw down to more empirically oriented economists has only recently been taken up. Urban Karlstrom (1985: 155) used a CGE model to estimate that the real wage in Sweden was 9.4 percent higher in 1890 than it would have been in the absence of twenty years of emigration after 1870. In chapter 9 we offer two more estimates for the wage impact of emigration, one for Ireland and one for Sweden.

What about other induced effects? Can these be captured in such models? First, what about possible crowding-out effects on the supply side? High native-labor supply elasticities would imply "discouraged" workers being crowded out of the labor force as native labor was displaced by immigrants at their occupational and locational ports of entry and as this displacement spread through the labor market economywide. If native labor supplies were very elastic, only small real wage declines would have been necessary to accommodate the immigrants. But it would also imply that some groups in America—women, blacks, and off-farm migrants—were marginalized in less dynamic sectors by competition in the major urban centers.

Second, it has sometimes been argued that more immigration reduced native births and hence there was a long-run offsetting effect on the labor force. This is known as the "Walker effect" after Francis A. Walker, who first suggested it in 1891. Such arguments have also been applied to sending countries, whose birth rates are sometimes said to have been enhanced as a result of emigration. However, these effects are difficult to measure. Using a CGE model, Alan Taylor (1995) found that immigration reduced the real wage in Argentina by 17 percent (allowing capital to chase after labor), but the addition of the Walker effect tends to diminish the immigration impact. Chapter 9 also offers estimates of the impact of emigration on Irish labor markets, allowing the Walker effect to operate in reverse.

On the labor demand side, large differences in population growth as a result of immigration or emigration would, of course, have led to profound changes in the structure of output and employment and to the economic returns to other factors of production, such as land and capital. The latter should alert us to a problem. One of the least plausible assumptions of a closed economy counterfactual is that the capital stock in the immigrant or emigrant countries would itself have remained unchanged in response to these dramatic differences in labor force growth. When the CGE models assume no capital mobility, they show that rental rates on capital would have decreased dramatically in the New World and increased dramatically in the Old World in the event of no migration. Yet we know that the international capital flows were very large in the late nineteenth century, with Britain at the center of this global capital market. Furthermore, the international capital market was highly integrated, probably as highly integrated as it is today (Edelstein 1982; Zevin 1992). Thus, much of the capital that "chased after labor" to the New World would probably have stayed at home had international migration been suppressed.

Factor Markets, Commodity Markets, and Economic Convergence

The literature on economic convergence has reached enormous proportions; started by Alexander Gerschenkron (1952), Moses Abramovitz (1979, 1986), and Angus Maddison (1982, 1991), it has flourished under the recent leadership of William Baumol (Baumol, Blackman and Wolff 1989) and Robert Barro (1991, Barro and Sala-i-Martin 1991). It has also generated a "new growth theory" in which human capital accumulation and endogenous technical progress play a richer role. Few of the economists working on convergence have paid serious attention to history. Even the economic historians among them have paid little attention to the contribution that international commodity, labor, and capital market integration has played in the process. Most of the recent attention has been on the period since 1950, but there was also substantial per capita real income and real wage convergence in the late nineteenth century. Indeed, the real wage convergence turns out to have been stronger than the convergence in per capita income (Williamson 1995; 1996: tables 3, 4).

How much of this real wage convergence can be accounted for by mass migration between the Old World and New? It must have made some contribution since migrations lowered real wages in the New World and raised them in the Old. The orders of magnitude may, at first sight, seem too small to account for much of the overall gap between the Old World and New. But appearances can be misleading. It is not just the effect of emigration on sending-country wages or immigration on receiving-country wages that matters, but rather these two effects taken together; and it is not the effect of migration on absolute wage levels that matters, but rather its impact on the convergence between poor and rich. Chapter 10 asseses the impact of mass migration on convergence between the two most important countries on either side of the Atlantic: Britain and the United States.

Clearly other forces were acting to produce convergence (and sometimes divergence) between the Old World and New. The standard model of economic growth (Solow 1957) emphasizes the rate of capital deepening in accounting for differences in real wage and per capita income growth between countries. Since economists have recently given renewed emphasis to capital deepening, it seems appropriate to ask whether differing rates of capital deepening were a key ingredient accounting for late-nineteenth-century real wage convergence as well. Evidence from five countries suggests not. The United States experienced faster capital deepening from 1870 to 1913 than any of the European countries, although Germany, Sweden, and Italy all experienced greater capital deepening than Britain (Wolff 1991; Hatton and Williamson 1994c: table 5; Maddison 1993).

A more important reason for real wage convergence between the Old World and New had to do with natural resource endowment. Since increases in capital and labor were applied to these resources at far greater rates in the New World than in the Old, labor's marginal product should have fallen relatively and that of land and natural resources should have risen relatively. These events would have been consistent with the writings of David Ricardo, John Stuart Mill, and other classical economists; they would predict a fall in the wage-rental ratio in the New World relative to the Old. New evidence dramatically supports this view, and econometric analysis confirms that these factor price ratios were being driven, in part, by trends in land-labor ratios (O'Rourke, Taylor, and Williamson 1996).

The moral of the story is this: migration of labor and capital must have contributed to economic convergence between the New World and Old in the late nineteenth century. But other forces were at work too, sometimes offsetting the effects of migration and sometimes reinforcing it. These additional forces were the fuller use of natural resources in the New World as more labor and capital were applied to them; the differential effects of technical change, particularly its factor-saving bias; and the trade boom resulting from commodity price convergence, which, in turn, resulted from the collapse in freight rates. Together, these forces integrated the world economy in the late nineteenth century and produced convergence in real wages and per capita incomes.

Migration may have been an important contributor to global real wage convergence, but what exactly was its contribution compared with other forces? We offer an answer in chapter 10.

Globalization, Inequality, and Policy

If international migration contributed to real wage convergence between the New World and the Old, did it also influence inequality? Was declining labor scarcity in the New World compared with the Old mirrored by increasing relative scarcity of other factors? Did trade or capital flows offset or reinforce the effects of migration? These issues have been at the heart of contemporary debate over rising inequality—and even stagnating wages for unskilled workers—in the United States since 1973. Economists have vigorously debated the contribution of immigration, trade liberalization, and technical progress to those trends. And if those forces mattered in the United States, they should have mattered in all corners of the global economy, including the very poorest exporting crude manufactures.

The late nineteenth century saw mass migrations, which tended to foster inegalitarian trends in the receiving New World and egalitarian trends in the sending Old World. Those decades also saw a dramatic increase in trade, induced in large part by a dramatic decline in transport costs. Standard trade theory suggests that a decline in trade barriers will cause countries to trade more, to specialize according to factor endowments, and to undergo some factor price equalization. Nineteenth-century endowments of labor and land were very different in the Old and New World. Thus, the New World tended to specialize in "grain" and the Old World in "manufactures" early on. But when transport costs dropped even more sharply later in the century, the New World completely swamped the Old World with grains, raising land rents relative to wages in the New World, and lowering them in the Old World.

We have two reasons, therefore, to expect that globalization increased income inequality in the New World relative to the Old: mass migration and a trade boom. Chapter 11 checks whether this globalization and inequality connection matches the facts of history.

The globalization debate in the late twentieth century has centered on the effects of trade liberalization. In the late nineteenth century, the situation was different. While falling transport costs fostered globalization, rising tariffs and trade barriers had the opposite effect. France, Germany, Italy, Portugal, and Spain all sought to protect landed interests from the grain invasion with tariffs, while Britain, Ireland, and, to some extent, Scandinavia, stuck with free trade.

What about migration and migration policy? The cause and effect of relatively free mass migration are the central topics of this book. But shouldn't we be asking why immigrant countries remained so open for so long? Liberal democracies might be expected to have enacted pro-labor policies sooner and with more drama than they in fact did—immigration restrictions being one such policy. Continued openness in countries with strong imperial ties (like Australia and Canada) can be easily understood. But what about Argentina and Brazil? What about the United States, especially in relation to the tight restrictions it imposed from 1917 onwards?

A large literature debates the political economy of immigration restriction, but almost none of it is formal or quantitative. A literature is now emerging that attempts to fill that gap (Foreman-Peck 1992; Goldin 1994; Timmer and Williamson 1996). Did xenophobia or markets dictate immigrant policy responses to rising mass migrations in the late nineteenth century? Chapter 12 reports some tentative answers.

THESE THEN ARE THE themes that will occupy the remainder of this book. Some of them have long been the staple diet of research on international migration, whereas others, we believe, have been starved for attention. And although the literature typically treats these issues in isolation, this book views them as intimately and globally connected.

3

Why Did Europeans Emigrate?

This chapter conducts a quantitative analysis of decade rates of emigration across 12 European countries between 1860 and 1913.[1] We seek answers to three of the questions raised in chapter 2. Why do emigration rates differ across countries? Can the same model account for rising emigration rates in some countries and falling emigration rates in others? Is the model equally effective in accounting for southern and northern European experience?

Modeling Emigration

The late-nineteenth-century European emigration experience is presented in table 3.1. These decade emigration rates were constructed from the authoritative study by Ferenczi and Willcox (1929). The original sources were taken from the origin country and were based chiefly on the issue of exit visas or on the registration of passengers on ships bound for extra-European ports. The data also include emigrations to other European countries if these were recorded. The decade averages are used to smooth out the sharp year-to-year fluctuations evident in many of the country time series. We do so since our interest here is in the long-run determinants of emigration rather than in the short-run timing of these long-distance moves. The observations are limited to western European countries since, although similar emigration data are available for some eastern European countries, they are often less reliable. In any case we do not have adequate information on the requisite explanatory variables to include these countries in the analysis. Nonetheless, the 12-country sample encompasses a wide range of experience. The observations range from the very low gross emigration rates for France to the very high rates for Ireland. The data also exhibit substantial variations for individual countries, contrasting, for example, the rising emigration rates of Italy and the Netherlands with the declining rates for Ireland. Gross emigration rates

Table 3.1 Gross (G) and Net (N) Emigration from Europe, 1850–1913 (emigrants per 1,000 population per annum decade averages)

	1850–1859	1860–1869	1870–1879	1880–1889	1890–1899	1900–1913
Belgium						
G	1.90	2.22	2.03	2.18	1.96	2.32
N	0.66	0.17	−0.93	−1.06	−1.80	−2.88
Denmark						
G	—	—	1.97	3.74	2.60	2.80
N	—	—	1.95	3.68	2.55	2.58
France						
G	—	0.12	0.16	0.29	0.18	0.15
N	—	0.11	0.09	0.19	0.11	0.01
Germany						
G	1.80	1.61	1.35	2.91	1.18	0.43
N	—	1.61	1.35	2.89	1.12	−2.45
Great Britain						
G	4.38	2.47	3.87	5.71	3.92	7.08
N	—	1.29	1.52	3.23	0.93	3.31
Ireland						
G	18.99	15.16	11.28	16.04	9.70	7.93
N	—	—	—	—	—	—
Italy						
G	—	—	4.29	6.09	8.65	17.97
N	—	—	—	—	6.78	13.01
Netherlands						
G	0.50	1.67	2.66	4.06	4.62	5.36
N	—	—	0.10	0.81	1.16	0.31
Norway						
G	—	—	4.33	10.16	4.56	7.15
N	—	—	—	—	—	—
Portugal						
G	—	—	2.91	3.79	5.04	5.67
N	—	—	—	—	—	—
Spain						
G	—	—	—	3.91	4.63	6.70
N	—	—	—	0.98	0.42	2.50
Sweden						
G	0.51	2.52	2.96	8.25	5.32	4.49
N	—	—	—	7.30	3.77	2.93

Source: See appendix A.

often differ substantially from net rates, although the difference varies from country to country. One of our objectives here is to note whether explanations of late-nineteenth-century emigration behavior are significantly different when return migration is included.

A number of studies have examined emigration trends across countries in Europe (Easterlin 1961; Tomaske 1971; Baines 1991) but often through qualitative analysis or simple bivariate comparisons. Whereas Easterlin concentrated on population growth and per capita income, Tomaske used a single cross-sectional econometric equation with relative income, excess births, and lagged migration as arguments. Since no adequate measure of internationally comparable real wage rates was available to these writers, they had to rely on Mulhall's crude estimates of per capita income. Easterlin did suggest, however, a negative relationship between home per capita income and emigration rates once lagged population growth was taken into account. The econometric evidence presented by Tomaske suggested that, across countries, the relationship between Mulhall's income per capita and emigration to the United States was insignificant, even in the presence of lagged natural increase, unless the lagged dependent variable was included.

Crippled by lack of adequate data, this important debate has lain dormant for about two decades. The appearance of a recently developed real wage database for internationally comparable urban unskilled male occupations (Williamson 1995) breathes new life into the debate. These data have three principal advantages over what was available to Easterlin and Tomaske. First, they offer an income measure far more relevant to the decision facing potential migrants. The wage rates were taken from unskilled urban occupations (such as the building trades) that were ubiquitous in all countries, and they were deflated by cost-of-living indices developed from purchasing-power-parity (PPP) constructs. Second, since these real wage indices are comparable across time and between countries, we can pool the country time series in the emigration analysis, something earlier studies could not do. Third, since we have comparable real wage estimates for major immigrant New World countries, we can develop a measure of the wage gap between sending and receiving countries that is also comparable across countries and over time.

Row A in table 3.2 reports the absolute real wage indexed on Britain, 1905 = 100. Row B reports the home real wage as a percentage of that in the relevant receiving countries. In most cases the destination wage is a weighted average of the most important receiving countries, including, where relevant, other European countries. The weights are based on the distribution of emigrant flows in the 1890s. The main exception is Spain, where the destination wage denotes Argentina alone, since we have no real wage observations for Cuba and only limited observations for Brazil.

Row A indicates that real wages were rising everywhere, although some countries, such as Denmark, Norway, and Sweden, were doing especially well while others, such as Belgium, France, and Spain, were not. If we compare these trends with emigration rate trends (table 3.1), the negative relationship would be weak since, with the exception of Ireland, there is no strong evidence of downward trend in emigration rates. Indeed, the correlation coefficient between gross emigration and the wage in our sample is −0.14, whereas it is −0.19 in the smaller sample of net emigration rates. Thus, at best only a very weak negative correlation appears between home wages and emigration.

A more appropriate measure of the overseas migration incentive, however, is the gap between home and destination real wages. As row B in table 3.2 shows, home wages were substantially below destination wages, but generally an erosion of the

Table 3.2 Internationally Comparable Wage Rates and Wage Ratios
(A = real wage rate, Great Britain 1905 = 100;
B = real wage ratio, home to receiving countries)

Country	1850–1859	1860–1869	1870–1879	1880–1889	1890–1899	1900–1913
Belgium						
A	37.7	43.7	51.5	59.7	71.3	76.3
B	—	89.9	92.0	91.0	100.8	96.6
Denmark						
A	—	—	41.6	52.5	70.9	92.4
B	—	—	35.1	39.8	47.6	56.9
France						
A	—	46.1	52.0	60.4	65.0	71.3
B	—	—	45.6	45.4	38.3	38.1
Germany						
A	52.7	55.4	62.5	68.6	78.1	85.9
B	—	—	54.2	53.4	53.9	52.7
Great Britain						
A	60.9	61.0	77.3	90.3	102.0	104.0
B	—	64.9	65.5	68.1	67.8	64.3
Ireland						
A	38.8	40.7	50.9	65.2	84.7	90.9
B	—	44.4	43.8	50.4	58.3	56.1
Italy						
A	—	—	26.2	34.3	37.3	46.5
B	—	—	37.8	42.8	40.6	45.6
Netherlands						
A	34.1	36.6	44.6	60.1	70.0	77.0
B	—	39.3	37.6	45.8	47.5	46.4
Norway						
A	—	—	35.1	44.0	59.7	66.6
B	—	—	29.6	33.5	40.5	40.1
Portugal						
A	—	—	35.1	47.9	40.8	43.3
B	—	—	58.9	63.1	44.0	42.1
Spain						
A	—	—	—	51.1	53.5	49.1
B	—	—	—	73.3	61.7	51.2
Sweden						
A	24.4	34.6	39.2	51.3	70.7	92.2
B	—	41.3	37.0	43.4	52.6	60.4

Source: Based on data in Williamson (1995).

wage gap favored the New World. For some, the convergence was dramatic. Between the 1870s and the early twentieth century, Danish real wages rose from about 35 percent to about 57 percent of those in the United States (the principal destination), a very impressive catch-up over only about three decades. Sweden's catch-up was also spectacular although Norway's was less so. Ireland, Belgium, and the Netherlands also enjoyed an appreciable convergence on their relevant

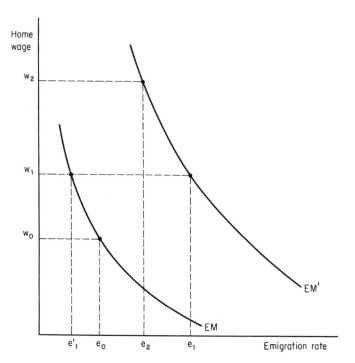

Figure 3.1 Stylized Emigration Responses

destinations, although for the European industrial leaders, Britain, France, and Germany, the convergence was less pronounced. Among the Latin countries, the impressive Italian catch-up was not matched in Spain and Portugal. Over the full intertemporal cross-section, the inverse correlation between the emigration rate and the wage ratio is modest: −0.20 for gross emigration and −0.39 for net emigration. This result implies that a more comprehensive model is needed to account for late-nineteenth-century emigration to the New World.

One central stylized fact makes it even more clear that real wage gaps will not suffice to explain emigration by themselves: during the course of modern economic growth, emigration rates rise steeply at first from very low levels, the rise then begins to slow, emigration rates peak, and subsequently they fall. As we pointed out in the previous chapter, this stylized fact has emerged from studies of both the time series of aggregate emigration for a number of countries (Akerman 1976) and of the local emigration rates within individual countries (Gould 1979), and it has been used to make predictions about the future of Mexican immigration into America (Massey 1988). Several explanations have been offered for this stylized fact, but each can be characterized by the time path captured by figure 3.1, where we isolate movements along some downward-sloping home country emigration function (EM) and shifts in that function. In preindustrial episodes, we observe low emigration rates (e_0) and low wages (w_0). Industrialization and other events then serve both to raise the emigration function to EM' and real wages to w_1. The former dominates in this example, since emigration rates have *risen* to e_1; in the absence of the shift in EM, emigration rates would have *fallen* to e_1'. In later stages of development, EM' is taken to be stable so that further improvements in real wages at home, to w_2, cut back emigration rates to e_2. Thus, the stylized emigration facts are reproduced in figure 3.1. If late-nineteenth-century European emigration is to be successfully explained, we need to identify factors that might account for the outward shift in the emigration function as well as the elasticity describing emigrants' response to wage gaps along that function. If these forces were operating in the same way in Latin and non-Latin countries, the latecomer surge in Latin emigration may be simply a repeat performance of what occurred in northern Europe 30 or 40 years earlier. What, then, accounts for the rightward shifts in EM during early industrialization and its stability thereafter?

Following Easterlin, one possibility is lagged population growth. As we have noted, Easterlin saw this as leading, with a lag, to labor market glut and lower real wages, in which case its effects would be captured in the home wage rate. However, alternative explanations would account for a *direct* effect for lagged demographic increase rather than (or in addition to) an *indirect* effect via the wage. First, if differences in natural increase were driven chiefly by variations in births and infant mortality, this could act as a proxy for the proportion of the population who, 20 or 30 years later, were in the prime emigration age group. Since this age cohort had a much higher propensity to emigrate than those older or younger, one might observe higher emigration rates associated with faster lagged natural increase even if real wage gaps between home and abroad remained unchanged. A second reason for a direct demographic effect is that genuine labor surplus developed, particularly in rural areas. As several studies of local emigration rates have suggested, access to land was often a critical determinant: those who were unable to inherit or marry into a tenancy or smallholding had little option but to leave. If these effects were important, they should be more powerful the more rural and less industrial the country.

We need also to take account of industrialization and urbanization. A higher share of the population in industry or urban occupations might be associated with greater employment opportunities in domestic industry, but it might also be associated with higher rates of mobility. The overseas mobility of rural populations was probably lower for three reasons. First, a significant share of those in the mobile rural age cohorts migrated toward their own cities. Second, the rural exodus tended to deplete the number of village residents in the mobile age cohort, while it augmented those cohorts in the cities. For that reason alone it must have created a relatively young urban labor force (Williamson 1988, 1990: ch. 2) that would have been more responsive to wage gaps favoring the New World. Third, city workers had more experience with urban labor markets at home, labor markets similar to those that absorbed so many of them when they arrived in the New World. In short, rising urban population shares and falling agricultural employment shares might have fostered greater overseas emigration, given the wage gap between the Old

World and the New, and we should account for this in our explanation of cross-country emigration rates.

What about persistence and path dependence? As we have seen, the influence of friends and relatives abroad sending letters containing information about prospects and remitting prepaid tickets is likely to have been a powerful force. Persistence is typically captured by the lagged dependent variable in time series studies, and it was found to be important in Tomaske's cross-country study. As Gould (1979: 658) notes, this is often the *most* significant variable in time series and some analysts have interpreted the result as reflecting the power of chain migration. However, it might also be interpreted as reflecting the formation of (adaptive) expectations about the future (see chapter 4). In any case one might have expected the friends and relatives effect to operate through the stock of all previous migrants, not just the previous year's flow, even though the more recent emigrants sent more frequent letters and remittances home than those who emigrated much earlier. But emigrants were also influenced by the possiblilty of migrating to a community that retained the language and some of the customs of the origin country—which strengthens the effect of the emigrant stock. We therefore need to account for the accummulated stock of previous emigrants as well as flows in the recent past. These variables are likely to have progressively increased the propensity to emigrate for a given real wage gap and, together with other structural variables, should help explain upward trends in emigration in the face of declining wage gaps favoring the New World.

Econometric Results

The dependent variable is the decade gross emigration rate. The sample of 48 includes the 60 cell observations in table 3.1, less 11 due to the presence of the lagged dependent variable, and less one due to the lack of data on an explanatory variable for Germany in the 1860s. The remaining sample (with the number of observations for each country) is therefore Belgium 1860–1913 (5); Denmark 1880–1913 (3); France 1870–1913 (4); Germany 1870–1913 (4); Great Britain 1860–1913 (5); Ireland 1860–1913 (5); Italy 1880–1913 (3); Netherlands 1860–1913 (5); Norway 1880–1913 (3); Portugal 1870–1913 (4); Spain 1890–1913 (2); and Sweden 1860–1913 (5).

Five main explanatory variables are introduced: the real wage gap between the home country and foreign destinations, entered as the log of the wage ratio (table 3.2); a demographic variable for lagged natural increase (20 years earlier); the share of the labor force in agriculture as an inverse proxy for industrialization; the stock of previous migrants living abroad at the beginning of the decade; and the dependent variable, the emigration rate, lagged one decade. The detailed derivation of these variables can be found in appendix A.

Table 3.3 reports estimates of several different variants of the model. They are generally quite successful with the adjusted R^2 around 0.7 in each case. The results strongly support a number of the hypotheses summarized above. We examined dummies for individual countries and found that only the ones for Belgium, Italy, Portugal, and Spain, which we combine into one dummy, were significant. The pos-

Table 3.3 The Determinants of Gross European Emigration Rates in the Late Nineteenth Century (n = 48): Overall Patterns

	1	2	3	4
Constant	−4.66	−1.56	−8.18	−6.08
	(2.66)	(1.34)	(0.14)	(3.25)
Share of male labor force	−4.04	−8.94	−4.10	−4.57
in agriculture	(1.26)	(2.45)	(1.20)	(1.29)
Log wage ratio	−6.86	−6.51	−6.81	−8.74
(home/destination)	(3.63)	(3.39)	(3.06)	(4.42)
Lagged natural increase	0.26		0.27	0.37
	(2.61)		(2.52)	(3.49)
Migrant stock/home population	0.09	0.08	0.09	0.22
	(1.89)	(1.62)	(1.84)	(8.40)
Lagged migration rate	0.52	0.56	0.52	
	(3.17)	(3.48)	(3.08)	
Lagged natural increase times		0.44		
labor force share in agriculture		(2.17)		
Log home real wage			1.86	
			(0.07)	
Log home real wage squared			−0.24	
			(0.07)	
Country dummy (Belgium,	4.43	4.27	4.41	5.64
Italy, Portugal, Spain)	(3.86)	(3.66)	(3.25)	(4.72)
$\bar{R}^2$	0.71	0.70	0.70	0.69
RSS	194.47	203.41	194.43	242.22
RESET	0.00	0.14	0.00	0.10

Note: t statistics are in parenthesis. RESET is the test for functional form using the square of the fitted values. The dependent variable is annual average emigration per 1,000 of population. Column numbers refer to different regression equations.

itive coefficients for the Latin countries may owe something to their high levels of temporary migration; we search for other possible explanations in chapter 6 (the Italian case). Migration within Europe was higher than the international wage gap would have predicted, partly because of shorter distances and lower moving costs, and partly because of cultural affinities. This was especially true of Latin and Belgian emigration rates.[2] None of the other country dummies was significant when entered separately in column 1. Thus, the observed low emigration rates from France and the high emigration rates from Ireland were not due to some deviant behavior, but rather to differences in the economic and demographic environment dictating their emigration experience. A time trend was also introduced to test for a secular change in emigration rates that might have been due, for instance, to falling transport costs. Although the time trend took a positive coefficient as expected, it was not significant.[3] Thus, the greater part of the variation across countries and through time can be explained by the variables in our model. Let us examine each variable in turn, focusing chiefly on column 1.

The real wage gap between source and destination had a powerful influence on emigration rates, and in the direction that conventional theory predicts: the higher the real wage at home, the lower the emigration rate. This result confirms the downward sloping emigration function in figure 3.1. The paradox of rising emigration coinciding with the convergence between Old World and New World wage rates is largely explained by those demographic and industrialization forces that induced rightward shifts in the emigration function. In column 3, we test the competing hypothesis that an inverted U-shaped emigration life cycle might arise from the growth of home wages alone: as the home wage first rises, the financial constraint is released and the emigration rate rises, but later, as the home wage continues to rise, and the wage gap closes, emigration begins to fall. The quadratic in the log of the home wage in column 3 gives the right signs for an inverted U but the level and the squared term give t statistics far smaller than one.[4] Furthermore, despite the inclusion of these terms, the coefficient on the log wage ratio remains stable (although its significance declines), suggesting that it was relative, not absolute, home wages that drove emigration from Europe in the late nineteenth century.

The results presented in column 1 suggest that a 10 percent rise in the real wage ratio reduced the emigration rate by $(0.1)(-6.86)/(1 - 0.52) = 1.27$ per thousand in the long-run steady state. This estimated impact is in the center of the range of those obtained from the annual time series models for individual countries explored in chapter 4. To anticipate those results, a 10 percent increase in the wage ratio lowered the United Kingdom emigration rate in the long run by 1.9–2.4 per thousand, the Swedish and Norwegian rates by 1.1 per thousand, and the Danish rate by 0.6 per thousand. Thus, annual time series and the cross-country analysis seem to be reporting consistent orders of magnitude. These effects were sufficiently powerful to exert an important impact on emigration.

The rate of natural increase was important, just as Easterlin suggested, and its influence was felt *directly* on emigration, not simply *indirectly* through an induced glut in home labor supply and thus on home wage rates. That is, the indirect effect that Easterlin stressed is already present in our wage variable, but additional direct demographic effects are significant and large in every column in table 3.3. The coefficient in column 1 implies that a permanent rise of one per thousand in natural increase led to a long-run increase in the emigration rate of 0.54 per thousand, a powerful effect indeed. The twenty-year generational lag implies that the impact was felt only in the long run, but the rise in the rate of natural increase was sufficiently pronounced on the upswing of the European demographic transition to have had a big impact on the mass migrations, as we shall see in a moment. It appears that a country's stage of demographic transition accounted for much of the intercountry variation in emigration rates as well as country trends across the late nineteenth century. Rightward shifts in the emigration function on the upswing of those surges in mass migration owed a good deal to direct demographic forces.

Although the impact of the share of the labor force in agriculture is always negative, it is not significant in columns 1, 3, or 4. This is consistent with our hypothesis that it had offsetting effects on emigration. While industrialization (a fall in the agricultural share) may have made labor more mobile in response to given incentives, if it also involved a shift from low-wage to high-wage sectors, it reduced emigration. The former dominated, although the latter must have served to mute the impact.[5] The coefficient in column 1 indicates, for example, that a fall in the agricultural share from, say, 50 percent to 40 percent raised the emigration rate by 0.84 per thousand. This effect may have been substantial although the estimate is imprecise. Column 2 explores the additional hypothesis that the share in agriculture should be interacted with the demographic variable, to the extent that direct demographic spillovers into emigration would be greater the more agricultural the economy. Column 2 supports the argument, and the size and significance of the agricultural share variable alone is also enhanced. However, when the variable lagged natural increase was added to the estimating equation, it was not significant, and the interacted variable also lost significance. The RESET test for functional form, which is easily passed in both cases, does not offer unambiguous evidence to discriminate between these alternative specifications.

What about persistence? We have already raised the question about whether the friends and relatives or chain migration effects would be best captured by the lagged dependent variable or by the emigrant stock. In fact, both mattered. The lagged dependent variable has an estimated coefficient of 0.52, suggesting that the effects of a once-and-for-all shock such as a famine should have died out almost completely after three or four decades. But the influence of past emigration (occurring cumulatively through the emigrant stock) had a much longer lasting effect. Column 1 suggests that the emigrant stock effect was quite powerful, although the coefficient is only significant at the 10 percent level. For every 1,000 previous emigrants still living, 20 more were pulled abroad each year. Even though this effect is large, it is not as large as the 90–130 per thousand previous emigrants estimated on annual time series in chapter 4. Is part of the chain migration effect being captured by the lagged dependent variable? As demonstrated in column 4, the coefficients on the relative wage and demographic variables hardly change at all when the lagged dependent variable is excluded. However, the coefficient on the emigrant stock variable *does* change, suggesting that the lagged dependent variable and the emigrant stock capture separate but closely related phenomena.

Finally, it has often been suggested that the appropriate variable for analysis should be net rather than gross emigration. Unfortunately, it is not possible to obtain net emigration for all country/decades included in the gross emigration sample. However, a smaller sample of 33 for those documenting net emigration rates was also used to estimate the model, and the results are compared with the estimates using gross emigration over the same sample in appendix B. The results are very similar to those in table 3.3. In both cases, the restricted sample gives slightly larger relative wage effects, and weaker labor-force-share-in-agriculture effects than when the dependent variable is measured gross. Apart from these minor differences, apparently net and gross emigration can be explained by the same set of variables, with roughly the same magnitudes on the estimated coefficients.

It is time to summarize this chapter's findings thus far. First, the ratio of home to receiving-country wages had a significant negative impact on emigration. While consistent with conventional theory, earlier studies—constrained by lack of comparative data on real wages (a constraint now released: Williamson 1995)—had been unable to isolate adequately this effect. Second, the rate of natural increase lagged 20 years had a powerful effect on emigration rates, just as Easterlin forcibly argued more than 30 years ago. This demographic effect stimulated emigration *directly* by raising the share of the population in the prime emigration age group rather than only *indirectly* by lowering the domestic wage, raising unemployment, or both. Third, emigration increased as the proportion of the labor force in agriculture fell. While this effect was never very strong, it does support the argument of Massey (1988) and a number of earlier writers who interpreted industrialization as a break with ties to the land leading to increased labor mobility (Semmingsen 1960: 152–53; Thistlethwaite 1960: 38).

There is also strong evidence of persistence in emigration rates as reflected in two variables, the emigration rate in the previous decade and the stock of previous emigrants living abroad. These variables reflect the important pull of earlier migrants—the friends and relatives or chain migration effect stressed by many historians. The first of the two variables may also reflect the lagged adjustment of expectations, but both proved very important and significant.

Were the Latin Countries Different?

The econometric model of European emigration estimated and reported in table 3.3 does indeed show that the Latin countries (and Belgium) were different, but only in one dimension. That is, holding everything else constant, emigration rates from late-nineteenth-century Italy, Portugal, and Spain were significantly higher than they were in northwestern Europe. Given that the gross emigration rate exaggerates the net emigration rate for these countries in the Mediterranean Basin more than for the rest of Europe,[6] the positive coefficient on the Latin dummy may be spurious. We will now pursue this important issue from three new directions. First, while table 3.3 showed that the Latin region had higher emigration rates *ceteris paribus*, did Latin emigrants also respond differently to any of the variables? Second, and more specifically, was Latin emigrant labor in more elastic supply to the New World? Third, were the same underlying economic and demographic fundamentals at work pushing the Latin emigrants abroad that we have seen at work elsewhere in Europe?

Table 3.4 provides some answers. The core model appears again as column 1, but this time the three Latin countries are separated from Belgium.[7] It indicates that the Latin countries alone had gross emigration rates 4.9 per thousand higher than the other countries of northwestern Europe, controlling for other influences. Column 2 examines the hypothesis that natural increase was a particularly potent force driving Latin emigration by interacting natural increase with the Latin dummy. The coefficient, though positive, is tiny and insignificant, offering no evidence to favor the hypothesis. In other regressions (not shown), we examined

Table 3.4 The Determinants of Gross European Emigration Rates in the Late Nineteenth Century ($n = 48$): Looking at the Latin Countries

	1	2	3	4
Constant	−3.51	−3.44	−3.82	−3.87
	(1.67)	(1.51)	(1.73)	(1.70)
Share of male labor	−4.77	−4.73	−5.63	−5.50
force in agriculture	(1.45)	(1.41)	(1.67)	(1.47)
Log wage ratio	−5.92	−5.86	−6.77	−6.62
(home/destination)	(2.81)	(2.56)	(2.93)	(2.48)
Lagged natural increase	0.26	0.25	0.26	0.27
	(2.50)	(2.27)	(2.48)	(2.50)
Migrant stock/home	0.10	0.10	0.12	0.10
population	(2.07)	(2.03)	(2.31)	(2.08)
Lagged migration rate	0.47	0.47	0.43	0.47
	(2.82)	(2.78)	(2.55)	(2.81)
Belgium dummy	3.16	3.12	3.65	3.62
	(1.85)	(1.70)	(2.01)	(1.79)
Latin dummy (Italy,	4.94	4.73	−68.88	6.96
Portugal, Spain)	(3.93)	(1.53)	(0.11)	(1.44)
Latin times lagged natural		0.03		
increase		(0.08)		
Latin times log home			31.98	
real wage			(0.10)	
Latin times log home			−3.24	
real wage squared			(0.08)	
Latin times log real wage ratio				2.52
(home/foreign)				(0.43)
$\bar{R}^2$	0.71	0.71	0.72	0.71
RSS	189.77	189.74	178.72	188.86
RESET	0.12	0.13	1.13	0.30

Notes: See table 3.3. Latin = Italy, Portugal, and Spain. Column numbers refer to different regression equations.

the effects of interacting in turn the share of the labor force in agriculture and the migrant stock with the Latin dummy. Neither produced a significant coefficient.

We next ask whether Latin emigration was *uniquely* constrained by poverty. Recall the argument from chapter 2 that potential emigrants in the poorest European countries were so income-constrained by their poverty that they could not afford the move; as real wages rose at home, the constraint was slowly released, but at some point further increases in home wages lost their influence. Table 3.3 rejected that hypothesis, but since it was developed primarily to account for Italian experience (Faini 1991; Faini and Venturini 1994b), table 3.4 tries again with this sharper focus. When column 3 adds the home wage in nonlinear form but now interacts it with the Latin dummy, the hypothesis is again rejected even as it applied to the Latin countries. It appears that the escape from poverty, associated with rising real wages, cannot account for much of the rise in Latin emigration after

Table 3.5 Sources of Changing Emigration Rates, 1890s–1900s

Country	1 Predicted change in emigration rate	2 Lagged natural increase	3 Due to Agricultural share	4 Real wage ratio	5 Migrant stock
Italy	0.350	1.305	0.079	−1.304	0.270
Spain	2.803	−0.340	0.711	2.102	0.330
Portugal	2.526	1.663	0.082	0.512	0.269
Sweden	−0.845	−0.140	0.619	−1.579	0.255
Great Britain	0.110	−0.500	0.181	0.633	−0.204

Notes: The predicted values in col. 1 refer to the change in gross emigration rates between 1890–99 and 1900–13, and they are derived by summing the four entries in cols. 2–5. The $\hat{\beta}_x$ used in cols. 2–5 refer to the estimated coefficients in table 3.4 (column 1), evaluated at their long-run values (e.g., each divided by one minus the coefficient on the lagged dependent variable). The ΔX refer to changes in each explanatory variable also between 1890–1899 and 1900–1913.

1880. Although table 3.4 does not report the results, we were also able to reject the hypotheses that the linear interaction alone mattered, although it does give a positive coefficient (t statistic = 1.55). We shall investigate the question of whether rising income stimulated emigration from Italy in more detail in chapter 6.

Is it true that Latin migration supplies to the New World were more elastic than was true of the rest of Europe? Column 4 tests this important hypothesis by adding an interaction term to column 1, the Latin dummy multiplied by the wage gap. The hypothesis is soundly rejected: it is simply not true that the Latin economies in the late nineteenth century were characterized by more elastic emigrant labor supplies than those in the rest of Europe, a revisionist result consistent with Alan Taylor's (1994) recent findings that immigration rates in Argentina were no more responsive to wage gaps than they were in Australia. It serves to damage the arguments of Sir Arthur Lewis (1978) and Carlos Diaz-Alejandro (1970) regarding Latin American development under (uniquely) elastic labor supplies.

If the Latin emigrants seem to have responded to their economic and demographic environment pretty much like those in the rest of Europe, perhaps it was the environment they left behind that was different. Table 3.5 explores this proposition by multiplying the estimated coefficients in table 3.4 (column 1 converted to long-run impact) by the change in the right-hand-side variable of interest. The multiplication yields a figure that tells us just how much of the predicted rise in decade emigration rates between, say, 1890–1899 and 1900–1913 (the sum of columns 2–5) can be explained by changes in natural increase, agricultural share, the real wage ratio and the migrant stock. The typical northern European patterns are illustrated by Sweden, which was on the downside of its emigration cycle after the 1890s, having reached peak emigration rates earlier (table 3.1). Thus, the decline in the predicted gross emigration rate for Sweden, -0.845, is explained entirely by two forces: the decline in the rate of natural increase two decades previously (-0.140) and the spectacular catch-up of Swedish real wages on those abroad (-1.579), the other two forces tending to have weaker effects serving to increase emigration.

Table 3.5 shows that very different economic and demographic forces were at work in the latecomer Latin countries. A boom in the natural rate of population increase two decades earlier was a powerful force serving to push up emigration rates in Italy and Portugal, experience on the upswing of the demographic transition that was replicated in the rest of Europe earlier in the century. These are by far the most powerful forces accounting for the surge in Italian and Portuguese emigration rates after the 1890s. Spain, however, is an exception: two decades earlier rates of natural increase were *falling*, not rising, a fact well appreciated by demographic historians (Moreda 1987). All three Latin countries shared additional underlying fundamentals that contributed to the surge in emigration: modest rates of industrialization and rising migrant populations abroad.

If emigrant-inducing demographic forces were absent in Spain after the 1890s, why the sharp rise in Spanish emigration rates? The answer seems to lie largely with economic failure at home. The wage gap between Spain and destination countries widened at the end of the century (table 3.2), and this event explains almost all of the surge in Spanish emigration. The same was true of Portugal, although the failure at home was not nearly as great. In contrast, Italian wages catch up with those in destination countries—the United States, Argentina, and Germany, and that wage success at home muted the surge in Italian emigration by partially offsetting those powerful emigrant-inducing demographic forces. What really made the Latin countries different after the 1890s was the delayed demographic transition and the economic failure in Portugal and Spain. In Italy, however, the combined effects are modest, and yet as table 3.1 showed, the surge in emigration was greatest. This puzzle deserves further examination—a task deferred until chapter 6.

Latin economic failure helps account for the surge of emigration after the 1890s; oddly enough, the same is true of Britain. British emigration rose to a peak in the 1880s, falling thereafter, thus obeying an emigration life cycle repeated by so many countries in nineteenth-century Europe. However, British emigration departed from this emigration life cycle pattern after the 1890s; that is, the emigration rate *rose* rather than continuing its fall. What made Britain different after the 1890s? Exactly the same forces that made Spain and Portugal different: economic failure at home.[8]

To summarize, contrary to conventional wisdom, the Latin emigrants did *not* exhibit a more elastic labor supply response to wages home and abroad. Nor did the Latin emigrations respond any differently to the demographic transition and industrial revolutionary events at home. What distinguished the late-nineteenth-century Latin countries from the rest of Europe to the northwest was their latecomer status and, with the exception of Italy, their weak economic and demographic performance when industrialization arrived late. With the exception of the Irish driven abroad by the famine, mass emigration in Europe had to await the forces of industrialization at home and a glut in the mobile age cohort driven by a demographic transition that industrialization produced. Furthermore, real wages in the industrializing European northwest were catching up with real wages in destination areas, and these forces held the mass emigrations in check, at least partially. As industrialization and the demographic boom slowed down in northwest Europe, real wage catch-up began to dominate, thus cutting back mass emigration. Italy seems to exhibit the same pattern, but with a lag. The differences lie with the Iberian peninsula. Spain never underwent a powerful demographic transition in the late nineteenth century; its mass emigration was driven instead by economic failure at home, especially after the 1890s. Portugal did undergo a powerful demographic transition in the late nineteenth century, but its mass emigration was also driven, at least in part, by economic failure at home.

Many have argued that nineteenth-century Latin labor markets were segmented from those in northwest Europe. After all, Latin laborers did not head north in large numbers. Had they done so, wages would have risen more at home due to greater labor scarcity, and wages would have risen less in northern Europe due to greater labor glut. They did not emigrate north in large numbers, and thus the Latins missed an opportunity—more rapid real wage growth even in the absence of dramatic industrialization at home. By not doing so, Latin labor markets remained segmented from the more dynamic parts of Europe. Furthermore, so the argument goes, with the exception of southern Italians, most Latin emigrants went overseas to South America, where real wages were lower, rather than to North America, where real wages were higher.

If segmentation was induced by discriminatory immigration policy or cultural preference, it should be possible to assess its impact. Imagine the following counterfactual: what would Latin emigration rates have been like had they faced the same overseas labor market options (as measured by destination wage rates) that faced the potential British emigrant? We do not have the space here to offer a detailed answer, but we calculate tentatively that Latin emigrations in the 1890s and 1900s would have been higher by 5 per thousand and would have doubled the emigration rates from the Iberian Peninsula. The more challenging question is to assess the impact of the counterfactually higher emigration on the Latin economies. Would the greater labor scarcity at home have raised Latin living standards considerably, perhaps helping the Latin economies join the convergence process much earlier?

The Stylized Facts of European Emigration

European emigration experience has often been characterized as following a life cycle pattern like that illustrated by figure 2.3. This stylized inverted U was origi-

Table 3.6 Quadratic Trends in Emigration Rates, 1860–1913

	Constant	Time	Time²/100	R^2
Belgium	0.273	−0.004	0.006	0.077
	(8.029)	(2.107)	(2.328)	
Denmark	−0.170	0.022	−0.024	0.272
	(1.760)	(3.774)	(3.209)	
France	−0.007	0.001	−0.002	0.053
	(0.594)	(2.224)	(2.162)	
Germany	0.004	0.013	−0.022	0.353
	(0.053)	(3.114)	(3.903)	
Great Britain	0.229	0.009	−0.001	0.286
	(1.435)	(0.928)	(0.073)	
Ireland	1.424	0.008	−0.035	0.401
	(5.263)	(0.518)	(1.593)	
Netherlands	−0.022	0.013	−0.005	0.708
	(0.291)	(2.890)	(0.820)	
Norway	0.036	0.034	−0.041	0.052
	(0.131)	(2.110)	(1.951)	
Sweden	−0.533	0.059	−0.073	0.328
	(2.767)	(5.162)	(4.875)	

Notes: Time runs from 1850 = 1. t statistics are in parentheses.

nally intended to describe late-nineteenth-century Scandinavian experience only, but Massey (1988) has recently asserted its generality. We have already argued that the upswing portion appears to be inconsistent with conventional theory and thus poses a challenge. Can our econometric results be used to explain the life cycle emigration pattern?

To begin, can the alleged life cycle pattern be identified in our sample? This question was explored by estimating a quadratic function of time for each country, using annual gross emigration rates from 1860 to 1913. Since Italy, Portugal, and Spain do not have a full-time series extending back as far as 1860, we excluded them, even though they exhibit a strong upward trend that might be viewed as the early portion of the emigration cycle. Regressions for the remaining nine countries are presented in table 3.6. With only one exception (Belgium), the regressions support the inverted U emigration pattern. This pattern is most marked for the three Scandinavian countries (Denmark, Norway, and Sweden) and Germany. These countries all experienced rapid rates of natural increase and rapid real wage growth over the period. The inverted U is also highly significant for France, although it is shallow and almost entirely due to the modest surge in emigration in the late 1880s. There is also some evidence of an inverted U for Great Britain, Ireland, and the Netherlands, but the coefficients on time and time squared are insignificant in all cases but one. In the British and Irish cases, the insignificance is largely due to the surge in emigration in the decade just prior to World War I. As we will show in chapter 4, this reflects the reversal of British and Irish real wage convergence on the New World.

The data therefore do not unambiguously support a late-nineteenth-century inverted emigration U, partly because some countries did not pass through the various phases at the same time. Some peaked early, some peaked late, and some had not yet passed a peak even by World War I. To analyze the forces driving the emigration rate over the European emigration life cycle, the emigration history of each country must be realigned so that the upswing, the peak, and the downswing coincide. To do so, the peak emigration decade must be located for each country. For all the countries in table 3.1 except Belgium and the three Latin, we simply select the decade when the estimated quadratic reached a maximum. For Belgium, Italy, and Portugal, we assume the maximum occurred in the final decade, 1900–1913, while for Spain we assume it would have occurred in the following decade, 1910–1920. Using these criteria, the peak decades are:

Belgium: 1900s   Great Britain: 1890s   Norway: 1890s
Denmark: 1890s   Ireland: 1860s   Portugal: 1900s
France: 1880s   Italy: 1900s   Spain: 1910s
Germany: 1880s   Netherlands: 1900s   Sweden: 1890s

Next, we force history to conform to what we call "emigration time." For each country, the peak decade is given a value of 5 with the decades 1 to 4 leading up to the peak and the decades 6 to 9 following on the downswing. The decade gross emigration rates featured in table 3.1 and analyzed in table 3.3 are then regressed on emigration time and emigration time squared, where the full set of country dummies (standardized on Britain) are included to allow for individual country

Table 3.7 Trends in "Emigration Time" ($n = 48$)

Dependent variable	Constant	Emigration time	Emigration time squared	$\bar{R}^2$
Gross emigration rate	−0.35	2.66	−0.27	0.74
	(0.21)	(3.65)	(3.39)	
Fitted values (from col. 1, table 3.3)	0.14	1.93	−0.18	0.88
	(0.15)	(4.57)	(4.02)	
Rate of natural increase	9.11	1.96	−0.15	0.78
	(6.82)	(3.35)	(2.25)	
Log wage ratio (home/destination)	−0.50	0.03		0.81
	(7.44)	(2.08)		
Share of male labor force in agriculture	0.28	−0.05	0.002	0.97
	(13.08)	(4.84)	(2.11)	
Log migrant stock/ home population	1.58	0.20	−0.01	0.96
	(9.10)	(2.67)	(1.39)	

Notes: Dummy variables were included for all countries with Great Britain as the excluded country. *t* statistics are in parentheses.

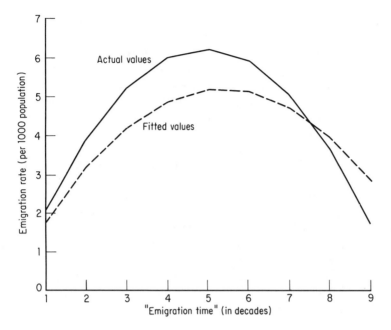

Figure 3.2 Stylized European Emigration Pattern

differences. The result appears as the first row of table 3.7 (although the country dummies are not reported), and it confirms a strong inverted U. This stylized pattern of late-nineteenth-century emigration is plotted in figure 3.2 ("actual values"): the life cycle begins in the first decade of emigration time recording an emigration rate a little above 2 per thousand; it then soars to over 6 per thousand in the peak decade before falling again to around 3 per thousand in the eighth decade and 2 per thousand in the ninth decade.

Can this emigration life cycle be explained by the evolution of the explanatory variables in our model of emigration? We search for the answer by first regressing the fitted values from table 3.3 (column 1) on emigration time and emigration time squared. This appears as the second row in table 3.7 and the result is also plotted in figure 3.2 ("fitted values"). Although the fitted values give a little flatter profile, it is apparent that the variables used to explain late-nineteenth-century emigration rates account for much of the upswing and downswing of emigration observed in the data.

Do the key explanatory variables also follow systematic trends over emigration time? The answers appear in the remaining rows of table 3.7.[9] The rate of natural increase lagged two decades reveals a strong quadratic: that is, it replicates the demographic transition. Lagged natural increase follows the same inverted U as does emigration itself, but with a difference: the peak occurs in decade seven, two decades after the peak in emigration. The log of the wage ratio does not follow a quadratic trend over emigration time, but rather exhibits a steep linear upward trend (table 3.7, row 3). This replicates real wage convergence as Old World real wages caught up with those in the New. For European countries in our sample, their real wages converged on the relevant destination real wage at an impressive average rate of 3 percent per decade (for more details, see Williamson, 1995, and chapter 9). Impressive real wage convergence such as this must have put powerful downward pressure on the emigration rate for the typical European country. This convergence would have been even greater (more than 4 percent per decade) but for the economic failures in Portugal and Spain.

We performed the same exercise for the share in agriculture. As the fifth row shows, it also exhibits a quadratic trend but the coefficients indicate a continued decline throughout the nine decades of emigration time. It first declines rapidly and then more slowly, replicating patterns noted long ago by Colin Clark and Simon Kuznets. Finally, we have the stock of previous emigrants as a proportion of the home population. This variable is endogenous in the very long run, but it is important to characterize its typical path over emigration time. To do this, we take the log of the variable to allow the quadratic to capture proportionate rather than absolute changes over time. It too exhibits an inverse U: it rises through most of the period, reaching a peak in the ninth decade of emigration time.

What role did each of these variables play in contributing to the observed emigration life cycle? The answer lies with the product of the estimated coefficients in Table 3.3 and the changes in the variables themselves implied by table 3.7. Since the estimated model is dynamic by virtue of the inclusion of the lagged dependent variable, it seems appropriate to use the long-run coefficients implied by column 1 of table 3.3. By so doing, we at least take some account of the cumulative impact of the explanatory variables embodied in the lagged dependent variable. The changing contribution of each variable is shown in figure 3.3, where each is normalized to zero in the first period of emigration time.

The long-run contribution of *direct* demographic events rises up until decade six when it contributes about two per thousand to emigration compared to decade one. This was clearly an important source of the upswing in emigration, but it gradually weakened as these countries passed through their demographic transitions. It was assisted by the weaker effects of industrialization, although we are less certain about the precise magnitude. This effect appears to have gradually raised emigration at a declining rate throughout the emigration cycle to an extent amounting to a little under one per thousand in decade nine. These two forces were enhanced by the cumulative effects of the stock of emigrants abroad. This rose strongly through the first six decades of emigration time, peaking in decade nine with a contribution of over 1 per thousand to the annual emigration rate. Of course, this effect was itself the product of economic and demographic fundamentals acting on emigration reaching far back in time.

These three variables together had a joint effect that traced out a quadratic trend rising at first strongly but then flattening out and reaching a peak in the eighth decade of emigration time. At the peak, the total contribution of these variables to

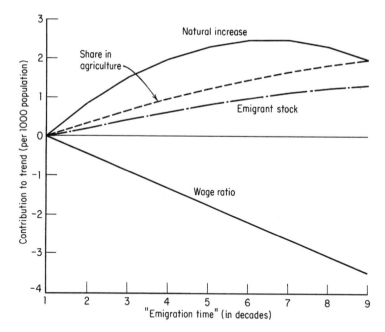

Figure 3.3 Factors in Trend Emigration

emigration compared with the first decade was 5.4 per thousand. This predicted profile is clearly very different from the actual or the fitted emigration trends as demonstrated in figure 3.2. The difference lies in the strong positive linear trend in the home-to-destination wage ratios. As figure 3.3 shows, the impact of the wage ratio was to reduce emigration by over three per thousand by decade nine of emigration time.

An emigration life cycle identified for so many European countries can be explained by demographic trends, industrialization, and real wage convergence. High rates of natural increase, rapid industrialization, and a growing stock of previous emigrants abroad dominated the upswing of the emigration cycle. Thus, early industrialization bred European emigration in the late nineteenth century, much like that observed for Mexico, Central America, the Middle East, and Asia since the 1950s. But European real wages were catching up with New World real wages from midcentury to World War I, and this convergence served to keep more potential emigrants at home, a force that tended to lower emigration rates throughout. When the forces of demographic transition eased and industrialization slowed, the forces of convergence began to dominate, aided by the weakening pull of the stock of previous emigrants as their numbers abroad leveled out. When the forces of the demographic transition reversed, they joined the forces of wage convergence, causing emigration rates to fall sharply, even before World War I and the quotas of the 1920s.

A European Model of Mass Emigration Emerges

The forces driving the European mass migration life cycle are now much clearer. In the early phases of emigration and modern development, the demographic transition, industrialization, and the cumulative impact of previous emigrants abroad outweighed the negative impact of real wage convergence. Thus, even though European real wages were catching up on real wages in the more labor-scarce New World, emigration rates did not ease but rather surged. But as demographic transition forces waned, as the rate of industrialization slowed down, and as the emigrant stock abroad began to level out, real wage convergence between labor markets at home and abroad increasingly dominated events. The continued fall in the wage gap between home and destination areas (due largely to European wages catching up with New World wages) finally caused emigration rates to drop. The fall in emigration rates accelerated on the downswing as *direct* demographic forces now joined these long-run labor market effects, that is, as the young adult cohort, most responsive to labor market forces, declined in relative importance. We suspect that these forces would have stemmed the European mass migration tide, at least from the Mediterranean Basin and the north, soon after World War I even in the absence of American quotas. But the quotas were imposed to deal with a new flood of emigrants coming from the south and east—countries on the upswing of their emigration cycle.

Appendix A. Data for Emigration Analysis

Four different sets of variables are used in the analysis carried out in this chapter. The first consists of the dependent variables: late-nineteenth and early-twentieth-century gross and net emigration rates of 12 European countries (Belgium, Denmark, France, Germany, Ireland, Italy, the Netherlands, Norway, Portugal, Spain, Sweden, and Great Britain). The second set of variables is based on estimates of the real wage in each of these 12 sending Old World countries as well as the real wages in four receiving New World countries (Argentina, Australia, Canada, and the United States). The third group of variables is a collection of estimates of the labor force share in the primary sector, the fourth consists of measures of the rate of natural increase in these same countries, and the fifth offers estimates of migrant stocks abroad.

Decade Averaging

The unit of observation for each variable is the decade average calculated in all cases from the underlying annual observations. Any country has at most six observation decades—from the 1850s through the first decade of the 1900s, although not all of these six decades are available for all 12 countries. In most cases, a decade is defined as the period of time running from a year ending in "0" to a year ending in "9." Thus, the 1860s are the years 1860–1869, the 1870s the years 1870–1879, and so on. The first decade of the 1900s is an exception to this rule, as averages for this "decade" are calculated from annual observations for the years 1900–1913. We also allow additional exceptions to our definition of a decade where doing so allows us to keep decade observations we might otherwise be forced to discard due to the lack of a small number of annual observations. Thus, we construct the first decade average for some countries using data starting in years ending in "1" or "2," as opposed to the usual "0." When an initial decade is shortened in this way, the abbreviated definition of the decade is used for the construction of all variable averages for that particular country and decade.

The years for which the earliest data are included are as follows: Belgium, 1850; Denmark, 1871; France, 1860; Germany, 1850; Ireland, 1851; Italy, 1871; Netherlands, 1850; Norway, 1870; Portugal, 1870; Spain, 1882; Sweden, 1851; Great Britain, 1851.

Emigration Rates

The gross and net emigration rates used as dependent variables are simple decade (or near decade) averages of the relevant annual emigration rates. The emigration rate is calculated as the number of emigrants (gross or net) in that year divided by the country's population in the same year. The result is expressed as a percentage. The population estimates used for the calculation of the emigration rates are from Mitchell (1980: 29–34), except for Portugal, which is taken from Baganha (1990: table 4.3, 213–14). Mitchell's estimates are for census dates only; the annual estimates used in this book are derived by linear interpolation.

All estimates of gross and net emigration flows are based on the data compiled in the "National Tables" section of Ferenczi and Willcox (1929), except for Portugal, which is taken from Baganha (1990: table 4.3, 213–14). Gross flows are based on the emigration estimates tabulated for each sending country, with preference given to measures that focus on the emigration of citizens of the country in question. Net flows are derived by subtracting the immigration estimates from the emigration flows. Most of our immigration estimates are derived from statistics compiled by each of the sending countries, although estimates for Belgium, Denmark, France, and Germany were constructed by aggregating estimates of emigration from each of these countries to various destination countries. (The data for these aggregations can also be found in the "National Tables" section of Ferenczi and Willcox.)

The gross emigration rates from Great Britain are modifications of those published in Ferenczi and Willcox, as the latter include emigrants from Ireland. To construct estimates for emigration from Great Britain alone, we subtract from Ferenczi and Willcox's values their estimates of emigration from Ireland and then use this alternative measure of gross emigration in both the gross and net emigration rate calculations for Great Britain.

Gross emigration rates are available for all country-decade combinations in our sample. Because of insufficient immigration data, however, we are unable to compile net emigration rates for the following countries and decades: Germany, 1850s; Ireland, all decades; Italy, 1870s and 1880s; Netherlands, 1850s and 1860s;

Norway, all decades; Portugal, all decades; Sweden, 1850s, 1860s, and 1870s; Great Britain, 1850s. However, since qualitative evidence suggests only trivial return migration to Ireland, we take Irish net and gross emigration to be the same. Also, net emigration from Great Britain is derived as net United Kingdom emigration less Irish intercontinental emigration.

Real Wages

All real wage data used in this chapter are PPP-adjusted estimates of the urban unskilled real wage rate in each of the sample countries. These estimates are compiled in table A2.1 of Williamson (1995) and described in detail in the same source. The values in his table A2.1 are calculated such that the level of the real wage in Great Britain in 1905 is equal to 100. Measures of real wages in the destination countries are also reported in table A2.1 of Williamson (1995), and they are used in this chapter to construct the relevant foreign wage index for each of the sending countries. The composites are constructed by averaging each destination country's real wage over the appropriate decade and then using weights derived from the composition of emigrant flows in the decade of the 1890s to calculate the weighted average. The weights used in constructing the destination wage are the following:

Belgium: France (0.805), Netherlands (0.110), United States (0.072),
                Argentina (0.013).
Denmark: United States (1).
France: Canada (1).
Germany: Canada (0.022), United States (0.930), Argentina (0.048).
Great Britain: Canada (0.168), Australia (0.115), United States (0.717).
Ireland: Canada (0.017), Australia (0.024), United States (0.905),
                Great Britain (0.054).
Italy: France (0.256), Germany (0.266), United States (0.214),
                Argentina (0.264).
Netherlands: United States (1).
Norway: United States (1).
Portugal: United States (0.102), Argentina (0.898).
Spain: Argentina (1).
Sweden: Norway (0.078), Denmark (0.079), United States (0.843).

Shares of the Labor Force in the Primary Sector

Our estimates of the share of the male labor force in the primary sector are based on results summarized in table C1 of Mitchell (1980), where he presents estimates by Bairoch et al. (1968) of male and female employment, by sector, in numerous European countries. From these data we construct estimates, at benchmark dates, of the share of the male labor force in agriculture, forestry, and fishing. We then exponentially interpolate between these benchmark estimates to generate annual observations of the labor force share, from which we finally calculate decadal averages. For three countries—Germany (1870–1881), Norway (1870–1874), and Sweden (1851–1859)—we also extrapolate backwards from the benchmarks to obtain additional annual observations for our decade averaging. Even with these extrapolations, however, there is insufficient data to calculate the first two decade observations for Germany.

Since there are no data on the agricultural share of the labor force prior to 1890 for Portugal, estimates were derived based on regressions reported in Crafts (1984). First, we converted per capita real GDP from Nunes, Mata, and Valerio (1989: table 1) to 1970 U.S. dollars by using the Kravis et al. (1978) estimates of Portuguese per capita gross domestic product (GDP) of $1432.21. Estimates of the agricultural share of the labor force were then generated by inserting the log per capita real GDP (1970 $) and log population into Crafts' fitted equation (Crafts 1984: table 3, AGLAB including British, French, and Russian dummies). The estimates generated by this method are close to those of Mitchell (1980: table B1, 58) for the years 1890, 1900, and 1910. The annual estimates generated by this method were then averaged over the decades.

Rates of Natural Increase

Rates of natural increase are based for the most part on birth and death rate estimates compiled in table B6 of Mitchell (1980). For all cases except that of Ireland, Great Britain, and Portugal, these data are sufficient to calculate the average rate of natural increase—i.e., the difference between the birth and death rate—20 years prior to each of the emigration rate dates in our sample. Extrapolation backwards of Mitchell's data is necessary in only two cases, that of Italy and the Netherlands. In the case of Italy, the rate of natural increase in each of the years from 1851 to 1861 is assumed to have been the same as the average rate of natural increase from 1862 to 1871. For the Netherlands, the rate of natural increase in the years from 1830 to 1839 is assumed to have been the same as the average rate of natural increase from 1840 to 1850.

Our estimates of the rate of natural increase for Ireland are derived differently for three separate periods of time. For the 1830–1851 period, they are based on Mokyr's (1983: tables 3.1 and 3.2) estimates of the birth rate and the death rate in Ireland in 1841. We assume that the rates derived by Mokyr for 1841 also hold for all years from 1830 to 1845 as well as 1851. (Mokyr's tables 3.1 and 3.2 both present upper- and lower-bound estimates of the birth and death rate; we use the average of these bounds.) For the famine years, 1846–1850, we assume annual birth rates to have been equal to 30.15 births per thousand inhabitants, which is the average of Mokyr's 1841 birth rate estimates minus his estimated drop in the birth rate during the famine years (Mokyr 1980: table 3). The death rate during the famine years is assumed to have been equal to 47.93 deaths per thousand inhabitants, which is the average of Mokyr's three lower-bound estimates (1980: table 3). (The upper-bound estimates equate averted births with deaths, and as such would not be appropriate for our purposes.)

For our estimates of the rate of natural increase in Ireland for the period 1872 and beyond, we once again use the birth and death rates in Mitchell (1980: table B6). For the years between 1851 and 1872, linear interpolation is used to generate the annual observations upon which the decade averages are based.

The rate of natural increase of the British population is estimated using two sets of data. For the period 1831 to 1871, they are based on the birth and death rates for England, excluding Monmouthshire, compiled by Wrigley and Schofield (1981) and summarized in Mitchell (1988: 41 and 53). For 1872 onward, our estimates are based on birth and death rates derived as population-weighted averages of the relevant rates in England and Wales, and Scotland. The birth and death rates we use for these calculations are from Mitchell (1980: table B6), while the population estimates are from Mitchell (1988: 11–12).

When calculating the rate of natural increase 20 years prior to decades that, in our sample, have been shortened or lengthened for reasons described earlier in this appendix, the annual observations used to calculate the rate of natural increase have been decreased or increased in a similar fashion.

The rates of natural increase for Portugal (lagged 20 years) were calculated using the Baganha (1990) population and emigration data. First, the change in population over a decade was calculated. Second, the sum of emigration over the decade was then added to the change in population to generate a raw figure for natural increase. The figure was then divided by the mid-decade population to construct the decadal rate of increase.

Migrant Stock Abroad

The emigrant stocks abroad for each sending country are the totals across receiving regions of those enumerated at Census dates. The sources are the following:

UNITED STATES: Foreign-born population, by country of birth: 1850 to 1970. United States, Bureau of Census, *Historical Statistics of the United States, Colonial Times to 1970, Part I* (Washington, D.C.: U.S. Government Printing Office, 1975), pp. 117–8. These census figures have been linearly interpolated to get the 1861–1921 figures for census dates ending in "1." For Portugal we use Baganha (1990: 307), which includes the sizeable Portuguese-born in Hawaii.

CANADA: Country of birth of other British-born and the foreign-born population, Census dates 1871 to 1951. M. C. Urquhart and K. A. H. Buckley (eds.), *Historical Statistics of Canada* (Cambridge: Cambridge University Press, 1965), p. 20. The year 1861 was computed by linearly interpolating from the 1871–1891 data.

AUSTRALIA: Birthplaces of the population, 1861–1981. *Australian Historical Statistics* (Australia: Fairfax, Syme and Weldon, 1987), pp. 8–9. The year 1861 for Denmark, Netherlands, and Spain was computed by linearly interpolating from the 1871–1891 data.

NEW ZEALAND: Birthplaces of the population, 1878 to 1911 for all countries except Spain, Netherlands, Italy, and Belgium. Results of a *Census of the Dominion of New Zealand, Birthplaces and Length of Residence, Part 3* (Wellington: Marcus F. Marks, Government Printer, 1918), p. 2. Birthplaces of the population from Spain, Netherlands, Italy, and

Belgium were obtained from the 1916, 1901, and 1896 census reports: New Zealand, *Report on the Results of a Census of Population of the Dominion of New Zealand, 1916* (Wellington: Marcus F. Marks, Government Printer, 1920), p. 48; New Zealand, *Results of a Census of the Colony of New Zealand, 1901* (Wellington: John Mackay, Government Printer, 1902), p. 126. New Zealand, *Results of a Census of the Colony of New Zealand, 1896* (Wellington: John Mackay, Government Printer, 1897). Data for 1861, 1871, and 1921 for all countries was linearly interpolated from reported figures.

SOUTH AFRICA: Union residents born in principal European countries and America, 1911 to 1926 and Europeans born in the United Kingdom, 1904–1926. *Fourth Census of the Population of the Union of South Africa, Report* (Pretoria: Government Printer, 1931), pp. 111–12. Stocks for 1861–1901 were computed by linear interpolation based on data for 1911, 1918, and 1921.

ARGENTINA: Population of the Republica Argentina by nationality. Republica Argentina, *Tercer Censo Nacional* (Buenos Aires: Tallercs Graficos do L.J. Rosso y Cia, 1916), pp. 398–99 for 1914 and 1895. The stocks for 1861–1891 were computed based on gross immigrant flows as stated in Ferenczi and Willcox, *International Migration*, Vol. 1 (New York: National Bureau of Economic Research, 1929), pp. 543–44. The following estimation technique was used: foreign-born stock in 1895 in Argentina from country j, M95j, and those in 1914, M14j. Call the gross immigrant flow to Argentina over the period 1895–1914 m10sj. Calculate (M14j − M95j)/(m10sj) = Bj. Using the immigrant flow from country j over the period 1891-1895, m90sj, and using the expression (M95j − M91j)/(m90sj) = Bj, M91j was calculated. This process was continued and adjusted for years going back to 1861. Data for census taken 1901–1921 were linearly interpolated from 1891, 1895, and 1914 figures.

CUBA: Population, classified by place of birth. Stocks for 1899, 1907, and 1919 are from census reports. Spanish stock for census dates 1861–1921 are computed by linear interpolation from known figures: Cuba, *Report on the Census of Cuba, 1899* (Washington, D.C. Government Printing Office, 1900), p. 220; Cuba, *Population, History and Resources, 1907* (Washington, D.C.: United States Bureau of the Census, 1909), p. 338; Cuba, *Report on the Census of Cuba, 1919* (Havana: Maza, Arroyo y Caso, S. en C., Printers, 1920), p. 435.

BRAZIL: The benchmark figures for the Portuguese-born in Brazil were based on the Brazilian census for 1872 and 1920, along with the partial census returns for 1890 and 1906. For the 1872 census, we use the figure for all Portuguese-born in "do Imperio Brazil." An all-Brazil figure for the Portuguese-born is also reported in the 1920 census. While similar figures are not reported in the incomplete 1890 and 1906 censuses, they do report such figures for the Districo Federal. We therefore assumed that the same proportion of the Portuguese-born lived in the Districo Federal in 1890 as in 1872, and in 1906 as in 1920. This made it possible to construct estimates of the Portuguese-born in Brazil for 1890 and 1906.

Appendix B. The Samples

Gross migration is better documented than net migration, so that analysis of the latter entails a smaller sample.

Tables 3.3 and 3.4 take the gross emigration rate as the dependent variable. The decade-country sample there is $n = 48$: Belgium 1860–1913 (5); Denmark

1880–1913 (3); France 1870–1913 (4); Germany 1870–1913 (4); Great Britain 1860–1913 (5); Ireland 1860–1913 (5); Italy 1880–1913 (3); Netherlands 1860–1913 (5); Norway 1880–1913 (3); Portugal 1870–1913 (4); Spain 1890–1913 (2); and Sweden 1860–1913 (5).

The table below takes the net emigration rate as the dependent variable and estimates the regressions of table 3.3 with a smaller decade-country sample ($N = 33$): Belgium 1860–1913 (5); Denmark 1880–1913 (3); France 1870–1913 (4); Germany 1870–1913 (4); Great Britain 1870–1913 (4); Ireland 1860–1913 (5); Italy 1900–1913 (1); Netherlands 1880–1913 (3); Spain 1890–1913 (2); and Sweden 1890–1913 (2). The net emigration figures for Ireland are the same as those used for the gross emigration regressions in table 3.3 since it is widely believed that there was very little return migration to Ireland (Ó Gráda 1994: ch. 8, 15), and, in any case, the gross emigration figures are likely to be underestimates of the true gross outflow. Treating the Irish emigration figures as both gross and net is consistent with our derivation of gross and net emigration for Great Britain detailed above. The regressions in the table here for gross emigration use the same data as in table 3.3, but, for the purposes of comparison, they are for the smaller decade-country sample underlying the net emigration regressions in the table below.

The Determinants of Net and Gross Emigration in Late Nineteenth Century Europe ($N = 33$)

	Net		Gross	
	1	2	3	4
Constant	−7.38	−4.75	−7.05	−3.76
	(3.35)	(2.94)	(3.33)	(2.53)
Share of male labor force	−0.07	−7.62	−3.99	−13.58
in agriculture	(0.02)	(1.87)	(0.99)	(3.32)
Log real wage ratio	−7.83	−8.51	−9.86	−10.63
(home/destination)	(3.20)	(3.30)	(3.95)	(4.05)
Lagged natural increase	0.20		0.26	
	(2.62)		(3.21)	
Lagged natural increase times		0.55		0.71
labor force share in agriculture		(2.32)		(2.96)
Migrant stock at beginning of	0.08	0.09	0.07	0.07
decade/home population	(1.65)	(1.68)	(1.46)	(1.38)
Country dummy (Belgium,	3.97	4.34	6.55	6.96
Italy, Spain)	(2.79)	(3.22)	(3.77)	(4.47)
Lagged dependent variable	0.58	0.59	0.64	0.67
	(3.26)	(2.90)	(4.43)	(3.96)
$\bar{R}^2$	0.84	0.83	0.82	0.81
RSS	100.94	105.73	100.18	104.65
RESET	0.13	0.18	0.48	0.40

Notes: t statistics are in parenthesis. RESET is the test for functional form using the square of the fitted values. The dependent variable is annual average emigration per 1,000 of population. Column numbers refer to different regression equations.

Cycles, Swings, and Shocks
Waiting to Make the Move

The preceding chapter explored European emigration over the long run; it focused on decade averages and abstracted from business cycles, long swings, and episodic shocks in the emigration time series. In contrast, much of the literature dwells on the short run. Does the analysis of annual fluctuations in emigration require a different explanation than that used successfully for long-run trends? In a sense, the answer is yes, although the two kinds of explanations can be readily reconciled. The economics and the demography are the same, but one concerns whether to move at all and where, while the other concerns when to make the move.

After a summary of the main issues in the time series literature on late-nineteenth-century emigration, this chapter develops a model of emigration that we believe encompasses most of the analytical insights of earlier work.[1] The model is then successfully estimated on annual emigration time series for the United Kingdom and for three Scandinavian countries—Denmark, Norway, and Sweden.

Explaining Swings and Cycles in Emigration

A sizeable literature attempts to account for time series movements in emigration, often from a single country and often to a single destination, although some studies examine several origin countries and some examine flows from one country to several destinations. As we pointed out in chapter 2, the debate over the determinants of fluctuations in emigration rates has a long history, dating back to the studies of Jerome (1926) and Thomas (1941). Many subsequent studies have used econometric methods to unravel the different forces at work determining the ebb and flow of migration. Much of this literature was admirably surveyed and subjected to a searching critique by Gould (1979), but unfortunately many of the issues Gould raised have received little further attention.

There are three main issues. First, much of the early literature was concerned with assessing the relative strengths of the pull factor of prospects abroad and the push factor of conditions at home that prospective emigrants faced. Although these terms are imprecisely defined, the discussion has often been about whether the coefficients on the variables representing conditions abroad are numerically larger or statistically more significant than those representing conditions at home. As we noted in chapter 2, among these studies, Kelley (1965), who analyzed immigration to Australia, Gallaway and Vedder (1971), who examined migration from the United Kingdom to the United States, and Richardson (1972), who examined United Kingdom emigration to four destinations, all found pull conditions abroad to be most important. By contrast, Wilkinson (1970), who analyzed emigration from seven European countries to the United States, Quigley (1972), who examined emigration from Sweden to the United States, and Magnussen and Siqveland (1978), who examined emigration from Norway to the United States, all emphasized the push of conditions at home. Given the different specifications used in these and other studies, it is not clear how much the differences are due to the variables included, the country analyzed, or the time period covered.[2]

In any case, it makes little sense to consider the prospective emigrant as acting only in the light of conditions at home or abroad: emigration decisions must surely have been based on some comparison, however approximate, between the two. In the absence of a formal model of the way different variables enter the migration decision, and an appropriate scaling of the variables, it is impossible to draw any inference from an asymmetry between the coefficient estimates.

Second, typically two types of variables have been included to represent conditions in sending and receiving regions. These represent prospective earnings, proxied either by GNP per capita or the average wage, and employment opportunities, proxied by the unemployment rate or some other cyclical variable. Clearly, relative incomes or wages must have mattered since we almost always observe net migration flows, in the long term, in the direction of countries with the higher wage rates. The cross-country evidence reported in chapter 3 strongly supports the view that relative wages were a key determinant of emigration in the long run. Yet when unemployment and wage rates have been included in the same regression, the former usually dominate, especially unemployment in the receiving country. As Gould (1979: 640) notes, where unemployment and wage rate variables are included, the latter prove largely insignificant (Kelley 1965; Gallaway and Vedder 1971; Richardson 1972; Pope 1968). By contrast, studies that exclude unemployment variables find significant wage rate effects (Quigley 1972; Magnussen and Siqveland 1978). In his study of Australian immigration, Pope (1981a) combined employment rates and wage rates to form expected income variables along the lines originally suggested by Todaro (1969). We extend this approach further below.

The dominance of unemployment variables no doubt reflects the correspondence between cyclical conditions and the sharp year-to-year movements in emigration rates emphasized by the early writers. Even this is something of a puzzle since migration is essentially a forward-looking variable. If migrants compared the net present value of future income streams over their lifetimes, it would not be greatly affected by short-run economic fluctuations, and hence we would not expect sharp fluctuations in emigration, but rather, a steady stream.

Third, most studies of time series have found lags to be important, particularly the lagged dependent variable. According to Gould (1979: 658), this variable is typically the most significant in the regression. When it is excluded from the regression, the equations are often characterized by severe serial correlation, leading some writers to use first differences rather than absolute levels of the variables (Gallaway and Vedder 1971). Some writers have interpreted the large and significant coefficient on the lagged dependent variable as a friends and relatives effect but, as we have seen, the migrant stock is probably a better indicator, although it has rarely been used in time series analysis. But if expectations about the whole stream of future earnings were formed and updated through an adaptive process, then the lagged dependent variable can be interpreted as reflecting that mechanism. Additional dynamics may enter the model on account of the timing decision: even though it might be worthwhile (in present value terms) to emigrate this year, it may be better still to wait a year (Burda 1993; O'Connell 1993).

In the following section, we specify a model that builds on microfoundations and encompasses many of the insights of the historical literature just summarized. The model suggests how asymmetries might emerge between the coefficients on the wage ratio and employment rates and between those on home and foreign employment rates, even where migrants take conditions at home and abroad fully into account. It also offers an explanation for emigration dynamics based on expectations of future relative earnings streams and includes a separate variable to capture the chain migration effect.

A Model of Emigration

The model incorporates two important features. It explicitly incorporates uncertainty into the migration decision and it explicitly (albeit simply) accounts for the formation of expectations about future income streams based on past information. These features have direct implications for the relative sizes of regression coefficients and for the dynamic structure of the model.

The probability of migration depends on the difference in expected utility streams abroad (f) and at home (h). For a given individual, i, in a given year, this difference can be written as:

[4.1]
$$d_i = Eu\left(y_f\right) - Eu\left(y_h\right) + z_i,$$

where y is income, z_i is the individual's nonpecuniary utility difference between the two locations and may also be taken to include the costs of migration. We assume that the individual's utility function is concave and, specifically, is given by $u(y) = \ln(y)$. Hence:

[4.2]
$$d_i = E\ln\left(y_t\right) - E\ln\left(y_h\right) + z_i$$

Expanding $E \ln(y_f)$ in a Taylor series around Ey_f gives:

$$E \ln(t_f) = \ln(Ey_f) + \frac{E(y_f - Ey_f)}{Ey_f} - \frac{E(y_f - Ey_f)^2}{2(Ey_f)^2}$$

[4.3]

$$E \ln(y_f) = \ln(Ey_f) - \frac{var(y_f)}{2(Ey_f)^2}$$

We follow Todaro (1969) in denoting $Ey = we$, the wage rate times the employment rate. Also, we assume that the variance of y is due to the uncertain prospects of employment rather than uncertainty about the wage. We can characterize employment probabilities as following a binomial distribution with expected value, e, and variance, $e(1 - e)$. Hence the second term in equation 4.3 can be written as:

$$\frac{1}{2} \frac{w_f^2 e_f (1 - e_f)}{w_f^2 e_f^2} = \frac{1}{2} \frac{(1 - e_f)}{e_f} \approx -\frac{1}{2} \ln(e_f)$$

Hence we can rewrite 4.3 as:

[4.4]

$$E \ln(y_f) = \ln(w_f) + \frac{3}{2} \ln(e_f)$$

Uncertainty about employment prospects as represented by the variance term leads to a greater weight on the employment rate than in the usual (risk neutral) expected income approach.[3]

Going abroad nearly always involves uncertainty because it involves finding a new job. Staying at home would typically involve less uncertainty if the individual had relatively secure employment. Hence, the expected utility from income at home can be written as:

[4.5]

$$E \ln(y_h) = \ln(w_h) + \frac{3}{2} \gamma \ln(e_h), \quad \gamma < 1$$

Substituting equations 4.4 and 4.5 into 4.2 gives:

[4.6]

$$d_i = \ln(w_f) + \frac{3}{2} \ln(e_f) - \ln(w_h) - \frac{3}{2} \gamma \ln(e_h) + z_i$$

The decision to migrate depends not just on the current value but also on future values of the stream of expected utility at home and abroad. The net present value of the difference in utility streams viewed at time t is d^*_{it}. The probability of individual i migrating at time t depends on d^*_{it} so that $Pr(m_{it} = 1) = Pr(d^*_{it} > 0)$. Aggregating over all individuals, the aggregate emigration rate, M_t, can be written as $M_t = \beta d^*_t$, where β measures the slope of the emigration function.

Assume that expectations about future utility are based on past values. If d^* is a geometric lag of past values of d, then:

$$d^*_t = \lambda d_t + \lambda^2 d_{t-1} + \lambda^3 d_{t-2} + \lambda^4 d_{t-4} \ldots$$

This would be equivalent to rational expectations if d follows an AR(1) process. Applying the Koyck transformation gives:

[4.7] $$M_t = (1-\lambda)d_t + \lambda M_{t-1}$$

Assume that $\bar{z}$, the mean of z_i over all individuals, is determined by the stock of previous emigrants and by a time trend (to proxy for the fall in emigration costs):

[4.8] $$\bar{z}_t = \varepsilon_0 + \varepsilon_1 MST_t + \varepsilon_2 t$$

where MST is the migrant stock per head of the home population.

From equations 4.6, 4.7, and 4.8, the following representation of the emigration rate emerges:

[4.9] $$M_t = (1-\lambda)\beta \ln(w_f/w_h)_t + (1-\lambda)\beta \frac{3}{2}\ln(e_f)_t - (1-\lambda)\beta\gamma \frac{3}{2}\ln(e_h)_t$$
$$(1-\lambda)\beta\varepsilon_0 + (1-\lambda)\beta\varepsilon_1 MST_t + (1-\lambda)\beta\varepsilon_2 t + \lambda M_{t-1}$$

This basic estimating equation can be modified or augmented in various ways. First, the dynamics may be more complicated than simply the lagged dependent variable. Such dynamics might be interpreted to reflect the fact that the timing of emigration depends not only on the current net present value of emigration but on the value of waiting (Hatton 1995a,b). Even if it were worth emigrating this year, it might be worth even more to wait until next year when an even higher present value might characterize the move. Another modification would be to allow other variables to enter by influencing $\bar{z}$ in equation 4.8. These might include demographic forces that shifted the emigration function by altering the age composition of the population or by changing prospects for access to land, events that would have an additional effect on emigration.

Now, can this model explain late-nineteenth-century emigration time series?

Emigration from the United Kingdom, 1871–1913

Emigration from the United Kingdom is plotted in figure 4.1. The data are for gross and net passenger movements from United Kingdom ports to extra-European ports per thousand of the United Kingdom population. The figures include Irish intercontinental emigration, experience that chapter 5 studies in more detail.

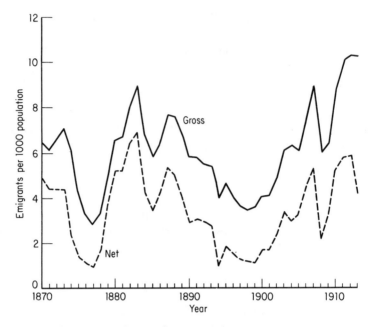

Figure 4.1 United Kingdom Emigration Rates, 1870–1913

Between 1871 and 1913 net outward passenger movements totaled 5.6 million or 131,000 per annum, and they averaged 3.4 per thousand of the population per annum. The overwhelming bulk of these emigrants went to the English-speaking parts of the New World: 53.8 percent went to the United States, 25.4 percent to Canada, and 16.5 percent to Australia and New Zealand combined. Of the small remainder, the majority went to Cape Colony and Natal (now South Africa).

The outward movement was very uneven over time. Sharp year-to-year movements were common: the net rate dropped by more than half from 1907 to 1908, dropped by about a third from 1883 to 1884 and doubled from 1878 to 1879. There is also clear evidence of what has become known as a long swing (or Kuznets Cycle) of about 15 to 20 years duration:[4] pronounced troughs characterized the mid–late seventies and the mid–late nineties; impressive peaks characterized the early seventies, the mid-eighties, and the period shortly before World War I. The rate of outflow varied between less than two per thousand in the late 1870s to over eight per thousand in 1882–1883, 1906, and 1910–1913. Gross and net emigration are positively correlated, indicating that variations in the net outflow were dominated by variations in the gross outflow.[5]

The explanatory variables in equation 4.9 are real wage rates, unemployment rates, and the emigrant stock. New World wages and employment rates are both constructed as a weighted average of all relevant overseas destinations.[6] The wage rates are the internationally comparable real wage series used in chapter 3 (from

Table 4.1 Emigration Regressions for the United Kingdom, 1871–1913

	1 Gross	2 Net	3 Gross	4 Net
Constant	−12.27	−9.30	−14.10	−11.59
	(3.04)	(2.28)	(3.73)	(2.72)
Log wage ratio (*t*)	14.28	11.27		
(foreign to home)	(4.38)	(3.53)		
Log foreign employment rate (*t*)	32.78	41.10		
	(4.36)	(4.87)		
Log wage ratio + 1.5 times log			16.22	15.13
foreign employment rate (*t*)			(6.23)	(5.05)
Log home employment rate (*t* – 1)	−14.81	−20.21	−14.29	−19.11
	(3.33)	(4.47)	(3.21)	(3.97)
Migrant stock (*t*)	60.14	49.68	60.92	41.62
	(2.47)	(1.99)	(2.48)	(1.57)
Time	0.13	0.07	0.14	0.07
	(3.65)	(2.15)	(4.03)	(2.26)
Lagged emigration rate (*t* – 1)	0.67	0.58	0.69	0.66
	(5.41)	(4.58)	(5.54)	(5.11)
Lagged emigration rate (*t* – 2)	−0.34	−0.38	−0.37	−0.42
	(2.92)	(3.15)	(3.22)	(3.29)
R^2	0.89	0.84	0.86	0.81
RSS	17.52	18.36	18.28	21.69
DW	1.92	2.02	1.98	2.04
LM(1)	0.04	0.09	0.06	0.18
RESET	3.49	3.13	0.94	0.27

Notes: *t* statistics in parentheses. LM(1) is the Lagrange multiplier test for first-order serial correlation and RESET is the test for functional form using the square of the fitted values. These are distributed as chi^2 (1). Column numbers refer to different regression equations.

Williamson 1995). The employment rates are obtained from Charles Feinstein (1972) for the United Kingdom, from James Vernon (1994) for the United States and from Noel Butlin (1946) for Australia. A series was constructed for Canada based on deviations of real GNP per capita from trend.[7] The immigrant stock variable was constructed from census reports on the numbers born in the United Kingdom who were enumerated in the United States, Canada, Australia, and New Zealand using net passenger movements to interpolate between census dates.

The model was first estimated in a more general form with an additional lag of each right-hand-side variable (including an additional lag of the dependent variable).[8] The only important modifications to the basic model were the addition of the second lag of the dependent variable and the substitution of the lagged for the current value of the home employment rate. The estimates are reported in table 4.1 for both gross and net emigration. The results are very impressive: all coefficents are highly significant, they give expected signs, and a very large share of the variance in annual emigration from the United Kingdom is explained. We start with the first two columns in table 4.1.

All three variables are highly significant, including the wage gap. Thus, it is worth emphasizing that most of the earlier studies that modeled all or part of British emigration failed to find significant coefficients on the relative wage in the presence of cyclical variables (Gandar 1982: 34). Furthermore, the foreign employment rate has a coefficient larger than that of the wage ratio or the home employment rate, just as the model predicts. The coefficient on the migrant stock is large in both columns but smaller in the net emigration equation. Since a larger emigrant stock would generate more return migration, this is exactly what would be expected. The time trend is also positive but smaller for net emigration. This finding is consistent with falling transport costs raising both gross emigration and return migration.

Columns 3 and 4 in table 4.1 combine the relative wage and foreign employment rate variables, giving a weight of 3/2 to the latter as the model suggests. This restriction tends to raise the size of the wage effects and to reduce the overseas employment effects. The restriction can be rejected for net emigration but not for gross.[9] The fact that the home employment rate gives smaller coefficients than the overseas employment rate suggests a value for γ less than one. But its effect is larger for net emigration than gross—probably because of the uncertainty attached to home employment prospects for return migrants.

The long-run coefficients derived for the four columns in table 4.1 are presented in table 4.2. These indicate that the relative wage and employment rates had powerful effects on the overall level of emigration. A permanent 10 percent increase in the overseas relative to the home wage (an overseas-British wage gap widening) would have increased the gross emigration rate by 1.9 to 2.4 per thousand, although the impact on the net emigration rate would have been somewhat smaller, 1.4 to 2 per thousand. A permanent 10 percent increase in the foreign employment rate (e.g., a fall in the unemployment rate from 10 percent to 1 percent) would have raised the gross emigration rate by 3.7 to 4.4 per thousand; a similar increase in the home employment rate would have lowered it by about 2 per thousand. Finally, the migrant stock term indicates that for every additional thousand migrants living abroad, 80 or 90 new migrants were generated each year—strong testimony indeed to the quantitative impact of chain migration.

The overseas real wage was, on average, 69 percent higher than that of the United Kingdom over the period. Had that wage gap evaporated and had wages been equalized, the long-run coefficients suggest there would have been a substantial reversal from net emigration to net immigration flows. In order to just eliminate net emigration from the United Kingdom, the wage gap favoring the overseas locations would need to contract from 69 percent to 27 percent higher, using column 2, or to 19 percent, using column 4. Trends in the wage gap also help explain the long swing in emigration from the United Kingdom. The gross emigration rate fell from 7 per thousand in 1879–1883 to 4 per thousand in 1894–1898 and then rose again to 7 per thousand in 1909–1913. The wage gap alone explains nearly two per thousand of the fall and one per thousand of the subsequent rise in the gross emigration rate. However, a lot of the long swing remains to be explained, presumably by fluctuations in the employment rate.

Table 4.2 Long-Run Coefficients for United Kingdom Emigration

	1 Gross	2 Net	3 Gross	4 Net
Log wage ratio	19.30	14.09	24.44	19.90
Log foreign employment rate	44.30	51.38	36.66	29.86
Log home employment rate	−20.01	−25.26	−21.01	−25.14
Migrant stock	81.27	62.10	89.59	54.76
Time	0.18	0.09	0.20	0.09

The average level of emigration and its long-run trend can be largely explained by the wage gap, but recursive simulations show clearly that the year-to-year fluctuations were attributable instead to employment rate shocks. A recursive simulation of the equation for gross emigration in column 1 of table 4.2, *holding the home and foreign employment rates constant at their means,* yields a fairly small coefficient of variation for the predicted emigration rate, 0.21. Compare this with a coefficient of variation of 0.32 for the actual emigration time series, or 0.30 when a full dynamic simulation of the equation in column 1 is generated. The coefficient of variation is, of course, a useful way to summarize the degree of instability in these series across the four decades, big numbers documenting more dramatic long swings and short-term business cycles. Using the equation for net emigration in column 2 of table 4.2, the simulated model with no variation in employment rates gives a coefficient of variation of 0.23, compared with 0.46 for the actual series and 0.42 for the full dynamic simulation. Note that even more of the net emigration series is explained by employment rate instability than gross, and for obvious reasons: return migration was also sensitive to state of the long swing or business cycle. The moral of the story is that much of the fluctuation in emigration, especially net emigration, can be explained by the short-run impact of business cycles and long swings on labor markets.

Emigration from Scandinavia: The Literature

Several of the most influential emigration studies have examined one or more of the Scandinavian countries, partly because the data for that part of the Atlantic economy are so good, and partly because Scandinavia represents the classic case of late-nineteenth-century emigration; it had high emigration rates, the emigration generated debate, emigration fluctuated widely, and the migrants went overwhelmingly in one direction—to the United States. The push-pull debate also apparently reached its height in the Scandinavian literature. This section applies our time series model to three Scandinavian countries between 1873 and 1913: Denmark, Norway, and Sweden.

The rates of intercontinental emigration averaged 4.33 per thousand of the population for Sweden, 6.64 for Norway, and 2.77 for Denmark. There were also small

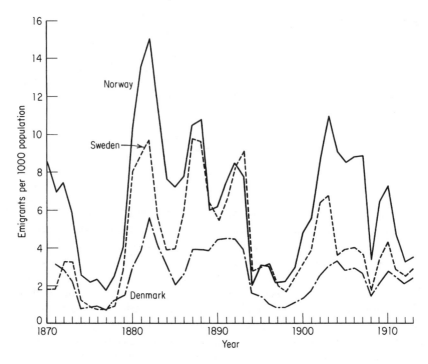

Figure 4.2 Scandinavian Emigration, 1870–1913 (to the United States)

numbers emigrating within Europe, chiefly to their Scandinavian neighbors and to
Germany. Migrant characteristics were similar across the three countries. They
were mainly young, 60 percent falling in the 15–29 age group; they were mainly
male, about three fifths; and they were mainly single, about four fifths. Although
about half the Swedish and Danish emigrants emigrated from urban areas, many
more had rural origins. A third of those declaring occupations were from agriculture, mainly laborers, and a large proportion of those from urban backgrounds
were general laborers or domestic servants.[10] Return migration was small—only
about 10 percent of the emigrants went back home. Finally, intercontinental
Scandinavian migrants went primarily to the United States: 90 percent of the
Danes, 97 percent of the Norwegians, and 98 percent of the Swedes. Thus, like previous studies, here we will concentrate on explaining the Scandinavian flow to the
United States.

Figure 4.2 reveals the same dramatic instability that characterized emigration
from the United Kingdom, indeed, even more so. Norwegian emigration rates show
the greatest amplitude, followed by Sweden and then Denmark. Each of the emigration streams exhibits distinctive troughs in the mid-1870s and the mid–late
1890s, with peaks in the early 1870s, the 1880s, and shortly after the turn of the
century—long swings strikingly similar to those observed for the United Kingdom

and strikingly similar with each other. There is also a fair degree of coincidence of shorter cycles among the three countries. The strong correlation of these movements across Scandinavia would appear to provide clear support for Jerome's conclusion that European emigration was driven by a common external influence. This is reinforced by the fact that the United States was the common destination for all three countries. However, following Dorothy Thomas's lead, other observers have suggested that contemporaneous fluctuations within the Scandinavian countries could account for emigration's instabilty, at least in part (Hvidt 1966: 171–4; Ljungmark 1992).

The econometric literature on Scandinavian emigration is rich, but the studies typically focus on a single country, each using different explanatory variables. Hence, it is difficult to determine whether divergent results are due to differences in specification or differences between countries. Important exceptions are the multicountry studies of Jeffrey Williamson (1974a) and Maurice Wilkinson (1970), which covered both Denmark and Sweden among other countries. The former study used a reduced form approach, eliminating the wage and estimating instead the effects on emigration of shifts in labor demand and supply in both origin and destination countries. Estimating a structural model of emigration, Wilkinson found that relative income was strongly significant even in the presence of business cycle indicators, but that the lag structures differed between countries.

Among the single-country studies, a variety of specifications has been used. The models estimated by Moe (1970) for Norway and Larsen (1982) for Denmark included both relative income and business cycle indicators. Both took five-year moving averages of relative GDP per capita rather than a direct measure of real wage gaps that would more closely approximate the income prospects of migrants.[11] In addition, the business cycle measures used are not generally comparable between origin and destination countries and hence little can be inferred about their relative effects. Yet both studies emphasized pull effects arising from the American business cycle, and neither found lags to be important. Norstrom (1988) reached similar conclusions about the dominance of business cycles in Swedish emigration, but lags were also found to be important. The models estimated by Quigley (1972) for Sweden and Magnussen and Siqveland (1978) for Norway include no explicit cyclical variable but rely only on wage rates or income at home and abroad. It is difficult to imagine how these models could fully explain the sharp year-to-year changes in emigration rates. Both based their push-pull assessment on the size and significance of coefficients on domestic and foreign wage rates and both stressed the importance of domestic push factors.

Although the importance of chain migration has often been stressed for the Scandinavian countries, attempts to confront this issue in the econometric models have been limited. Many studies include lags of the dependent variable, but only Magnussen and Siqveland (1978) included a measure of the stock of previous emigrants. Chapter 3 and the time series model for emigration from the United Kingdom showed that migrants from the country in question living abroad had a powerful impact on current emigration, and this finding will be reinforced later in the book. Thus, there is good reason for this chapter to explore the impact of

Scandinavians living in the United States on Scandinavians emigrating. Some attempts have also been made to capture the quantitative influence of those demographic events discussed so widely in the qualitative literature. Quigley (1972) introduced a variable for the birth cohort lagged 26 years but found it to be insignificant for Sweden. In contrast, Moe (1970) included the ratio of those aged 20–29 to the total population, which turned out to be strongly significant for Norway. For Denmark, Larsen (1982) included the rate of population growth five years earlier, but it is difficult to see why a lag as short as five years would be appropriate.

Emigration from Scandinavia, 1873–1913

The basic model is estimated on the Scandinavian time series from 1873 to 1913. The emigration rates to be explained are the series displayed in figure 4.2. As before, the relative real wage data are taken from Williamson (1995). In the absence of direct observations on unemployment or employment rates, a measure of economic activity is derived by taking the deviations of the log of real GDP per capita from a linear trend.[12] The migrant stock series were obtained by using annual gross emigration to interpolate between Scandinavian-born populations in the United States recorded at census dates.

The model was estimated with various lag structures but, as with the United Kingdom, only the two lags for the dependent variable were relevant in all but one case.[13] In the case of Denmark, the first lag of the domestic activity term performed better than the current value and hence this was preferred. The time trend never gave significant coefficients, so it was eliminated from the final regressions. Furthermore, the restriction on equal and opposite coefficients for foreign and home wages could not be rejected; hence, there is no asymmetry between the effects of home and foreign wages, just as the model asserts.[14]

The results are reported in table 4.3. All the coefficients yield the expected signs and, with the exception of a couple of the Danish explanatory variables, all are highly significant. United States economic activity has large positive coefficients, supporting Jerome, while domestic economic activity has coefficients with roughly similar magnitude and opposite sign, supporting Thomas. Thus, in the Scandinavian case at least, both forces were working equally hard. The wage ratio has a significant but somewhat smaller coefficient than economic activity. The migrant stock variable also has a strongly significant coefficient in all three Scandinavian cases, once again testifying to the importance of chain migration. The long-run impact of these variables can be summarized in this way: 10 percent increase in the foreign to home wage ratio would have raised the emigration rate by 1.1 per thousand in Sweden, by 1.1 in Norway, and by 0.6 in Denmark. These effects are a little lower than those ranging between 1.9 and 2.4 per thousand that emerged from the United Kingdom time series. The coefficients on the migrant stock term indicate that in the long run, for each additional thousand migrants living in the United States, 108 more emigrants were drawn abroad each year from Sweden, 90 for Norway, and 130 for Denmark—chain migration effects only a little higher than for the United Kingdom (80 to 90).

Table 4.3 Emigration Regressions for Scandinavia, 1873–1913

	Sweden	Norway	Denmark
Constant	−12.40	−12.76	−5.14
	(2.83)	(1.96)	(1.70)
Log wage ratio (t)	10.15	8.85	3.41
(foreign/home)	(3.33)	(2.09)	(1.78)
U.S. economic activity (t)	21.53	34.60	9.22
	(4.36)	(4.60)	(3.33)
Domestic economic activity (t)	−30.34	−20.45	−10.98
	(5.53)	(2.31)	(1.65)
Migrant stock (t)	0.10	0.07	0.07
	(3.42)	(2.75)	(2.05)
Emigration rate ($t − 1$)	0.53	0.56	0.84
	(4.29)	(4.39)	(5.92)
Emigration rate ($t − 2$)	−0.45	−0.34	−0.38
	(3.86)	(2.78)	(2.59)
R^2	0.84	0.83	0.79
RSS	47.32	80.60	13.03
DW	2.16	1.92	2.02
LM(1)	0.63	0.07	0.03
RESET	0.76	1.35	0.06

Notes: See table 4.1. The domestic activity index is lagged one year in the case of Denmark. t statistics are in parentheses.

Two additional issues remain. First, note that the coefficient on domestic activity is larger than that on foreign activity for Sweden, smaller for Norway, and about the same for Denmark. These results suggest that, in terms of the model set out above, we might impose the restriction $\gamma = 1$. Second, we have not investigated the role of demographic events, which might be expected to matter for the Scandinavian countries. Table 4.4 reports the results when the restriction on the wage ratio and activity terms is imposed, and when a five-year moving average of the rate of natural increase lagged 26 years (following Quigley, 1972) is introduced. The restriction is rejected at the 5 percent level (but not at the 10 percent level) for Sweden, but not for either Norway or Denmark. On the other hand, the lagged rate of natural increase, though positive in each case, is only significant at the 5 percent level for Sweden. But the long-run coefficients of 0.35 for Sweden and 0.41 for Norway largely bear out the orders of magnitude obtained in the cross-country analysis of chapter 3.

What impact did these variables have over Scandinavia's long swing in emigration? Figure 4.2 clearly documents the surge in emigration rates from the mid-1870s to the 1880s, the subsequent decline to the mid-1890s, followed by a renewed surge to the mid-1900s, and then a further decline. Table 4.5 reports the contribution of the log wage ratio, the migrant stock, and the lagged rate of natural increase over these booms and busts using the long-run coefficients from table 4.4: that is,

Table 4.4 Restricted Regression Model with a Demographic Variable: Scandinavia, 1873–1913

	Sweden	Norway	Denmark
Constant	−21.15	−25.66	−8.66
	(6.06)	(5.45)	(3.84)
Log wage ratio + 1.5 times	13.74	14.32	5.18
U.S. economic activity − 1.5 times domestic economic activity	(6.30)	(5.03)	(4.03)
Migrant stock (t)	0.13	0.10	0.09
	(5.32)	(4.56)	(3.35)
Lagged natural increase (5- year moving average, $t − 26$)	0.33	0.37	0.10
	(2.24)	(1.39)	(1.03)
Emigration rate ($t − 1$)	0.54	0.53	0.83
	(4.36)	(4.02)	(3.52)
Emigration rate ($t − 2$)	−0.47	−0.44	−0.44
	(4.39)	(3.99)	(3.53)
R^2	0.83	0.82	0.79
RSS	50.71	86.42	13.32
DW	2.09	1.97	2.02
LM(1)	0.22	0.00	0.01
RESET	0.74	1.80	0.06
Restrictions [chi^2 (2)]	8.02	2.91	1.06

Note: See table 4.1. t statistics are in parentheses.

it presents the changes in the emigration rate per thousand of population that are predicted by these variables over each long swing boom and bust. The predictions strongly bear out the qualitative findings of chapter 3. For all three countries, the declining wage ratio tended to lower Scandinavian emigration rates, although at a diminishing rate after 1895. That is, the rapid Scandinavian catch-up (O'Rourke and Williamson 1995, 1996) served to keep a larger and larger share at home. This influence was largely offset by the effect of the rising stock of previous migrants early in the period, but this effect diminished after 1895, so much so that the negative impact of wage catch-up began to offset the positive effect of chain migration. These effects by themselves would, therefore, have caused Scandinavian emigration rates to drop as the late nineteenth century progressed, results fully consistent with chapter 3. The lagged rate of natural increase also made a contribution, but with changing effects over time. For all three countries, it helped drive up the emigration rate in 1875–1885 and helped to drive it down in the following decade. After 1895 demographic influences turned positive again, but they faded away after 1905. So, plenty of evidence supports the traditional emphasis on Scandinavian demographic forces, but it is important to note that these demographic forces were often reinforced, and sometimes dominated by, the combined impact of relative labor market conditions and chain migration.

These long-run forces only partly explain the booms and busts over the long swing in Scandinavian emigration. Cyclical forces were important in contributing

Table 4.5 Long-Run Forces in Scandinavian Long Swings (effect on emigration per 1,000 population)

	Sweden	Norway	Denmark
1875–1885			
Log wage ratio	−2.84	−3.10	−0.48
Migrant stock	2.85	3.33	1.59
Natural increase	0.81	1.33	0.30
1885–1895			
Log wage ratio	−2.81	−2.42	−2.09
Migrant stock	3.51	1.67	2.00
Natural increase	−1.28	−1.50	−0.18
1895–1905			
Log wage ratio	−1.48	0.61	−0.93
Migrant stock	1.45	1.28	0.47
Natural increase	1.03	1.23	0.31
1905–1913			
Log wage ratio	−1.42	−0.26	−1.13
Migrant stock	0.14	−0.73	0.20
Natural increase	0.18	−0.43	0.10

to the emigration slump after 1874 and 1893, as well as during the emigration boom after 1879 and 1901. For all three countries the surge in American economic activity in 1877–1880 contributed strongly to the surge in emigration and the American slump of 1892–1894 sharply magnified the collapse in emigration after the mid-1880s. Similarly, the rise in American economic activity contributed to the upswing at the turn of the century and the sharp downward spike of 1908, but these movements were sometimes reinforced and sometimes attenuated by domestic cyclical fluctuations and by shifts in the wage ratio and lagged natural increase. The effects

Table 4.6 Results of Dynamic Simulations: Scandinavia, 1873–1913 (coefficients of variation)

	Sweden	Norway	Denmark
Actual emigration rate	0.626	0.543	0.502
Simulated, table 4.4 coefficients			
Full model	0.537	0.407	0.487
Foreign activity = 0	0.487	0.345	0.406
Domestic activity = 0	0.467	0.389	0.466
Foreign and domestic activity = 0	0.417	0.301	0.407
No dynamics			
Full model	0.481	0.364	0.445
Foreign and domestic activity = 0	0.338	0.259	0.351

of purely cyclical forces are isolated in table 4.6, applying the same technique used above for the United Kingdom. The coefficients of variation are derived from dynamic simulations, first from the full model and then suppressing the variation in foreign and domestic activity. Compared with the full dynamic simulation, the effects of suppressing foreign activity reduce the coefficient of variation surprisingly little—only by 10 or 15 percent. But suppressing domestic activity reduces it less still, and in this limited sense one might say that pull forces were the more important. When both foreign and domestic activity are suppressed, the coefficients of variation fall by more, except in the case of Denmark, suggesting that the impact of foreign and domestic fluctuations was reinforcing rather than offsetting. Much of the variabilty remains because of the long swing forces and the equation dynamics. As the last two lines of table 4.6 illustrate, when the effects of the two lags of the dependent variable are eliminated, the coefficients of variation fall further, both for the full model and especially when the business cycle components are suppressed.

Conclusion

Time series models used to study emigration often emphasize either business cycle fluctuations or relative incomes, and sometimes both, as determinants of the sharp fluctuations in late-nineteenth-century emigration. They also seem to unanimously suggest that unemployment rates mattered more than wages in generating relative income movements and thus emigration. Our model suggests why both should matter and why the coefficients on employment rates might be different from those on the wage ratio. The results for Britain and Scandinavia strongly support this view and demonstrate an important role for both domestic and foreign activity and for the wage ratio. In addition, the migrant stock, often omitted in earlier studies, confirms a powerful role for chain migration.

The results are largely consistent with the country cross-section results of chapter 3. The effect of a 10 percent increase in the wage ratio was to raise emigration rates by somewhere between 0.6 and 1.5 per thousand in Scandinavia and by somewhat more for the United Kingdom. The migration stock effects are substantially larger than in the cross section, suggesting that the chain migration effect estimated in chapter 3 was partly captured by the coefficient on the lagged dependent variable. The effects of lagged natural increase can be identified even in the time series, although somewhat imprecisely, and not surprisingly the effects are a little lower than in the cross section. Our examination of long swings in the Scandinavian time series indicates that the forces that influenced the long-run trends also contributed to the long swing. Variations in economic activity or employment were largely responsible for fluctuations around the long swing pattern, but they account for a relatively modest proportion of the overall variation in emigration rates.

After the Famine
Irish Experience

Introduction

Over 4.5 million men and women left Ireland in the six decades after the famine in the late 1840s. The emigrant flood continued long after actual famine conditions had disappeared, and the number who eventually left was about five times the famine deaths. The rate of Irish emigration was more than double that of any other European country (table 1.1), with as many as 13 per thousand emigrating on average each year. Largely as a consequence of this mass exodus, the Irish population fell from 6.5 to 4.4 million between 1851 and 1911.

What were the causes of Irish emigration? This is, of course, the same question raised more generally of European emigration in chapters 2 and 3. Here we want to look in detail at one of the most spectacular examples of European mass emigration.[1] Our basic goal is to understand why the Irish emigration rate was so high and why it declined so much across the late nineteenth century. We seek the answers in two ways. First, we offer explanations for fluctuations in the annual time series, both for total emigration and for emigration to the main destination country, the United States. This detailed country analysis will confirm and enrich the more general European findings of chapter 4. Second, we explore the determinants of county-level emigration rates at four census dates in an effort to learn more about the domestic factors—or long-run "fundamentals"—that drove so many Irish abroad. Overall, our findings reinforce those of chapters 2 and 3, although they urge that real wage gaps between home and abroad be augmented wherever possible to capture broader dimensions of living standards.

Trends in Irish Emigration

The principal source of Irish emigration data is the emigration reports of the Registrar General for Ireland. These statistics were collected and recorded by the police at the ports of embarkation from 1851 onward. These records are for gross outflows only, but we know that Irish return migration was relatively rare. Return migrants from the United States, for example, were only about 6 percent of the outflow (Fitzpatrick 1984: 7).

The data are plotted in figure 5.1 as a rate per thousand of the total Irish population. The figure documents a very sharp fall in emigration rates immediately following the Great Famine: between 1852 and 1855 alone, the rate halves from around 30 to around 15. Yet, the fall persisted, dropping from about 15 per thousand in the 1860s to about 8 per thousand in the years immediately before World War I. While annual rates of 8 per thousand were *still* high by the standards of that time, the significant fact remains that Irish emigration rates fell by three quarters between the Great Famine and the Great War.

These data substantially understate the true level of emigration, chiefly because the movement across the Irish Sea to Great Britain was only partially recorded. Cormac Ó Gráda (1975) estimates that between 1851 and 1911 the shortfall was around half a million. The true figure for migrants moving across the Irish Sea was therefore probably double what the statistics suggest and perhaps even more.[2]

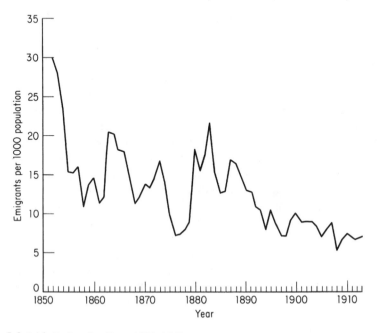

Figure 5.1 Irish Emigration Rate, 1852–1913

Table 5.1 Emigration from Ireland to Various Countries, 1876–1913

	Irish immigration to United States	Emigration to				
		United States	Canada	Australia	New Zealand	Great Britain
1876–1880	28,356	27,924	1,300	3,408	2,159	(33,901)
1881–1885	69,080	62,736	5,497	2,234	753	(18,480)
1886–1890	56,016	59,965	2,460	3,319	167	(9,832)
1891–1895	45,440	46,494	842	927	109	(4,306)
1896–1900	32,243	33,006	475	779	59	(6,878)
1901–1905	36,819	30,768	1,447	418	91	(8,634)
1906–1910	30,996	24,125	3,538	542	165	(6,224)
1911–1913	27,622	21,411	5,980	841	192	(2,012)

Sources: Based on Ferenczi and Willcox (1929: 731) and Ó Gráda (1975: 44).

Hence, emigration to Britain was probably a fifth to a quarter of the total rather than an eighth, and the true Irish emigration rate was larger accordingly. Furthermore, since the share of the Irish going to Britain declined over time, the true decline in the emigration rate was probably even greater than that documented.

Irish emigration statistics are broken down by country of intended destination after 1875. These are given as five-year averages in table 5.1. Following Ó Gráda (1975), we have doubled the recorded emigrants headed across the Irish Sea. Even with this adjustment, the outstanding feature of the table is the overwhelming (and increasing) dominance of the flow to the United States. For the purposes of comparison, the first column of the table reports five-year averages of the number of Irish immigrants arriving in the United States.[3] Despite differences in definition and source, the United States–Irish immigration series and the Irish–United States emigration series are reasonably close (although significant discrepancies emerge after the turn of the century). Examination of year-to-year fluctuations also indicates a close association between the two series.[4]

These statistical flaws are unlikely to undermine the conclusion that the emigration rate fell significantly across the late nineteenth century. The numbers emigrating to Britain decline up to 1890. If there was a relatively constant rate of underenumeration of Irish emigrants to Britain, then the true aggregate emigration rate would have fallen even faster than figure 5.1 suggests. Any possible improvement over time in reporting accuracy too would indicate a steeper decline in the true compared with the measured emigration rate. Even if the flawed Irish emigration statistics to Great Britain are eliminated altogether, the impressive decline in the Irish emigration rate would persist. After all, a dramatic decline was apparent for Australasia, for the United States, and for North America as a whole.

What accounts for the fall in Irish emigration? It has been suggested that the declining rate was linked to the changing position of Catholics under

British rule. It was widely held at one time that land and religious reforms were accompanied by growing economic opportunity for Catholics, not to mention the rise of Irish nationalism. Thus "the achievement of Irish independence in 1921 climaxed a set of changes which reduced the reasons for Irish Catholic emigration from Ireland" (Kennedy 1973: 39). This view has, however, received little support in more recent studies, thus eroding its popularity (Fitzpatrick 1980a; Miller 1985, 1991). Miller asserts that "the vast majority of Catholic emigrants left home for essentially mundane reasons similar or identical to those which produced mass migration from other European countries" (1991: 339). It is the phrase "similar or identical to" that we wish to confirm in this chapter.

Another possibility is that the share of the population in the mobile age range decreased, what we called the *direct* Easterlin effect in chapters 2 and 3. This demographic effect may not have been the dominant force accounting for the decline, but it was not trivial. The percentage of the population in the mobile age range, 15 to 34, fell from 35.3 percent of the population in 1861 to 32.7 percent in 1911; this fact alone can account for about a one per thousand fall in the aggregate emigration rate, or for a seventh of the total fall between 1861 and 1911.[5] Of course, other demographic changes might have contributed to the falling emigration rate, and we shall discuss these further. Other forces, such as declining costs of emigration, may have had offsetting effects: the cost of passage to North America fell in the early 1870s and, relative to Irish wages, declined by more than a half between 1850 and 1913.

What about the friends and relatives effect? According to Fitzpatrick (1984: 21), chain migration "became the main agency trans-planting the young adults of each generation," and nowhere were these forces likely to have been more powerful than among the Irish. Indeed, the evidence for American immigrants in the 1850s and 1860s seems to confirm this, since the average per migrant remittance to England and Ireland combined was $28.43 (North 1960: 616–18), or almost 8 percent of average annual earnings of United States nonfarm employees (Williamson 1990: 73), and most of this was to Ireland (Baines 1985: 85). Emigrant remittances in 1838, prior to the famine, may have paid for half of the expense of the Irish sailing for Liverpool (Adams 1932: 181, 226).

Clearly, the large stock of Irish emigrants abroad partly accounts for the high rates of postfamine emigration. Indeed, the sharp jump in the stock during the famine decade may account for much of the rise in the emigration rate between prefamine and postfamine periods (Ó Gráda and O'Rourke 1997). But did it also contribute to the declining rate of emigration in postfamine Ireland? The emigrant stock, after rising to over three million in 1881, declined to just over two million by 1911.[6] Even though the Irish population was declining, the ratio of Irish-born living abroad to those living at home fell from a peak of 0.62 in the late 1880s to 0.49 in 1911. Declining chain migration effects therefore help account for the fall in the Irish emigration rate after the 1880s, but they cannot account for any of the decline prior to the late 1880s when the ratio of Irish-born living abroad to the Irish living at home was still rising.

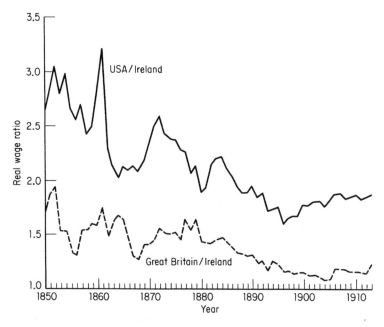

Figure 5.2 Irish Real Wage Ratios, 1850–1913 (United States and Great Britain to Ireland)

Yet there is a far more important explanation for the decline in Irish emigration, central to the theme of this book: changing labor market conditions at home and abroad. As Ó Gráda has reminded us, "it must not be forgotten that no matter how poor people were, living standards were rising so that, other things being equal, there was less incentive to move" (1980a: 100). Furthermore, Irish economic conditions did not just improve across the second half of the nineteenth century, they improved *relative* to the countries of traditional Irish emigration. The important point is that between the Great Famine and the Great War the Irish laborer began to catch up in bread and butter terms with the Australian, the American, and the British laborer. It follows that the average Irish laborer had less and less to gain from the move overseas.

As we shall see further on in this chapter, most of the Irish who emigrated were unskilled laborers. It makes sense therefore to compare the urban unskilled real wage in the receiving countries with that prevailing in Ireland. As we pointed out in chapter 2, real wage rates for urban unskilled laborers have recently been constructed for Ireland and for all those countries to which the Irish emigrated, at least for the postfamine nineteenth century (Williamson 1995; Boyer, Hatton, and O'Rourke 1994). The ratios of American-to-Irish and British-to-Irish real wages are plotted in figure 5.2, and the ratios of Australian-to-Irish and Canadian-to-Irish real wages are plotted in figure 5.3. Figure 5.2 shows that both the American and British wage ratios relative to Ireland fell sharply over the period. The ratio of American to Irish wage rates fell from 2.85 in 1850–1854 to 1.67 in 1895–1899

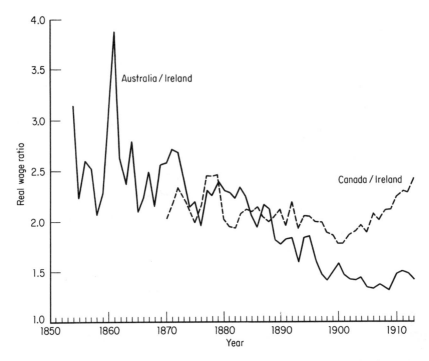

Figure 5.3 Irish Real Wage Ratios, 1850–1913 (Australia and Canada to Ireland)

before rising slightly to 1.85 in 1909–1913. The British/Irish ratio declined from 1.71 in 1850–1854 to 1.16 in 1909–1913. Repeating the American experience, the Australian-to-Irish wage ratio fell from 2.51 in 1870–1874 to 1.44 in 1909–1913. Although the Canadian labor market absorbed only a small share of the Irish (table 5.1), the experience there was an exception to the rule: the Canadian-to-Irish wage ratio increased slightly from 2.18 in 1870–1874 to 2.28 in 1909–1913.

If the wage ratio is the appropriate measure of the relative attraction of moving compared with staying, these trends should help explain why the Irish emigration rate fell over time. Compared with the two major emigration destinations (America and Britain), all of the fall in the relative wage occurred before 1896, as did almost all of the decline in the Irish emigration rate. This simple correlation should, however, be treated with caution since, when the Irish wage fell relative to the American wage after 1896, the emigration rate did not accelerate. We need to explore more formal tests of the relative wage hypothesis so that other influences on the emigration decision can be assessed simultaneously.

Irish Emigration: Explaining the Time Series

To investigate the causes of the long-term decline and the short-term fluctuations in the Irish emigration rate, a time series model is estimated similar to that used

Table 5.2 Determinants of Time Series for Irish Emigration Rates, 1878–1913

	Dependent variable					
	Total emigration	Adjusted total	Inter continental emigration	Emigration to the United States	Total male emigration	Total female emigration
Constant	−18.39	−24.97	−12.04	−11.76	−20.20	−16.32
	(3.48)	(4.21)	(2.51)	(2.36)	(3.52)	(3.23)
Foreign employment	77.46	88.18	57.04	46.00	91.07	62.92
rate (t)	(3.84)	(4.39)	(2.89)	(2.72)	(4.16)	(3.25)
Deviation of log	−25.89	−28.04	−27.34	−27.55	−25.77	−26.30
farm output $(t-1)$	(3.82)	(3.66)	(3.24)	(3.63)	(3.01)	(3.43)
Relative wage (t)	15.48	23.55	9.64	6.90	20.92	10.51
	(3.67)	(4.67)	(2.27)	(1.81)	(4.22)	(2.79)
Migrant stock (t)	37.52	46.68	33.06	40.27	37.58	36.09
	(3.64)	(4.27)	(2.91)	(3.04)	(3.55)	(3.45)
Emigration rate	0.39	0.34	0.50	0.55	0.38	0.41
$(t-1)$	(2.87)	(2.64)	(3.65)	(4.17)	(2.84)	(2.92)
Emigration rate	−0.16	−0.27	−0.12	−0.14	−0.18	−0.12
$(t-2)$	(1.21)	(2.01)	(0.88)	(1.02)	(1.42)	(0.89)
R^2	0.85	0.88	0.80	0.80	0.85	0.84
Residual sum of squares	86.67	80.56	95.64	79.54	100.27	78.53
Durbin-Watson	1.79	1.91	1.85	1.93	1.98	1.82
LM(1)	0.45	0.03	0.24	0.02	0.55	0.41

Notes: The t statistics are given in parentheses. LM(1) is the Lagrange Multiplier test for serial correlation obtained from the regression of residuals on lagged residuals and right-hand-side variables. Foreign wage and employment rate variables and the migrant stock term are defined differently across equations to be consistent with the destinations reflected in the dependent variable.

for the United Kingdom as a whole and the Scandinavian countries in chapter 4. The model is estimated on annual observations for 1878 to 1913 to secure more reliable data and to separate emigration by destination (from 1876). As in figure 5.1 and table 5.1, the source of the emigration data is Ferenczi and Willcox (1929). The overseas wage and employment rates are (geometric) weighted averages of the United States, Great Britain, Canada, and Australia with the weights reflecting emigration shares.[7] Internationally comparable real wage rates for these countries and Ireland are those depicted as ratios in figures 5.2 and 5.3 and are taken, as before, from Williamson (1995). The overseas employment rates are from the same sources as those used for the United Kingdom as a whole in chapter 4 but with the addition of Great Britain, taken from Feinstein (1972). No series is available for Irish unemployment, so domestic employment fluctuations are proxied by deviations in the log of agricultural output from trend.[8] The stock of previous emigrants was constructed by using the emigration series to interpolate between census benchmarks for Irish-born living in the four countries listed above plus New Zealand.

Table 5.2 reports regression results for total Irish emigration, emigration to various destinations, and emigration by gender. As with the U.K. as a whole, the domestic activity term worked best when lagged one year and, for comparability with the earlier estimates, two lags of the dependent variable were included. When we tested the restriction that foreign and home wage rates had equal and opposite signs, we found that this restriction could not be rejected in any of the regressions reported. In initial experiments a measure of the rate of natural increase lagged 25 years was included, but it did not take a significant coefficient in any of the regressions. Although the share of the Irish population in the mobile age range mattered in the long run, it did not change enough in the short run to influence fluctuations in annual emigration rates. A time trend added to the regressions did not take on a significant coefficient either. Thus, no omitted variables correlated with time were influencing annual emigration rates from Ireland. It appears, therefore, that Irish emigration can largely be explained by the variables listed in table 5.2: after all, they account for more than four fifths of the variance in the late-nineteenth-century Irish emigration rate.

The coefficients on the first regression reported in table 5.2 imply that the overseas employment rate had a very powerful impact on the timing of Irish emigration. A 10 percent increase in the employment rate (for example, a change in the unemployment rate from 10 percent to 1 percent) raised the emigration rate by 7.7 per thousand in the short run and by more than 10 per thousand in the long run. Predictably, changes in real wage ratios mattered far more in the long run. A fall of 10 percent in the foreign-to-domestic wage ratio led ultimately to a decrease in the emigration rate of 2.0 per thousand. (Although this elasticity is much smaller than that for the employment rate, the actual change in the wage ratio over the period was much larger than the change in the overseas employment rate, which has no appreciable long-run trend). Similarly, a 10 percent deviation of farm output above trend would tend to lower emigration by 3.3 per thousand in the long run. The migrant stock term indicates that in the long run, for every thousand previous Irish emigrants living abroad, an additional 50 were attracted overseas each year. This implies a very large and persistent effect and suggests that Irish emigrant history had a potent impact on current emigration rates through this chain effect.

We noted above that the official statistics understate the Irish flow to Britain. In the second column of table 5.2 the emigration rate has been adjusted by doubling the recorded flow to Britain. This major adjustment serves only to raise slightly the size and significance of the estimated coefficients on the relative wage and overseas employment rate variables: explanations for the long-run decline in the Irish emigration rate are little affected. The third column is for intercontinental emigration alone (i.e., excluding Britain). The estimated coefficients diminish in size but the pattern is pretty much the same. The same comments apply to the fourth column, which is for emigrants to the United States only. Indeed, these coefficients indicate that much of the short-run variation in Irish emigration can be attributed to changing employment conditions in the United States.[9]

The final two columns in table 5.2 indicate that the model fits both male and female emigrants. The result for women, particularly interesting given that the wage rates are for male occupations, suggests that our wage and employment variables are good proxies for conditions facing potential emigrating Irish women. However, the results do suggest that women were slightly less responsive to variations in economic activity overseas and to the relative wage than were men, but slightly more responsive to variations in economic activity at home.

What do the coefficients in table 5.2 imply for the long-run fall in the Irish emigration rate? Using the coefficients from the first column of table 5.2, a 10 percent fall in the foreign/Irish wage ratio would have caused the emigration rate to decline by 2 per thousand. Thus, the actual 17 percent fall in the foreign/Irish wage ratio between 1876–1880 and 1909–1913 accounts for a fall in the total emigration rate of 4 per thousand. More than half of this influence would be accounted for by the 13 percent fall in the United States/Irish wage ratio itself. Projecting these influences back to 1852–1856 implies that the 43 percent fall in the foreign-emigration-destination/Irish wage ratio must have lowered the long-run emigration rate by as much as 8.6 per thousand, a very large share of the secular decline in the actual emigration rate.

In short, the fall in the ratio of overseas to Irish real wages—Irish catching up—was central in accounting for the long-run decline in the emigration rate after 1850. But a significant part of the decline after the 1870s was due to the fall in the stock of Irish-born abroad from 59 percent of the Irish population in 1876–1880 to 49 percent in 1909–1913. In fact, it accounted for a 4.8 per thousand decline in the emigration rate over those 30 years. Since this decline was an indirect result of the declining wage gap, its impact on the secular decline in the emigration rate was even greater than these calculations imply. The migrant stock was a less powerful force over the period as a whole because it was rising prior to the 1880s as a result of the very high rates of postfamine emigration. Thus, with these modifications, Irish emigration appears to fit the stylized European pattern identified in chapter 3, which emphasizes the wage gap and the migrant stock abroad. In the first half of the period from 1851 to 1911, declining emigration was driven chiefly by economic convergence. After the 1880s, the fall in the emigration rate was driven instead by the decline in the relative migrant stock abroad, which in turn was the result of the prior slowdown in emigration, a powerful force that offset the impact of the slowdown in wage convergence after the mid-1890s.

Thus, there seems to be strong evidence of a long-run equilibrium process at work linking Irish to overseas labor markets: big wage gaps between home and abroad during and shortly after the famine induced an unusually large exit rate; this large exit rate induced fast Irish catch-up (via diminished pressure of labor on Irish resources) and an impressive erosion in the wage gap; the decline in the wage gap induced a decline in the exit rate, an event reinforced by the decline in the Irish-born abroad relative to the Irish at home. A new equilibrium was approached at the end of the century when wage gaps between home and abroad were far smaller and when emigration rates were much lower.

Who Were the Irish Migrants?

Chapter 2 suggested that we can clarify the forces that drove so many Irish to emigrate by examining the composition of the Irish emigrant cohort. To draw inferences from such evidence, we must compare the composition of the emigrant

Table 5.3a Irish Emigration Rates per 1,000 by Age Group: Census Years

Age (years)	1881 Male	1881 Female	1891 Male	1891 Female	1901 Male	1901 Female	1911 Male	1911 Female
0–4	7.6	7.5	4.8	4.7	3.8	3.9	2.2	2.1
5–9	6.2	6.2	3.5	3.6	2.6	2.7	1.8	1.5
10–14	5.0	5.9	2.9	3.0	1.7	2.0	1.6	1.6
15–19	21.0	35.1	17.8	31.8	6.8	16.6	9.7	18.9
20–24	67.1	55.1	59.3	53.3	34.9	41.2	37.8	29.0
25–34	31.6	16.9	23.1	13.3	16.6	12.7	16.8	8.5
35–44	8.9	6.2	6.5	4.8	5.4	5.3	3.2	2.0
45–54	5.1	4.5	3.5	3.1	2.3	2.2	1.3	1.1
55+	1.5	1.4	0.8	0.8	0.8	0.9	0.3	0.4
Total	15.9	14.5	13.0	12.4	8.3	9.5	7.8	6.4

Source: Calculated from *Emigration Statistics of Ireland* and *Census of Ireland*. See the appendix for further details.

cohorts with the population at risk. Such studies have been undertaken for emigrants from England and Scotland (Erickson 1972), and from Ireland (Fitzpatrick 1980a; Blessing 1985). Once again, the Irish evidence comes from the emigration reports of the Registrar General for Ireland. The accuracy of the returns before 1876 has been questioned,[10] so we concentrate on the years following, looking at census years when emigrants can be compared with the source population.

Compared with emigration from other European countries, which was male-dominated, Irish emigration was unusual in that it was composed almost equally of men and women. Women accounted for 48 percent of all recorded emigrants over the period as a whole. Emigration of both genders was highly concentrated in the 15–34 age groups: these young adults constituted over 80 percent of all the emigrants. The enormous age-specific emigration rates are given in table 5.3a for four census years. For example, the emigration rate for men aged 20–24 in 1881 was 67.1 per thousand, and it was 55.1 per thousand for women. The main difference between male and female emigration rates is that they were higher for women in the 15–19 age group and lower in the 25–34 age group.

Table 5.3b Irish Emigration Rates per 1,000 by Region: Census Years

Region	1881 United States	1881 Other	1891 United States	1891 Other	1901 United States	1901 Other	1911 United States	1911 Other
Leinster	10.9	1.8	6.9	0.8	2.4	0.6	2.6	11.1
Munster	12.7	3.7	18.3	2.9	12.4	2.8	6.8	0.6
Ulster	8.8	5.0	6.7	1.5	3.1	2.4	3.5	4.1
Connaught	18.7	1.3	16.3	0.9	16.7	0.4	10.5	0.4

Source: Calculated from *Emigration Statistics of Ireland* and *Census of Ireland*. See the appendix for further details.

The total number per thousand emigrating in the 15–34 age group fell from 35.9 in 1881 to 25.2 in 1911. Indeed, the decline in the aggregate emigration rate was common to all age groups, and the age structure of the emigrant cohorts varied little over time. For the cohort aged 15 in 1876, the probability of having departed from Ireland by the age of 55 was about 47 percent for men and 42 percent for women (Fitzpatrick 1980a: 126).

Most of the emigrants were single. The percentage of all emigrants aged 15 and over who were married or widowed amounted to only 10 to 15 percent of the total. Children under 15 had much lower emigration rates, typically emigrating as part of a young family. The lower emigration rates for those aged 10–14 compared with the 0–4 age group reflect the lower emigration rates of older parents compared with younger parents.

Where did these emigrants come from? Emigration rates varied greatly across regions (table 5.3b) and were higher in the rural counties to the south and west. At the provincial level, emigration rates were much higher from Connaught and Munster than from Ulster and Leinster. But there was also considerable variation within provinces. What stands out most is the low emigration rates from County Dublin and to a lesser extent from the most urbanized parts of Ulster, such as County Antrim and County Down. The overall variation in county emigration rates increased and then decreased after 1881: there is no evidence confirming the diffusion hypothesis identified by Gould (1980b) for Italy and Hungary, discussed briefly in chapter 2. Indeed, the coefficient of variation of county emigration rates *rose* over the period, while the diffusion hypothesis predicts a fall: 0.31 in 1881, 0.44 in 1891, 0.71 in 1901, and 0.41 in 1911.[11] Furthermore, there was considerable persistence in county emigration rates, as in the time series. The correlation coefficient between rates in 1881 and 1911 is 0.42.

Table 5.3b reports the Irish emigrants per thousand population heading for the United States and for all other destinations combined. Even though the latter figure is known to be downward-biased, the differences across the four provinces is so pronounced that any correction in that bias is unlikely to reverse the bottom line: not only were the emigration rates far higher from Leinster, Munster, and Connaught than from Ulster, but the high emigrating regions of Ireland strongly favored the United States as a destination while the preference was much weaker for Ulster. Emigrants from Ulster showed a greater preference for Britain, Canada, Australia, and New Zealand.

The emigration reports also break down the occupational structure of the emigrants, although these are somewhat harder to compare with population census data because of differences in classification. Clearly, however, the unskilled were a much bigger share of the emigrants than of the occupied population. Laborers were 80 percent of the emigrating men reporting an occupation in 1881, and the figure was still 65 percent in 1911. In contrast, laborers were only 22 percent of the occupied population in 1881, and 21 percent in 1911. Similarly, of the female emigrants who reported an occupation the vast majority were servants: 84 percent in 1881 and 85 percent in 1911. Compare these figures with the far lower servant shares of the occupied female population at the 1881 and 1911 censuses: 33 and 34 percent.

Thus, the emigration rates for unskilled men and women were very high: the emigration rates were 35 per thousand for male laborers and 26 per thousand for female servants in 1911.

What inferences can be drawn from such evidence? As we argued in chapter 2, the costs of migrating were lower for the single, unskilled, young adult than they were for the population at large. They had little investment in skills specific to firms, to industries, or to Ireland as a whole. The present value of emigration likely was much greater for these young, unskilled workers than for those who were older, more established, and more skilled.

There are, of course, other reasons for the dominance of unskilled young adults among the Irish emigrants. It has long been argued that diminishing opportunities in agriculture were a major reason for emigration. This fact is certainly consistent with the observed high emigration rates from counties in the rural west and south. The decline of the potato culture, underemployment, low wages, and limited opportunities to move up the agricultural ladder to become a small farmer all contributed to the flow of emigration from rural areas. The decline in the small farm probably made opportunities for women even more bleak than for men. Fitzpatrick (1980a: 138) has found a strong correlation across counties between the emigration rate and the population resident on agricultural holdings, and also between the emigration rate and the decline in the share of agricultural laborers in the population. A related debate has focused on the link between the system of inheritance in rural households and emigration. Some have argued that the "stem family" system prevailed in Ireland, although its extent has been debated (Gibbon and Curtin 1978; Fitzpatrick 1983; Guinnane 1992a). After the famine, the division of farms became relatively rare; one child inherited the family farm, leaving the others to seek their fortunes elsewhere. The inheritor was generally a son, though not necessarily the eldest (Ó Gráda 1980b; Kennedy 1991). In a recent study of household data at the turn of the century, Guinnane (1992b) has shown that the incidence of departure among sons and daughters depended on economic and demographic characteristics of the family, including the age of household head and the presence of siblings. In general, large families should have had high rates of emigration since emigration was surely preferable to low wages and underemployment as a farm laborer.

Some have argued that extreme poverty both encouraged and suppressed emigration. Cousens has noted that emigration rates in the 1860s and 1870s were more alike across counties than they were later in the century, despite the greater relative and absolute poverty of the west earlier than later. And he offers an explanation not unlike that we examined in chapter 2 for the European mass migration "life cycle" more generally: "The very poverty of these western areas partly explained the lack of mass emigration" (Cousens 1964: 311). The central idea, of course, is that only the very poor Irish were unable to find the resources to invest in the move. However, the lower-than-predicted emigration rate in the west of Ireland may be due in part to underenumeration before the late 1870s. In addition, Cousens' argument has trouble explaining why the very poor from the west of Ireland did not emigrate in greater numbers to Britain (which would have been a relatively modest investment) and why so many of them chose the more expensive passage to America (Fitzpatrick 1984: 9; Ó Gráda 1977: 70).

Other factors also may have served to limit Irish emigration from the more backward areas. Illiteracy and inability to speak English may have attenuated knowledge of opportunities abroad and reduced the potential gain from the move. This factor could have mattered for many potential emigrants. Among the population over the age of five in 1881, one third could neither read nor write and 3.4 percent spoke only Irish. These percentages had fallen in 1911 to 8 percent illiterate (aged nine and over) and 1.5 percent who spoke only Irish. If these characteristics retarded emigration, their effects must have weakened over time.

A final set of characteristics sometimes associated with emigration relates to religion and republicanism. Although it is not clear that Catholics had a higher propensity to emigrate once other factors are taken into account, it has been suggested that Protestants and Catholics emigrated to different destinations. Since Protestants clustered in Ulster while Catholics clustered elsewhere, this is certainly true as we have already seen (table 5.3b). But Ulster Protestants also tended to emigrate more often to Britain or to Canada. To what extent these destination patterns reflected political preference is unclear. Fitzpatrick (1980a: 129), for example, has argued that these destination patterns arose from regional differences in emigration established after the famine and sustained through chain migration.

Although rich and suggestive, this literature suffers a serious limitation: it derives from simple bivariate comparisons or cross tabulations that do not control simultaneously for the full set of influences. Hence, this literature does not determine whether the presence of industry, the height of wages, or the extent of urbanization deterred emigration. Similarly, it does not tell us how much poverty, illiteracy, and differences in religion contributed to emigration since they were correlated across regions and counties. We need multivariate analysis to answer these questions.

Irish Emigration: Explaining County Differences

To enrich the time series analysis already reported, this section explores the determinants of emigration by examining county data for the four census years from 1881 to 1911, yielding a pooled cross section of 128 observations. Fortunately, these census years were generally close to the trend in emigration rates.[12]

The demographic variables include the share of the population in the prime emigration 15–34 age group, average family size, and the number of persons per house. We expected these variables to correlate positively with emigration. The proportion of county population who were born there was intended to test the hypothesis that those who had moved once were more likely to move again. We expected the Catholic share to raise the emigration rate, and the share who were illiterate and who spoke only Irish to lower it.

The economic characteristics of the counties are described by several variables. The share living in towns of 2,000 or more measures the degree of urbanization whereas the share of the labor force in industry and in agriculture reflect differences in the occupational composition of the labor force. Potential access to a small farm is proxied by the share of agricultural holdings of less than five acres. This variable is interacted with the share of the male labor force in agriculture to give it a greater weight for the more agricultural counties. Irish employment conditions are measured by the farm wage and, to capture the incentive to emigrate, divided by a weighted average of the real wage in destination countries, just as we did in the time series analysis.[13] The extent of poverty is measured by two variables: the proportion of families living in third- and fourth-class housing and the proportion of the population receiving poor relief.[14]

Preliminary tests showed that a number of variables attained very low significance levels and could be excluded from the analysis: the proportion born in the county of residence, the proportion of the labor force in industry, the number of persons per house, and the proportion speaking Irish only. Regressions with the remaining variables appear in table 5.4 for total emigration, emigration to the United States, and intercontinental emigration. These regressions perform very well by cross-sectional standards, explaining more than two thirds of the variation in the dependent variable in each case. We tried year dummies but found, on a chi-squared test for joint significance, that they could be excluded. This result suggests stability in the factors determining Irish emigration across the late nineteenth century.

The regression for total emigration is reported in the first column of table 5.4. The point estimate for the proportion of the population aged 15–34 indicates, plausibly, that emigration would be 13.6 per thousand higher for this group than for the population as a whole, although, surprisingly, it is not significant. The proportion of the population in towns has a small, positive but insignificant coefficient, indicating that urbanization had little independent influence on the emigration rate. The agricultural variables are more important: the greater the proportion of the labor force in agriculture, the greater was emigration; the higher the proportion of smallholdings, the smaller was emigration (given the share of the labor force in agriculture). These results strongly suggest that lack of opportunities in agriculture (including opportunities to obtain or inherit a small farm) was an important cause of emigration.

The relative wage term was constructed to facilitate comparison with the time series results and was entered in logarithmic form. The point estimate from table 5.4 is noticeably smaller than the short-run coefficient estimated from the time series in table 5.2, and much lower than the long-run coefficient. The estimates in table 5.4 suggest that a 10 percent fall in the relative wage (foreign to Irish) would have lowered the emigration rate by 0.64 per thousand, while table 5.2 implies a long-run response three times as big, 2 per thousand. However, real wages appear to be too narrow a measure of relative labor market conditions since the poverty variables also had significant and independent effects on emigration. A 1 percent decline in the share on poor relief would have lowered the emigration rate by 1.96 per thousand, and a 1 percent fall in the share living in third- and fourth-class

Table 5.4 Regression Estimates for Irish County Emigration Rates, 1881–1911

	European emigration			Population aged 15 to 34		
	Total	United States	Intercontinental	Total	Men	Women
Constant	−45.92	−50.96	−45.18	−113.78	−96.96	−129.84
	(4.20)	(5.20)	(4.38)	(5.19)	(4.26)	(5.39)
Proportion aged 15–34	13.60	21.82	16.44			
	(0.88)	(1.58)	(1.13)			
Proportion in towns >2,000	3.02	3.17	2.03	3.88	−4.47	11.27
	(0.50)	(0.60)	(0.36)	(0.26)	(0.28)	(0.68)
Proportion of labor force in agriculture	16.39	15.90	15.46	41.60	34.28	48.03
	(2.38)	(2.56)	(2.37)	(2.46)	(1.95)	(2.59)
Proportion of holdings <5 acres times percent of labor force in agriculture	−41.98	−42.42	−46.50	−127.48	−123.63	−130.65
	(3.26)	(3.68)	(3.84)	(3.91)	(3.65)	(3.65)
Log of foreign wage relative to Irish wage	6.43	6.49	7.54	18.86	21.23	16.26
	(2.12)	(2.33)	(2.61)	(2.48)	(2.69)	(1.95)
Percentage of population on poor relief	1.96	1.56	1.88	4.14	5.78	2.51
	(4.40)	(3.95)	(4.53)	(3.67)	(4.95)	(2.03)
Proportion of third- and fourth-class houses	7.69	8.88	9.17	16.31	7.79	24.27
	(1.45)	(1.89)	(1.86)	(1.29)	(0.60)	(1.75)
Average family size	7.93	7.15	6.83	21.22	20.55	22.07
	(5.24)	(5.30)	(4.82)	(5.57)	(5.20)	(5.28)
Proportion Catholic	−4.97	1.04	−1.43	−1.38	−14.07	10.59
	(1.79)	(0.42)	(0.55)	(0.20)	(1.97)	(1.40)
Proportion illiterate	1.53	−0.80	−1.13	−9.70	−3.30	−15.44
	(0.19)	(0.11)	(0.15)	(0.50)	(0.16)	(0.73)
R^2	0.70	0.74	0.72	0.72	0.68	0.71
Residual sum of squares	1,420.9	1,188.6	1,309.9	9,646.6	10,360.2	11,590.0
HETERO	0.73	2.99	1.77	1.09	1.53	1.49

Notes: The *t* statistics are given in parentheses. HETERO is the test statistic for heteroscedasticity, based on regressing squared residuals on squared fitted values. It is distributed as chi-squared with one degree of freedom; critical value at 5 percent = 3.84.

housing would have lowered the emigration rate by another 0.08 per thousand. We shall have more to say about these living standard forces.

Average family size has a large and highly significant coefficient. It implies that a reduction in average family size by one person would have lowered the emigration rate by 7.93 per thousand. This would support those who have argued that demographic forces had a powerful *direct* influence on emigration throughout the late nineteenth century, an influence in addition to any *indirect* effect of population growth by creating a glut in Irish labor markets, lowering wages, raising poverty rates, and thus inducing more emigration. High birth rates led to large families, which directly contributed to larger emigration flows. Furthermore, family size rather than household size dominated when both variables were included in the regression. Finally, the Catholic share has a negative sign and the illiterate proportion has a positive sign, contradicting the conventional wisdom, although the coefficients are almost always insignificant in both cases. Income, poverty, and demography were the key determinants of county emigration rates. In Kerby Miller's words, Irish "emigrants left home for essentially mundane reasons" (Miller 1991: 339). Economics and demography mattered.

The second regression in table 5.4 is only for emigration to the United States, and the results are very similar to those for total emigration. There is some increase in the size of the coefficients on the proportion of the population aged 15–34 and the proportion living in towns, but these variables are still insignificant. The other minor difference is the fall in the size of the coefficient on the Catholic share, which becomes positive but is still insignificant. Given the small size and insignificance of this coefficient, Protestants and Catholics apparently were equally likely to emigrate to the United States, but Protestants were more likely than Catholics to emigrate to other destinations. The third column in table 5.4 indicates that the coefficients remain largely unchanged for intercontinental emigration.[15]

Because the emigration data are available by age and gender, we can explore the impact of the variables on the key emigration group: young men and women aged 15–34. The results are reported in the last three columns of table 5.4, and for the most part the coefficients are similar to those for total emigrants (column 1), but *much* bigger. Thus, for the age group 15–34 alone, a fall in the foreign/Irish wage ratio of 10 percent would have raised the age-specific emigration rate by 1.9 per thousand. Similarly, a rise in the share on poor relief by 1 percent would have raised the emigration rate by 4.1 per thousand, and an increase in family size by one person would have raised it by 16 per thousand.

When men and women are treated separately, only minor differences emerge. The results for the wage and poverty variables again suggest that these variables capture the market incentives for both men and women, although the estimated coefficients are a bit lower for women. In contrast, women were more responsive to the housing quality variable. Another point of difference is that the urban share has a negative effect on male emigration and a positive effect on female emigration, although in neither case is the coefficient significant. In addition, women were more likely to emigrate the higher the proportion of the labor force in agriculture. On the whole, however, table 5.4 tends to stress the similarities by gender rather than the differences.

How much did each of these variables contribute to emigration across the late nineteenth century? In particular, which variables were most important in accounting for the pronounced decline in Irish emigration rates? We can get an answer by taking the means of the variables across counties for beginning and ending census years, and then, using our estimated coefficients, we can decompose the change in the (unweighted) mean of county emigration rates between the two dates.[16] We offer answers for the shorter 1881–1901 period along with the longer 1881–1911 period because some of the variables, specifically the relative wage and the proportion on relief, changed their trend in the last decade. We want to determine whether that peculiar last decade matters. We use the first column of table 5.4 to decompose changes in the total emigration rate.

What we want to explain is fall in the emigration rate by 8.44 per thousand between 1881 and 1901, and by 9.52 per thousand between 1881 and 1911. The

Table 5.5 Decomposition of Changes in Irish Emigration Rates, 1881–1911

	1881–1901	1881–1911
Proportion aged 15–34	0.26	−0.02
Proportion in towns >2,000	0.08	0.11
Proportion of labor force in agriculture	−0.05	−0.29
Proportion holdings <5 acres times percent of labor force in agriculture	−0.68	−1.12
Log foreign wage relative to Irish wage	−0.92	−0.82
Percentage of population on poor relief	−2.08	−1.38
Proportion third- and fourth- class housing	−0.97	−1.63
Average family size	−2.71	−3.63
Proportion Catholic	0.01	−0.02
Proportion illiterate	−0.18	−0.20
Total predicted change	−7.24	−9.00
Actual change	−8.44	−9.52

Note: Effects on unweighted means of county emigration rates from first column, table 5.4.

answers are reported in table 5.5. The decomposition results indicate, once again, that the key variables that reduced the emigration rate over time were economic and demographic. The decline in family size served to reduce the emigration rate by 2.7 per thousand between 1881 and 1901 and by 3.6 per thousand between 1881 and 1911. If the relative wage, the share on relief, and housing quality together are taken to reflect labor market conditions and living standards, these contributed even more to the decline in the emigration rate. Together, they account for a 4.0 per thousand fall between 1881 and 1901 and a 3.8 per thousand fall between 1881 and 1911. In both periods, these combined demographic and labor market variables account for three quarters of the decline in the emigration rate. In the period ending 1901, the labor market variables dominate, accounting for almost half of the decline. Irish catch-up ceases between 1901 and 1911, so it is not surprising that the labor market variables lose a bit of their influence for the period ending 1911, but they still account for about 40 percent of the decline in emigration. The agricultural variables, the share of the labor force in agriculture, and this variable interacted with the proportion of holdings over 5 acres together contributed more modestly to the fall in emigration, reducing it by 1.4 per thousand over the whole period—that is, about 15 percent of the emigration decline. There is not much left to explain when the impact of labor market, demographic, and agricultural variables are added up.

These cross-sectional findings may seem, at first sight, to be at variance with the time series results, which stressed even more the importance of the relative wage and labor market forces in driving Irish emigration. The cross-sectional results suggest that wage rates alone had a relatively small impact on the emigration decline. But wage rates can be viewed as a summary statistic representing various components of the living standard package. Thus, the different relative wage effects

Table 5.6 Restricted Regressions for Irish County Emigration Rates, 1881–1911

	Total emigration	Emigration to the United States	Intercontinental emigration
Constant	−54.42	−57.85	−55.83
	(10.07)	(11.34)	(10.52)
Log of foreign wage relative to Irish wage	11.91	12.74	13.14
	(4.15)	(4.61)	(4.62)
Average family size	12.17	12.21	11.92
	(10.58)	(11.59)	(10.82)
R^2	0.57	0.59	0.57
Residual sum of squares	2,145.9	1,866.1	2,030.4
HETERO	0.66	2.09	1.62

Note: See table 5.4.

in time series and cross section may be more apparent than real. We can easily test this assertion by estimating a much reduced version of the equation in table 5.4, one that includes only the family size variable and the log relative wage.

The results appear in table 5.6 and suggest that the wage does indeed capture a range of variables representing living standards. The coefficient of 11.9 on the relative wage in the first equation in table 5.6 is nearly twice as large as in table 5.4. It indicates that a 10 percent fall in the relative wage would have reduced emigration by 1.2 per thousand, about the same as the short-run coefficient in the time series equation and about half the long-run coefficient. If the family size variable is excluded, the wage coefficient rises still further to approximate the long-run time series estimate.[17] Hence, the time series and cross-sectional results can be largely reconciled.

Conclusions

This chapter argues that the secular decline in the Irish emigration rate from its immediate postfamine peak owes a good deal to the impressive rise in Irish wage rates and living standards. And the important point is that Irish wages and living standards were catching up with those in destination countries overseas—Britain across the Irish Sea, the United States across the Atlantic, and Australasia even more distant. Time series analysis suggests that this catch-up was especially true of Irish emigration to the United States. The cross-sectional evidence argues, however, that living standards need to be construed more broadly than simply real wages. Just as they had during and immediately after the famine, the Irish in the late nineteenth century were still emigrating to escape poverty, as reflected in the numbers on poor relief and the share in low-quality housing.

The cross section analysis also illuminates a number of additional hypotheses that have had long lives in the literature and that we stressed in chapters 2 and 3. Our results strongly support the view emphasized in demographic studies, namely, that large families led to high emigration rates. Although our family size variable is only a proxy, the results are consistent with the hypothesis that one or two children either inherited or married an inheritor, and the surplus siblings essentially faced the choice of becoming poor landless laborers or emigrants. Second, and consistent with this hypothesis, we find that agricultural variables were important in determining county emigration rates. In particular, the greater the access to small holdings, the lower the emigration rate. Third, we find little evidence that poverty inhibited emigration after 1880. Both the numbers on poor relief and the share living in low-quality housing had positive effects on emigration. While the "poverty constraint" may have been relevant around the Great Famine, it was no longer relevant in the late nineteenth century: by then, we suspect that most prospective emigrants could obtain financial help from relatives abroad, thus easing the poverty constraint. Finally, there is little evidence that personal characteristics such as religion or illiteracy were important determinants of emigration. But there is some evidence that Catholics were less likely than Protestants to emigrate, especially to destinations other than the United States.

This chapter has stressed the role of Irish living standards as a central force causing the decline in Irish emigration, but it also raises another question. Did the decline in population and labor force, driven by emigration, lead to those rising Irish living standards? Almost all of the population decline was centered in agriculture and, as Schrier (1958: 73–75) noted almost 40 years ago, many contemporaries associated it with the rise in wages. More recently, Kevin O'Rourke (1991: 428) has argued that between 1856 and 1876 rural depopulation and changes in the structure of agriculture, particularly the reduction in tillage, can be explained by increasing labor scarcity as a result of foreign labor market conditions. We think the global labor market forces were more general and that as the wage gap between Ireland and the countries of immigration declined, the Irish emigration rate decreased, as did the rate of population decline and the rate of increase in real wages and living standards. Before we conclude that emigration was a central factor contributing to long-run convergence of Irish wages on those prevailing in Australia, Britain, and America, we need to know more about the impact of emigration on wages and living standards at home. This topic receives our full attention in chapter 9 as we search for the forces creating an increasingly integrated global labor market in the late nineteenth century.

Appendix

Means of Variables Used in Cross-Sectional Regression

Variable	1881	1891	1901	1911	Pooled
Emigration rate	16.55	12.63	8.11	7.03	11.08
Proportion aged 15–34	0.32	0.34	0.35	0.32	0.33
Proportion in towns	0.18	0.19	0.20	0.21	0.20
Proportion of male labor force in agriculture	0.66	0.65	0.66	0.65	0.66
Proportion holdings <5 acres	0.17	0.17	0.19	0.21	0.19
Foreign wage/Irish wage	1.88	1.73	1.62	1.65	1.72
Percentage of population on poor relief	2.51	2.37	1.45	1.80	2.03
Proportion of third- and fourth-class housing	0.46	0.40	0.33	0.25	0.36
Average family size	5.10	4.93	4.76	4.64	4.86
Proportion Catholic	0.82	0.81	0.81	0.81	0.81
Proportion illiterate	0.25	0.18	0.13	0.11	0.17

Sources: The numbers of emigrants in the total by age and country of destination were taken from *Emigration Statistics of Ireland: 1881* (C. 2828), 1891 (C. 6679), 1901 (Cd. 976) and 1911 (Cd. 6131). The total population, numbers aged 15–34, numbers in towns, proportion on poor relief, average family size, proportion Catholic, and proportion illiterate are from *Census of Ireland, Provincial Summary Tables*: Leinster, 1881 (C. 3042), 1891 (C. 6575), 1901 (Cd. 847), 1911 (Cd. 6049); Munster, 1881 (C. 3418), 1891 (C. 6567), 1901 (Cd. 1058), 1911 (Cd. 6050); Ulster, 1881 (C. 3204), 1891 (C. 6626), 1901 (Cd. 1123), 1911 (Cd. 6051); Connaught, 1881 (C. 3268), 1891 (C. 6685), 1901 (C. 1059), 1911, (Cd. 6052). The proportion of holdings less than five acres and the proportion of third- and fourth-class housing from *Census of Ireland, General Report*: 1881 (C. 3365), 1891 (C. 6780), 1901 (Cd. 1190), 1911 (Cd. 6663). The proportion of the male labor force in agriculture is from Fitzpatrick (1980*b*). For the derivation of the wage ratio see text.

6

Segmented Markets, Multiple Destinations
Italian Experience

Introduction

Italian emigration accounted for a large part of the surge of southern European migrations in the late nineteenth century. From the 1890s onward Italy became the leader in sheer numbers emigrating and in rate of emigration. An estimated 14 million left Italy between 1871 and 1914; 44 percent went to other European countries, 30 percent went to North America, and 24 percent went to South America (Nugent 1992: 95). Indeed, John Gould sees late-nineteenth-century Italy as *the* classic case of mass migration:

> In many respects, ... Italy is ... the country of emigration par excellence—not merely for its sheer importance as a source of migrants but as a country in and from (and back to) which migrants' motives and choices reached perhaps their highest and most developed level of sophistication, and from whose history many of the characteristics and motivations of migrant behaviour can generally be laid bare. (1980a: 78)

Given the importance of the Italians, one would have expected far more quantitative attention to them in the migration literature.

Conditions in some parts of Italy bear strong resemblance to those in Ireland highlighted in chapter 5. Thus, Dennis Mack-Smith called Sicily "a country like Ireland, of great estates, absentee landlords, secret societies, rebellion and emigration" (1969: 234). Yet Italian emigration patterns differed sharply from those of Ireland. While the Irish annual emigration rate declined over time, the Italian rates rose sharply from about 5 per thousand in 1880 to a peak of 25 per thousand in 1913. Furthermore, unlike Irish and Scandinavian emigration, Italian emigration was accompanied by a rising tide of return migration. In addition, the intensity of emigration varied greatly between Italian regions. Emigrants came chiefly from the north of Italy in the 1870s, but emigration from the center and the south increased to comparable levels as the period unfolded. And Italians emigrated to a far wider variety of destinations than did emigrants from any other European country. The Italians went to Germany, France, Switzerland, and Austria-Hungary in Europe; they went to Argentina and Brazil in South America; and, of course, they went to the United States. The Irish emigrated almost exclusively to Anglo-Saxon destinations, and the vast majority went to Great Britain and the American northeast.

This chapter is motivated by familiar questions that have not yet received serious quantitative attention for Italy. To what extent can Italian emigration be explained by the same economic and demographic forces identified in the cross-country analysis of chapter 3, the time series analysis of chapter 4, and the Irish regional analysis of chapter 5? To what extent must these explanations be modified when applied to Italy? There is no shortage of additional hypotheses in the rich qualitative literature on Italian emigration, but for the most part they have been explored only by simple bivariate correlation, when explored quantitatively at all. The determinants of Italian emigration are much too complex to be isolated by that kind of analysis: they need instead an explicit multivariate framework wherein the simultaneous impact of more than one influence can be explored. This chapter shows that conventional wisdom is often badly bruised when exposed to multivariate analysis.

Chapter 3 showed that the same forces drove emigration in southern and northern Europe. But recall that the Latin dummy had a significant and positive coefficient even when embedded in a model rich in economic and demographic variables. Furthermore, the model could not account fully for the surge in Italian emigration after the 1890s. Is this uniquely large Italian emigration surge simply an artifact of inadequate data? Or was it influenced by Italian emigration policies and the immigration policies of destination countries? Are the effects of the emigration "fundamentals" masked by the unusually high levels of return migration? Were there additional economic or demographic factors that applied to Italian and other Mediterranean emigrations but not to Northwest Europe? Two candidates were nominated earlier in this book: rising levels of education and literacy, which released an information constraint, and rising levels of Italian real income, which released a poverty constraint. We explore both of these candidates here.

Other questions relate to the variation in emigration rates across Italian regions. Differences in the magnitude and composition of emigration between the Italian north and south have received much attention. Can these be explained by a single model of emigration or are different explanations required for north and south? If the same model applies, what, then, accounts for the enormous variation in emigration rates across regions? Did the differences result from persistence and path dependence, as many observers have claimed? Or were regional differences in the fundamentals driving emigration? And what explains the regional variance in emigrant destinations?

These questions are important enough to warrant a separate chapter for Italy. It will offer quantitative answers to all of them.

Explaining Italian Emigration

Was the "Big Surge" Spurious?

Italian emigration statistics come from the Instituto Centrale di Statistica and are based on the authorization or issue of passports collected from 1876 onward and are widely accepted as the best available estimates of gross emigration. The statistics cover intercontinental emigration and emigration to other countries within Europe and offer a breakdown of emigration flows by region of origin.[1] Figure 6.1 shows the strong upward trend in gross emigration per thousand population with increasingly sharp fluctuations after the turn of the century.[2]

Is this a true representation of the increased flow of migrants settling permanently abroad? Probably not, since estimates of net migration fail to show the same surge after the turn of the century. The true volume of net migration is hard to judge because we do not have comprehensive estimates of return migrants.[3] One estimate of net migration appears as the lower plot in figure 6.1. This estimate, from Giusti (1965), is constructed using vital rates to infer net migration as the residual between census benchmarks. It is consistent with other estimates that put 1881–1911 net emigration at about one third of the gross flow (Di Comite 1976: 153; Livi-Bacci 1961: 39).

An important implication of these estimates is that they identify a *fall* in the net emigration rate in the first decade of the twentieth century in contrast to the sharp

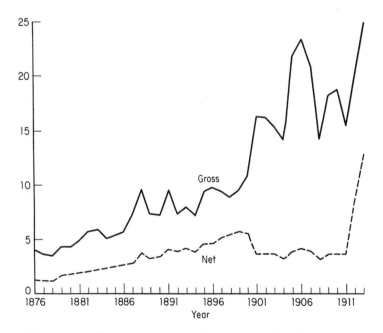

Figure 6.1 Emigration from Italy, 1876–1913 (per 1,000 population)

rise in the gross emigration rate![4] Indeed, the ratio of net-to-gross emigration falls from 52 percent in 1891–1900 to 20 percent in 1901–1910. Although the return migration rate almost certainly rose between these two decades, it cannot have risen from a half to four fifths. One reason for the large gap between gross and net is that changes in passport regulations probably exaggerate the rise in the measured gross emigration rate around 1901 and hence would tend to understate the return migration rate from that date on. Passports were not obligatory for travel before 1901 and there was a charge for them; they were obligatory but free after 1901.[5] Between 1879 and 1900 Italian emigration to the United States, based on Italian emigration statistics, was 11 percent lower than that based on American immigration statistics. Between 1901 and 1911, it was 14 percent *higher*, for an enormous net swing of 25 percent. Smaller upward shifts in the ratio of emigration-to-immigration totals also apply to other countries, such as Argentina and Brazil (Foerster, 1919: 17–18; Gould, 1980a: 90).

All of these statistics suggest that the surge in Italian gross emigration around the turn of the century is exaggerated. The exaggeration likely matters, but we simply do not yet know how much.

Was the Big Surge Uniquely Italian?

Even though official Italian sources may overstate the rise in Italian emigration after the 1890s, a substantial growth in Italian emigration undoubtedly took place. This big surge is well documented by immigration statistics from destination countries. Italian immigrants to Argentina, Brazil, and the United States combined rose from an annual average of about 400,000 in the early 1880s to nearly a million a decade later and exceeded 1.5 million in 1902–1906. A big surge is also reflected in the rise in the stock of Italian-born enumerated in receiving countries censuses from about a million in 1881 to over 5 million in 1911. Chapter 3 argued that rising European emigration was driven chiefly by natural increase, industrialization, and the rising emigrant stock itself. These forces help explain why emigration so often surged when industrial catch-up was narrowing gaps between low-wage European sources and high-wage destinations. Such was the case in Italy but, as we have seen, other explanations have also been offered to explain the surge, citing Italy as the prime example. Is it possible that Italy may be a special case?

Riccardo Faini and Alessandra Venturini (1994a) have forcibly restated the argument that rising per capita income in Italy had a potent impact on emigration. By releasing the poverty constraint for an ever-widening group of potential emigrants, economic growth in Italy led to a surge in the emigration rate despite the declining income gap between Italy and destination countries. The rise in Italian income per capita reflects more than simply income changes: it also serves as a proxy for changing patterns of production, rising urbanization, and the accumulation of human capital.[6] Based on the analysis of time series data for emigration to Germany, France, and the United States, they argue that nearly a third of the surge in Italian emigration between 1900 and 1913 can be explained by domestic per capita income growth.

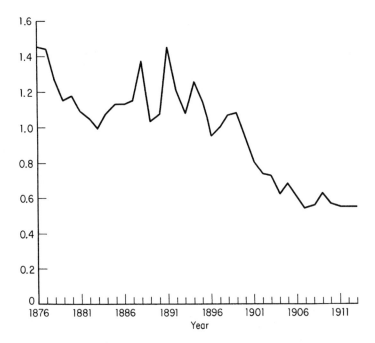

Figure 6.2 Coefficient of Variation of Compartimenti Emigration Rates

Drawing on Italian experience, John Gould (1980b) argued that a process of diffusion occurred whereby information about emigration opportunities spread from one area to the next as time passed and as the volume of emigration itself increased. He suggested that emigration from different localities should each trace out an "S" curve with emigration at first low, then advancing rapidly and finally leveling off as saturation is reached. Gould cited declining inequality of Compartimento-level emigration rates to help clinch his case. This is confirmed by the declining coefficient of variation of these rates in figure 6.2. However, such evidence might be explained in other ways and, because of the difficulty in measuring information flows, Gould's hypothesis cannot be tested directly. One indirect corollary is that local emigration rates were dominated by persistence rather than by economic and demographic variables; another is that levels of education and literacy, by mediating the flow of information, would be correlated with regional emigration rates. We test these hypotheses in the following analysis.

Was Italian Emigration Segmented?

There are two dimensions along which segmentation in Italian emigration might be observed: across Italian regions and across different emigrant destinations. If there were separate and independent emigration streams by source and destination, each driven by different forces, any attempt to explain Italian emigration that

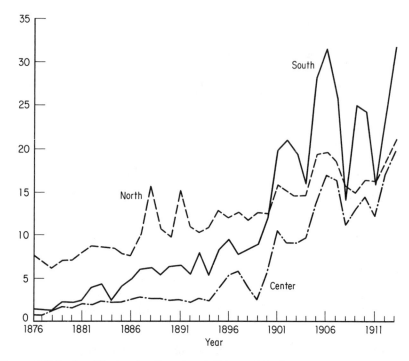

Figure 6.3 Regional Emigration Rates (per 1,000 population)

did not recognize this heterogeneity is likely to fail. One of the major themes in Italian modern history is north-south dualism.[7] Were these regions so different that a common model of emigration is inappropriate? Certainly their experience over time looks different. While the northern emigration rate showed a steady increase from 1876 to 1913, more dramatic increases occurred from relatively low initial levels in the center and south (figure 6.3).[8] Even though the Italian statistics over-state the surge, the fact remains that regional experience differed and raises the question about whether a common approach can explain them.

The contrasts in regional experience are heightened by differences in destina-tions (table 6.1). Over 70 percent of the northern emigrants left for European coun-tries, while only a quarter headed for the Americas. The pattern was reversed in the south, where only a tiny and declining fraction departed for European countries. The share going to north America increased in each region, although it rose most dramatically and from a very low base in the south and center. Gould has argued that the rise in the share going to the United States, and the decline in the shares going to Brazil and Argentina, derived from the rise in overall emigration from the south. Applying the 1881–1886 destination shares to the 1908–1913 emigration totals for 16 Compartimenti, he found that about half of the increase in the United States' share in the three-country emigration total could be accounted for by shifts

Table 6.1 Italian Emigration by Major Destinations

	1876–1885	1886–1895	1896–1905	1906–1915
Annual averages (000s)				
Total	131.5	239.1	432.2	599.9
Europe	85.0	97.0	189.1	242.6
France	40.7	28.6	39.6	62.6
Germany	7.1	12.8	43.5	59.2
Austria-Hungary	22.4	35.2	50.3	35.2
Switzerland	10.2	9.7	39.7	74.5
Americas	42.4	138.6	234.1	347.3
Argentina	17.6	41.4	49.0	71.6
Brazil	6.0	50.4	45.0	21.1
United States	8.8	37.7	130.6	238.6
Shares of total emigration (%)				
Total	100	100	100	100
Europe	64.6	40.6	43.8	40.4
France	31.0	12.0	9.2	10.4
Germany	5.4	5.4	10.1	9.9
Austria-Hungary	17.0	14.7	11.6	5.9
Switzerland	7.7	4.1	9.1	12.4
Americas	32.2	58.0	54.2	57.9
Argentina	13.4	17.3	11.3	11.9
Brazil	4.6	21.1	10.6	3.5
United States	6.7	15.8	30.2	39.8

Source: Annuario Statistico Emigrazione Italiana dal 1876 al 1925, table 1.

in the overall levels of emigration towards Compartimenti that favored the United States. The remainder was due to destination shifts within Compartimenti.[9] Alternatively, one might argue that conditions favoring emigration to North America raised southern Italian emigration relative to northern. Indeed, the increase in emigration to North America from all Italian regions suggests that increasing pull in North America rather than increasing push from southern Italy was at work. Either interpretation is consistent with segmented Italian labor markets and thus segmented emigration streams.

Were the Motives of Italian Emigrants Different?

Were the motives of Italian emigrants different from those of emigrants leaving other countries like Ireland or Scandinavia? Italian emigrants were typically young and single, like other European emigrants: over half were aged 15–34 and three quarters traveled alone rather than in family groups. Among those reporting occupations, a large share was from agriculture (though many more were from agricultural backgrounds)[10] and more than 80 percent were unskilled. The major difference in the emigrant profile is the predominance of men, who accounted for

80 percent of the emigrants, a percentage similar to Spain's.[11] This fact is closely connected with temporary emigration and with the high rates of return migration (even more heavily male) that characterized southern European emigration. Most qualitative accounts of Italian emigration stress that the overwhelming bulk intended to return to their families after a few years, though many of them failed to do so.[12] This raises the question of whether population pressure, wage gaps, and conditions in agriculture and industry operated with different effects on Italian emigration.

Seasonal emigration is one of the most well-known features of Italian emigration, although not the most important quantitatively.[13] These *golondrinas* or birds of passage often traveled to South America in October or November to take part in the southern wheat or flax harvests, returning in February or March for the northern harvest season (Foerster 1919: 244). Differences in agricultural seasonality might therefore be an important factor in emigration, but seasonal migrations also flowed to the United States and Europe, where seasonal movements in labor demand were certainly pronounced yet not inverted with the Italian harvest season.[14] Destination choice was linked perhaps to the degree of underemployment in agriculture: the greater the seasonal unemployment, the lower the opportunity cost of seasonal emigration to northern-hemisphere labor markets.

Did Policy and Prejudice Make a Difference?

During the 1860s Italian political leaders were much concerned with emigration, and many disapproved of it (as was true in Germany and Sweden as well). In 1868 and 1873 laws were passed to restrict the issue of passports only to those deemed to have sufficient abilities and resources to thrive abroad and to finance their return. But laws had little impact on local officials or on individual emigrants, and thus in 1888 a new law gave official sanction to all emigration (Dore 1968: 104–05), suggesting that emigration was "a phenomenon more apt to make laws than to obey them" (Foerster 1919: 475). As part of a major policy shift, the minister for foreign affairs was given the power in 1901 to ban emigration to any specific country. This power was used against Brazil in 1902 following reports on the conditions faced by Italian emigrants there (and later against other South American countries). But by that time the Brazilian coffee bubble had burst, and, notwithstanding the Prinetti decree, only a modest flow of emigrants to Brazil continued.

The effect of destination-country policy may have been more powerful. The Brazilian subsidy to Italian emigrants during the great coffee boom surely must have influenced destination choices. Three quarters of the Italian immigrants entering Sao Paulo during this period came on essentially free passages, although the subsidy was offered selectively to northern Italians from Lombardy, Piedmont, Veneto, and Liguria (Maurette and Siewers 1937: 236; Merrick and Graham 1979: 92, 95). Subsidies were not offered to Italians going to Australia, a policy that effectively shut them out even though they could have earned substantially higher incomes there compared with Argentina and Brazil (Taylor 1994). But culture and language, not policy and prejudice, kept Italian immigration to the United States low at first. Both the gradual breakdown of these barriers and the declining fortunes of South America fueled the late-nineteenth-century emigration surge to America.

Analyzing the Time Series

What explains trends and fluctuations in Italian emigration? To explore this question, we estimate a time series model similar to that used in chapter 4 to explain emigration from northern Europe. The gross emigration rates to be explained are plotted in figure 6.1, and the variables representing foreign conditions are weighted averages for five major receiving countries: France, Germany, Argentina, Brazil, and the United States. Since direct measures of employment rates do not exist for all these countries, we constructed instead indices of economic activity based on deviations from per capita GDP trend.[15] We constructed the migrant stock series using annual gross emigration data to interpolate between census benchmarks to estimate the foreign-born in destination countries for each year. The rate of natural increase lagged 20 years was also included to capture the impact of demographic events, as we did in chapter 3.[16] Finally, a dummy for the years 1901–1913 was included to account for that spurious surge in the official statistics.

The results appear in table 6.2 and strongly support the model.[17] In the equation for total emigration, all the coefficients give the expected signs and the t statistics are usually high enough to pass significance tests. Foreign activity has the usual large, positive, significant coefficient whereas home activity has the usual small, negative, insignificant coefficient: in this sense, Italian emigration was no different from that of the rest of Europe. The coefficient on the wage ratio is positive and strongly significant: in the long run, a rise in the wage ratio of 10 percent would have increased the emigration rate by about 1.3 per thousand per annum, a figure much like those we obtained earlier for northern European countries. This result reinforces chapter 3, where we also found little evidence to support the view that Italian emigration was more wage-elastic than the northern European emigrations. To repeat, no evidence supports an Arthur Lewis–like hypothesis of relatively elastic labor supply coming from this part of the Mediterranean Basin.

The lagged rate of natural increase has a plausible but not significant coefficient; nevertheless, it implies that in the long run an increase of one per thousand in the rate of natural increase raised the emigration rate by 0.5 per thousand, a powerful effect and, once again, consistent with the cross-country analysis in chapter 3. The migrant stock also has the important influence we have come to expect: for every thousand previous emigrants living abroad, in the long run 87 more were drawn abroad every year. This is also similar to our earlier estimates for the United Kingdom and Scandinavia, suggesting that chain migration, or the friends and relatives effect, was important for Italian emigration. This finding is consistent with the emphasis placed on chain migration in both the Italian emigration literature (Gould 1980a) and in the Latin American immigration literature (Cortes Condé 1982). Finally, the dummy for 1901–1913 confirms an upward shift in the

Table 6.2 Time Series Regressions for Italian Emigration, 1878–1913

	Total emigration	European emigration	Intercontinental emigration
Constant	−17.78	−1.43	−8.63
	(2.58)	(0.81)	(1.80)
Foreign activity (t)	39.84	17.54	18.75
	(3.01)	(3.29)	(3.19)
Home activity (t − 1)	−6.81	−6.79	−11.45
	(0.89)	(2.93)	(1.41)
Log wage ratio (foreign/home) (t)	19.22	2.20	4.90
	(2.95)	(1.42)	(1.78)
Lagged rate of natural increase	0.73	0.06	0.78
	(1.19)	(0.43)	(1.32)
Migrant stock (t)	0.13	0.34	0.07
	(4.42)	(4.11)	(2.87)
Dummy for 1901–1913	4.75	2.79	1.74
	(3.05)	(4.54)	(1.15)
Lagged emigration rate (t − 1)	0.06	−0.01	0.16
	(0.38)	(0.04)	(1.00)
Lagged emigration rate (t − 2)	−0.55	−0.52	−0.44
	(4.10)	(3.39)	(2.93)
R^2	0.95	0.98	0.88
RSS	64.15	3.88	66.32
DW	1.90	2.46	1.78
LM(1)	0.01	4.61	1.01
RESET	7.09	0.27	0.57

Note: Figures in parentheses are t statistics.

emigration rate unassociated with the other variables: in the long run this "exogenous" force amounted to an increase in the emigration rate of 3.2 per thousand, but we think this exogenous force is simply exaggerated official statistics. If so, we have successfully derived an estimate of the size of the "spurious" exaggeration—3.2 per thousand or, as we shall see, 17 percent.

Separate estimates for emigration to European and intercontinental destinations are reported in the remaining two columns of table 6.2. These give qualitatively similar results, although the magnitudes of the coefficients sometimes differ substantially between the two equations. The coefficient for home activity is strongly significant for European emigration but not for intercontinental emigration. The reverse is true for relative wage effects, which appear to be more powerful for intercontinental emigration, although still significant only at the 10 percent level. The difference in the coefficients on lagged natural increase suggests that demographic forces were more powerful in driving intercontinental than European emigration, although the coefficients are not significant. By contrast, the migrant stock coefficient is *much* larger for European emigration than for intercontinental emigration. Apparently chain migration was a far more potent force influencing Italian emigration to Europe than overseas. Alternatively, it reflects the fact that the stock of European emigrants was small relative to the flow, largely because the return migration rate was higher for the European than for the intercontinental stream. The smaller migrant stock coefficient for intercontinental emigration is consistent with a larger proportion of permanent emigrants.

These results confirm that the Italian emigration time series was determined by much the same forces as those underlying the emigrations from northern Europe. Furthermore, the unique big surge in Italian emigration after the 1890s disappears when we control for the appropriate economic and demographic variables, as well as for the effect of the upward shift resulting from the changing passport regulations.

The estimated long-run coefficients can be used to examine the relative contributions of each variable to trends in the total emigration rate between 1878 and 1913. The emigration rate increased 21.5 per thousand over those years, or 18.3 per thousand based on a quadratic trend. Multiplying the long-run coefficients by each variable's change over the period implies that the falling wage ratio (Italian catch-up) produced a *decline* of 3.1 per thousand in the emigration rate, an influence only partially offset by an increase of 2.33 per thousand produced by the rise in the lagged rate of natural increase. The most powerful force contributing to the surge in Italian emigration was quite simply the rise in the migrant stock abroad: it contributed 12.6 per thousand to the rise in the emigration rate. Adding to these forces the rise of 3.18 per thousand accounted for by the dummy variable (that spurious part of the surge due to faulty official statistics), the model predicts a rise of 15 per thousand, not far short of the actual trend increase of 18.3 per thousand. These results can be stated another way. Of the 18.3 per thousand increase, 17 percent was due to faulty official reporting, leaving a true increase of 15.1 per thousand to be explained. The model can account for 78% (11.8 per thousand), while 22% remains unexplained.

One force missing from the model in table 6.2 is Italian incomes and wages. Did they in fact contribute to the surge in emigration as Faini and Venturini (1994a) suggest? This hypothesis can be tested by adding the Italian real wage (for prospective migrants, a more relevant variable than per capita income) to the specification in table 6.2. The result is shown in the first column of table 6.3. Although the coefficient is positive as predicted, it is small compared with that on the wage ratio and, more importantly, it has a 't' value of only 0.2. Therefore, we reject the hypothesis that rising real wages in Italy were an important cause of rising Italian emigration.[18]

The second column in table 6.3 shows how the results change when the wage level is included but the migrant stock is excluded. The result is a dramatic increase in size of the coefficient on the Italian real wage together with a rise in its t value to 3.0. According to this equation, the long-run effect of the rise in the Italian real wage between 1878 and 1913 was to increase the emigration rate by 8.9 per thousand. However, the result is due entirely to the absence of any other strongly upward-trend variable in the equation (with the exception of the lagged rate of natural increase), and we think the missing variable is the migrant stock. To illustrate, we added a time trend to the specification that omits the migrant stock; the result

Table 6.3 Alternative Specifications for Italian Emigration, 1878–1913 (dependent variable: total emigration rate)

	1	2	3
Constant	−22.96	−66.99	−33.90
	(0.92)	(3.14)	(0.83)
Foreign activity (t)	39.71	43.38	45.10
	(3.03)	(2.98)	(3.08)
Home activity ($t − 1$)	−7.27	−17.07	−12.30
	(0.90)	(2.12)	(1.30)
Log wage ratio (foreign/home) (t)	19.23	13.32	9.67
	(2.91)	(1.81)	(1.31)
Log Italian real wage (t)	1.56	16.31	6.19
	(0.21)	(3.02)	(0.52)
Lagged rate of natural increase ($t − 20$)	0.72	1.07	1.07
	(1.16)	(1.58)	(1.58)
Migrant stock (t)	0.13		
	(2.75)		
Dummy for 1901–1913	4.85	5.94	5.91
	(2.95)	(3.35)	(3.32)
Time trend			0.19
			(0.95)
Lagged emigration rate ($t − 1$)	0.06	0.29	0.25
	(0.04)	(1.88)	(1.56)
Lagged emigration rate ($t − 2$)	−0.55	−0.46	−0.49
	(4.01)	(3.12)	(3.24)
R^2	0.95	0.94	0.94
RSS	64.03	82.71	79.88
DW	1.92	1.95	1.97
LM(1)	0.00	0.01	0.05
RESET	0.98	1.05	1.05

Notes: Figures in parentheses are t statistics. Column numbers represent alternative regressions.

appears in the final column of table 6.3. This again reduces the coefficient on the Italian real wage to insignificance.[19] Thus, if a poverty constraint did affect potential emigrants, it seems to have been released through remittances from previous emigrants rather than through rising real wages at home.

Italian Regional Experience

Background Hypotheses

To many observers the key to unlocking the secrets of the forces driving Italian emigration lies with understanding the wide variations in emigration across regions. Italian emigration rates varied widely between the 16 Compartimenti and even more so among the 69 provinces. The variation across Compartimenti is documented in table 6.4 for 1882 and 1912, a period over which this variation declined

Table 6.4 Italian Emigration Rates by Compartimento, 1882 and 1912 (per thousand)

	1882			1912		
	Total	European	Intercontinental	Total	European	Intercontinental
Piedmont	12.29	9.53	2.76	18.97	11.21	7.76
Liguria	6.75	1.99	4.76	7.34	2.52	4.82
Lombardy	6.09	3.77	2.32	15.54	12.17	3.37
Veneto	12.79	11.29	1.50	31.82	27.01	4.82
Emilia	3.19	2.97	0.22	13.15	9.99	3.17
Tuscany	4.21	3.48	0.73	15.06	10.11	4.95
Marches	0.77	0.17	0.60	29.40	12.76	16.64
Umbria	0.05	0.03	0.02	20.30	16.00	4.31
Lazio	0.01	0.00	0.01	13.49	2.03	11.46
Abruzzi-Molise	3.56	0.64	2.92	32.27	4.25	28.02
Campania	4.82	1.21	3.61	20.14	1.65	18.48
Apulia	0.49	0.39	0.10	13.54	2.02	11.53
Basilicata	14.72	0.86	13.86	31.09	1.14	29.95
Calabria	8.29	2.12	6.17	33.32	0.91	32.41
Sicily	1.08	0.52	0.56	25.06	1.49	23.57
Sardinia	0.30	0.29	0.01	10.63	5.67	4.96
Italy	5.62	3.54	2.08	20.31	8.80	11.51

Source: Annuario Statistico Emigrazione Italiana dal 1876 al 1926, table 1.

dramatically while the overall gross emigration rate increased; the coefficient of variation fell from 1.09 in 1882 to 0.55 in 1912. By the turn of the century, north-south differences in emigration rates that had been so prominent earlier had disappeared and the south had overtaken the north.[20]

The Compartimento emigration rates hide even greater variations at the provincial level. The coefficient of variation for total emigration rates among the 69 provinces declined from 1.57 in 1882 to 1.05 in 1902 and 0.63 in 1912. Even though regional variances in Italian emigration experience declined dramatically, they were still higher than those in Ireland: chapter 5 reported the coefficient of variation for emigration rates among the 32 Irish counties as 0.31 in 1881, 0.71 in 1901, and 0.41 in 1911. In 1882 10 Italian provinces had emigration rates above 10 per thousand while at the other extreme six had rates less than 0.1 per thousand. By 1902 six had rates over 40 per thousand while eight had rates less than 5 per thousand. Furthermore, of the six provinces with highest emigration rates in 1902, three were in the north and three were in the south; similarly, the eight with the lowest rates were evenly split between the north and either the center or the south. These figures suggest that any adequate explanation of Italian regional variation in emigration rates must be developed to explain provincial differences, not just to explain north-south differences.

What explanations have been offered? As we have seen, John Gould has argued that local Italian variations can be explained by a process of information diffusion. This argument stresses persistence in emigration rates and predicts a convergence in the cross-sectional variation as the persistence only slowly erodes. Cases of persistence can easily be identified; Belluno and Sondrio in the north consistently had the highest emigration rates, while Ferrara in the north and Lecce in the south consistently had the lowest. A gradual erosion in this persistence is documented by the decline in the correlation coefficient between the log of provincial emigration rates in 1882 and 1902, 0.45, to that for 1882 and 1912, 0.23. Although all of this evidence is consistent with Gould's argument, it is also consistent with provincial persistence in *other* determinants of emigration. The evidence in chapter 5 suggested that the latter argument wins in the Irish case.

Although Gould's hypothesis is not directly testable, this is a corollary: education and literacy, by mediating the flow of information, must have had an important influence on emigration. According to this corollary, southern educational backwardness must have inhibited migration up to the 1870s: as southern literacy converged on northern literacy, emigration rates in the south caught up with those in the north. Significant gaps in north-south literacy still persisted by 1911; hence, the effects should still be discernible. Literacy rates of those aged six or over averaged about two thirds in the north and the center by then, and they had reached 89 percent in the Piedmont. In the south they were about 50 percent and as low as 30 percent in Calabria. Not only were these gaps apparent in literacy and primary education, but they were also evident in secondary education and in craft and industrial skills. Since literacy and education were more important to the labor market in 1900 than in 1850, they might have been more important for the assimilation and adaptation of Italian migrants, who emigrated in great numbers later in the nineteenth century, than for the Irish, who emigrated in great numbers earlier in the century.

The qualitative literature on Italy suggests many other determinants of interregional emigration rates, most echoing the economic and demographic forces we identified in the cross-country analysis in chapter 3 and the Irish cross-county analysis in chapter 5. Livi-Bacci (1961) and Sori (1979) have both argued for a strong link between demographic pressure and emigration both over time and across regions. Although we found only weak evidence of demographic effects in the time series analysis, perhaps such forces are more likely to be revealed in the provincial cross section. Demographic forces are unlikely to have accounted for much of the north-south difference in emigration rates because demographic differences between north and south were small by the end of the century. They were considerable, however, at the provincial level. Some of the provinces with the highest rates of natural increase, such as the Venetian provinces of Belluno, Treviso, and Udine, also had some of the highest emigration rates.

High natural increase might also have been absorbed by rural-urban migration to expanding industry in regional cities and towns. Indeed, labor force growth was on the rise just when Italy's industrial production began to accelerate. According to Stefano Fenoaltea's index, industrial production grew at nearly twice the rate after 1881 as in the two preceding decades. Others think the acceleration was more modest (Zamagni 1993: 79), but most agree that there was an acceleration. Much of this growth was concentrated in the industrial triangle marked out by Milan,

Table 6.5 The Italian Agricultural Labor Force in 1911

	Share of labor force in agriculture (%)	Agricultural Labor Force Composition (%)				Farm daily wage (1913; lira)
		Owner-operator	Tenant farmer	Share cropper	Day laborer	
Piedmont	58.4	43	7.5	5	39	2.20
Liguria	39.2	39	8	14	34	1.73
Lombardy	47.3	18	10	18	39	2.28
Veneto	64.2	22	19	12	38	1.76
Emilia	63.8	13	9	31	38	2.44
Tuscany	56.9	12	2	55	25	2.05
Marches	71.6	12	1	58	25	1.64
Umbria	74.3	12	1	47	32	1.62
Lazio	56.3	12	1.5	13	58	1.86
Abruzzi-Molise	54.9	32	6	11	46	1.96
Campania	80.3	17	10	8	57.5	1.85
Apulia	65.2	8	5	1.5	76.5	1.84
Basilicata	78.8	16	9.5	3	61	2.10
Calabria	73.7	9	4	10	68	1.93
Sicily	54.3	7.5	5	8	68.5	2.16
Sardinia	60.9	12	3	4	53	1.90

Source: Zamagni (1993: 32, 68), Arcari (1936: 324).

Turin, and Genoa. But even in booming Piedmont and Liguria the emigration rate continued to increase, although not as rapidly as in most other regions, and although much of the emigration from the triangle had its source in the poorer alpine provinces. This apparently paradoxical event—rising emigration when conditions improve at home—was not unique to northern Italy, as we have seen earlier in this book. Chapter 2 offered explanations for this aspect of the European mass migrations, and chapter 3 gave those explanations empirical content.[21]

Italian urbanization may have promoted labor mobility and emigration, but it likely had stronger effects in the north. Whereas the fastest urban growth took place in the northwest, which was associated with industrialization, medium-sized communities grew in the south as well. But urban growth was not associated with industrialization in the south (De Rosa 1988). Southern agricultural workers typically lived in towns and large villages, often traveling miles to work.

A number of observers have postulated important links between emigration and patterns of farm tenure and landholding. Low wages and lack of opportunity to acquire land generated emigration in some areas, while in others better opportunities to ascend the agricultural ladder generated temporary emigration as a strategy to acquire capital to become an owner-operator. Italian agriculture was dominated by peasant farming, and tenure systems varied greatly across regions and localities. These variations are discernible in the agricultural labor force census classifications reported in table 6.5. In the north, many small farms were owner-occupied or rented directly from landowners. Wage labor could often be combined with subsistence farming on smallholdings in these areas. In Tuscany and other central regions, the sharecropping system (*mezzadria*) was common. Here peasant farmers subsisted on yearly but easily renewable contracts (overseen by the landlord's bailiffs (*fattori*), especially in Tuscany). All of these were mixed farms, and half the realized value of farm produce went to the landlord. Large estates were more common in the south and in Sicily: these were worked by large tenant farmers (*gabelloti*), who often subrented to smaller farmers, or by the land-lord relying on wage labor.

Peasant smallholdings were usually insufficient to support more than one family. Unless the second or third sons could acquire a tenancy or marry into a small-holding, there was little alternative but irregular wage labor or emigration. This plight gave additional impetus to emigration in areas where there was a market in small plots of land.[22] Temporary emigration became the means to acquire land or of extending an existing family smallholding. Cinel (1982) has argued that emi-gration to the United States was motivated principally by the desire to accumulate capital for the purchase of land, explaining why emigration was particularly heavy from areas of peasant agriculture and active land markets. Areas dominated by large estates and wage labor offered less opportunity to acquire land and resulted con-sequently in less emigration. Rural workers chose instead to "voice" rather than exit, exhibiting a greater degree of working class solidarity and engaging in various forms of reform agitation (MacDonald 1963; Surace 1966: chs. 9, 10; Cinel 1982: 59–70).

Most observers believe that the critical factor driving emigration was poverty from low wages and underemployment. Yet regional income levels and emigration are not well-correlated (Coletti 1911; MacDonald 1963; Cinel 1982: 45).[23] It seems unlikely that wage rates alone can provide much of the explanation. Despite huge differences in the levels of economic development between north and south, the spatial variation in daily agricultural wages were remarkably small, at least in 1913 (table 6.5).[24] It follows that levels of unemployment and underemployment must have been far more important determinants of annual earnings for farm laborers. Underemployment and seasonal unemployment were certainly important in Italian agriculture[25] and especially marked in the wheat-growing areas of the south where agriculture was not diversified and where few opportunities for off-season craft industry were available. However, making these qualitative assertions is one thing; getting good measures of farm labor use at the provincial level is quite another.

A Model of Provincial Emigration

The only way to test the hypotheses reviewed above is to apply cross-sectional analysis to Italian regional emigration rates. Previous scholars have typically framed their arguments in terms of bivariate correlations (often qualitative), but to discriminate among their hypotheses requires multivariate analysis. The Italian data seem adequate for the task. Italian emigration is analyzed at census dates because the census is the principal source for documenting explanatory variables. The province offers the lowest level of aggregation for which emigration data are available; thus, we analyze the determinants of emigration rates in 69 provinces across the two census years 1901 and 1911, giving us a panel data set with 69 × 2 = 138 observations in all. Alas, there was no census in 1891, so we could not obtain the full set of variables using only the 1881 census. We use the census variables to explain the variations in (gross) emigration in 1902 and 1912 rather than 1901 and 1911 to avoid the change in the coverage of the official statistics in 1901. The appendix presents the sources and methods used to construct the data.

Demographic pressure is measured by the rate of natural increase 15 to 30 years earlier. Hence natural increase between 1871 and 1886 is used for 1901 while natural increase between 1881 and 1896 is used for 1911.[26] Other structural characteristics were captured by the share of the labor force in agriculture and the proportion of the population living in towns and cities of 15,000 or more.[27] We also interact these variables with regional dummies to allow for north-south differences asserted in the literature. Thus, the share of the labor force in agriculture is interacted with a dummy for the south to reflect the poverty, backwardness, and underemployment of southern agriculture. The urban share is interacted with a dummy for the north to reflect the essentially industrial nature of urbanization there. Recent views of regional homogeneity (Zamagni 1978, 1993) suggest that the econometric analysis that follows now limit the north to the industrial triangle including Liguria, Lombardy, and Piedmont; the south remains as before, with the center now expanding to include Emilia and Venetia.

To test for the effects of access to land and the agricultural ladder, we include some tenure variables. The census divides agricultural workers into a number of different occupations, mainly owner-occupiers, renters, sharecroppers, and agricultural laborers. As shares of the total agricultural labor force, these four groups are assumed to reflect the structure of relationships to the land. The variables for renters and agricultural laborers were excluded from the final regressions because these never proved to be statistically significant. It was not necessary to interact these variables with region.[28]

Once again, the log of the wage ratio between destination countries and the emigrating province is included, but with some modification. In sharp contrast with the Irish, the Italians headed in different directions depending on the province of emigration. Thus, we weight the destination wage rates to reflect the destination composition in each province. We have no direct measure of per capita income, poverty, or wealth at the provincial level, but an index of relative "prosperity" of the 16 Compartimenti was developed for 1900–1902 and 1910–1912 by Mortara (1913). Although this crude index was built from a variety of economic indicators, a number of writers have regarded it as fairly reflecting differences in per capita income (e.g., MacDonald, 1963). Therefore, we assigned the Mortara index for a given Compartimento to all provinces within.[29]

The influence of education is measured by literacy rates for those aged six and above in the province.[30] To account for persistence effects and emigration "traditions," the provincial emigration rate in 1882 was also included. If emigration rates were driven chiefly by persistence or by traditions, this variable should dominate the equation.

Finally, the proximity of the province to the main immigrant-receiving labor markets of Europe should be noted. Even a cursory glance at the map of emigrant destinations confirms that proximity mattered, especially in the northern provinces. This is important since we want to examine continental and intercontinental emigration separately. Proximity was calculated as the straight-line distance between the provincial capital and either Lyons (France) or Munich (Germany), whichever was closest.[31] This distance measure is entered in a quadratic form to reflect the decaying effects of proximity to continental Europe for more distant provinces. Proximity mattered hardly at all to the overseas move because the distance to Buenos Aires or New York from the Italian north and south were essentially the same.

Econometric Results for 1902 and 1912

A version of the model with the log of the emigration rate as the dependent variable fitted the data best, so this version is reported in table 6.6.[32] The equations give a high level of explanatory power judged by the R^2, but the signs, size, and significance of the coefficients differ between the separate continental and intercontinental emigration regressions, in some cases sharply. We start with total emigration.

The lagged rate of natural increase gives the significant positive sign predicted, and the implied impact is substantial. Across provinces, an increase of one per thousand per annum in the rate of natural increase 15–30 years earlier would have raised the emigration rate by 1.09 per thousand. The result strongly supports those historians who have emphasized demographic effects on Italian emigration. It offers further support to our prediction for Italy in chapter 3, and the effect is even more significant than the one we identified there.[33]

The share of the labor force in agriculture reduced emigration everywhere except in the south. The strongly significant coefficient on the interaction with the south dummy supports the argument that limited opportunities in southern agriculture led to emigration. This effect by itself increased the emigration rate by 0.26 per thousand for every 1 percent increase in the agricultural share. The urban share gives negative coefficients that suggest that higher mobility among the urban population was offset by other urban forces—such as the growth in industrial or service sector employment. Consistent with this hypothesis, the effect was greater in the north. A rise across provinces in the urban share by 1 percent lowered the emigration rate by 0.1 per thousand in Italy as a whole but by 0.7 per thousand in the north.[34]

The agricultural tenure variables also give strongly significant coefficients for both the percentage of owner-occupiers and of sharecroppers relative to all other agricultural occupations. The magnitudes of the coefficients are quite large too. An increase of 1 percentage point in the owner occupier share raised the emigration rate by 0.45 per thousand and in the sharecropper share by

Table 6.6 Regression Results for Italian Provincial Emigration Rates, 1902 and 1912 (dependent variable: log emigration rate)

	Total emigration	European emigration	Intercontinental emigration
Constant	4.55	8.08	0.03
	(3.54)	(4.55)	(0.01)
Lagged natural increase	0.41	0.62	0.64
	(1.88)	(2.15)	(2.24)
Share of labor force in agriculture	−0.80	−1.49	−0.03
	(1.44)	(1.95)	(0.05)
Share in agriculture times south dummy	1.21	−0.87	1.43
	(3.38)	(1.85)	(3.07)
Share of population urban	−0.46	0.08	−0.04
	(1.35)	(0.18)	(0.10)
Share urban times north dummy	−1.08	−1.82	−0.69
	(2.39)	(2.87)	(1.15)
Share of owner-occupiers in agriculture	1.78	0.80	2.42
	(3.83)	(1.28)	(3.90)
Share of sharecroppers in agriculture	1.03	1.02	0.14
	(3.31)	(2.41)	(0.33)
Log wage ratio (foreign to home)	0.35	−0.47	0.27
	(1.37)	(0.98)	(0.81)
Mortara index of development	−0.87	−1.24	−0.21
	(4.35)	(4.62)	(0.78)
Proportion literate (age >5)	−0.08	−0.96	−0.84
	(0.08)	(0.71)	(0.63)
Log emigration rate in 1882	0.07	0.08	0.10
	(3.00)	(2.64)	(4.89)
Distance from European centers	−1.29	−3.01	0.87
	(2.13)	(3.73)	(1.11)
Squared distance from European centers	0.19	0.39	−0.12
	(1.92)	(3.02)	(0.97)
Dummy for 1912	0.56	0.19	0.77
	(3.50)	(0.84)	(3.63)
R^2	0.61	0.71	0.72
RSS	36.38	65.83	64.95
RESET	0.00	1.95	7.07
HETERO	3.32	2.83	4.21

Note: Figures in parentheses are t statistics.

0.22 per thousand. These results suggest that the prospect of ascending the agricultural ladder actually increased emigration rather than lowered it, as happened in Ireland.

The wage ratio gives the expected positive sign and the coefficient implies that a 10 percent rise in the foreign-to-home wage ratio raised the emigration rate by 0.57 per thousand—a smaller effect than that implied by the cross-country results in chapter 3, but consistent with our argument that Latin emigration was not any more wage-elastic than that in the rest of Europe. The coefficient on the Mortara development index is significant and negative, implying that the more developed the province, the lower the emigration rate. An index of development 10 percent below the Italian average raised the provincial emigration rate by 1.0 per thousand, a powerful effect. To the extent that the Mortara index can be viewed as an effective indicator of living standards, the result is consistent with our findings for Ireland, where living standards were also negatively correlated with emigration, *after* one has controlled for emigration-inducing forces correlated with early development.

What about persistence and information diffusion stressed by Gould and others? It appears that emigration traditions were significant, but their effect was small. A difference of 1 per thousand in the emigration rate in 1882 resulted only in a difference of 0.29 per thousand in 1902 and 1912. Thus, even though tradition, habit, and persistence mattered, they did little to obscure the impact of other more fundamental and contemporaneous economic and demographic forces within these provinces, forces that themselves persisted with such tenacity. Literacy seems to have had no discernible effect on emigration rates either. This finding casts doubt on the view that literacy was the key to unlocking a flood of emigration, either as a means of improving knowledge about foreign labor markets or as a valuable asset in those labor markets. Both of these findings must be viewed as revisionist, and they illustrate how essential it is to embed these contentious propositions from the Italian literature into an explicit multivariate model. When we do so, their influence disappears!

Finally, the distance variables confirm that proximity to labor markets in continental Europe had a potent impact on the overall emigration rate. As the squared term indicates, the gradient becomes flatter further south. The effect of distance was very strong; due to proximity alone, the area around Naples would have had an emigration rate about 8 per thousand lower than the area around Milan. Hence, the poverty and underdevelopment that drove up emigration in the south was counterbalanced by its remoteness from European labor markets. Indeed, that remoteness helps explain Neapolitan poverty.

Interesting contrasts emerge when continental and intercontinental emigration rates are considered separately. The rate of natural increase seems to have had a quantitatively important effect on both streams. But whereas the share of the labor force in agriculture had a negative effect on emigration to Europe, especially from the south, the effect was strongly positive for intercontinental emigration from the south. Urbanization in the north apparently had a much smaller damping effect on intercontinental emigration than on European emigration. The percentage of owner-occupiers and sharecroppers had positive influences on emigration to both destinations, although owner-occupation was more important for intercontinental emigration. If Italians emigrated to earn the income to buy land later in Italy, emigration both to Europe and overseas would have resulted.

The other economic variables also show interesting contrasts. The wage ratio appears to have been less important probably because of our inability to control for days worked per year. The Mortara development index had much weaker effects on intercontinental than on continental emigration. The persistence effects were about

Table 6.7 The Source of South-North Differences in Emigration

Difference in predicted emigration rate due to	Total	European	Intercontinental
Lagged natural increase	1.02	0.78	0.69
Share of labor force in agriculture	15.01	−6.34	8.29
Share of population urban	4.03	3.68	−0.64
Share of owner-occupiers in agriculture	−4.00	−1.20	−2.42
Share of sharecroppers in agriculture	−1.93	−0.94	−0.17
Log wage ratio	2.76	0.41	0.02
Mortara index of development	6.69	3.95	2.51
Proportion literate	−1.55	2.24	1.34
Emigration rate in 1882	−1.82	−1.45	−1.52
Distance from European centers	−11.02	−19.14	12.84
Explained difference	9.19	−18.01	20.94
Actual difference	5.75	−14.62	20.36

the same for both types of emigration, equally weak, and neither was influenced by the literacy rate. Finally, whereas the north-south gradient had strong effects on continental emigration, it had only marginal effects, and in the opposite direction, for intercontinental emigration.

The Sources of South-North Differences in Emigration

How do these estimates explain the differences in emigration between the Italian north and south? Table 6.7 provides a decomposition of the sources of the south-north differential by influence (excluding the center).[35] By the first decade of the century, south-north differences in lagged rates of natural increase had only marginal effects favoring southern emigration. However, the share of the labor force in agriculture and the proportion of the urban population had a powerful combined effect on raising southern emigration rates relative to the north. The wage ratio and the Mortara development index drove up emigration in the south relative to the north even more. The former was due largely to the fact that New World real wages were higher than European real wages, thus producing a larger wage gap for the south, whose emigrants favored the New World. The latter reflects the fact that the north was more than twice as "developed" as the south.

These powerful positive influences were partially offset by the large negative impact on the south-north emigration differential that arose from proximity to European labor markets. In addition, owner-occupiers and sharecroppers were more common in the north, offsetting a bit more of the differential. We discuss the remaining negative offsets later, but why the south had higher emigration rates than the north is now clear (9.19 percent higher predicted, and 5.75 percent higher actual). It had nothing to do with literacy, chain migration, and agricultural tenure. It had very little to do with rates of natural increase. The high rate was mainly due to poverty: a dominant agriculture, low urbanization, illiteracy, low wages and underdevelopment. The differential would have been two or three times as high had it not been for the longer distance to European labor markets from the south.

For European emigration alone, the agricultural share and urbanization effects were roughly offsetting, and, although the development index still contributed strongly to southern emigration, these effects were swamped by the role of distance from European markets so that the overall south-north differential was negative. But not only distance was at work; while the more agricultural south meant more emigrants, it also meant fewer European emigrants. For intercontinental emigration alone, high agricultural shares, underdevelopment, and illiteracy generated higher emigration rates from the south. But distance from European labor markets mattered most in augmenting the south-north intercontinental differential: distant from those labor markets, southerners were encouraged to seek their fortunes overseas in relatively large numbers.

New World Destinations

The Issues

One of the more intriguing aspects of Italian emigration is the destinations that emigrants to the New World selected. Unlike most other Europeans, Italians emigrated in almost equal numbers to North and South America. The three main destinations were Argentina, Brazil, and the United States, but the timing of the flows to these three countries differed. Argentina dominated the emigrant flow in the late 1870s and early 1880s, followed by a surge to Brazil in the late 1880s and early 1890s. Although Argentina reestablished its dominance over Brazil after the turn of the century, these were years when emigration to the United States surged to exceed the combined total of *both* countries.

The story must be told in part, of course, by reference to shifting fortunes in the three economies: the strong but intermittent growth of the Argentine economy, the boom and bust of Brazilian Sao Paulo coffee growing, followed by the leap to world industrial leadership by the United States after 1890. These shifting fortunes influenced the composition of emigration by destination within and between regions. Until late in the period, northerners favored Argentina, although there was an extraordinary surge in emigration to Brazil (largely from Veneto) in the early 1890s (table 6.8). Those from the center emigrated to both Americas but particularly to Brazil. By contrast, emigrants from the south headed primarily to the United States. As time wore on, more emigrants from the north and center were drawn to the United States, particularly after the turn of the century, but the regional differences in destination persisted.

So why did northern Italians typically go to South America while the southern Italians typically went to North America? On the surface, this trend seems paradoxical. One would think that the more agricultural economies of South America with their ample opportunities for agricultural labor and their less sophisticated social structure would have suited best the agrarian southern Italian. One would

Table 6.8 Destination Shares in Regional Emigration
(of three-country total: %)

	Argentina	Brazil	United States
North			
1881	68.3	20.2	11.5
1891	11.4	85.4	3.2
1901	57.8	17.0	25.2
1911	24.7	14.9	60.4
Center			
1881	39.5	45.7	14.8
1891	29.9	52.2	17.9
1901	20.9	54.9	24.2
1911	15.9	9.8	74.3
South			
1881	21.6	17.7	60.7
1891	16.0	18.2	65.8
1901	17.9	29.3	52.8
1911	9.8	7.4	82.7

Source: *Annuario Statistico Emigrazione Italiana dal 1876 al 1926*, table 3.

think that the more industrial, urban, and literate northern Italians would have been more suited to the booming urban-industrial labor market in the United States. Perhaps it was simply a matter of timing: based on cultural and language preferences, the earlier emigrants from the north chose Argentina; a little later, and for similar reasons, the northern and central Italians started going to Brazil with the added inducement of subsidized passage from the Sao Paulo government. Whether a prejudiced or an accurate assessment of relative skills, these subsidies were not offered to southern Italians, so they headed for cities in the United States. Once in motion, these patterns persisted through habit, tradition, and the friends and relatives effect.

Or so the argument goes. But surely these destinations were viable alternatives for all emigrants by the turn of the century. Why didn't the regional destination pattern break down more quickly? Are we observing segmented markets? The answers will not emerge easily because the questions need to be embedded in a fuller explanation that admits other influences at the same time.

One explanation for this behavior is that land-hungry northerners took advantage of the concessionary land sales that were a feature of settlement in both Argentina and Brazil. Two thirds of Italian emigrants to Argentina but only one third of emigrants to the United States were agricultural workers and farmers. Emigrants from Piedmont, Lombardy, and Veneto dominated immigrant small-holders in Argentina and Brazil. According to one observer, Brazilian immigrants were "never hired farm hands but all [were] proprietors and most [were] secure in their possessions. The crops they [grew resembled] those of Italy" (Foerster 1919:

310). The Argentinian immigrant could either acquire a land concession or move up the agricultural ladder from day laborer (*peon*) to sharecropper, then to tenant farmer, and eventually to small proprietor (Foerster 1919: 243). Given these routes to landownership, there seems no reason why southern Italians should not have joined in. Even if they lacked the entrepreneurial skills, they could have joined the large numbers who migrated to the Brazilian coffee plantations, although not on passages subsidized by the state of Sao Paulo. Yet even among these (often seasonal and short-term) immigrants, there were relatively few southerners. Insofar as they did go to Argentina or Brazil, southern Italians were more often found in unskilled urban occupations (bootblacks, barbers, street sellers, or building laborers).

A second explanation rests on human capital. Northern Italians clearly had higher levels of literacy, education, industrial skills, and experience as proprietors. But perhaps the value of these attributes in the United States was limited. The evidence is certainly consistent with this view. Italians flooded into United States manufacturing and service occupations often at the lowest level. At the turn of the century, they were significantly overrepresented in domestic and personal service, among barbers and bootblacks, and among laborers in manufacturing and on the railways. Very few entered the skilled or white-collar ranks. If Italians found it hard to use their skills in cities like New York, they stood a better chance in Buenos Aires, where Italian language, customs, and skills were more widely accepted. The proportion of skilled workers among Italians in Buenos Aires was about twice that in New York (Baily 1983: 285). Thus, high-skilled northern Italians may have had more to gain by migrating to Argentina whereas low-skilled southern Italians had more to gain by going to the United States where work at the bottom of the job hierarchy commanded such a high wage.

A third (and related) explanation focuses on permanence. Temporary emigrants would be less interested in making long-run investments in country-specific skills than would the emigrant who intended to stay. Emigrants to Buenos Aires appear to have assimilated more quickly and completely than emigrants to the United States: they were occupationally more upwardly mobile, more often joined labor organizations and mutual aid societies, and more frequently became proprietors or employers (Baily 1983: 286–87). They had a much lower rate of home ownership in the United States, even compared with other immigrants (12 percent against 24 percent in 1903), and a much higher savings rate (7 percent against 4 percent) despite having lower incomes. As one observer puts it, "the perceptions they held of the two labor markets determined their decisions to migrate, their willingness to remain in the country and their ideas about developing a local community. Even patterns of savings and investment were largely determined by their perceptions of the possibilities within the two labor markets" (Klein 1983: 319).

A Model of Overseas Destination Choice

Distance mattered in influencing the choice between emigrating to Europe or overseas. But where overseas? Despite the interest in emigrant destination, no quanti-

Table 6.9 Regression Results for the Composition of Italian Intercontinental Emigration 1902, 1912 (dependent variable log[$S_i/1 - S_i$])

	Argentina	Brazil	United States
Constant	−0.89	−2.45	−1.12
	(0.80)	(1.90)	(0.60)
Share of labor force in agriculture	−0.23	2.25	−2.32
	(0.21)	(1.99)	(2.03)
Share L.F. in agriculture times South dummy	−1.58	−0.62	2.50
	(2.46)	(0.84)	(3.60)
Share of population urban	0.10	0.11	0.53
	(0.15)	(0.15)	(0.72)
Share of owner-occupiers in agriculture	0.21	−3.33	3.76
	(0.21)	(3.28)	(3.64)
Share of sharecroppers in agriculture	−1.16	−0.45	2.15
	(1.77)	(0.65)	(3.12)
Relative wage	1.88	1.56	0.37
	(2.61)	(1.61)	(0.15)
Mortara index of developement	0.61	0.25	−0.69
	(1.56)	(0.58)	(1.54)
Proportion literate	−2.53	1.58	1.02
	(1.91)	(1.09)	(0.69)
Share of emigrants to country i in 1884	2.27	1.58	1.50
	(6.59)	(3.42)	(3.35)
Dummy for 1912	0.65	−1.10	0.75
	(2.08)	(3.62)	(2.58)
R^2	0.42	0.31	0.41
RSS	167.03	204.67	203.40
RESET	0.95	0.22	0.05
HETERO	0.17	0.48	1.81

Note: Figures in parentheses are t statistics.

tative efforts have identified factors that determined choice of overseas destination across Italian regions. We intend to do so by focusing on Argentina, Brazil, and the United States. The dependent variable is the logistic transformation of migration to each country as a share of the three-country total: log[$S_i/(1 - S_i)$], where S_i is the share for country i. As before, the data cover the 69 provinces for the two years 1902 and 1912.

We should confess at the outset that explaining Italian emigrant overseas destination with conventional economics is difficult at best. In fact, table 6.9 indicates that only between 40 and 45 percent of the variation in destination is explained for Argentina and the United States and even less, about a third, for Brazil. Nonetheless, some variables mattered in clear and unambiguous ways.

The share of the labor force in agriculture yields significant coefficients for Brazil and the United States: those in agricultural regions preferred Brazil to the United States. But note that the impact is revised when this variable is interacted with the south dummy: agricultural regions in the south were *less* likely to send emigrants to South America (especially Argentina) and *more* likely to send them to the United States. This supports the claim that underemployed southern laborers preferred the United States. If they were seasonal migrants, they had less to lose and more to gain by spending the summer in the high-wage United States. Farm labor in the north had more to lose, to the extent that employment rates were higher in the summer. Urban regions showed a preference for the United States, but the estimated coefficients are uniformly insignificant everywhere but in the north, where urban regions clearly preferred Argentina.

The landholding and land tenure variables yield interesting results. They did not influence the emigrant's choice of Argentina, but they did influence the choice between the other two countries in opposite ways: negatively for Brazil and positively for the United States. Since the prospects for becoming a sharecropper or owner-occupier were clearly better in South America than in the United States, the result seems paradoxical. But if we interpret the result as reflecting the possibility of ascending the Italian agricultural ladder, it makes more sense. In localities with no prospects for obtaining a sharecropping contract or of acquiring a smallholding, Italian emigrants were more likely to emigrate to the United States with the intention of returning with enough savings to start farming.

The relative wage term is for country *i* relative to a weighted average of the other two; hence it is driven by the weights that vary across provinces. It takes a significantly positive sign for Latin America (although only at the 10 percent significance level for Brazil), but it is statistically insignificant and small for the United States. The coefficients imply that a 10 percent increase in the wage ratio would increase the share of emigrants going to Argentina by 3.4 percent and to Brazil by 3.1 percent. The results also suggest that Argentina and Brazil were closer substitutes than either was for the United States, an intuitively plausible finding.

The Mortara index confirms that the more developed the region, the more likely the emigrant would have gone to Latin America, but the estimated coefficients are never statistically significant. There is no evidence to support the view that regions with higher literacy went to Latin America while those with lower literacy went to the United States. If anything, the opposite was true. This result illustrates again the advantage of pursuing multivariate analysis so that we can control for all other factors while isolating the independent influence of one under debate.

Finally, there is strong evidence of persistence in the choice of destination as represented by the share of emigrants going to the relevant destination in 1884. The strongly significant coefficients further support the view that the choice of destination contributed to at least partially segmented Italian labor markets. The magnitudes are also large: for Argentina a 10 percent difference across provinces in 1884 persisted as a 3.7 percent difference in 1902 and 1912. For the United States this number was 3.5 and for Brazil 2.3. Persistence was therefore very important in determining the *composition* of intercontinental emigration, although we have already seen that it had little effect on *total* emigration. No doubt destination choices were reinforced by friends and relatives effects and by information from returning emigrants. But they were also modified over time.

Conclusions

What have we learned about Italian emigration?

The big surge in gross emigration after the 1890s was not matched by a big surge in net emigration, and that big surge was in large part the spurious result of a change in passport regulations. While a surge in Italian emigration *did* take place, the uniquely "big" surge was simply the product of defective official statistics. When adjustments are made (perhaps a 17 percent deflation), the Italian emigration surge looks pretty much like those that northern Europe went through in earlier decades.

The (adjusted) trend increase in Italian gross emigration was largely the result of stronger chain migration through the impact of a rising emigrant stock abroad. These chain migration effects were augmented by booming natural increase, a relationship revealed more clearly in the cross-sectional analysis. The gradual fall in the foreign-to-home wage gap tended to mute the rise in Italian emigration, but it was overwhelmed by the chain migration and demographic forces. These results are fully consistent with chapter 3.

Finally, there is no evidence that Italian real wages by themselves had any independent positive effect on emigration: rather, their sole influence was through the wage *gap* between home and abroad. Although the wages-at-home thesis is popular in the qualitative literature on Italy, multivariate analysis rejects it. This example is perhaps the best illustration of the strength of multivariate analysis and the weakness of simple bivariate correlations.

Cross-sectional analysis indicates that a common model *can* be used to explain the oft-cited wide variance in provincial emigration rates. Larger wage gaps and lower levels of economic development drove emigration up. Forms of agricultural land tenure also influenced emigration. But by contrast with emigration in northwest Europe, opportunities for Italians to ascend the agricultural ladder stimulated emigration (and return migration) rather than retarded it. Furthermore, while such forces mattered, there is little evidence that persistence or literacy dominated provincial emigration rates with anything like the force often assigned them in the qualitative literature.

All of these forces had a common and consistent influence across regions. But some of these forces *did* differ regionally: urban development in the north reduced emigration while agricultural underdevelopment in the south raised it. These factors raised southern emigration relative to northern: by the turn of the century, these forces had almost completely offset the north's advantage of closer proximity to immigrant-absorbing European labor markets.

Finally, although segmentation did not dominate total provincial emigration rates, it did matter for intercontinental destination choice. This supports the links between specific regions of origin and destination historians so often emphasize. But it would be a mistake to regard these links as the sole or even the most important determinant of total provincial emigration. Destination choices were influenced by a number of local characteristics. In particular, whereas agriculturalists as a whole were less likely to go to the United States than to Argentina or Brazil, those with opportunities to ascend the agricultural ladder at home were more likely to emigrate to the United States as target earners. By contrast, little evidence supports the view that those emigrants with higher levels of human capital were more likely to prefer south America.

Appendix. Sources of Province Level Data

Total, European, and intercontinental emigration data for 1882, 1902, and 1912 are from Commissariato Generale dell'Emigrazione, *Annuario Statistico Emigrazione Italiana dal 1876 al 1926* (Roma, 1926: 45–65). Emigration data for Argentina, Brazil, and the United States for 1902 and 1912 are from Ministerio Agricoltura, Industria e Commercia (MAIC), *Statistica della Emigrazione Per l'Estero* (Roma, 1904 and 1915); for 1884, they are from MAIC, *Statistica della Emigrazione Italiana* (Roma, 1886).

Census data are from Direzione Generale della Statistica, *Censimento della Popolazione del Regno D'Italia al 10 Febbraio 1901* (Roma, 1904) and *Censimento della Popolazione del Regno D'Italia al 10 Guigno, 1911* (Roma, 1914). Population: 1901, Vol. 5. table 3; 1911, Vol. 1, table 1. Labor force, share in agriculture, and proportion of owner-occupiers, tenant farmers, sharecroppers and laborers: 1901, Vol. 3; 1911, Vol. 4, table 6. Share of population in towns of over 15,000: 1901, Vol. 5, table 8; 1911, Vol. 7, table 15. Proportion of population aged 6 and above literate: 1901, Vol. 5, table 28; 1911, Vol. 2, table 4.

Natural increase: for 1871–1886, MAIC, *Popolazione: Movimento dello Stato Civile, Anno 1881* (Roma, 1882), Table 54, and *Annuario Statistico, 1887–88* (Roma, 1888); for 1881–1896, MAIC, *Popolazione: Movimento Dello Stato Civile, Anno 1896* (Roma, 1897), table 1. Daily wage rates in agriculture (for 1905 and 1913) are from P. M. Arcari, "Le Variazione dei Salari Agricoli in Italia della Fondazione del Regno al 1933," *Annali di Statistica*, Series 5, Vol. 36 (1936), table 27. Index of development (16 Compartimenti, 1900–1902 and 1910–1912) is from G. Mortara, "Numeri Indici dello Stato e del Progresso Economico delle Regioni Italiane," *Giornale degli Economisti e Rivista di Statistica*, 47 (1913): 28.

Assimilating the Immigrant
An American Melting Pot?

This chapter explores immigrant assimilation in the New World and the next explores their labor market absorption. The focus is exclusively on the United States, where about three fifths of European emigrants went and where a far wider range of origin countries was represented than was true of any other New World country. Indeed, this fact alone accounts for most of the unusual intensity of the American political debate over the migrations after the 1890s, a debate that was much more subdued in more immigrant-homogeneous Australia, Argentina, Canada, or Cuba. As a by-product of this debate about immigrant assimilation and absorption, a rich statistical database was generated by which the issues can be evaluated.

The debate stimulated investigations such as the massive report of the Immigration Commission initiated in 1907 and completed in 1911. The themes raised by the Commission were controversial then and provoke congressional debate even today. One set of questions dealt with immigrant assimilation and are more micro-related: how quickly were immigrants assimilated into American life and culture? Did immigrants arrive disadvantaged and did they face discrimination in labor markets? How long did it take them or their offspring, the second-generation immigrants, to catch up with natives? Was economic performance related to their European cultural, religious, ethnic, and economic background? Did the more recent immigrants from southern and eastern Europe assimilate less rapidly and less completely than their predecessors from the north and west?

Another set of questions, more macro-related and less fully explored, dealt with immigrant absorption: did immigrants fill the jobs that were being created most rapidly in the expanding American economy? Did they displace some sections of the native American workforce? Did they raise unemployment in the industries and occupations they entered? Alternatively, did they provide the kind of flexible labor supply sometimes claimed for the "guestworkers" in post–World War II Germany? Did the rhythm of migration lead to smaller variations in unemployment than would have been true in their absence? Above all, to what extent did the burgeoning immigrant labor supply lower wage and living standard improvement for unskilled workers in America? This last question was perhaps *the* major question addressed by the Immigration Commission, and the answers have proved the most elusive.

In this chapter and the next we reexamine the evidence on the speed and extent of immigrant assimilation and analyze the process through which immigrants were absorbed in the American labor market. We also provide preliminary estimates of their macro impact on wage rates. This macro impact theme is taken up again for both source and destination countries in chapters 9 and 10.

Debating Immigrant Assimilation, Past and Present

Attitudes toward immigration and immigrants ebbed and flowed in late-nineteenth-century America. Anti-immigration movements such as the Know-Nothing movement of the 1850s, came and went. Renewed anti-immigrant sentiment emerged in the 1880s, and heightened public concern was reflected by a series of official enquiries, notably by the Industrial Commission (1901), into the problems of immigrant assimilation in labor markets as well as their wider social and political impact.[1] After a series of attempts in the House of Representatives to limit immigration through the imposition of a literacy test in 1905 and a renewed attempt in 1906, Congress, supported by President Theodore Roosevelt, set up a fact-finding commission that it hoped would resolve the issue once and for all. After devoting four years and considerable resources investigating almost every aspect of the immigration problem, the Immigration Commission published its mighty 41-volume report in 1911.

The "chief basis of the Commission's work was the changed character of the immigration movement to the United States during the past twenty-five years" (Vol. 1: 13). Influenced by the eugenics movement and techniques of phrenology, the Commission drew a sharp racial distinction between the old immigrants (those from Belgium, Great Britain, Ireland, France, Germany, the Netherlands, Scandinavia, and Switzerland) and the new immigrants (those from Austria-Hungary, Bulgaria, Greece, Italy, Montenegro, Poland, Portugal, Romania, Russia, Serbia, Spain, and Turkey).[2] The Commission concluded that the new immigration was "largely a movement of unskilled laboring men who have come, in large part temporarily, from the less progressive and advanced countries of Europe" and that, on the whole, they were "far less intelligent" and were "actuated by different ideals" than the old immigrants. In addition, they "have almost entirely avoided agricultural pursuits, and in cities and industrial communities have congregated together in sections apart from native Americans and the older immigrants to such an extent that assimilation has been slow as compared to that of earlier non-English-speaking races" (Vol. 1: 14).

The Commission's report was long on evidence but short on analysis and it is doubtful that it was read in full by many contemporaries. But the main ideas were amplified and presented more forcefully by one of the leading members of the commission, Jeremiah Jenks, together with J. B. Lauck. Their book, *The Immigration Problem*, reached a wide audience and went through six editions between 1911 and 1926. The Commission (and Jenks and Lauck) argued that on most socioeconomic criteria the new immigrants were inferior to the old. Table 7.1 summarizes some of the evidence collected in the Commission's survey of households, divided up by the "race" of the household head. On the basis of statistics such as these, they argued that the new immigrants earned lower wages, had larger families, lived in more crowded conditions, were concentrated in ghettos, had lower rates of literacy, and had less ability to speak English than either native-born Americans or old immigrants. These findings were well substantiated by the evidence. However, their most politically sensitive assertions were not well documented: that the new immigrants assimilated only slowly and that they undermined the living standards of unskilled old immigrants and native-born.

The Commission's report received criticism right from the start, and its politically sensitive assertions are now widely discredited (Hourwich 1922; Handlin 1957; Jones 1992: 152–56). Critics have argued that (1) there was no firm basis other than prejudice for the racial distinction between new and old immigrants;[3] (2) the Commission failed to draw on the abundance of statistical evidence in State Labor Bureau reports and elsewhere, preferring to make its own investigations; (3) in comparing new immigrants with old, the Commission at worst misread or distorted the evidence, or at best failed to allow for the fact that more recent immigrants had had less time to assimilate than the old; and (4) influential members of the commission (such as Jeremiah Jenks) had made up their minds beforehand and in the rush to produce the final report simply ignored the volumes of statistical evidence. Although these four criticisms have much substance, the most important assertions of the commission have not been unambiguously overturned by subsequent analysis: was the assimilation of new, mostly unskilled immigrant arrivals "slow"? Did these new immigrants lower wage improvement among unskilled resident Americans?

The historian Oscar Handlin was one of the foremost critics of the Commission. Handlin argued that the pace and degree of assimilation of the new immigrants was no different than, say, that of the Irish in the decades after the famine. Of the Irish in Boston, Handlin wrote:

> Thousands of poverty-stricken peasants, rudely transposed to an urban commercial center, could not readily become merchants or clerks; they had neither the training nor the capital to set up as shopkeepers or artisans. The absence of other opportunities forced the vast majority into the ranks of an unemployed resourceless proletariat, whose cheap labor ultimately created a new industrialism in Boston. But for a long time they were fated to remain a massive lump in the community, undigested, undigestible (1959: 55).

Table 7.1 Summary Statistics from the Immigration Commission's Household Survey

Race/ nationality	Annual earnings of men aged 18 and over ($)	Annual family income ($)	Percentage owning own home	Household size (persons)	Persons per room	Percentage aged 10 and over literate	Percentage aged over 5 who speak English	Percentage aged 21 and over in United States for over 5 years who are naturalized or have filed papers
Armenian	454	730	8.6	4.98	1.03	89.6	74.8	79.1
Bohemian/Moravian	549	773	67.3	5.14	1.18	96.3	69.8	85.3
Bulgarian	255	—	—	6.19	2.53	73.1	7.4	—
Canadian (French)	538	903	7.5	5.82	1.17	84.2	67.9	32.8
Croatian	410	702	23.5	7.65	1.88	58.1	44.0	38.5
Dutch	555	772	70.3	5.68	0.97	95.6	90.6	99.8
English	673	956	15.6	4.52	0.87	96.2	—	80.7
Finnish	683	781	56.3	4.92	1.37	95.7	63.8	80.2
French	479	757	26.1	3.90	0.88	88.1	66.3	59.1
German	579	878	39.7	5.19	1.02	96.9	83.1	79.5
Greek	300	632	1.5	6.13	1.48	72.0	21.7	10.1
Hebrew	513	685	6.3	5.27	1.36	85.2	75.7	53.5
Irish	714	999	30.2	5.45	1.02	92.5	—	86.2
North Italian	636	657	27.8	5.50	1.42	83.4	57.1	54.9

South Italian	480	569	14.9	5.65	1.47	54.5	46.6	28.0
Lithuanian	454	636	18.0	5.89	1.44	54.6	50.9	33.7
Magyar	395	611	13.7	6.44	1.72	88.2	41.5	34.3
Polish	428	595	18.1	6.06	1.58	70.6	45.8	35.5
Portuguese	335	790	9.5	6.68	1.38	58.6	48.4	6.2
Romanian	402	805	2.6	12.47	2.57	74.3	30.1	4.2
Russian	400	494	1.2	5.93	1.77	59.2	33.9	16.6
Ruthenian	418	569	6.7	6.66	1.84	57.5	42.9	23.0
Scottish	703	1,142	33.6	5.40	1.08	99.2	—	78.1
Serbian	212	462	4.4	9.62	1.97	52.2	13.7	5.7
Slovak	442	582	17.6	5.87	1.62	78.3	52.2	31.8
Slovenian	484	684	25.3	5.82	1.43	91.5	61.3	48.8
Swedish	722	974	44.5	4.90	0.92	99.5	94.2	96.0
Syrian	370	594	4.7	4.80	1.15	69.2	72.9	35.0
Turkish	281	—	—	8.92	1.42	4.5	1.4	—
Welsh	623	893	51.6	5.26	0.96	95.0	—	94.0
Foreign-born	455	843	21.6	5.81	1.38	74.8	52.3	45.7
Native-born	600	704	22.1	4.28	0.82	98.0	—	—

Source: Reports of the Immigration Commission (1911), Vol. 1: Col. 1, 407–8; Col. 2, 412; Col. 3, 468; Col. 4, 429; Col. 5, 431; Col. 6, 444; Col. 7, 475–6; Col. 8, 486. Blank entries reflect either insufficient data or not applicable.

In *The Uprooted* (1951) Handlin paints a dismal picture of the assimilation of immigrants, both new and old. Like many other writers, he argued that the background, culture, and mentality of these simple peasants left them helpless in understanding and adapting to American life. Not until the second generation did the process of immigrant assimilation really begin. Handlin's "helpless peasant" image has, in turn, been much criticized.[4] John Bodnar, one of the leading post-Handlin revisionists, has written that

> [b]ecause immigration was structured and selective, notions and myths about immigrants being tradition-bound, provincial peasants or excited and eager men on the make can no longer be sustained. These people did not leave preindustrial worlds but worlds which were already encountering capitalism and experimenting with ways to deal with its realities. Credit cooperatives, mutual aid societies, agricultural improvement societies, and forms of political agitation such as peasant protests and Jewish socialism all demonstrated that these people were struggling for ways to cope with new and present economic realities and not captured by future hopes or even past glories (1985: 56).

A large literature has accumulated that places the assimilation experience of immigrant groups in a new light. It argues that the old notions of assimilation as a simple linear process of "acculturation" or "Americanization" are misleading. Immigrants and their offspring did not Americanize uniformly, but rather formed ethnic groups that adapted and adopted American culture according to their own needs. Nor did assimilation always involve a melting-pot progression from ghetto to suburb, from foreign to English language communication, by formal education and gradual movement up the occupational ladder (Nelli 1983; Zunz 1982). Successful immigrants often stayed in the ghetto and often leaped up the occupational ladder without formal education or English language skills.

Yet for all the revisionist literature, many of the studies of the social and economic mobility of immigrants argue that first-generation immigrants improved their economic status only very slowly, particularly for the new immigrant arrivals. Thus, in his study of occupational mobility in Boston, Stephan Thernstrom found that "the rate of upward mobility for natives exceeded that for immigrants, leaving the latter further behind at the end of the race than they were at the starting gun" (1973: 119). Similarly, Bodnar concluded that although "most immigrants had no direction to go but upward if they remained in the United States, the overall impression is that such movement was an unrealistic expectation in their lifetimes" (1985: 170).

Second-generation immigrants may have fared somewhat better, but immigrant disadvantage allegedly often persisted. Table 7.2, based on data drawn by the Immigration Commission from the 1900 census, shows that first-generation immigrants were substantially overrepresented in low-status (and low-income) occupations. There were exceptions, but almost all of these were among the old immigrant groups. There were much smaller occupational gaps between those born of native parents and second-generation Americans of immigrant parents. But residual effects sometimes persisted into the second generation, especially for immigrants

Table 7.2 First- and Second-Generation Male Immigrant Breadwinners in Certain
Occupations, United States, 1900 (in percentages)

Nationality	General laborers		Miners and quarrymen		Clerical	
	1st	2nd	1st	2nd	1st	2nd
Austrian	18.8	7.4	18.9	4.9	1.1	8.4
Bohemian/Moravian	14.0	8.1	2.2	0.8	0.9	3.9
Canadian (French)	15.1	13.4	1.0	0.8	1.0	2.4
Danish	10.0	9.5	1.2	1.2	1.5	4.0
English and Welsh	6.4	6.9	10.2	5.7	3.8	5.9
French	7.8	7.9	5.7	1.8	2.1	5.8
German	10.2	7.5	1.5	1.1	1.8	5.3
Hungarian	22.3	7.0	30.0	10.2	1.0	11.9
Irish	22.3	10.2	3.2	2.6	2.2	6.4
Italian	33.2	12.4	9.2	3.1	0.6	6.4
Norwegian	9.5	7.2	1.3	0.5	1.2	2.9
Polish	29.1	15.7	7.7	5.0	0.6	4.0
Russian	7.3	4.7	4.0	1.3	2.2	11.7
Scottish	5.7	6.2	7.5	5.6	4.2	6.2
Swedish	12.8	9.5	4.2	2.1	1.3	5.4
Swiss	8.7	7.3	1.8	1.4	1.5	4.0
Other foreign-born	14.1	9.4	7.1	2.7	2.5	6.2
All foreigh-born	14.4	8.6	5.1	2.3	2.0	5.7
Native-born, native parents	8.0	—	1.5	—	3.4	—

Source: Reports of the Immigration Commission (1911), Vol. 1: 780–83, 791–92.

from French Canada, Ireland, Italy, Poland, and Hungary. For New York Italians in the 1880s, Thomas Kessner observed that "the peasant shovel was passed on from one generation to the next; no longer working the soft earth of Italy's farms it was now used to excavate sewers and aqueducts. Like it or not, Italian youth wore the heavy yoke of their parents' past" (1977: 79). However, Kessner found that both first- and second-generation Italians had significantly improved their economic status by 1905.

While renouncing the labels new and old, studies of first- and second-generation immigrants have pointed to considerable differences in the upward occupational mobility by nationality or ethnic group. Thernstrom found that the British and east Europeans did rather better than the Irish in Boston: "What was thought to be the old-immigrant pattern applied to the British but not to the Irish: what was taken to be the new-immigrant pattern applied to the Italians but not to the East Europeans" (1973: 135). Similarly, New York Jews were more upwardly mobile than New York Italians (Kessner 1977), and first-generation Romanians in Cleveland climbed faster than either Slovaks or Italians (Barton 1975: ch. 5).

Thus, the literature suggests the rung on which immigrants stepped on the occupational ladder, as well as the rate at which they climbed it, varied. These differences have been traced back to immigrant origins whether rural or urban, skilled or unskilled, educated or not. They reflected both the economic attributes of the origin countries and the selectivity of the immigration process.

Analyzing Immigrant Earnings

Economists studying immigrant assimilation in the United States after 1950 have been concerned with the same micro issues that preoccupied late-nineteenth-century observers. Has the quality of immigrants declined? If so, how fast has it declined? How quickly do immigrants climb the occupational ladder? Do their earnings catch up to those of native-born Americans? If so, how fast do they catch up? This debate has involved estimating earnings functions based on human capital theory for immigrants and natives. Immigrants would be expected to invest heavily in human capital upon their arrival, the more so the less human capital they bring with them at the start. Accordingly, we expect their wages initially to be low relative to those for natives but that they rise faster over time. Their wages would also rise as they gather more information about how to exploit their skills more profitably in the new environment and to signal their productivity to employers.[5]

Barry Chiswick (1978) estimated earnings functions for natives and foreign-born by regressing the log of earnings on years of education, labor market experience, experience squared, and for immigrants, years since migration and its square. He found that earnings functions for immigrants sloped upwards steeply with their time in the United States and that, for given years of education, they actually *overtook* native Americans after 10–15 years. George Borjas (1985, 1987) argued that this result arose from the fact that immigrant quality had declined and thus that later (and therefore younger) cohorts were likely to have lower earnings than their predecessors, biasing upwards the cross-sectional estimate of the assimilation effect. This issue has been widely debated in the recent literature (Chiswick 1986; Jasso and Rosenzweig 1988, 1990; Borjas 1987, 1990, 1994, 1995; LaLonde and Topel 1992). Its significance for the late-nineteenth-century debate should be obvious given all the attention devoted to the differences between immigrant and native earnings and given the alleged lower quality and slower assimilation of new immigrants.

The cliometric literature has been more concerned with the issue of immigrant discrimination in the labor market. Did late-nineteenth-century immigrants attain lower occupational status and therefore lower earnings than comparable native-born workers? Did they receive lower rates of return on their human capital and therefore experience lower rates of wage growth over their lifetimes than natives? Robert Higgs (1971) explored the issue using the Immigration Commission's published data which take the form of group averages of earnings and worker characteristics. He estimated that, if immigrants had had the same levels of literacy and ability to speak English as the native-born, their earnings would have been similar. Paul McGouldrick and Michael Tannen (1977) analyzed the same data as well as data for individual unskilled workers reported in the 1890 Commissioner of Labor survey. Controlling for age and industry, they uncovered no significant difference between the earnings of immigrants from northwest Europe and the native-born, but those from southeast Europe received 5–10 percent less. Francine Blau (1980) found that immigrants covered by the Commission's report were initially at a disadvantage but that their wages grew faster than those of native-born. She found that immigrants from northwest Europe had an initial disadvantage of 12.2 percent, but caught up (and overtook) after 11.4 years; new immigrants from southeast Europe had a 17.8 percent disadvantage on arrival but caught up after 16.6 years.

More recently, a number of studies have used data for individual workers drawn from a variety of State Labor Bureau reports, which make it possible to explore these issues in greater detail, to estimate separate earnings functions for the native-born and foreign-born, and to disaggregate by ethnic background. Joan Hannon examined data for Michigan copper workers in 1888 (1982a) and for workers in the Michigan agricultural implements and ironworking industries in 1890 (1982b). Both studies indicated a modest gap between native-born and foreign-born workers but also very different age-earning profiles. The foreign-born caught up with native-born workers only after 40 years in the copper industry, more rapidly in the ironworking industries in small-town Michigan, but in Detroit and Grand Rapids they fell progressively behind (1982a: 39; 1982b: 842–43). Hannon argued that the generally slow growth of immigrant earnings was due largely to discrimination blocking their progress up the occupational ladder. However, second-generation immigrants experienced more rapid wage growth than natives and in some cases overtook them.

Barry Eichengreen and Henry Gemery (1986) found in Iowa labor markets in the mid-1890s that immigrants who had aquired their skills abroad experienced slower earnings growth than natives but U.S.-trained immigrants experienced earnings profiles more similar to natives. Their results are consistent with those of Hannon and a number of other studies, indicating that education and training acquired abroad yielded lower rates of return than that acquired in the United States. More recently, Christopher Hanes (1996) examined a variety of datasets and concluded that slower relative earnings growth for immigrants was pervasive. Immigrant earnings were similar to native-born earnings around age 20 but grew much more slowly over the following 30 years. He obtained similar results for the individual national groups of British, Irish, and Germans. Hanes argues that these results are not due to some peculiarity of individual datasets for the late nineteenth century but genuinely reflect poor immigrant assimilation.

These findings suggest slower rates of assimilation than is typically found for the post–World War II years. The difference can be seen clearly in table 7.3, which presents the proportionate difference over 10-year intervals of wage growth for the foreign-born and the native-born predicted from regression estimates of existing studies. For each of the four nineteenth-century estimates, the predicted wage of an immigrant arriving at the age of 20 grows substantially slower over the following decade than that of the native-born. The difference narrows over the 30–40 age interval and then becomes positive in the later decades as predicted foreign-born wages begin to grow faster than those of the native-born. Census data from 1970 and 1980 tell a different story. Chiswick's estimates for white men in 1970 predict

Table 7.3 Relative Growth of Immigrant and Native-born Earnings in the United States (percentage per decade)

Year(s)	Age 20–30	Age 30–40	Age 40–50	Age 50–60
A. Past assimilation evidence				
Michigan 1888 (clay and stone) (Hanes 1996: table 2, eqs. 7–8)	−14.64	0.71	0.16	41.29
Michigan 1890 (ironworkers) (Hanes 1996: table 2, eqs. 11–12)	−6.39	−0.64	4.98	11.55
California 1892 (Hanes 1996: table 2, eqs. 3–4)	−28.51	−10.01	3.10	17.82
Iowa 1894/5 (Eichengreen and Gemery 1986: table 3, eqs. 4, 5)	−13.10	−4.60	2.73	10.76
B. Present assimilation evidence				
United States 1970 (whites) (Chiswick 1978: table 2, eqs. 1, 5)	5.44	6.19	7.03	7.98
United States 1970–1980 (whites) (Borjas 1985: table A2)	2.37	2.94	2.31	0.71

Notes: These figures are the difference between growth rates of predicted earnings of the foreign-born and the native-born. Growth rates are calculated as $\log(W_{a+10}) - \log(W_a)$, where W_a is the predicted wage at age a. Immigrants are assumed to have arrived in the United States at age 20. For the nineteenth-century estimates, 9 years of schooling is assumed, and for the twentieth-century estimates, 12 years. The wage growth from the Borjas study is that predicted from the 1980 regression for age $a + 10$ and the 1970 regression for age a. These predictions also take account of the cohort arrival dummies. For the 20–30 age interval, the 1965–1969 cohort arrival dummy was used, for the 30–40 age interval, the 1950s dummy was used, and for the 40–50 and 50–60 age intervals, the 1940s dummy was used.

faster growth for the foreign-born throughout the life cycle. Borjas's estimates for 1970 and 1980 make it possible to predict the wage growth of each cohort over the decade of the 1970s. These still indicate that earnings growth is faster for the foreign-born, although the difference is smaller than that suggested by Chiswick's evidence.

Historical analysis has therefore painted a pessimistic picture of immigrant assimilation before the turn of the century. The most recent findings suggest that they did considerably worse than immigrants in the 1970s, almost a century later. This result is puzzling given that the immigrants from northwestern Europe who arrived before the 1890s are thought to have assimilated better than those from southern and eastern Europe who came later. But note what the figures in table 7.3 imply. In the estimated earnings profiles for the late nineteenth century, faster relative wage growth for natives at the younger ages is followed by slower relative wage growth later. This implies that the age-earning profiles for the native-born are much more "humped" than those estimated for immigrants. Perhaps the puzzle is only an artifact of the analysis rather than a real difference in immigration assimilation. As we shall see, the specification of the age-earning profile turns out to matter significantly in the results.

Another Look at Immigrant Earnings in Late-Nineteenth-Century Michigan

This section reexamines data from the survey of male workers in the agricultural implement and ironworking industries taken by the Michigan Bureau of Labor and Industrial Statistics in 1890 and published in its *Eighth Annual Report* (1891), the same data source used previously by Hannon (1982b) and Hanes (1996).[6] The survey has several important advantages. It was one of the largest worker surveys ever taken by a State Labor Bureau: 8,838 workers were canvassed—about half of all Michigan workers enumerated in these industries at the 1890 Census. The survey was also implemented with exceptional care by officials who visited the workplace rather than by a postal survey. Consequently, selectivity bias in the responses was kept to a minimum as were nonresponses to individual questions. In addition, the survey contains a large proportion of foreign-born workers and those with foreign-born parents and reflects a variety of nationalities from the immigrant wave of the 1880s. But the data also have limitations. Since the evidence comes from only one industry and one state, it cannot speak to career progression that involved migration across industries or states. The data also do not contain many of the new immigrants who arrived mostly after 1890 and who preoccupied the Immigration Commission. Still, many of the foreign-born in the data were recent immigrants, although only a minority were from new regions.

The Michigan labor market is, nevertheless, an especially good place to confront immigrant assimilation issues. The population of Michigan grew rapidly in the 1880s—about 2.5 percent per annum, and urban places grew much faster. Almost half of this growth was due to immigration (both native-born and foreign-born). A quarter of the state's population was foreign-born at the time of the 1890 Census and nearly 30 percent were native-born of foreign parents. Although 38 percent of Michigan's labor force was still in agriculture in 1890, the rapidly growing manufacturing sector occupied a quarter of the labor force. Michigan's industrial growth was based on the extraction of minerals and on the manufacture of metal goods such as agricultural implements, wagons, and carriages. The foreign-born population share was nearly twice as big as that for the United States as a whole, but its composition was fairly typical of the two postbellum waves of immigrants. In addition to British and Irish, it included substantial numbers of Germans, Dutch, Scandinavians, and eastern Europeans, particularly Poles. Michigan immigrants were also fairly similar to the American immigrant population as a whole in terms of age, literacy, and ability to speak English.

The Michigan survey yields 8,493 usable observations for workers aged 16 and older, divided into four groups: the native-born of native parents, the native-born of foreign parents, the foreign-born who arrived in the United States after they were 15, and the foreign-born who arrived before they were 16. The distinction between the two groups of foreign-born turns out to be important.[7] Table 7.4 presents summary statistics that confirm that the two groups of native-born workers received almost identical annual earnings and weekly wages even though those with foreign-born parents were about five years younger on average than those

Table 7.4 Michigan Ironworkers, 1890: Descriptive Statistics

Origin	Number of observations	Annual earnings ($)	Weekly wage ($)	Age	Years in the United States
A. Total sample					
Native-born, native parent(s)	3,412	479.0	10.4	31.4	—
Native-born, foreign parent(s)	2,163	475.4	10.4	26.6	—
Foreign-born arriving >15	1,890	485.9	10.4	36.0	11.1
Foreign-born arriving <16	1,028	461.7	9.9	26.9	17.9
B. Immigrant groups					
British-born	380	558.9	12.4	35.4	15.7
Irish-born	272	521.6	11.2	37.2	20.4
Scandinavian-born	83	547.2	11.2	32.9	10.9
French/Belgian/Dutch-born	258	482.1	10.2	33.2	13.4
German-born	1,721	449.8	9.7	31.6	12.4
East European-born	191	414.2	8.8	30.6	9.7

Source: Michigan Bureau of Labor and Industrial Statistics, *Eighth Annual Report* (1891).

whose parents were native-born. The foreign-born who arrived as adults earned a wage similar to that of the native-born and a little higher than those who arrived as children. Those who arrived as adults were, on average, slightly more than nine years older than those who arrived as children and had been in the United States for almost seven years.

As a preliminary step, figure 7.1 plots by age the average earnings for both the foreign-born and the native-born. Wages rose very steeply for both groups after the age of 16 until about the mid-twenties, when their ascent began to brake sharply. After the late-twenties, the wage profiles are virtually horizontal although foreign-born wages tend to stay a bit below native-born wages. The smooth curves represent the predictions from quadratic equations in age, fitted to these average wage observations. Two findings are unambiguous. First, there is no evidence of dramatically slower earnings growth for foreign-born in the early years. Between the ages of 20 and 50, the predicted wage of both groups grows by about 50 percent, and the average rates of growth are identical at 1.6 percent per year of age. This contrasts sharply with the findings of recent studies that estimate over all the individual observations (rather than on the average wage for each age). Second, the quadratic equations fit the data very poorly.[8] They underpredict the wage between the age of 20 and the early 30s and overpredict it between the mid-30s and the early 50s.[9] As we shall see, together, these findings imply that the results of previous studies might have been misled by fitting an inappropriate functional form for the experience- or age-earning profiles of these nineteenth-century workers.

Figure 7.1 suggests that we estimate age-earning functions that deviate from convention. In essence, we follow the earnings function approach first used by

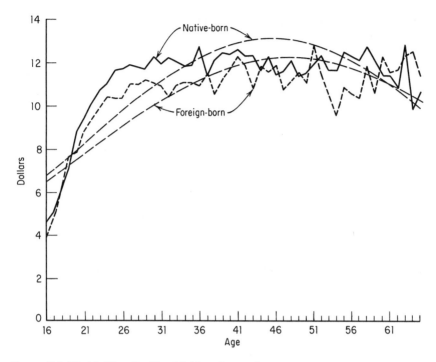

Figure 7.1 Weekly Wage Profiles: Michigan ironworkers, 1890

Chiswick (1978) and then, in the historical literature, by Hannon (1982a, 1982b), Eichengreen and Gemery (1986), and Hanes (1996). But in order to allow for the kink in the earnings functions (most evident for the native-born), the coefficients on age and age squared are allowed to shift after age 25 by introducing the extra terms age-25 and (age-25)^2.[10] Furthermore, we do not control for occupation since moving up the occupational ladder can be seen as the means by which life-cycle earnings evolved. Because the Michigan data contain no information on education or the age at which individuals began work, we proxy experience by age. We also include intercept dummies for residence in big cities such as Detroit or Grand Rapids (Hannon 1982b) and for whether the worker was married.

The results for weekly wages appear in table 7.5. The estimated coefficients for the native-born of native parents and the native-born of foreign parents are strikingly similar; both exhibit highly significant coefficients on the shift term for (age-25)^2. This result strongly reinforces the view that the simple quadratic in age and age^2 is not an adequate representation of the data.[11] It matters, as we shall see. Turning to the foreign-born who arrived aged 16 or older, the coefficients on age differ somewhat from those of the two native-born groups, but the most striking feature is the highly significant coefficients on years in the United States and its square.[12] This provides strong support for an assimilation effect among immigrants who arrived as adults. Hanes (1996) found much smaller and less significant

Table 7.5 Weekly Wage Functions for Michigan Ironworkers (dependent variable: log weekly wage)

Variable	Native-born, native parent	Native-born, foreign parent	Foreign-born, arriving >15	Foreign-born, arriving <16
Constant	−4.243	−4.973	−2.583	−5.962
	(9.70)	(10.92)	(1.88)	(9.82)
Age	0.508	0.570	0.358	0.668
	(12.09)	(12.86)	(2.87)	(11.22)
Age^2/10	−0.098	−0.110	−0.068	−0.135
	(9.84)	(10.33)	(2.41)	(9.46)
(Age−25)/10	−0.139	−0.153	−0.250	−0.200
	(1.53)	(1.39)	(1.40)	(1.30)
(Age−25)^2/10	0.096	0.108	0.068	0.129
	(9.83)	(10.14)	(2.43)	(9.31)
Years in United States/10			0.274	0.017
			(9.58)	(0.39)
(Years in United States)^2/100			−0.044	0.007
			(5.60)	(0.76)
Big city	0.084	0.041	−0.012	0.068
	(7.38)	(3.06)	(0.85)	(3.26)
Married	−0.018	0.022	−0.031	−0.097
	(0.59)	(0.37)	(0.80)	(1.03)
R^2	0.43	0.58	0.19	0.60
RSS	299.75	192.15	147.23	86.41
Log-likelihood	−692.27	−450.98	−269.84	−185.88
No. of observations	3,412	2,163	1,890	1,028

Note: t statistics in parentheses.

coefficients on the terms for years in the United States in his regressions on the same data. The final column in table 7.5 suggests why. For immigrants who arrived in the United States younger than 16, the coefficients for years in the United States and its square are both insignificant. Combining these different immigrant groups into one tends to dilute the assimilation effect.

What do the implied age-earning profiles look like? Figure 7.2 plots the four estimated profiles. The plot for immigrants who arrived as children assumes an age of arrival of nine, and the plot for those who arrived as adults assumes an age of 26 at arrival (the respective means in the data). Consequently, the plot for adult arrivals begins at age 26. Figure 7.2 illustrates that the age profiles of wages are very flat for the two groups of native-born, with the second generation having slightly higher wages in the early years. The profile for immigrants who arrived as children is slightly more humped, but its mean after the age of 25 is close to that of second-generation immigrants. By contrast, the immigrants who arrived as adults have lower wages throughout. But the important point to note is that from the age of 26 until the mid-forties, the wages of the two immigrant groups grow slightly *faster*

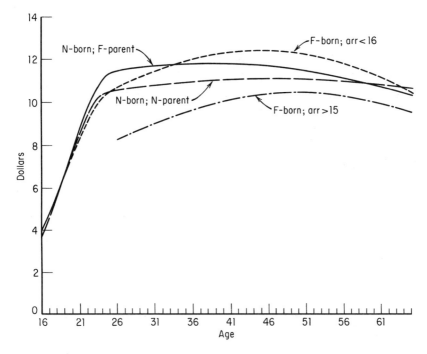

Figure 7.2 Estimated Weekly Wage Profiles: Michigan ironworkers, 1890

than those of the native-born—not slower, even dramatically slower, as some previous studies have suggested.

The similarity of the age-earning profiles of the two groups of native-born and
the immigrants who arrived as children suggests that the profiles might not be significantly different. In fact, we can reject the hypothesis that these three groups can
be pooled in one regression, largely because with a large number of observations,
small differences tend to be statistically significant. In absolute terms, however, the
differences in the predicted wage are small and suggest strongly that the two groups
of native-born and the immigrants who arrived as children competed on almost
equal terms and received almost identical wages. Between the ages of 26 and 65,
the wages of these three groups grew hardly at all.[13] For immigrants who arrived as
adults, wages grew by 16 percent over the 40 years. Their predicted wage grew 0.35
percent per year faster than that for the native-born.

Just how misleading the quadratic age-earning profiles can be is illustrated in
figure 7.3. These are derived in exactly the same way as those in figure 7.2, but they
are based on estimates that omit the shift terms in age-25 and (age-25)^2. They look
nothing like the plots of average wages by age in figure 7.1. For second-generation
immigrants and immigrants who arrived as children, the age-earning profiles are
extremely humped, and the predicted wage collapses to very low levels after age
50. The reason is clear: these two groups are relatively young. For the second-

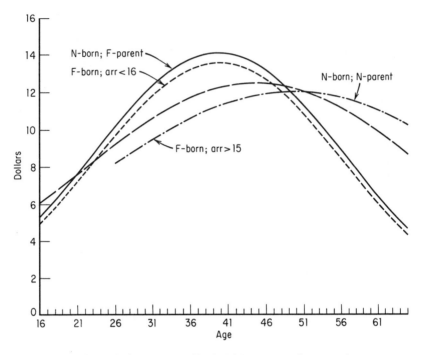

Figure 7.3 Quadratic Weekly Wage Profiles (Michigan ironworkers, 1890)

generation immigrants, 53 percent of the observations are for workers aged 16–25; for the immigrants who arrived as children, 58 percent. Hence, the age-earning profiles are disproportionately influenced by the steep upward slope of the wage profile in the early years, as documented in figure 7.1. By contrast, 38 percent of the native-born of native parents and only 16 percent of immigrants who arrived as adults are 16–25 in the data. Hence, the bulk of these workers are on the flat part of the age-earning profile and their estimated profiles, though still unrealistic, reflect this.

Our results in table 7.5, very different from those obtained in earlier econometric studies, even using the same data, indicate that immigrants assimilated better than others have suggested. It is worth reiterating the reasons for the difference. Separating immigrants who arrived as children and those who arrived as adults is important; otherwise, the assimilation effect will be underestimated. And allowing for the flatter earnings profiles after the mid-twenties is important; otherwise, the estimated age-earnings profile for natives will be more steeply humped because of the greater proportion of workers at younger ages. This point is further illustrated in figure 7.1: when observations at each year of age are equally weighted, the shape of the quadratic profiles for immigrants and natives, although they fit poorly, are rather similar.

The surprisingly flat age-earning profiles beyond the age of 25 raise the question of whether our results might suffer from a selectivity bias. Since the native-

Table 7.6 Age Distributions of Michigan Ironworkers and U.S. Workers, 1890

Worker group	Age group (years)				
	15–24	25–34	35–44	45–54	55–64
Michigan ironworkers, 1890					
Native-born, native parent	34.97	32.45	18.73	9.93	3.91
Native-born, foreign parent	48.89	34.18	12.30	3.98	0.65
All native-born	40.41	33.13	16.22	7.60	2.64
Foreign-born	26.99	33.97	22.37	13.12	3.56
United States Census white male workers, 1890 (%)					
Native-born, native parent	26.30	27.80	21.55	15.01	9.34
Native-born, foreign parent	42.25	34.32	15.32	5.90	2.21
All native-born	29.98	29.31	20.11	12.91	7.70
Foreign-born	16.62	28.08	23.61	19.64	12.07
Ratio of Michigan to United States					
Native-born, native parent	1.33	1.17	0.87	0.66	0.42
Native-born, foreign parent	1.16	1.00	0.80	0.67	0.29
All native-born	1.35	1.13	0.81	0.59	0.34
Foreign-born	1.62	1.21	0.95	0.67	0.29

born in the sample were, on average, younger than the foreign-born, could it be that the older native-born had left the industry for higher-paying jobs faster than the foreign-born? If so, the true earnings profile for natives might slope upward more than those of the foreign-born.

In table 7.6, which rejects this view, the age distribution of the Michigan sample is compared with that of all white male workers from the 1890 Census.[14] The Michigan data show much higher proportions in the 15–24 and 25–34 age groups than does the Census. But this is true of both the native-born and the foreign-born. In the last two rows of the table, the ratio of the share of each age group in the Michigan data to that in the Census is reported for native-born and foreign-born. Both show declines with rising age, but the foreign-born show a greater decline than do the native-born. Hence, the foreign-born are more underrepresented at the higher ages in Michigan ironworking than are the native-born, the opposite of what we would expect if the native-born were disproportionately leaving the industry for higher-paying employment. In short, we may be underestimating the relative growth of foreign-born earnings, a bias that would support our case.

It is possible that *both* immmigrants *and* the native-born left the industry for higher-paying, possibly white-collar, jobs as they gained maturity. But the Michigan ironworking industries do not appear to have been low-paid. The mean weekly wage of $10.35 compares favorably with Lebergott's figure of $9.5 for all nonfarm employees (1964: 528). Nor does it seem likely that the native-born left the industry for higher-paying jobs while immigrants left for lower-paying jobs. Kirk's study of social mobility in Holland, Michigan, indicates that rates of upward mobility from blue-collar jobs were not much lower for the foreign-born than for the native-born. Furthermore, upward mobility declined rather than increased with age (Kirk 1978: 87–88). The most likely reason for the relative youth of the Michigan ironworkers was the rapid expansion of the industry.

Earlier we noted that Joan Hannon (1982b) used the same Michigan data to identify differences in immigrant earnings growth between big-city and small-city locations. In Detroit and Grand Rapids, predicted earnings for the native-born of native parents were 25 percent higher than for the foreign-born at age 20 and 33 percent higher at age 50. Thus, Hannon thought she could point to immigrant cohorts falling behind natives in these two big cities. In the smaller Michigan cities, however, the native-born advantage fell from 21 percent to -9 percent over the same age interval. Thus, immigrants appeared to have been catching up on natives in the smaller cities and towns. Hatton showed elsewhere (1997) that this apparent difference in assimilation experience largely disappears when the specification used in table 7.5 is applied to big and small cities separately. Immigrants who arrived as adults actually had faster wage growth than the native-born of native parents between ages 26 and 46: faster by 0.9 percent per year in Detroit and Grand Rapids and by 1.2 percent per year in the smaller Michigan cities and towns. Thus, there is no evidence of immigrants' progressive falling behind in Michigan, even in the two biggest cities.

Does a similar pattern of immigrant assimilation emerge for other states and other industries? Would the results differ if we were able to control separately for years of schooling and years of labor market experience, rather than simply for age?[15] Hatton has answered these questions by extending the analysis to a mixed-industry sample of California workers in 1892 (1997). Four key findings emerged. First, the earnings profiles of native-born workers in California also exhibited a kink, again around age 25 or after about 11 years of labor market experience. Second, the earnings function for the foreign-born who arrived as children was insignificantly different from that of native-born. Third, the foreign-born who arrived as adults evidently had a smaller return for years of schooling (more accurately, years before beginning work). Fourth, years-since-migration had a potent influence on the earnings of foreign-born who arrived as adults: between the ages 26 and 46, their predicted wage grew about 1 percent faster than that for native-born. In short, the evidence from California strongly supports the Michigan findings.

The results reported here seem far more consistent with the view of the Immigration Commission and other contemporary observers of the assimilation of the old immigrant groups. In contrast with some recent studies of immigrant wages from around 1890, they suggest that these immigrants assimilated relatively easily into the American labor market. It is also consistent with recent studies of immigrant progress in the antebellum period. Joseph Ferrie (1994) has shown that between 1850 and 1860 immigrant wealth, in the form of real estate, increased with years in the United States. As a result, immigrants accumulated wealth faster than the native-born and faster than earlier studies had suggested.

Finally, how do our results for Michigan compare with those reported for the post–World War II period? The cohort analysis of Borjas (1985: 481) documented earnings growth of white immigrants relative to natives of 8 percent per decade. Borjas has found roughly the same rate for white immigrants arriving in the late 1960s and 1970s (1995: 230–31), somewhat faster than the rates reported here. Postwar white immigrants received earnings shortly after arrival similar to those for natives, and subsequently received higher wages. Late-nineteenth-century immigrants seem to offer a contrast since they experienced an initial wage disadvantage. However, postwar white *and* nonwhite immigrants combined did experience an initial wage disadvantage of 18 percent for new arrivals in 1970 rising to 38 percent in 1990 (Borjas 1995: 201), consistent with nineteenth-century experience.

Earnings and National Origins

The recent debate on postwar immigrant assimilation suggests that we should pay attention to the differences in the labor market performance of immigrants from different countries of origin. Borjas has argued that successive waves of immigrants over the postwar period have declined in "quality" as measured by their educational attainment and their earnings soon after arrival. He estimates that 90 percent of the decline in educational attainment and relative wages of recent immigrants between 1960 and 1980 reflects changing immigrant mix by country of origin (1994: 1685).[16] One implication is that cross-sectional estimates that do not allow for the heterogeneity among immigrant groups may suffer from upward bias in the estimates of immigrant wage growth. This is because the older immigrants, from the earlier cohorts, receive higher wages not only because of age and assimilation effects but also because they are drawn from cohorts with higher earnings capacity than those who arrived later. The same argument might be applied to the late nineteenth century when differences in labor market performance are at the heart of the debate. If true, our estimates of the earnings profiles of immigrants relative to natives might be biased, potentially overestimating the degree of immigrant assimilation.

The lower panel of table 7.4 gives summary statistics for individual nationalities or groups of nationalities for which significant numbers are represented in the Michigan ironworkers' data. The highest earners were the British followed by the Scandinavians, the Irish, the French/Belgian/Dutch, the Germans, and, finally, the somewhat heterogeneous east Europeans.[17] These rankings reflect differences in age and years in the United States as well as inherent performance or quality. The British and Irish were considerably older than the other immigrant groups. Whereas the Irish had been in the United States somewhat longer than average, the east Europeans were relatively recent arrivals. We need to control for these differences.

In preliminary analyses, separate regressions were estimated for each of these national or regional groupings for the immigrants who arrived as adults. We found

Table 7.7 Weekly Wage Functions for Michigan Ironworkers with Dummies for National Origin (dependent variable: log weekly wage)

	Foreign-born arriving >15	Foreign-born arriving <16	Native-born, foreign parent
Constant	−1.807	−5.867	−4.812
	(1.37)	(9.78)	(10.55)
Age	0.304	0.672	0.558
	(2.54)	(11.38)	(12.57)
$Age^2/10$	−0.055	−0.136	−0.107
	(2.04)	(9.59)	(10.07)
(Age-25)/10	−0.341	0.198	−0.168
	(2.00)	(1.29)	(1.53)
$(Age-25)^2/10$	0.055	0.131	0.105
	(2.05)	(9.45)	(10.16)
Years in United States/10	0.278	0.008	
	(10.22)	(0.19)	
(Years in United States)^2/100	−0.047	0.008	
	(6.20)	(0.88)	
Big city	−0.002	0.082	0.048
	(0.13)	(3.86)	(3.53)
Married	−0.005	−0.116	0.027
	(0.14)	(1.25)	(0.45)
Origin dummies			
Ireland	−0.207	−0.074	0.007
	(7.63)	(1.97)	(0.42)
Germany	−0.255	−0.131	−0.047
	(13.67)	(4.52)	(2.56)
Scandinavia	−0.099	−0.207	−0.132
	(2.78)	(2.45)	(1.52)
France/Belgium/Holland	−0.225	−0.109	−0.002
	(8.42)	(2.75)	(0.11)
Eastern Europe	−0.328	−0.178	−0.105
	(11.79)	(3.42)	(2.10)
R^2	0.28	0.61	0.58
RSS	130.43	83.89	190.31
Log-likelihood	−159.10	−172.04	−441.07
No. of observations	1,881	1,024	2,161

Note: *t* statistics in parentheses.

that these could be legitimately pooled in a regression that simply includes a dummy variable for each national group.[18] This implies constant proportions between the predicted wages of each group over the life cycle. The result in the first column of table 7.7 indicates appreciable differences among these immigrant groups compared with those from Great Britain—the excluded group.[19] The coefficients indicate that, allowing for age and time in the United States, the Irish, Germans, and French/Belgians/Dutch earned at least 20 percent less while the Scandinavians earned about 10 percent less.

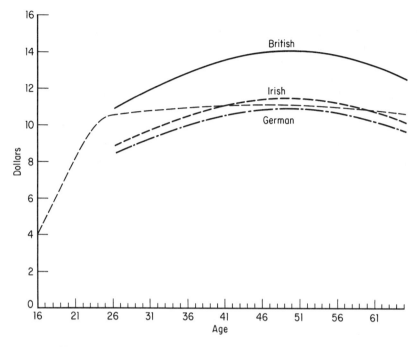

Figure 7.4 Estimated Profiles by Nationality (immigrants arriving aged 16 and over)

The important issue is whether allowing for the differences in earning power of different nationalities alters the overall conclusion about immigrant assimilation. The coefficients on age differ slightly from those in table 7.5 (column 3) but those on the key assimilation variables, years-in-the-United States and its square, change very little. The predicted wage profiles for the three national groups represented by more than a hundred observations are plotted in figure 7.4. The dashed line is the wage profile of the native-born of native parent from table 7.5 (column 1). The wage profile of the British-born lies above that for the native-born throughout, and those for the Irish and the Germans show the same pattern of convergence towards the native-born wage observed in figure 7.2. They therefore confirm the finding of faster wage growth for the immigrants who arrived as adults than for the native-born. Between the ages of 26 and 46, the predicted wage of these immigrants grows at 1.0 percent a year faster than that of the native-born—almost identical to the result when the national groups were not distinguished.

Are differences by nationality important for immigrants who arrived as children and do they persist across generations? The regressions in columns 2 and 3 of table 7.7 introduce the same region dummies for immigrants who arrived as children and for second-generation immigrants—in the latter case the dummies are for parents' place of birth. For immigrants who arrived as children, the dummies are generally significant and, with the exception of the Scandinavians, smaller in value than those for the immigrants who arrived as adults. For the second-generation immigrants the coefficients are smaller still; they are significant only for the Germans and the eastern Europeans. With the exception of the Scandinavians, for whom there are relatively few observations, there is a clear pattern of nationality- or region-specific effects declining from immigrants arriving as adults to those arriving as chidren to second-generation immigrants. Although one should be careful of applying cross-sectional effects across generations, this pattern does offer evidence of the dramatic fading of nationality effects with assimilation in the United States. But to return to the major theme, in the case of both immigrants who arrived as children and second-generation immigrants, adding nationality or region dummies has very little effect on the slopes of the estimated age-earning profiles (compare tables 7.5 and 7.7) and does not alter our conclusions from the previous section.

Our results for the Michigan ironworkers do not imply the slow wage growth for immigrants relative to natives that previous studies have indicated. They seem much more consistent with the traditional view that pre-1890 immigrants assimilated easily into the American labor market. Previous cliometric studies of individual earnings have been misled on this point largely by the use of an inappropriate specification for the earnings function. It is also important to distinguish between immigrants who arrived as children and those who arrived as adults. On average, the former have earnings experiences similar to those for the native-born. The latter suffered some initial disadvantages but these eroded over time. Disaggregating into national groups reveals some heterogeneity, with the British doing better than the other groups, particularly the eastern Europeans. Such differences suggest that quality gaps between new and old immigrants could have been considerable.

The Assimilation Performance of Old and New Immigrants

The Michigan data allow us to say little about the performance of the so-called new immigrants. Italians, Russians, Bohemians, Poles, Slovaks, and other new immigrant groups did not arrive in large numbers until the 1880s. Thus, they are not represented well enough in surveys taken around 1890 to enable a full analysis of immigrant performance by race and origin. There are no suitable microdata sets for the early twentieth century either, an unfortunate fact since these new immigrants came to dominate the inflows in the early twentieth century—the key feature that exercised the Immigration Commission.[20] If we want to examine these new immigrant groups, we must use the Immigration Commission's own data.

The Commission conducted two surveys, one of households, the results of which form the basis of table 7.1, and one of employees surveyed at the workplace. The latter is the most suitable for analysis of immigrant earnings, but unfortunately the underlying microdata do not survive. The results of the survey are presented in the form of averages cross-tabulated by industry and "race." These cells form the basis of the studies by Higgs (1971), McGouldrick and Tannen (1977), Blau

(1980), and Chiswick (1992). Most observers agree that the survey results are unbiased, even if the inferences drawn from them by the Commission were not. The survey covered over half a million employees in a variety of manufacturing and mining industries. Wage rates and employee characteristics were reported by industry for about 60 different races or nationalities, including the native-born of native parent and the native-born of foreign parent. Previous studies have included a variety of variables to explain immigrant earnings such as literacy, ability to speak English, and industry characteristics, but they did not examine each race or nationality separately, distinguishing only between old and new immigrant groups. The only study to distinguish the individual race is that of Chiswick (1992), who compared the performance of Jewish immigrants with that of old and new immigrant groups.

We take a somewhat different approach here since, as with the analysis of the Michigan data, we want to control only for age and the number of years in the United States. This approach allows us to include more observations, 409 in total, including the two groups of native-born.[21] Even so, there are relatively few observations for some races or nationalities, and aggregating some of them into larger groups, 26 in all, was necessary and this was guided by the classification of immigrants adopted after 1899 by the United States Immigration Bureau.

Our approach is to estimate a model for the log of the wage using dummy variables for each industry (16 industries, 15 dummies) and for each race as well as for the share of employees in certain age groups.[22] We also develop a single variable reflecting the average duration in the United States. The duration variable can be expressed as $[(A/20)*S1 + S2]$, where $S1$ is the share of the immigrants in a cell who had been in the United States for less than 20 years and $S2$ is the share who had been in the United States for 20 years or more. A is the average duration in the United States of those who had been present for less than 20 years (based on 5-year duration categories) and it is divided by 20. Thus, the variable would take a value of 0 for newly arrived immigrants and a value of 1 for immigrants who had been present for 20 years or more. The duration variable embodies the plausible assumption that the assimilation effects are only important for the first 20 years. On a more practical level, it allows us to deal with the open-ended category "20 years or more" in the United States and also summarizes assimilation effects in a single variable.

The main results are presented in table 7.8.[23] Industry dummies were included in the regression but are not reported in the table.[24] The variables for the shares in younger age groups yield negative coefficients, declining with age, and consistent with the sharply rising age-earning profiles observed for Michigan. The dummy variable for the native-born of foreign parent(s) indicates that their earnings were about 7 percent higher than the native-born of native parent(s) (the excluded group)—a result also consistent with our findings for Michigan and with Chiswick's (1977) for the postwar era. The coefficient of 0.206 on the assimilation duration variable indicates that immigrant earnings grew by 20.6 percent relative to native earnings in the first 20 years in the United States or at about 1 percent per year—again consistent with the evidence from Michigan.

Table 7.8 Weekly Wage Functions: Immigration
Commission Data (dependent variable: log weekly wage)

Constant	2.772
	(93.208)
Share aged 18–19	−0.649
	(6.53)
Share aged 20–24	−0.195
	(2.99)
Native-born, foreign parent	0.065
	(2.25)
Foreign-born assimilation duration variable	0.206
	(4.17)
Race dummies: "old" immigrant group	
Danish/Norwegian/Swedish	−0.151
	(3.52)
Dutch/Flemish	−0.157
	(3.88)
English	−0.089
	(1.99)
Finnish	−0.158
	(3.67)
French/Belgian	−0.142
	(3.26)
German/Swiss	−0.205
	(4.42)
Irish	−0.242
	(4.93)
Scottish/Welsh/Scots-Irish	−0.127
	(2.76)
Race dummies: "new" immigrant group	
Armenian	−0.285
	(7.29)
Bohemian and Moravian/other Austrian	−0.192
	(5.51)
Bosnian/Dalmatian/Herzegovinian	−0.142
	(2.75)
Bulgarian/Montenegrin/Serbian	−0.236
	(7.43)
Croatian/Slovenian	−0.200
	(6.14)
Greek/Macedonian	−0.281
	(8.91)
Hebrew Russian/Hebrew other	−0.157
	(4.57)
Northern Italian/other Italian	−0.219
	(6.19)
Southern Italian	−0.282
	(8.39)
Lithuanian	−0.249
	(6.96)

Table 7.8 (*continued*)

Magyar	−0.259
	(7.40)
Polish	−0.245
	(6.89)
Portuguese/Spanish	−0.193
	(3.78)
Romanian	−0.239
	(6.38)
Russian	−0.237
	(7.10)
Ruthenian	−0.269
	(6.91)
Slovak	−0.238
	(6.46)
Syrian/Turkish	−0.302
	(8.52)
R^2	0.837
RSS	2.432

Notes: Industry dummies are included in the regression, but are not reported in the table. See text. Figures in parentheses are *t* statistics.

The intercept dummies for each racial or national group provide an estimate of the proportionate wage disadvantage (relative to the native-born of native parent[s]) on first arrival in the United States. With two exceptions, all new immigrant groups had initial wage disadvantages of 20 percent or more. The most disadvantaged were southern Italians and eastern Mediterraneans, with entry wages more than 28 percent below the native-born. With the exception of the Germans and the Irish, all old immigrant groups had initial wage disadvantages less than 20 percent. The least disadvantaged were the English, Scots, and Welsh, who had entry wages of 9 and 13 percent less than the native-born. These results again seem broadly consistent with our Michigan findings. Using unweighted averages, we found that the old immigrants had a starting disadvantage of 15.9 percent and the new immigrants, 23.5 percent.[25] The 7.6 percent difference is consistent with the 5–10 percent found by McGouldrick and Tannen (1977: 731) and Blau (1980: 27).

The wage differential after 20 years in the United States can be calculated by adding the individual race or nationality coefficient to the coefficient on the assimilation variable. To illustrate, the wage differential for the Scandinavians would be 0.206 − 0.151 = 0.055 and that for the Poles would be 0.206 − 0.245 = −0.039. On average, the old immigrant groups' wages after 20 years in the United States exceeded those of the native-born of native parent by 4.7 percent. By contrast, only a few of the new immigrant groups did. On average they still lagged behind by 2.9 percent after 20 years.

The Immigration Commission was right: immigrants from new regions did not do as well as immigrants from old regions. But it is important to emphasize that these differences are relatively modest: immigrant earnings *did* gradually approach parity with native earnings and, in some cases, overtook them. So how do these differences in the labor market performance of immigrant groups relate to their characteristics upon arrival in the United States? Then and now there has been much discussion of the decline in immigrant quality, but little consideration of how the differing quality of immigrant groups related to their performance in the labor market. On the other hand, the literature on immigrant wages, focusing on variables such as literacy and skill, says little about how immigrant performance related to the characteristics exhibited by imigrants *on arrival in the United States*. We now have a measure of labor market performance for different immigrant groups and can compare it with some of their arrival characteristics.

After 1899 the Immigration Bureau distinguished immigrants by race or nationality rather than by country of origin as it had done previously. These races or nationalities correspond roughly to the groups distinguished by the Immigration Commission in its survey of employees. The Bureau reported the composition by age, gender, previous occupation, and literacy, although the latter two were not reported separately by gender. The Commission compiled this data by race for the period 1899 to 1909 (Vol. 1: 97–109). These reported characteristics of the immigrant flow between 1899 and 1909 can be used to explain the variation in immigrant performance across races or nationalities estimated above for 1909. Of course, some of the immigrants observed in 1909 would have arrived earlier than 1899 and some of the flow would have returned in the meantime, but the aim is to capture broad compositional differences across different ethnic or racial groups.

Our dependent variable is the predicted wage relative to the native-born wage, calculated as 1 minus the value of the race or nationality dummy estimated in table 7.8.[26] We distinguish 28 different races or nationalities, compared with 26 in table 7.8, because the Portuguese and Spanish are separated as are the Scots and Welsh, each taking the relevant value estimated for the combined group in table 7.8.

Regression results are presented in table 7.9. Column 1 indicates a strong relationship between the proportion of skilled workers or professionals (as a share of those reporting previous occupations) and immigrant wage performance, evidence always considered an important proxy for immigrant quality. The coefficient indicates that increasing the proportion of immigrants in the skilled category from the level of the Lithuanians (6.8 percent) to that of the English (57.7 percent) would increase the wage by 8.4 percent, a significant but modest amount. In column 2 we use as an explanatory variable the proportion who were illiterate on arrival in the United States.[27] This takes on a significant negative coefficient, as might have been expected. In this case, increasing literacy from the level of the Lithuanians to that of the English raises the wage by 7.4 percent, an even more modest amount. When both variables are entered, as in column 3, the size and significance of each coefficient diminish. The proportion of skilled and illiterate gradually lost significance as further variables were added[28] because these variables and others, such as the proportion of farm laborers, are highly collinear across immigrant groups: high proportions of illiterate, low proportions of skilled, and high proportions of farm laborers went together.

Table 7.9 Explaining Immigrant "Quality" (dependent variable: immigrant wage relative to native-born wage)

	1	2	3	4
Constant	0.959	1.036	0.911	1.056
	(75.05)	(74.65)	(44.78)	(6.31)
Proportion of skilled	0.165		0.117	0.090
or professional workers	(4.09)		(2.46)	(1.47)
Proportion illiterate		−0.155	−0.085	
		(3.53)	(1.72)	
Proportion farm laborers				−0.123
				(1.61)
Proportion adult				−0.057
				(0.31)
R^2	0.39	0.32	0.46	0.47
RSS	0.05	0.06	0.05	0.05
RESET	0.31	3.10	5.82	3.74
HETERO	0.00	0.06	0.31	0.20

Notes: t statistics are in parenthses. RESET is the test for functional form based on the regression of the residuals on the squared fitted values. HETERO is the test for heteroskedasticity based on the regression of the squared residuals on the squared fitted values. Both are chi-squared (1): critical 5 percent value 3.84. Column numbers represent different regression equations.

In column 4 the proportion of adults and the proportion of farm laborers (among those claiming previous occupations) are included and illiteracy is excluded. The proportion of farm laborers takes a negative coefficient (though it is not significant) whereas the skilled proportion loses further significance.[29] The proportion of adults takes a negative coefficient consistent with the finding from Michigan that immigrants who arrived as children had higher wages than those who arrived as adults, but the variable has a very low significance level.

Did Immigrant "Quality" Decline in the Late Nineteenth Century?

The Immigration Commission lamented the progressive shift in the sources of immigration away from northwestern and toward southern and eastern Europe, perceiving it as a decline in immigrant quality. Jenks and Lauck emphasized the same point. Drawing on data assembled by the Commission, they showed that in the decade following 1899 the proportion of immigrants classified as either professional or skilled was 22 percent among the old immigrant group but only 9.2 percent among the new immigrant group (1926: 32). For the same decade, they calculated that 2.7 percent of old immigrants were illiterate on arrival, compared with 35.8 percent of new immigrants (1926: 36), and concluded that immigrant quality had fallen dramatically.

Paul Douglas (1919) took issue with Jenks and Lauck. He pointed out that they had excluded Hebrews from their new immigrant group. More important, he argued that a more reasonable comparison would be between new immigrants from 1899 to 1909 and old immigrants from, say, 1871 to 1882, when these formed the bulk of the immigrant inflow. Douglas showed that in the earlier period 12.2 percent of immigrants from northwestern Europe were either skilled or professional, whereas for the later period 17 percent from southern and eastern Europe were so classified. Hence, the immigrants from southeastern Europe appeared to have been *more* skilled than were their counterparts from the northwest 20–30 years earlier. But when the comparison was made only for those who reported any occupation (rather using all immigrants as the denominator, whether they reported an occupation or not), the proportion skilled or professional among immigrants from northwestern Europe from 1871 to 1882 was 22.6 percent while that for immigrants from southern and eastern Europe from 1899 to 1909 was 18.6 percent. Douglas concluded that there was little evidence one way or the other confirming that new immigrants were less skilled than old when one controls for stage in a country's emigration life cycle.

The question Douglas answered is, however, not quite the same as that implicitly asked by the Immigration Commission and more explicitly by Jenks and Lauck. Their question might be restated: what effect did the shift in the sources of immigration have on the average industrial quality of immigrants? We now know that the proportion of immigrants in skilled or professional occupations was closely correlated with labor force performance. So how much difference did the changing composition by source make to immigrant quality judged by this criterion? Our approach is to compare the change in this and other immigrant characteristics for all European immigrant groups with calculated indices that hold constant the shares of each country in the total. That way we can isolate the effects from the country composition alone (and not just that from the changing weights of old and new immigrant groups). We base our comparison on 24 European countries and focus on the years 1873, 1893, and 1913. The fixed weight indices use the immigrant composition for 1893, the central year in the period.[30]

Table 7.10 presents the results of these comparisons. Rows 1 and 2 show that the proportion of men in the European immigrant flow rose by nearly 10 percentage points between 1873 and 1913, but that in the absence of compositional shifts the rise would have almost disappeared. The trends in the percentages of skilled or professional workers among those reporting a specific occupation are given in rows 3 and 4. The proportion from skilled backgrounds fell by 5.9 percentage points between 1873 and 1913, but the fixed weight index shows an *increase* of 2.2 percentage points over the whole period. Thus, changing composition accounted for an 8.1 percentage points decline in the share of skilled and professionals (5.9 + 2.2). Alternatively, since the skilled and professional workers were predominantly men, and given the rise in male shares among the immigrants, it might be even more relevant to consider the ratio of those reported as skilled or professional to total male immigrants. Rows 5 and 6 show that while this index rose by 0.7 percentage points, the fixed weight index increased by 10.6 percentage points—so that the compositional effect implies a decrease of about 10 percentage points. The same comparison is made in rows 7 and 8 for the share of literates (among those aged 14 or over).[31]

Table 7.10 Composition and Skills of European Immigrants, 1873–1913

	1873	1893	1913
Percentage Men (weights: all immigrants)			
(1) Actual	58.6	62.5	68.0
(2) 1893 weights	62.0	62.5	63.2
Percentage skilled or professional			
(weights: immigrants reporting occupations)			
(3) Actual	24.1	19.6	18.2
(4) 1893 weights	22.1	19.6	24.3
Skilled or professional/men			
(weights: male immigrants)			
(5) Actual	19.6	15.6	20.3
(6) 1893 weights	17.7	15.6	28.3
Percentage literate (weights: immigrants			
aged 14 and over)			
(7) Actual	—	77.4	73.0
(8) 1893 weights	—	77.4	83.8
Starting wage 1909 (weights: male			
immigrants)			
(9) Year weights	81.9	79.5	77.1

Notes: The 24 countries used for the weights are Austria, Belgium, Bulgaria/Serbia/Montenegro, Denmark, Finland, France, Germany, Greece, Hungary, Netherlands, Norway, Poland, Portugal, Romania, Russia, Spain, Sweden, Switzerland, Turkey (in Europe), England, Ireland, Scotland, and Wales. For 1913, Finland and Poland were counted as parts of the Russian empire and England, Ireland, Scotland, and Wales as the United Kingdom. In the calculation for 1913 each country in these aggregations is allocated the value of the group as a whole. In the fixed weight indices, Bulgaria/Serbia/Montenegro has a zero weight.

Sources: Calculated from Annual Report of Bureau of Commerce and Navigation for Fiscal year 1873, Washington, D.C.: GPO, 1874: 759–783. Treasury Department, Immigration and Passenger Movement at Ports of the United States during the Year ended June 30, 1893, Washington, D.C.: GPO, 1894: 11–12, 21–38; Department of Labor, Annual Report of the Commissioner General of Immigration for Fiscal Year 1896, Washington, D.C.: GPO, 1897: 12; Department of Labor, Annual Report of the Commissioner General of Immigration, Washington, D.C.: GPO, 1914: 46, 53–54, 64–69.

Immigrant literacy declined by more than 4 percentage points between the mid-1890s and 1913, but in the absence of compositional shifts it would have *increased* by more than 6 percentage points.

In short, those, like the Immigration Commissioners, who associated shifts in immigrant composition with declining immigrant quality were quite correct. Even though the actual decline was small, in the absence of shifting composition it would have improved. This changing mix was the inevitable consequence of the shifting locus of demographic and industrial revolutions in Europe (chapter 3). But how did the American labor market value this decline in quality? Did the decline in immigrant skill characteristics significantly affect immigrant quality as measured by earning power?

If we weight the immigrant arrival wages estimated in table 7.8 by male immigrant shares, we can construct an index of quality as reflected in earning power, which appears in the last row of table 7.10. The index of 77.1 for 1913 reflects the average wage on arrival of immigrants relative to the native-born (i.e., a 22.9 percent disadvantage). Applying 1873 immigrant weights to the same starting wages gives an index of 81.9 (i.e., an 18.1 percent disadvantage); hence, compositional shifts account for a 4.8 percent decline in arrival wages. Suppose we now include assimilation effects and give the immigrants a chance to adjust as duration in the United States lengthens. Adding the effect of the assimilation estimated in table 7.9 implies that after 20 years the 1873-weighted-average immigrant would have reached 102.5 percent of the native-born wage while the 1913-weighted-average immigrant would have reached 97.7 percent. Calculations such as these take no account of the fact that the quality of immigrants from a given country changed over time and at different rates from that of the native-born. However, the little evidence we have suggests that the earning power of old and new immigrants did not change much relative to that for the native-born between 1890 and 1909 (McGouldrick and Tannen, 1977: 740). If so, we might speculate that the changing relative earning power of immigrants was driven largely by compositional shifts and it probably declined by no more than 5 percent, hardly a number big enough to provoke anti-immigration alarm.

How does this number compare with those fueling current debate about the quality of America's immigrants? The source of America's immigrants underwent a dramatic shift between the 1950s and the 1980s. Europeans and Canadians fell sharply from two thirds to slightly more than a tenth, while those from the western hemisphere (excluding Canadians) surged upwards to almost half and those from Asia to more than a third (Borjas 1994: 1669). Both Chiswick (1986) and Borjas (1992) have associated the decline in immigrant relative earnings and schooling with the changing composition by national origin. According to Borjas, the composition change was responsible for about a two-year decline in schooling achievement and for a decline of more than a third in the wages of recent immigrants relative to wages for natives (Borjas 1992: 25).[32] Even when wages are adjusted for age and education, changing composition still accounts for a relative earnings decline of almost a quarter. Thus, most of the quality decline has not resulted from education. Yet even the smaller of these two figures is about four times as large as our estimate of the decline for the late nineteenth century. In short, even though the late-nineteenth-century shift from old to new European sources was dramatic, its impact on immigrant performance was modest compared with that for the late twentieth century.

Conclusion

Views on immigrant assimilation have always differed widely. Immigrant wage performance has been central to debate since the Immigration Commission's *Report* appeared in 1911. We have argued that most of the pessimistic assessments of immigrant labor market performance are misplaced, particularly for the so-called old immigrants who arrived before 1890. The Michigan evidence shows that second-generation immigrants and those who arrived in the United States as children had wage profiles much like those of the native-born of native parents.

Although immigrants who arrived as adults earned less initially, their earnings grew faster than those of the native-born, and they gradually caught up during their own lifetimes. Some even overtook the native-born. The traditional view of easy assimilation of the old immigrants apparently was right after all.

But did the new immigrants from southern and eastern Europe do worse? After all, these are the immigrants who excited so much controversy. Evidence from the Immigration Commission's survey suggests that they also started at an earnings disadvantage upon arrival. But in contrast with the old immigrant groups, many first-generation new immigrant groups failed to catch up with the native-born. The Immigration Commission's view seems to be justified. Furthermore, plenty of evidence confirms the Commission's view that the shifts in the source composition of the new immigrant flow lowered the industrial quality of the immigrants. What the Commission did not assess, however, was the impact of the quality decline on immigrant earning power. If the Commission's concern was largely America's industrial capacity, then this quality deterioration should have been exposed to market test. Did American labor markets place a high value on this quality decline? The answer is that the immigrant switch from old to new had a very modest impact on immigrant earning power. It simply did not matter much.

Had the literacy test been implemented earlier or had the quotas been introduced in 1890, immigrant quality would have risen, but only at the cost of a drastic reduction in numbers. No doubt both these effects would have pleased restrictionists, but the trade-off would have been a large decline in immigrant numbers for a small rise in quality. In any case, the absorption of numbers rather than ethnic or national origins really lay at the heart of the immigration debate.[33] Thus, chapter 8 turns to labor market absorption issues.

8

Absorbing the Immigrant
The Impact on Americans

The macro impact of the immigrants on employment conditions, living standards, and wages in American labor markets has received far less attention than has the process of assimilation. Yet this was the major preoccupation of contemporary observers, discussed at length by the Immigration Commission Reports. Here we confront three questions just as relevant today as they were almost a century ago: did late-nineteenth-century immigrants act as a flexible labor supply in America much like late-twentieth-century guestworkers in Europe? Did immigrants flow into occupations in which job creation was fast, or did they displace natives in occupations in which job creation was slow? Did immigration reduce wage growth and increase unemployment for native workers?

The Guestworker Hypothesis

Late-twentieth-century governments have sought to regulate the flow of immigrants and their composition in order to bring total labor supply closer to total labor demand and to manipulate the composition of immigration, thus helping erase growth-induced imbalances across different sectors and occupations. These workers, often given only temporary immigrant status and usually relatively unskilled, have become widely known as guestworkers. The prime example is Germany, which signed a guestworker agreement with Italy in 1955, with Spain and Greece in 1960, with Turkey in 1961, and by 1968 with Morocco, Portugal, Tunisia, and Yugoslavia. Another example is offered by Belgium, where official recruitment of Italians for Belgian coal mines started even earlier, in 1946. And France established an Office National d'Immigration to recruit workers from southern Europe in 1945.[1]

Analysis of the impact of this questworker labor supply on the host country probably starts with Charles Kindleberger's *Europe's Postwar Growth* (1967). The central idea of Kindleberger's book is the role of elastic labor supplies in facilitating fast growth in labor-constrained western Europe. Not only did he think that the guestworker supplies from Portugal, Spain, Greece, and Turkey helped release important bottlenecks in the host countries, but he thought it would help contribute to sending-country economic catch-up. Individual country studies have since concluded the same (e.g., Marshall 1973: 3–19, 77–111; Rogers 1985; Straubhaar 1988). Why is it, then, that most observers now believe that an effective and efficient European guestworker system is largely a myth? In the words of one, any "hopes of using immigrants as guestworkers to manage labor supply and solve problems of unemployment were dashed by the failure of repatriation policies in the late 1970s" (Hollifield 1992: 77). Many, of course, went home. Indeed, one study focuses exclusively on the role of cyclical downturn on return migration of the guestworker (Kayser 1972). Still, the failure of the guestworker system cited in these accounts is that too many stayed on when employment conditions deteriorated.[2] Thus, while the guestworker system worked well on the upswing, it worked badly on the downswing, or so the critics say.

Is there any reason to believe that the open migration system of the late nineteenth century worked any better than this modern guestworker system? It seems likely. The so-called new American immigrants in the late nineteenth century behaved pretty much the same way as the late-twentieth-century European guestworkers: like Michael Piore's characterization of postwar industrial-country immigrants, the American immigrants were unskilled, took low-wage jobs avoided by natives, saw themselves as temporary, and responded to booms and busts in the host country labor market (Piore 1979: 3). Furthermore, American immigrants in the late nineteenth century did not have access to the elaborate safety net and social contract offered by the late-twentieth-century welfare state. Thus, they had less reason to remain during hard times. In addition, over the 1890–1915 quarter century immigrants had a far bigger impact on the U.S. labor market (foreign-born were about 15 percent of the total labor force) than the guestworkers had on west European labor markets over the 1950–1975 quarter century (with the exception of Switzerland, from 4 to 8 percent of the total labor force: Rogers 1985: table 1.1, 11). Thus, there is reason to believe that the guestworkers were more effective then in smoothing out unemployment over industrial booms and busts than they are now.

Some observers—mostly historians—have seen these parallels and suggested that open United States immigration policy provided just such an elastic labor supply that cushioned the effects of cyclical booms and busts on the domestic labor market. In their view, it also fed the growing sectors of the economy, thus minimizing bottlenecks that more inelastic domestic labor supply might have otherwise created. Thus, Ian Tyrrell has recently argued that the United States "was, like some West European countries in the 1970's, able to export its' unemployment problem by massive repatriation of Mediterranean labor . . . in the era before World War I" (1991: 147). Similarly, Alexander Keyssar asserted that "workmen in Europe and Canada constituted a reservoir of labor that was tapped when needed and that reabsorbed jobless workers when business was slow in Massachusetts" (1986: 79). Two economists, Vernon Briggs (1985: 158) and Thomas Muller (1985: 113) agree. Indeed, they have lamented the loss of the flexibility that temporary foreign workers offered prior to World War I, now restricted by quotas and thus operating only through illegal immigration.

Contemporary observers certainly saw some advantage in the seasonal and cyclical flow of immigrants and the increasing rates of return migration, particularly to southern Europe. Indeed, "birds of passage" was a popular phrase some 70 or 80 years before it reappeared as the title of Michael Piore's book (1979). When W. B. Bailey wrote in 1912, the term birds of passage was sufficiently common to persuade him to use it as the title of his article. He then went on to describe the southern European immigrants:

> [T]he arrival of tens of thousands of this class in good seasons undoubtedly tends to limit the rise in wage rates in this country and thus furnishes grounds for the criticisms of labor leaders, but when hard times come these same laborers return home and reduce the supply at the very time when demand is beginning to fall off. (1912: 394)

A contemporary of Bailey's, Cyrus Salzberger, said in the same year that "the so-called bird of passage instead of being a menace to our industrial conditions is their greatest help. He gives flexibility, comes when there is demand for his work and departs when the demand is over" (quoted in Nelli 1983: 44). The phrase birds of passage was used so commonly around the turn of the century that it even appears in the 1901 *Report of the Industrial Commission* (1901, Vol. 15: lxxviii).

It appears that the questworker notion was as popular before World War I as it was after World War II.

A New Look at Jerome

The most comprehensive investigation of the relationship between immigration and domestic conditions in the United States remains Harry Jerome's, completed in 1926. Jerome's primary concern was to identify the role of host-country employment conditions in pulling Europeans overseas to the United States. This has become the more famous Jerome immigrant-demand hypothesis in the literature. His second concern, less well known, is an early version of the guestworker hypothesis: to determine whether immigration acted as a safety valve, thus making unemployment less severe in U.S. slumps than it would have been otherwise. Jerome did not have access to comprehensive measures of employment or output to confront the first question, but he documented in great detail the strong positive correlation between immigration and various indicators of economic activity. Although most of his time series analysis used index numbers, Jerome did pause to ponder the second question by looking at immigrant magnitudes relative to levels and changes in factory employment (1926: 95–122). He concluded that immigration was likely small compared with absolute changes in numbers unemployed, but that continued immigration in slumps certainly tended to aggravate the unemployment problem (1926: 122).

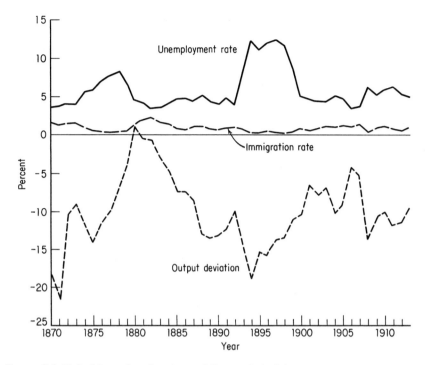

Figure 8.1 United States Immigration and Economic Activity

We can shed further light on this issue by comparing net *worker* immigration with unemployment—both of which were unavailable to Jerome—taking each as percentages of the labor force. The series for net immigration has been constructed for separate groups by age and gender based in the studies by Simon Kuznets and Ernest Rubin (1954) and by Everett Lee and his associates (1957). As the appendix shows, each age- and sex gender-specific net immigration series is multiplied by the relevant United States age- and gender-specific activity rate to obtain a measure of net worker immigration. This series is then divided by the civilian labor force estimates of David Weir (1992) for 1890–1913, and J. R. Vernon (1994) for 1870–1889. This series can then be compared with the unemployment estimates from the same sources. In addition, they can be compared with percentage deviations from trend in Christina Romer's (1989) real output series, output aggregates that were also unavailable to Jerome.

These comparisons appear in figure 8.1. In the average year, net immigration augmented the labor force by 0.87 percent, although that figure fluctuated widely between a low of 0.18 percent in 1895 and a high of 1.65 percent in 1883. Jerome was right: swings in the net worker immigration rate were small relative to the much wider swings in the unemployment rate, and smaller still when compared with the percentage swings in real output. But there is that clear inverse correlation between

Table 8.1 The Relationship between United States Immigration and Employment
(dependent variable: immigrant workers)

Variable	1870–1913	1870–1913	1870–1889	1890–1913
Constant	−1,507.60	157.89	126.94	288.77
	(7.13)	(3.03)	(1.37)	(0.56)
Employment level	0.15			
(thousands)	(8.07)			
Employment change		0.06	0.001	0.07
(thousands)		(1.89)	(0.014)	(1.89)
Time	−59.57	−4.75	2.49	−16.52
	(7.81)	(0.94)	(0.14)	(0.51)
Time^2	−0.53	0.17	0.11	0.38
	(4.89)	(1.63)	(0.14)	(0.80)
R^2	0.71	0.29	0.10	0.44
RSS/1000	162.53	391.78	163.74	191.22
DW	1.24	0.78	0.53	1.05
LM(1)	6.05	17.85	11.79	6.51
RESET	0.19	0.90	5.60	0.48

Notes: *t* statistics are in parentheses. LM(1) is the test statistic for the Lagrange Multiplier test for serial correlation. RESET is the test for functional form based on the regression of the residuals on the squared fitted values. Both tests are chi-squared (1): critical value 3.84.

unemployment and the immigration rate, a testimonial to the importance of United States employment conditions on the timing of the European emigrant's move. This correlation was explored at length in the 1950s and 1960s by scholars interested in the long swing (Thomas 1954; Abramovitz 1961, 1968; Easterlin 1966, 1968; Williamson 1964), and our exploration of European emigration amply demonstrated the same in chapter 4.

The first column in table 8.1 reports a Jerome immigrant-demand equation where the number of worker immigrants is regressed on the total number employed and time; it implies that every increase of 100 workers employed raised the number of worker immigrants on average by 15. This strongly supports the most famous of Jerome's hypotheses that late-nineteenth-century immigration was very sensitive to employment conditions in the United States. But Jerome's immigrant-demand hypothesis deals with the *determinants* of immigration. In contrast, the guest-worker hypothesis deals with the *impact* of immigration and thus focuses on the relationship between the change in the employment rate (a flow) and the immigration rate (another flow), not the level of the employment rate (a stock) and the immigration rate. The second column of table 8.1 reports a guestworker regression of the number of worker immigrants on the change in employment; it yields a coefficient of only 0.06, a tiny guestworker effect. The third and fourth columns show that the guestworker effect was even smaller (and statistically insignificant) before 1890. Apparently, the guestworker effect became significant only after 1890, but stayed tiny.

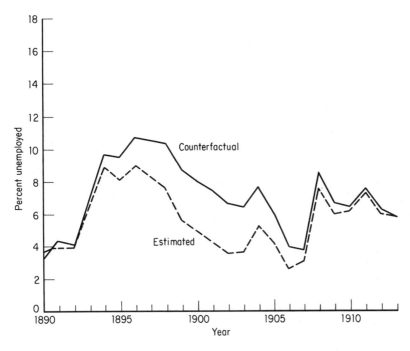

Figure 8.2 The "Guestworker Effect," 1890–1913 (unemployment rates)

But have we asked the wrong question? If immigration remained low over a protracted and serious recession such as the 1890s (due to the low level of employment), then the *cumulative* effect of immigrant scarcity would be to retard labor force growth and attenuate the unemployment bulge. To explore this alternative test of the guestworker hypothesis, we adjusted Weir's labor force estimates to account fully for the impact of worker immigration (see appendix). A counterfactual labor force is then calculated that would have emerged had the annual number of immigrants between 1890 and 1913 been constant at the average for the period as a whole. Under the "no guestworker" counterfactual, more of the immigrants would have arrived earlier in the period and fewer later on. Holding worker immigration constant over long swings and business cycles implies a new counterfactual no guestworker labor force and a corresponding counterfactual unemployment rate. Figure 8.2 plots the result: the unemployment bulge in the 1890s would have been bigger and persisted longer than it did in fact. The no guestworker unemployment rate would have reached 10.7 percent at the 1896 peak, rather than 9 percent. Alternatively, the no guestworker unemployment rate would have risen by 6.7 percentage points between 1892 and 1896, rather than by 5.1 percentage points (e.g., the guestworkers muted the impact of industrial crisis on unemployment by [6.7 − 5.1]/6.7 = 24%). The no guestworker unemployment rate would have been 7.6 percent in 1904 rather than 5.2 percent,

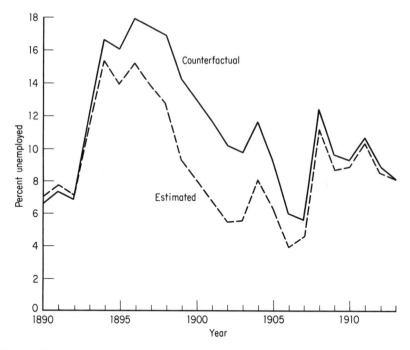

Figure 8.3 The "Guestworker Effect," 1890–1913 (nonfarm unemployment rates)

and it would have risen by 1.1 percentage points between 1902 and 1904, not 1.8 percentage points.

Foreign immigrants went to northern cities in overwhelming numbers. Indeed, Gavin Wright (1986) has argued that labor markets in the south were segmented from the north until World War I. Others have argued that the farm and city labor markets were far less than perfectly linked, especially in the short run (Hatton and Williamson 1992). Thus, it could be argued that we should be looking at the impact of the immigrants on labor markets in the urban north. The data do not make it possible to separate north from south, but we can distinguish between farm and nonfarm. The nonfarm unemployment levels were, of course, higher in both actual and counterfactual labor markets. Under the plausible assumptions that overt unemployment was absent in agriculture and that European immigrants entered nonfarm labor markets exclusively (see appendix), figure 8.3 plots the urban guest-worker effects. While the levels are bigger, the share of unemployment changes explained by immigrants is the same as before in figure 8.2. Between 1892 and 1896, the no guestworker nonfarm unemployment rate rose by 10.8 percentage points compared with 8.4 percentage points in fact (muting the impact of industrial crisis on nonfarm unemployment by 22 percent).

Are these figures big or small? Surprisingly small, we think.[3] Immigration did not operate as a very important safety valve on a year-to-year basis. Whereas the cumulative impact during a series of boom or depression years could have been more significant, as it evidently was in the 1890s, the guestworker impact was still relatively modest for an age of free migration, serving to mute the rise in unemployment during the biggest pre–World War I depression, 1892 to 1896, by only a quarter.

The Guestworker Effect: Easing Labor Supply Bottlenecks?

A second pair of questions underlies the guestworker hypothesis: did the immigrants flow disproportionately into rapidly growing, high-wage industries and occupations, thereby lessening the need for intersectoral migration of the existing native labor force and easing short-run bottlenecks? Or did they crowd into slow-growing, low-wage industries and occupations undergoing relative decline, thus crowding out unskilled natives? These competing views can be examined by comparing the share of immigrants in a given occupation with the growth of the total numbers in that occupation. If that share was high and rising in rapidly expanding industries and occupations, immigrants could be regarded as the "shock troops" of structural change.[4] We have examined the share of male immigrants in 106 occupations in 1900 and the change in that share between 1890 and 1900—the only pair of census years in which both the same occupational definitions and the share of immigrants are available. These occupations can be divided into the socioeconomic classification suggested by Alba Edwards (1917) and placed on a six-point scale from the highest to the lowest skill (e.g., unskilled = 6 and professional = 1). Unemployment incidence is measured as the proportion of the workers in a given occupation who experienced some unemployment in the previous year. Of course, the data are for native-born and foreign-born stocks, not the current inflows. However, they are all we have.

The first column of table 8.2 reports a regression for the share of the (male) foreign-born across occupations in 1900. The coefficient on occupational score is positive and significant, confirming that immigrants found employment more frequently in unskilled jobs, compared with natives. The coefficient on unemployment incidence is insignificant and close to 0, indicating that the foreign-born did not move disproportionately into industries and occupations with low unemployment rates. The coefficient on total occupational growth is negative, suggesting that immigrants located in slow-growth rather than high-growth sectors. But perhaps the second column of table 8.2 is more relevant, where the correlates with the *change* in the foreign-born share between 1890 and 1900 are reported. These were years of high unemployment and consequent low immigration, so the share of foreign-born among all occupied men fell across the decade, from 23.1 percent to 20.9 percent. Nonetheless, the foreign-born share tended to fall most in the fastest-growing occupations and least in the slowest-growing occupations.[5]

There is no evidence to support the view that occupations dominated by the foreign-born in 1890 grew faster over the subsequent decade or that immigrants in the 1890s flowed disproportionately into high-growth sectors and high-growth occupations. In fact, the evidence suggests the contrary: immigrants flowed

Table 8.2 Immigrant Share, Occupational Growth, and Unemployment Incidence

	Dependent variable	
Variable	Proportion of foreign-born in total labor force, men, 1900	Change in foreign-born proportion, men, 1890–1900
Constant	0.18	−0.003
	(4.46)	(0.26)
Occupational rank	0.03	−0.006
	(3.63)	(2.04)
Unemployment incidence, 1900	−0.02	0.02
	(0.17)	(0.70)
Growth of total occupied, 1890–1900	−0.09	−0.03
	(1.66)	(1.61)
R^2	0.15	0.07
RSS	1.76	0.18
RESET	1.74	2.23
HETERO	2.92	2.95

Notes: t statistics are in parentheses. RESET is defined in Table 8.1. HETERO is the test for heteroskedasticity based on the regression of the squared residuals on the squared fitted values. The index of occupational rank is based on Edwards (1917): 1 = professional; 2 = proprietor, manager, and official; 3 = clerk and kindred worker; 4 = skilled worker and foreman; 5 = semiskilled worker; 6 = unskilled worker.

disproportionately into the slowest-growing occupations, a fact that holds for the late twentieth century as well.

We have a ready explanation for this result: assuming occupational growth reflects shifting comparative advantage, and assuming that the United States was exploiting its comparative advantage in skill-, resource-, and capital-intensive industries, relatively fast-growing sectors should have generated relatively bouyant demand for skilled labor and sluggish growth for unskilled labor (Williamson and Lindert 1980: chs. 9 and 10). Thus, unskilled immigrants *should* have flooded into unskilled labor-intensive industries (and thus occupations) where growth was slower. Indeed, and to repeat, these findings are consistent with those from the 1980s and 1990s when the flood of new less-skilled immigrants into services and import-competing manufacturing has raised concern (Baumol et al. 1989; Borjas 1994). The evidence from the 1890s also seems to confirm a mismatch between labor demand that was shifting away from unskilled occupations (e.g., becoming more skilled) and booming immigrant labor supplies that were declining in quality (e.g., becoming less skilled). It had, of course, inequality implications a century ago (Williamson and Lindert 1980; Williamson 1982), just as it does today (Goldin and Margo 1992; Borjas, Freeman, and Katz 1992). It crowded out native unskilled (including southern blacks; Thomas 1972: 130–34 and ch. 18) and thus widened the gap between the working poor and the rest. In this sense, the Immigration Commission of 1911 and today's Congress share the same concern.

Table 8.3 Changing United States Foreign-born Shares and Regional Growth by Decade, 1880–1910

Variable	Dependent variable: change in foreign-born share	
	Population	Labor Force
Constant	−0.01	−0.01
	(1.34)	(0.37)
Growth of population/labor force in		
New England	0.21	0.21
	(4.55)	(3.10)
Mid-Atlantic	0.15	0.13
	(3.57)	(2.27)
South Atlantic	0.08	0.04
	(2.34)	(1.12)
East north-central	0.04	−0.11
	(0.86)	(1.82)
West north-central	−0.04	−0.03
	(3.66)	(1.28)
East south-central	0.09	0.05
	(1.58)	(0.73)
West south-central	0.04	0.02
	(1.05)	(0.04)
Mountain	−0.03	−0.04
	(2.66)	(2.86)
Pacific	0.02	−0.03
	(1.59)	(1.85)
1890s dummy	−0.004	−0.01
	(0.82)	(1.09)
1900s dummy	−0.02	−0.02
	(3.53)	(2.63)
R^2	0.41	0.33
RSS	0.085	0.24
RESET	2.10	2.55
HETERO	1.55	6.06

Notes: See notes to table 8.2. Units of observation are 48 states observed over three decades, 1880–1990, 1890–1900, and 1900–1910.

What we have said about occupations need not, of course, apply to regions. Even though immigrants may not have flooded the fastest-growing industries, surely they flooded the fastest-growing regions. So, did immigrants move into the most rapidly expanding states, thus easing excess demand in local labor markets? This time we examine the proportion of foreign-born in the total population across states for the intercensal periods 1880–1890, 1890–1900, and 1900–1910. These data are pooled to produce the regression in the first column of table 8.3. The result shows that for three regions—New England, the mid-Atlantic, and the south Atlantic—states whose populations grew rapidly experienced a significant rise in foreign-born density. This reflects the well-known fact that immigrants moved to the cities in the most rapidly growing states on the eastern seaboard. By contrast, the more rapid was the growth of a state's population in the west north-central or in the mountain regions, the more the share of foreign-born (native-born) in the population fell (rose). They avoided most of the south. Thus, while immigrants moved disproportionately into the most rapidly growing centers on the East Coast, they did not do so elsewhere in the United States. Given that movers (whether native or foreign-born) have higher labor participation rates than stayers, these results should be even stronger for foreign-born labor force shares regressed on state labor force growth. Although the second column in table 8.3 fails to confirm that prediction, it *does* suggest that the Pacific and the east north-Central (with Chicago at its center) should join our characterization of the western states.

Were immigrants crowding out the natives in the fast-growing East Coast regions and pushing them west? Or did the westward movement of natives pull foreign immigrants into the East Coast?

Were Immigrants and Natives Substitutes? Was There Crowding Out?

A number of studies have examined the intended destinations of immigrants arriving in the United States at the turn of the century (Dunleavy and Gemery 1977, 1978; Dunleavy 1980, 1983; Dunleavy and Saba 1992) and have found that immigrants made consistent destination choices in response to a number of well-defined variables. They migrated toward states on the eastern seaboard (close to New York), toward those offering relatively high incomes, and toward those with high population densities. These studies also confirmed that the stock of previous emigrants from a given country and the lagged emigration rate both significantly influenced the current emigrant's decision: that is, there was strong historical persistence operating on the foreign-born location decision in the United States. The presumption, therefore, is that foreign-born destinations differed from those of the native-born. Mere inspection of the regional distributions of immigrants and natives suggests differences in their migration behavior within the United States, and more sophisticated studies support this view (Gallaway and Vedder 1971; Gallaway, Vedder, and Shukla 1974). A recent study of the intended destinations of Canadian immigrants in 1912 argued that immigrants systemmatically also selected destinations and sectors that offered the best use of their skills (Green and Green 1993). Insofar as their skills differed from those of natives, immigrant settlement patterns might be expected to differ from those of the native-born.

These studies certainly confirm that immigrants were guided to labor market destinations by economic opportunity, but they do not tell us whether immigrants displaced or crowded out natives in the occupations and regions they entered. There are, of course, crude but compelling correlations, the best example of which was offered almost a quarter of a century ago by Brinley Thomas (1972: 130–34 and ch. 18), who noted an inverse rhythm between southern black emigration to the north and foreign immigration over the long swing. The exit rate out of the south was high in the 1870s, high in the 1890s, high during World War I, and high after the quotas, all of which were years of low European immigration. Is this evidence of unskilled European immigrants crowding out unskilled (black, male, southern) Americans? Or is it evidence that during a slump, when unemployment was high in eastern cities and immigration low, things were even worse for southern agriculture, thus pushing farm labor north in spite of the high unemployment incidence there? Thomas's correlations do not necessarily imply crowding out until we have controlled for labor demand.

Some economists have recently addressed the same crowding-out issue for the 1970s and 1980s. Perhaps the most notable natural experiment was performed by Fidel Castro when the Mariel boatlift brought the 1980 influx of Cubans into Miami. David Card (1990) found that this influx of 45,000 Cubans, equivalent to 7 percent of the Miami labor force at that time, had almost no long-run effect on the overall size of the city's labor force or on the wages of competing groups of whites, blacks, and other Hispanics. This occurred "because of a change in the net migration of natives and older cohorts of immigrants rather than a change in the inflow rate of new immigrants" (Card 1990: 256). That is, employment and wages in the local Miami labor market were left unaffected since so many natives vacated the market, apparently one-for-one, and moved on to other United States cities. On a more general level, Randall Filer (1992) examined native-born migration patterns for 272 geographical areas in 1975–1980. After controlling for local labor market characteristics, he found that an influx of foreign-born to an area crowded out native workers about one-for-one, a striking vindication of the crowding-out hypothesis.[6] Other studies suggest that the same results might not hold for different periods (Butcher and Card 1991), including, we suppose, the late-nineteenth-century free migration period.

It all depends on how well labor markets were linked between cities. Perhaps a truly well-integrated national labor market was absent then (Rosenbloom 1990, 1996; Sundstrom and Rosenbloom 1993). Perhaps, but even so there was that enormous and continuing westward movement that was so much a part of United States internal migrations at that time. Census evidence testifies to the large-scale migration of the native-born. While 13.7 percent of the United States population in 1900 was foreign-born, a larger share, 17.7 percent, was interstate migrants (not living in their state of birth: Hill 1906: 279). Net migration of the native-born was dominated by the movement toward the west north-central, mountain, and Pacific states. Thus, while 42.6 percent of the residents of western divisions were migrants from other divisions, only 4 percent of the north Atlantic residents were. While some foreign immigrants went west upon arrival or subsequently (Ferrie 1992), the westward movement largely involved natives. Immigrants tended to concentrate in the urban northeast.[7]

Was therefore some proportion of the northeastern native-born crowded out (pushed west) by the mass immigration from Europe? Intercensal estimates of net migration of native-born and foreign-born have been offered by Hope Eldridge and Dorothy Thomas using the method of cohort depletion. The resulting migration patterns "produced a sort of 'dovetailing' of native migration losses with

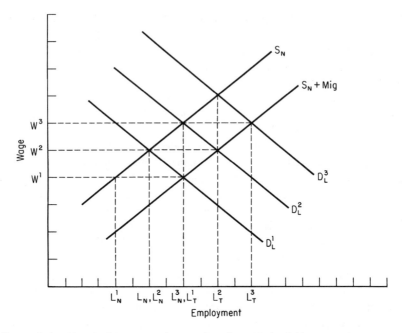

Figure 8.4 Did United States Immigrants Crowd out Natives? (three cases)

foreign-born migration gains in the industrial sections of the Northeast and the North Central, especially in the decades before World War I" (1964: 65). Table 8.4, based on their figures, documents net migration of native-born and foreign-born both divided by the regional native-born population. But before we examine the table, consider the three possibilities offered in figure 8.4. Native-born labor supply (S_N) to a given region slopes upward to reflect migration across borders, exogenous foreign immigration is added to give total labor supply (S_N + Mig), and the three cases of regional labor demand (D_L) are stagnant, modest boom, and big boom. In case 1, stagnant regional labor demand ensures massive native-born crowding out (L_N retreats to the left to L_N^1, reflecting native out-migration to another region); in case 2, modest regional labor demand results in no crowding out at all (L_N remains the same in the presence of the new immigrants, and there is no native out-migration); and in case 3, regional labor demand dominates so that native-born are crowded in (L_N moves to the right to L_N^3, reflecting native in-migration) even though immigrants have flooded the region.

Figure 8.4 has an obvious moral: we have to control for regional labor demand. Thus, the crude correlations suggested by table 8.4 may or may not tell us much about crowding out. Nonetheless, the table illustrates that the small and somewhat intermittent net out-migration of natives from New England, the mid-Atlantic, and the east north-central was accompanied by high rates of net foreign-born in-migration. Although native out-migration was modest, it must be remembered that

Table 8.4 United States Native Net Internal Migration and Immigration (average per 1,000 per year)

Region	Rate of native immigration			Rate of foreign-born immigration		
	1880s	1890s	1900s	1880s	1890s	1900s
New England	−1.27	−1.50	−1.60	14.16	12.98	14.07
Mid-Atlantic	−1.92	1.42	−0.05	11.95	9.97	16.09
South Atlantic	−2.98	−2.99	−2.40	0.85	0.57	1.17
East north-central	−5.16	0.36	−3.40	9.43	5.26	7.21
West north-central	8.14	−5.46	−5.99	11.48	3.55	4.46
East south-central	−6.26	−4.31	−7.11	0.42	0.17	0.28
West south-central	6.60	7.31	7.62	1.87	1.70	1.89
Mountain	32.04	14.06	24.79	17.96	7.59	11.66
Pacific	32.79	14.00	38.78	20.83	7.69	19.37

Source: Calculated from Eldridge and Thomas (1964), tables A1.11, A1.12, and A1.14. Migration rates are per 1,000 of the average native-born population per decade.

very rapid industrial growth was taking place in the northeast between 1880 and 1910 (Wright 1990). Strong labor demand crowding in and foreign-born immigrant crowding out were both at work in this case (case 2 in figure 8.4). The old south exhibits higher rates of native out-migration and very small foreign-born in-migration. Weak labor demand was the primary force at work in this case (case 1 in figure 8.4). The pull of the west is clearly seen in the large rates of in-migration to the mountain and Pacific regions and, to a lesser extent, the west south-central. In this case, very strong labor demand was the primary force at work (case 3 in figure 8.4). Thus, the evidence in table 8.4 cannot be used to test for immigrant crowding out without controlling for labor demand, even in the east.[8]

What follows is an effort to control for labor demand and to focus on the region where crowding out was likely to have mattered most—the northeast. We explain the net in-migration rate of natives to the 14 states comprising New England, the mid-Atlantic and the east north-central across the three intercensal periods, yielding a panel dataset consisting of 42 observations. Native migration is explained by wages and other structural characteristics such as the manufacturing employment share, the urban population share, and the share of the population aged 15–24, all at the beginning of the decade. To test the displacement hypothesis, the net in-migration of foreign-born as a proportion of the native population is included. We also include total employment growth as a proxy for bouyant labor demand.

Table 8.5 reports ordinary least squares (OLS) and instrumental variables (IV) regressions. The OLS results in the first column of the table confirms immigrant crowding out, and the other significant variables in the regression are employment growth, the manufacturing labor force share, and the 1890s dummy (the 1890s being a poor growth decade compared with the ones preceding and following). However, neither immigrant influx nor employment growth can be viewed as

Table 8.5 Displacement of Natives by Immigrants, United States Northeast, 1880–1910 (dependent variable: native net in-migration rate)

Variable	1 OLS	2 IV
Constant	−0.18	−0.11
	(0.74)	(0.41)
Foreign-born in-migration	−0.22	−0.40
	(1.88)	(2.55)
Employment growth	0.38	0.44
	(5.78)	(5.24)
Share of labor force in manufacturing	0.18	0.16
	(2.26)	(1.93)
Share of population urban	0.03	0.07
	(0.60)	(1.27)
Share of population aged 15–24	−0.01	−0.01
	(1.10)	(1.45)
Log real manufacturing earnings	0.02	0.01
	(0.50)	(0.30)
1880s dummy	−0.02	−0.01
	(1.20)	(1.01)
1890s dummy	0.04	0.04
	(3.96)	(3.99)
R^2	0.85	0.84
RSS	0.011	0.012
RESET	2.44	3.84
HETERO	0.04	0.08

Notes: See notes to table 8.2. In the instrumental variable regression, foreign born in-migration and employment growth are treated as endogenous. The instruments used are the proportion of the population foreign-born and the proportion living in cities with a population greater than 100,000 (both measured at the beginning of the decade), the growth in the value of gross manufacturing output between manufacturing census years (1879–1889, 1889–1899, 1899–1909), and dummies for New England and the mid-Atlantic states. OLS = ordinary least squares. IV = instrumental variables, Column numbers refer to different regression equations.

exogenous since both should have been influenced by native migration, as figure 8.4 has already suggested. Hence, we must instrument these two variables. The instruments used are the proportion of the population foreign-born and the proportion living in cities with a population of 100,000 or more, both measured at the beginning of the decade. Since these variables are evidently important determinants of the immigrant inflow, they ought to be good instruments for the in-migration of foreign-born, though not necessarily for demand growth. Our instrument for demand growth is the decade growth in the value of gross manufacturing output. The second column of table 8.5 reports a much more powerful foreign-born crowding-out effect and the level of statistical significance has risen as well. It suggests that an additional 100 foreign-born in-migrants to these northeastern states increased native-born out-migration by 40. While this is not quite the one-for-one Filer found for late-twentieth-century America or that Card found for Miami in 1980, it is substantial crowding out nonetheless.

The net westward movement in search of better economic opportunities brought with it a convergence of regional wage rates (Easterlin 1960; Williamson 1965, 1980; Rosenbloom 1990, 1996; Barro and Sala-i-Martin 1991), although the south was not part of the process (Wright 1986). Fewer immigrants arriving on the East Coast would have led to less competition in eastern cities, bigger wage increases there, and a slower westward movement of population (both native-born and foreign-born). It also would have led to bigger wage increases in the west, but perhaps not so much bigger as back east.

The Immigration Commission lamented the concentration of immigrants in the cities and their unwillingness to enter agriculture even though so many of them came from rural backgrounds. But this is hardly surprising given that real wages in agriculture were lower than those in unskilled urban occupations.[9] If more immigrants had entered agriculture, the urban-rural wage gap would have increased and more rural native-born Americans would have migrated to the cities. This is not simply speculation; our own recent analysis of rural-urban migration and wage gaps (Hatton and Williamson 1992) has shown that if immigrant entry into urban labor markets led to higher unemployment or lower real wages there, then this in turn slowed the rate of rural-urban migration and kept the rural wage lower than otherwise. Similarly, in the absence of the immigrant inflow to the industrial north, blacks would have moved up from the south in greater numbers in the late nineteenth century as they ultimately did during World War I and after the imposition of the immigration quotas in the early 1920s (Thomas 1972: 130–34; Collins 1997).

The Impact of Immigration on Wages: Looking at Cross Sections

The key immigrant absorption question, however, has always been this: what effect did current immigration have on the wage rates of natives and those of past immigrants? Although the preceding sections have something to say about the way immigrants were absorbed in the late-nineteenth-century American economy, we, like the Immigrant Commission before us, have failed so far to confront this key question. It is time to do so.

The evidence surveyed above argues that, for a given occupation and region, immigrants received roughly the same wages as natives. The Immigration Commissioners would have agreed: their report firmly stated that it was unusual for employers to engage immigrants at wages lower than those prevailing in the industry and occupation to which they were recruited. In modern terminology, the Commission observed little evidence of labor market segmentation between immigrants and natives. Cliometric analysis concurs. But were immigrants (less skilled labor) complements or substitutes for natives (more skilled labor) in production? If they were complements, then immigration could have raised the productivity and hence the wages of the more skilled native workers. James Foreman-Peck (1992) recently estimated a translog production function for United States manufacturing in 1890, treating immigrant and native labor as separate factors of production. His results showed that these two types of labor were not complements: bigger immigrant labor supplies did not increase the marginal product of native labor.[10]

These results, generated by different methods and sources, suggest that immigration lowered wages in American labor markets (or lowered the increase in workers' wages there), a view strongly held by the Immigration Commission but derided by critics such as Hourwich. According to the Commission, immigrant labor supply "has undoubtedly had the effect of preventing an increase of wages to the extent which would have been necessary had the expansion of local industries occurred without the availability of the southern and eastern Europeans" (1911, Vol. 8: 440; see also Jenks and Lauck 1926: 206–07). As Hourwich pointed out, the same should apply to all immigrants, and not just the southern and eastern European immigrants. But he rejected the idea implicit in such counterfactual statements, preferring instead to emphasize that substantial gains in real wages had in fact taken place since the 1880s and to infer from this that immigration had not retarded the growth of wages (1922: 295–307). However, comparing real wage growth in the period from the 1890s to 1914 with that in the 1920s has led such authorities as Paul Douglas (1930: 564) and Stanley Lebergott (1964: 163) to conclude that mass immigration slowed the rate of growth of real wages in the earlier period.[11]

We have already noted that economists have generated a sizeable literature dealing with the effects of the immigration of the 1970s and 1980s. One of the largest estimated effects of modern United States immigration on native wage rates comes from a recent study by Joseph Altonji and Card (1991), who examined the effects of changes in the share of immigrants across SMSAs between 1970 and 1980 on low-skilled natives' wages. They found that a 1 percentage point increase in the share of foreign-born lowered the wage of low-skilled natives by between 0.3 and 1.2 percent. Such effects are somewhat smaller than, but consistent with, late-nineteenth-century assessments. However, the Altonji and Card study appears to be the exception to the rule since several influential surveys concluded just the opposite, that the impact of immigration on wage rates in the post–World War II period has been tiny (Greenwood and McDowell 1986, 1994; Simon 1989: ch. 12; Borjas 1990, 1994). The studies cited in these surveys and elsewhere have often tried to infer the effects of immigration by looking across local labor markets within the United States.

In a recent historical study, Claudia Goldin (1994) estimated the impact of immigration on wage changes across cities between 1890 and 1915. She found that a 1 percentage point increase in the foreign-born population share reduced unskilled wage rates by about 1 to 1.5 percent. Furthermore, her results also apply to artisans and to different industry groups. Her objective, however, was to identify local relative wage impacts rather than to infer the economy-wide effect of immigration. She associates these local wage effects with voting behavior in the House

of Representatives to override the presidential veto on the introduction of a literacy test in 1915 (Goldin 1994: 254).

Local labor market studies almost certainly understate (or miss entirely) the
economy-wide impact of immigration on wages. After all, immigration will only
lower wages in a local labor market insofar as it increases the total supply of labor.
If instead there is completely offsetting native emigration, as seen in the study of
Filer cited before, then a rise in the immigrant share is consistent with no change
in the size of the local labor force and no wage effect of immigration *compared with
other local labor markets in which natives relocate.* But wages should fall (perhaps
equally, perhaps not) in all locations. These effects are not measured by the local
labor market studies if local labor markets are well connected.[12] Even if there was
no correlation between the inward movement of immigrants and the migration
patterns of natives, the latter would probably obscure the total labor force impact
of immigration.[13] Our own state-level evidence for the northeast presented in table
8.5 indicates a powerful crowding-out effect but that it was not complete and thus
an immigrant influx to a given state typically did increase the total state labor
supply but by less than the influx.

The Impact of Immigration on Wages: Looking at Time Series

One way to examine directly the impact of immigration on the real wage is to estimate the wage adjustment mechanism from time series.[14] By altering labor supply
and unemployment in the short run, immigration should drive down the wage
along a long-run Phillips curve. The wage adjustment mechanism we favor is the
standard Phillips curve that follows:

[8.1]
$$\Delta \log(W)_t = \alpha_0 + \alpha_1 \Delta \log(P)_t + \alpha_2 \log\left(\frac{E}{L}\right)_t$$

where W is the nominal wage, P is the price level (cost of living), E is employment,
L is the civilian labor force, and both α_1 and α_2 are expected to be positive. Labor's
marginal product condition (assuming a CES production function) implies:

[8.2]
$$\log(E)_t = \beta_0 + \beta_1 \log\left(\frac{W}{P}\right)_t + \log(Q)_t + \beta_2 t$$

where Q is real output and t is a time trend to capture technical change. We expect
β_1 to be negative, and in the special Cobb-Douglas case it should equal −1.
Substituting equation 8.2 into 8.1 and rearranging gives:

[8.3]
$$\Delta \log\left(\frac{W}{P}\right)_t = \frac{\alpha_0 + \alpha_2 \beta_0}{1 - \alpha_2 \beta_1} + \frac{\alpha_1 - 1}{1 - \alpha_2 \beta_1} \Delta \log(P)_t + \frac{\alpha_2}{1 - \alpha_2 \beta_1} \log\left(\frac{Q}{L}\right)_t$$
$$+ \frac{\alpha_2 \beta_1}{1 - \alpha_2 \beta_1} \log\left(\frac{W}{P}\right)_{t-1} + \frac{\alpha_2 \beta_2}{1 - \alpha_2 \beta_1} t$$

This model is consistent with many empirical Phillips curve formulations although it includes a term for output relative to the labor force, rather than simply detrended output (or the "output gap") and it includes the lagged real wage level (the error correction term).[15] This formulation clearly produces an inverse relationship between the real wage and the total labor force (holding output constant). In long-run steady state, where wages and prices are constant, the equation can be written:

[8.4]
$$\log\left(\frac{W}{P}\right) = -\frac{\alpha_0 + \alpha_2\beta_0}{\alpha_2\beta_1} - \frac{1}{\beta_1}\log\left(\frac{Q}{L}\right) - \frac{\beta_2}{\beta_1}t$$

An increase in the labor force due to immigration would cause the wage to fall until the "natural" rate of unemployment was restored.

This model has been estimated on annual observations for 1890 to 1913, using the immigrant-adjusted labor force estimates reported in the appendix. The real wage and price indices are from Williamson (1995) and real GNP is from Romer (1989). The first equation in table 8.6 offers strong support for the model with all coefficients significant. The price change coefficient is negative, a plausible result consistent with incomplete short-run adjustment of nominal wage to price change, and the output/labor coefficient is positive, also consistent with theory. The lagged real wage coefficient is negative, results again consistent with theory.[16]

When the output and labor force terms are entered separately in the second equation, the coefficients are predictable—of opposite sign and almost equal in magnitude, but the labor force has a low level of significance because of its collinearity with the time trend, which also loses significance. When the time trend is eliminated in equation 3, the labor force term also becomes strongly significant. Finally, equation 4 imposes the restriction that output/labor and the lagged real wage take on equal coefficients with opposite signs, consistent with a Cobb-Douglas world. This restricton cannot be rejected against either equation 1 or equation 2.[17]

The long-run solution to these equations suggests that, holding output constant, an increase in the labor force by 1 percent would lower the real wage by from 1 percent (table 8.6: equation 4) to 1.25 percent (table 8.6: equation 1), other things constant. But other things were not constant because a larger immigrant-augmented labor force would have caused output to expand as well. Under perfect competition and CES assumptions, the long-run impact of labor force growth on output is simply the labor share multiplied by labor force growth. Adding this endogenous output response, and taking labor's share to be 0.6 (Taylor and Williamson 1997), implies that a 1 percent rise in the labor force due to immigration would have reduced the real wage in the long run by 0.4 percent (table 8.5: equation 4) or 0.5 percent (table 8.6: equation 1). Based on the stock of foreign-born and their children enumerated in the 1910 Census (see chapter 10), immigration after 1890 accounted for 11.8 percent of the 1910 labor force and immigration after 1870 accounted for 27.3 percent of the 1910 labor force.[18] These

Table 8.6 Wage Adjustment Equations, United States
1890–1913 (dependent variable: $\Delta\log(W/P)$)

Variable	Equation			
	1	2	3	4
Constant	5.31	4.55	6.47	5.33
	(4.71)	(1.04)	(4.49)	(4.29)
$\Delta\log P_t$	−0.53	−0.53	−0.53	−0.45
	(2.38)	(2.30)	(2.34)	(2.56)
$\log(Q/L)_t$	0.60			
	(4.11)			
$\log Q_t$		0.61	0.57	
		(3.83)	(4.16)	
$\log L_t$		−0.52	−0.71	
		(1.12)	(3.43)	
$\log(W/P)_{t-1}$	−0.49	−0.50	−0.47	
	(3.21)	(2.80)	(2.93)	
$\log(Q/L)_t - \log(W/P)_{t-1}$				0.55
				(4.82)
Time	−0.003	−0.006		−0.002
	(1.69)	(0.46)		(3.51)
R^2	0.56	0.57	0.56	0.56
RSS	0.004	0.004	0.004	0.004
DW	1.93	1.90	1.96	1.78
LM(1)	0.001	0.02	0.01	0.27
RESET	0.13	0.06	0.26	0.001

Note: See notes to table 8.1.

magnitudes suggest that the real wage would have been 4.7–5.9 percent higher in the absence of immigration after 1890, and 10.9–13.7 percent higher in the absence of immigration after 1870.[19]

Conclusions

The measured impact of mass migration on late-nineteenth-century America sheds light on several important debates. Migration's ebb and flow did little to ease the wide swing in unemployment associated with business cycles and industrial crises. Immigration was simply not the effective guestworker safety valve contemporary observers often imagine. Nor did immigrants fill excess labor demand gaps in a way that eased the labor market disequilibria created by a spectacular industrialization performance that was the envy of the world. Instead, immigrants filled less skilled niches in slower-growing activities while natives filled more skilled niches in faster-growing activities. Not only did immigrants compete with those natives (and previous immigrants) left behind in unskilled jobs, but their concentration in the urban northeast caused a geographic displacement of native northeastern workers to the west. Presumably, it also helped postpone the Great Black Migration from the rural south until war and quotas removed much of the unskilled European competition in northern labor markets.

Given that immigrants displaced natives in local labor markets, it follows that macroeconomic analysis should be preferred to local labor market analysis when assessing the impact of immigration on wages. Local labor market studies typically conclude that late-twentieth-century immigration has had a trivial impact on American wages and living standards. In contrast, this chapter concludes that immigration in the late nineteenth century had an important impact on real unskilled wages—just as the Immigration Commission argued.

But these partial equilibrium estimates may overstate the case. After all, they make no allowance for output shifts induced by immigration's impact on relative endowments. Nor do they allow capital to chase labor across the Atlantic, muting the decline in the capital-labor ratio implied by immigration alone. The best way to accommodate such complications—all of which served to ease the impact of immigration on American labor markets—is to evaluate the effects in general equilibrium. The next two chapters will do just that by exploiting CGE models for both source and destination countries.

Appendix. Revised Estimates for United States Net Worker Immigration, 1870–1913, and the Civilian Labor Force, 1890–1913

Net Worker Immigration, 1870–1913

To determine the impact of immigration on the labor force, we need an annual series describing net immigration of working age immigrants. The series for gross immigration are well-known; not until 1908 did the Immigration and Naturalization Service begin to collect data on gross emigration. There is, however, information on steerage passenger movements to and from the United States. The various biases in these statistics have been discussed many times by Jerome (1926), Davis (1931), Thompson and Whelpton (1933), Kuznets and Rubin (1954), Thomas (1954), and others. Their main drawbacks are that they understate true gross flows, exclude some nonsteerage passengers, and ignore movements across the land borders (especially with Canada). The most widely accepted estimates of the net movement of aliens are those offered by Kuznets and Rubin (1954: 95–96), who applied a series of adjustments to the raw data.

We base our 1870–1913 estimates on the Kuznets and Rubin net arrivals, applying to it estimates of immigrant composition to emerge with annual estimates of net immigration by age and gender. Finally, we convert each age-gender net population flow into labor force or worker equivalents. The first step uses the decade estimates of age- and gender-specific net migration that Lee et al. (1957) constructed for foreign-born and native-born whites using forward census survival techniques. These estimates are used to allocate the Kuznets and Rubin net arrival totals into

Table A.1 Net Immigration Estimates: Totals and
Equivalent Workers, 1870–1913 (000's)

Year	Total	Equivalent workers	Year	Total	Equivalent workers
1870	365.6	184.1	1892	480.1	244.1
1871	300.0	151.2	1893	380.9	193.7
1872	378.9	190.7	1894	137.2	69.8
1873	401.7	202.3	1895	94.8	48.2
1874	245.1	123.4	1896	204.7	104.0
1875	132.8	66.8	1897	105.0	53.4
1876	100.2	50.5	1898	121.0	61.5
1877	71.0	35.9	1899	201.0	102.2
1878	89.2	44.9	1900	385.1	223.5
1879	132.0	66.4	1901	287.9	167.1
1880	423.4	219.6	1902	386.2	224.1
1881	644.7	334.3	1903	532.1	308.9
1882	751.7	389.8	1904	530.0	307.7
1883	578.7	300.1	1905	662.4	384.6
1884	473.7	245.7	1906	697.5	404.9
1885	283.7	147.2	1907	767.2	445.5
1886	250.0	129.6	1908	210.1	122.0
1887	415.8	215.6	1909	544.0	315.9
1888	437.9	227.0	1910	818.5	391.7
1889	314.7	163.2	1911	512.1	245.1
1890	328.0	166.9	1912	402.2	192.4
1891	426.2	216.7	1913	815.2	390.0

age-gender groups (five-year intervals, e.g., 15–19, 20–24, etc.). The decade age-gender composition is applied to every year within that decade, and we assume that the age and gender distribution of white migrants applied to the much smaller flow of nonwhites as well. This procedure yields annual net immigration for each age-gender category. Finally, we apply the labor force participation rates from the 1890 Census to these age- and gender-specific series (by the same five-year age intervals, e.g., 15–19, 20–24, etc.) to derive the labor force or equivalent-worker content of net immigration. The data are reported in table A.1 for total immigrants and equivalent workers for 1870 to 1913.

Labor Force Estimates, 1890–1913

The debate surrounding Stanley Lebergott's (1964) unemployment estimates for 1890–1913 focused on the numerator, number unemployed, but it also generated some discussion about the denominator, the civilian labor force. Christina Romer (1986a, 1986b) and David Weir (1986, 1992) have both offered adjustments, particularly for the 1890s.[20] Lebergott himself made some allowance for the effect of

Table A.2 Alternative United States Labor Force Estimates, 1890–1914 (000's)

Year	Total labor force (Weir)	Adjusted total labor force	Adjusted nonfarm labor force	Counterfactual total labor force	Counterfactual nonfarm labor force	Total employment (Weir)
1890	22,772	22,682	12,391	22,736	12,445	21,868
1891	23,382	23,283	12,916	23,341	12,974	22,332
1892	24,038	23,930	13,487	23,965	13,522	23,003
1893	24,649	24,559	14,040	24,621	14,102	22,981
1894	25,168	25,060	14,465	25,274	14,679	22,834
1895	25,679	25,568	14,897	25,955	15,284	23,501
1896	26,220	26,129	15,383	26,632	15,886	23,788
1897	26,712	26,634	15,812	27,305	16,483	24,439
1898	27,209	27,140	16,243	27,971	17,073	25,090
1899	27,753	27,678	16,704	28,627	17,653	26,130
1900	28,374	28,345	17,295	29,291	18,241	26,956
1901	29,153	29,174	18,258	30,175	19,259	27,947
1902	29,904	29,916	19,163	30,913	20,160	28,874
1903	30,698	30,723	19,854	31,632	20,763	29,616
1904	31,441	31,548	20,472	32,370	21,294	29,894
1905	32,299	32,388	21,201	33,047	21,860	31,042
1906	33,212	33,248	21,769	33,723	22,244	32,398
1907	34,183	34,173	22,680	34,423	22,930	33,135
1908	34,916	34,944	23,706	35,293	24,055	32,310
1909	35,721	35,839	24,676	36,093	24,930	33,704
1910	36,709	36,831	25,571	36,914	25,654	34,559
1911	37,478	37,601	26,494	37,661	26,554	34,845
1912	37,932	37,987	26,851	38,076	26,940	35,708
1913	38,675	38,686	27,712	38,686	27,712	36,454

fluctuations in net immigration for the 1900s, and Weir did the same for the 1890s. Rather than rely on their adjustments for the annual contribution of immigration, we made our own. We therefore removed the immigration adjustments from the Weir-Lebergott series and added back in our own series from table A.1 (equivalent workers) to adjust for the contribution of net immigration.

The resulting figures used to derive the unemployment rates in figures 8.2 and 8.3 are given in table A.2. The total labor force is taken from Weir, and the adjusted total labor force reflects our effort to adjust for the contribution of net immigration, as already explained. The adjusted nonfarm labor force is constructed by applying Weir's nonfarm labor force shares (Weir 1992: appendix D, 336–44) to our adjusted total labor force series.

The counterfactual total labor force is derived by computing the average annual net (worker equivalent) immigration for the whole 1890–1913 period, and then applying that average to every year. The counterfactual nonfarm labor force is calculated similarly. These are called the no guestworker counterfactuals in the text since they do not allow the immigrants to respond to U.S. business cycles and long swings. Given the total and nonfarm employment figures in table A.2, it is a simple matter to calculate the actual and counterfactual unemployment rates cited in the text and plotted in figures 8.2 and 8.3. The nonfarm unemployment rate, actual and counterfactual, assumes that all the immigrants went to nonfarm occupations (an assumption only weakly violated by the end of the century) and that there was no overt unemployment in agriculture.

Labor Market Impact at Home
Ireland and Sweden

A Solution to Problems at Home?

Late-nineteenth-century emigration generated no shortage of political debate and moral judgment.[1] Some feared that these emigrations drained the home country of the best and the brightest, jeopardizing the future. Post-famine Irish commentators, for example, viewed the emigrant flood as the result of Ireland's failure to industrialize and thus its inability to create enough good jobs (Ó Gráda 1994: ch. 13). But some saw the flood in even more negative terms, as one more *cause* of industrial failure because they thought the best was being creamed off the top of the labor force. Some even argued that Ireland failed to industrialize because its home market for industrial goods was too small; once too small, scale economies were hard to achieve, Irish manufacturing lost its competitive edge, and industrial job creation faltered; emigrants fled the stagnant Irish labor market; and the market got even smaller. Such commentary would imply that a dismal path-dependent historical process was at work that ensured Irish industrial failure (Ó Gráda 1994: 342–47).

On the other hand, though there was industrial failure, after the famine Ireland *did* undergo an impressive catch-up on both Britain and America. Economics as old as Adam Smith can explain why: emigration made labor more scarce in Ireland, thus raising real wages and living standards at home even compared with conditions overseas where immigration made labor more abundant. This kind of Smithian economics exploits diminishing returns: given land, capital, technology, and resources, more labor means lower labor productivity, real wages, and living standards; less labor means higher labor productivity, real wages, and living standards. While the movers may have been able to escape to higher wages abroad, the now scarcer stayers found conditions improving at home. Thus, Arnold Schrier firmly concluded:

there can be little doubt that the over-all impact of emigration on the Irish economy was generally favorable. To some extent it relieved the pressure of unemployment and improved the condition of the laborers and tenantry by raising wages and leading to better living accommodations for a larger portion of the population. It also facilitated the consolidation of small holdings and helped place agriculture on a more economic basis. . . . Whether in itself it appreciably retarded the development of Irish industry is doubtful. (1958: 82)

Swedish commentators also viewed emigration as a sign of failure: surely, they seemed to be saying, it is a poor economy that cannot generate enough good jobs to keep our young Swedes at home. The Swedes left in especially large numbers in the 1880s, when the debate became most intense. And this happened even though Sweden in particular, and Scandinavia in general, was in the midst of the most impressive European catch-up by far that, in contrast with Ireland, seemed to be carried by vigorous industrialization (Williamson 1994; O'Rourke and Williamson 1995; 1996; 1997). In 1882, Knut Wicksell, a young neo-Malthusian theorist, wrote a popular essay that argued the Smithian case: emigration would eventually solve the pauper problem which blighted labor-abundant and land-scarce Swedish agriculture and thus was a good thing, to be tolerated, perhaps even stimulated (Wicksell 1882, cited in Karlstrom 1985: 155).

What *was* the impact of mass emigration on the home country? The literature is loud on assertion but quiet on evidence, even though more than a century has passed since Wicksell's essay appeared. This chapter offers some evidence for Ireland and Sweden. Chapter 10 augments the evidence to include all emigrating and all immigrating countries in the greater Atlantic economy so that the impact of mass migration on late-nineteenth-century convergence can be assessed more generally. But first let's look at labor markets at home for two major emigrating countries. We begin where the mass migrations started, with Ireland.

Irish Wages and the Labor Market, 1850–1914

Estimates of Irish national income for the late nineteenth century are sketchy, but Cormac Ó Gráda (1994: 242, 379) uses what we have to suggest that Irish national income grew at about 0.7 percent per annum between 1845 and 1913. Per capita income grew more than twice as fast, 1.6 percent per annum. That is not a typographical error: per capita income grew much faster than did total income because the Irish population fell over the period. Per capita income growth is somewhat slower if we skip over the famine, say about 1.29 percent per annum. Irish income per capita rose from about two fifths to about three fifths that of Britain. Furthermore, the share in poverty declined and the families living in low-quality housing (third- and fourth-class) dropped from 63 percent in 1861 to 29 percent 50 years later.[2]

Although GNP per capita and other indicators of well-being suggest significant improvement, it can also be documented by real wages, information more directly relevant in describing the labor market conditions that were driving emigrants abroad and in describing the market that had to adjust most to their departure.

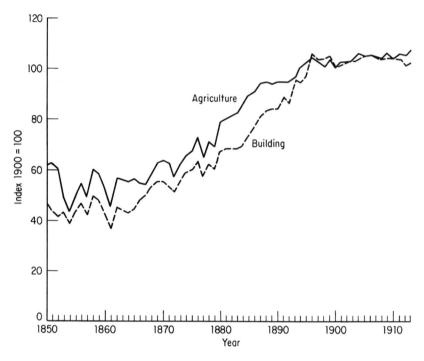

Figure 9.1 Irish Real Wage Rates: Rural and Urban Laborers

Figure 9.1 plots the real wage for Irish building laborers used in chapter 5 as an index of labor market conditions and, in addition, an index of the real wage for agricultural laborers.[3] Two features stand out. First, the two indices move quite closely together over the whole period, confirming the representativeness of the series for building laborers alone. This comparison suggests that the market for unskilled labor was relatively well integrated within Ireland.[4] The second feature is the substantial real wage growth that these series exhibit. Between 1855 and 1913 real wages for these laborers more than doubled, building laborers' wage growing by nearly 1.5 percent per annum and agricultural laborers' by more than 1.3 percent per annum. These rates of growth are highly consistent with the available evidence on the growth of national income per capita. Third, most of the growth is concentrated in the period between 1860 and 1895; indeed, both real wages more than doubled in this period alone, growing at 2.4 percent annually for building laborers and 1.9 percent for agricultural laborers.

We can compare the trends in Irish real wages with those in the major receiving countries, Britain and the United States, using the same purchasing power parity adjusted wage rates as in chapter 5. Figure 9.2 plots the ratios for building laborers (the same series as in figure 5.2 but inverted). As we noted earlier, these ratios exhibit significant Irish real wage catch-up with those in the main overseas destinations. Irish building wages rose from about 60 percent of British in the early

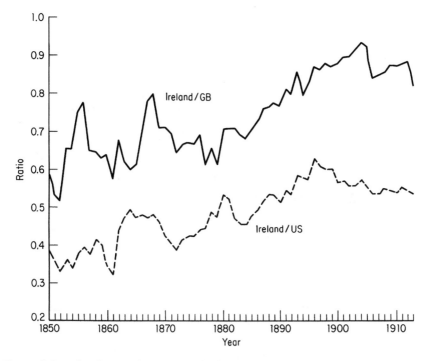

Figure 9.2 Irish Relative Urban Wage: Ireland/Great Britain and United States

1850s to about 85 percent after the turn of the century, while over the same period they rose from about 35 percent to about 55 percent of American. The Irish catch-up ceased after the turn of the century, Irish wages actually falling relative to American.

This Irish convergence was part of the more comprehensive trend in the greater Atlantic economy (Williamson 1994), although it was attenuated towards the end of the period when America leapt to industrial leadership (Wright 1990). Given that Ireland did not industrialize rapidly during the period, and given that the Irish population declined, it is tempting to conclude that the labor force contraction was the main source of the convergence. This appeal to Smithian diminishing returns—or an easing of pressure on the land—is certainly consistent with the relative rise in Irish wages and a decline in the rural labor surplus.

Most of the decline in Irish population and labor force from the Great Famine to the Great War took place in rural areas and on the farm. Between 1851 and 1913 the rural population fell by over 2.6 million, almost halving its level! Meanwhile, the population living in towns and cities rose by about a half million, so that the share living in urban areas more than doubled, jumping from 12 to 29 percent. In fact, only two of the 32 Irish counties experienced a population increase over the six decades. These were County Dublin and County Antrim, including Dublin and Belfast, the latter accounting for about half of the urban population growth by itself.

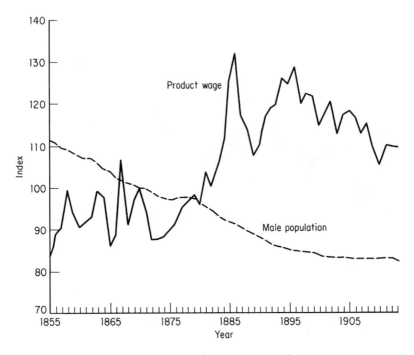

Figure 9.3 Farm Real Wage and Male Population (1870 = 100)

Reflecting the slow rate of industrialization, the proportion of occupied men engaged in farming fell only gradually over the period, from 66.3 to 54.7 percent (Fitzpatrick 1980b: 87). Predictably, the ratio of farm workers to farmers contracted sharply, from 2.3 to 1.3: farm laborers were becoming an increasingly small minority of the farm work force while smallholdings were on the rise. True, the line between farm laborer and farmer was blurred. Many farm families, particularly on smallholdings, combined work on their own farm with hiring out as wage labor. But this implies that farm wage should accurately reflect the opportunity cost of labor, even where little wage labor was directly employed.

Figure 9.3 plots the weekly farm wage, this time divided by an index of farm output price.[5] The resulting product wage rose considerably over the period. The striking upward drift in the farm product wage could have resulted from a sustained upward shift in the marginal product of labor schedule associated with improved farming techniques and more capital per acre, or it could have resulted from a movement along some stable marginal productivity schedule as the labor force declined. We do not have good information on the former, but we plot the decline in the total male population, from 2.95 to 2.17 million over the period.[6] The inverse trends in figure 9.3 certainly encourage the view that we are observing an easing of diminishing returns; that is, we are observing the result of movements back up the labor productivity schedule as farm labor inputs shrank. However, that

Table 9.1 Time-Series Equations for the Irish Agricultural
Product Wage: Ireland, 1866–1913 (dependent variable: log
product wage)

	1	2
Constant	11.65	11.06
	(2.15)	(2.20)
Log male population (t)	−1.45	−1.41
	(2.20)	(2.21)
Log agricultural production (t)	−0.05	—
	(0.30)	—
Log product wage (t-1)	0.56	0.58
	(3.95)	(4.47)
Time	−0.005	−0.005
	(1.76)	(1.85)
R^2	0.80	0.80
RSS	0.12	0.12
DW	1.96	1.95
LM (1)	0.06	0.10

Note: t statistics in parentheses. LM(1) is the Lagrange Multiplier test for
serial correlation, distributed as chi-squared (1), critical value = 3.84

schedule must also have shifted up, to the extent that Irish agriculture underwent substantial improvement. Did it? The most notable change was the pronounced shift in the composition of output away from relatively labor-intensive arable production towards land-intensive livestock activities (Crotty 1966; Ó Gráda 1988). If this was an agricultural event that took place independent of labor's rising cost, it may have been sufficiently labor-saving to have *lowered* the labor productivity schedule. But was the shift really independent of rising labor costs? Apparently not. Using a multisector computable general equilibrium model, Kevin O'Rourke (1991) has shown that almost all of the decline in tillage between 1856 and 1876 was due to the increasing scarcity of labor and the rise in the real product wage. More evidence for movements along that labor productivity schedule, it seems, but certainly no evidence for upward shifts in the schedule. Towards the end of the period, Irish farming also saw the introduction of threshers and tractors, although these capital-intensive innovations were surely the result of the need to save on increasingly expensive labor, and thus still more evidence for movements along the schedule. Still, a number of agricultural historians have shown that there was *some* improvement in agricultural techniques independent of labor's rising cost, but it seems unlikely to have been very much.[7]

So, to what extent can the rising product wage be attributed to a declining farm labor force? As a first step, we estimate the relation between the real farm wage and the total male population. The explanatory variables are the total male population, an index of farm output, and the lagged product wage. It simply represents a dynamic marginal productivity equation for the agricultural sector,[8] although we note that we have only the total male population, not the agricultural labor force as our labor supply variable. The result appears in the first column of table 9.1. This equation confirms the inverse relation between the real farm wage and the male population for the period 1866 to 1913, even in the presence of other variables. It implies a long-run elasticity of −3.3, which is surprisingly large. Agricultural output gives a negative and insignificant rather than the expected positive coefficient. Possibly output reflects largely supply-side rather than demand-side forces, including emigration and the declining labor force. The second column of table 9.1 excludes the output term, and the coefficient on the male population is hardly changed. The coefficient on the time trend is again negative, suggesting that in the absence of declining population, the product wage would have fallen.[9]

To summarize, economic conditions facing Irish laborers improved dramatically in the half century following the famine not only in absolute terms but relative to Britain and the United States. Agricultural wages rose strongly relative to agricultural prices as the labor force declined. These results certainly support the view that the real farm wage in post-famine Ireland was being driven by the farm labor force, and thus that the wage was intimately tied to emigration. Although supportive, these results need reinforcement. After all, the economics is very simple, and the total male population is unlikely to be a perfect proxy for the farm labor force. We need to estimate the impact of emigration on the labor force, and we need a more complete model to measure its effects.

A Model of the Irish Economy

Enormous labor force shocks such as the Irish mass emigration can best be assessed by a general equilibrium approach that allows for the full set of influences felt throughout the domestic economy. The CGE approach is certainly not new to economists; these CGE models have become common in the development, trade, and public finance literature.[10] Economic historians have also been finding many useful applications since the early 1970s, including most recently the problem of convergence and mass migrations. In fact, CGE models have been used successfully to estimate the impact of Irish immigration on British labor markets between 1821 and 1861 (Williamson 1990: ch. 6), to assess the impact of emigration on Irish agriculture between 1856 and 1876 (O'Rourke 1991), to evaluate the effects of immigration on United States labor markets (Williamson 1974a, b) and to identify the impact of United States immigration and British emigration on convergence between them (O'Rourke, Williamson, and Hatton 1994).

What follows is a brief description of a model of the Irish economy in 1907–1908, designed to assess the effects of post-famine emigration on Irish real wages and living standards.[11] A similar model will be applied to Sweden later in this chapter. The appendix supplies the details for both.

There are three producing sectors in the Irish model: agriculture (A), manufacturing (M), and services (S). Agriculture produces food by using as inputs agricultural labor (L_A), capital (K), land (R), and imported manufactures (M_{FA}, denoting imported fertilizers). Manufacturing produces output by using as inputs nonagricultural labor (L_{NA}), capital, agricultural goods (food processing was an important industrial activity in nineteenth-century Ireland), imported manufactures (M_{FM}, denoting, for example, cotton yarns) and "exotic imports" (F, goods for which no [or almost no] domestic substitutes were produced at home, such as raw cotton and coal). Services are produced by using nonagricultural labor, capital, and agricultural goods (horses and horsefeed sold to the transport part of the sector). These production functions can be written formally as:

[9.1]
$$A = A\left(L_A, K_A, R, M_{FA}\right)$$

[9.2]
$$M = M\left(L_{NAM}, K_M, A_M, M_{FM}, F_M\right)$$

[9.3]
$$S = S\left(L_{NAs}, K_S, A_S\right)$$

All production functions are CES and constant returns are assumed; competition assures that price equals cost everywhere in Ireland.

Food and manufactures are internationally traded: Ireland exports domestic manufactures (linen) and food (cheese and meat) and imports foreign manufactures (cotton textiles and machines) and "exotic" intermediate inputs. With one exception, we view Ireland as fulfilling the so-called "small country" case: prices of all tradables but one are taken as exogenous, determined in world markets over which Ireland has no control. The exceptions are those domestically produced manufactures: Irish manufactures face a constant elasticity demand function abroad, a standard treatment in the trade literature. Ireland is allowed to run the (tiny) trade deficit that was observed in 1908, but it is exogenous. Services are non-traded and thus their price is determined by supply and demand at home, not by conditions abroad.

It seems to us that capital moved quite freely between sectors in nineteenth-century Ireland, seeking out highest returns. The same was not true of labor, however. Farm labor was not perfectly mobile, and thus wage gaps between city and countryside were common, and they often widened during supply-side slumps in agriculture at home or during demand-side booms in manufacturing at home or abroad. The model reflects these real-world factor market forces. Thus, capital is perfectly mobile between sectors. Irish labor is less than perfectly mobile between sectors: technically, what might be called "raw labor"—$L(L_R)$—is transformed into agricultural and nonagricultural labor via

[9.4]
$$\left(L_A, L_{NA}\right) = L\left(L_R\right),$$

which is in constant elasticity of transformation form. The elasticity of transformation reflects the sensitivity of the distribution of labor between town and country to rural-urban wage gaps. This formulation allows labor to be mobile between town and country, while at the same time allowing for the existence of persistent (and endogenous) rural-urban wage gaps.[12] Land, of course, is only used in agriculture.

The model determines relative prices of the tradables, outputs, demand, a cost-of-living index (with the weights coming from the budgets underlying those demands), wages per laborer (and thus real wages, and living standards), land rents per acre, and returns on capital invested.

How Much of the Rise in Irish Wages Was Due to Emigration?

By applying the no-emigration population and labor force actuals and counterfactuals to our 1907–1908 CGE model of the Irish economy, we can assess how much of the post-famine rise in real wages was due to emigration. First, we calculated the impact on wages of both the actual and the counterfactual change in the Irish labor force from 1851 onward. Next, the difference between the two is calculated and an estimate of the independent impact of the post-famine Irish emigration on labor markets at home is derived.

First, we need an estimate of what the Irish population and labor force would have been in 1911 in the absence of emigration from 1851 onwards. The simplest method is to begin with the 1851 population and simulate its growth assuming no emigration and that birth and death rates would have been the same as those actually observed. This gives a 1911 no-emigration population estimate of 9.773 million, 1.5 times the 1851 population and 2.2 times the actual population in 1911. However, it has been argued that a set of demographic responses would have been set in train by the absence of emigration that would have reduced the birthrate, perhaps by half the amount of emigration (Ó Gráda 1988: 164). If we reduce births by half the amount of emigration and rerun the simulation, we get a 1911 counterfactual population of 6.527 million, close to the actual population size in 1851, or 1.5 times the actual 1911 population.[13]

These alternatives represent a wide range, but its plausibility can be confirmed with other evidence. The total stock of Irish living abroad in 1911 was 2.134 million. Adding these back would raise the 1911 Irish population close to its 1851 level. A few of these would have been elderly pre-1851 emigrants, but this small number would have been dwarfed by the second-generation Irish living abroad. In the United States alone there were 2.141 million children of unmixed Irish parentage and over a million with one Irish parent, although many of these would have been the children of pre-1851 emigrants. Alternative estimates based either on the stock of emigrants living abroad or on cumulating the emigration flow are likely to fall into the range suggested here, and indeed we offer one such alternative in chapter 10. In principle such estimates should measure the impact of emigration on the labor force rather than on the population, although the difference will not be very great over a period as long as 60 years. In short, we assume that the no-emigration Irish labor force would have fallen between an upper bound of 2.2 and a lower bound of 1.5 times the actual in 1911.

The 1907–1908 CGE model for Ireland is fully capable of dealing with the fundamental insight of Eli Heckscher and Bertil Ohlin, both Swedes writing about Sweden and both writing (in 1919 and 1924) right at the end of this mass emigration from Ireland and Sweden (Flam and Flanders 1991). They believed that trade

Table 9.2 The Impact in 1911 of Irish Emigration, 1851–1911: Computable General Equilibrium Analysis (in %)

	Capital immobile		Capital mobile	
	lower	upper	lower	upper
Labor force decrease	−32.9	−55.2	−32.9	−55.2
Impact on				
Agricultural real wage	+19.0	+40.1	+6.4	+12.4
Nonagricultural real wage	+23.5	+51.5	+6.4	+12.4
GNP	−22.5	−39.8	−29.6	−50.5
GNP per capita	+14.9	+33.3	+5.2	+9.9
Gross output in				
Agriculture	−35.1	−57.4	−23.1	−47.4
Manufacturing	−7.4	−7.4	−32.4	−54.5
Services	−16.7	−29.1	−30.6	−52.2
Real rental rates				
Land	−33.3	−54.5	−28.1	−49.0
Capital	−27.5	−45.4	−2.0	−2.9

Source: Based on Boyer, Hatton, and O'Rourke (1994, table 11.2).

can be a partial substitute for lack of factor mobility between countries. The Irish CGE model allows trade to have an offsetting impact on real wages, just as Heckscher and Ohlin insisted. Even though we have used the model here only to assess the impact of emigration, changes in labor scarcity induced by movements abroad will change trade patterns (Ireland will shift into less labor-intensive exports) and change output mix (producing less labor-intensive products).[14] Those changes in economic activity and trade will tend to diminish (but not eliminate) the impact of rising labor scarcity on real wage improvement. Heckscher and Ohlin would be happy on that score. But what about world capital markets? Can capital not serve as a substitute for labor migration by moving in the opposite direction? If emigration had been only a trickle from a labor surplus area like Ireland, wouldn't capital have flooded in to exploit the cheap labor? Since Irish emigration was actually a flood, shouldn't capital have retreated from the now more expensive labor market area? Cormac Ó Gráda (1994: chs. 12–14) makes a persuasive case that international capital *was* mobile over Irish borders prior to the Great War, at least as far as Ireland was financially connected to Britain. How mobile? We do not know, so we offer two cases in the tables that follow: "capital-mobile," in which the rental rate on capital is taken as exogenous, implying that small Ireland could have borrowed (or loaned out) as much additional capital as it wished from (to) world capital markets (e.g., London) without influencing world interest rates;[15] and "capital-immobile," in which Ireland had to go it alone and thus could not have borrowed (or loaned out) any additional capital from (to) foreign markets.

Table 9.2 reports the percentage change in each variable in 1911 that resulted from emigration over the no-emigration counterfactual values. We will discuss all of the table 9.2 findings in terms of ranges, bounded by "lower" and "upper."

Consider the internationally capital-immobile case first. The real wage in agriculture was 19 to 40 percent higher as a result of emigration, whereas the nonfarm wage was 24 to 52 percent higher. The implied elasticity of the real agricultural wage with respect to the labor force ranges between −0.50 and −0.75. Although these elasticities are large, they are not nearly as large as the effects of population on the product wage estimated earlier.[16]

Irish workers who stayed home in Ireland—as opposed to landlords and capitalists—enjoyed the biggest gains from the emigration of their brothers and sisters or would have been hit hardest had the emigration to Britain, America, and elsewhere not taken place. Per capita GNP rose by between 15 to 33 percent due to emigration, figures not quite as big as those for real wages. Thus, wages rose by more than per capita income due to emigration. Total GNP, of course, decreased since the wage elasticity is less than unity. This result certainly confirms who gains and who loses from emigration. Landlords lose, since increasing labor scarcity cuts into their rents: rents were reduced by 33 to 54 percent due to emigration. Capitalists lose, since increasing labor scarcity cuts into their profits (recall that, for the moment, capital is assumed to be internationally immobile): rates of return on capital were reduced by 28 to 45 percent.

How did Irish emigration influence industrialization? To the extent that agriculture was labor-intensive, emigration should have favored the relative expansion of urban-based manufacturing and services in Belfast and Dublin. As a result of emigration, there were fewer workers everywhere in Ireland. But agriculture contracted most; in fact, agricultural output declined by 35 to 57 percent, while manufacturing declined by 7 percent in both cases and services by 17 to 29 percent. The counterfactual underlying table 9.2 implies that emigration and rising labor scarcity helps account for the relative decline of agriculture in late-nineteenth-century Ireland. As a share of gross output agriculture was a third in 1911, but in the absence of emigration it would have been 40 or 50 percent. This would also help account for the relative rise of Dublin, Belfast, and the smaller towns as manufacturing and services, though reduced in absolute size due to emigration, nevertheless increased their shares.

Suppose, instead, capital is viewed as having been completely mobile over Irish borders. What then? While still big, all of the effects of emigration just discussed would have been somewhat smaller.[17] In the absence of emigration, more labor and lower wages would have attracted more foreign capital (or kept more Irish capital at home); more foreign capital would have meant better equipped Irish workers than in the capital-immobile case; and the glut of workers in the counterfactual world without emigration would have been at least partially offset by more capital. Under the capital-mobile case, both farm and nonfarm wages increase by 6 to 12 percent as a result of emigration, not the 19 to 40 percent seen in the capital-immobile case. No doubt the truth lies somewhere in between. The average of all of these emigration-induced wage increases is about 21 percent.

Table 9.3 converts all of these results into per annum growth terms covering the half-century 1851–1911: perhaps the implications of Irish emigration can be seen

Table 9.3 Growth Rates of Irish Wages and Income, 1851–1911: Growth per Annum (%)

| | | Counterfactual | | | |
| | | Capital immobile | | Capital mobile | |
	Actual	lower	upper	lower	upper
Labor force	−0.66	0.00	0.68	0.00	0.68
Agricultural real wage	1.27	0.98	0.70	1.19	1.08
Nonagricultural real wage	1.46	1.09	0.76	1.33	1.26
GNP	0.70	1.12	1.54	1.28	1.87
GNP per capita	1.36	1.06	0.88	1.27	1.20

Note: These figures differ from those given in Boyer, Hatton, and O'Rourke (1994, table 11.3) because of the different period covered and the different wage series used.

even more starkly there. In the capital-immobile case the growth in farm wages would, in the absence of emigration, have plunged from 1.27 to 0.98 or 0.70 percent per annum; and the growth in nonfarm wages[18] would have plunged from 1.46 to 1.09 or 0.76 percent per annum. Thus, roughly 40 to 50 percent of the observed growth can be attributed to emigration. The figure is smaller for farm wages but is still as much as a quarter even on the lower estimate. For the growth of GNP per capita, we assume a benchmark of 0.7 percent per annum based on Ó Gráda's estimate, implying 1.36 percent per capita income growth over the 60 years, 1851–1911. Growth rates of GNP per head would have dropped to 0.88–1.06 percent per annum in the absence of emigration, not as big as the reduction in farm wage growth, but big enough, that is, a quarter to a third lower.

How Much of the Irish Catch-Up Was Due to Emigration?

Post-famine Irish emigration accounted for as much as a half of the growth in real wages at home and for as much as a third of the growth of income per head. Can it also explain a large share of Irish catch-up on the leaders abroad, Britain and the United States? Some answers are offered in table 9.4 where we explore the impact of Irish emigration on American-Irish and Anglo-Irish wage gaps. Recall that between 1851 and 1911, the Irish unskilled in the building trades caught up a bit with their counterparts in Britain. In fact, the ratio rose from 0.59 to 0.88, an increase of 0.28, the figure recorded in the upper left of table 9.4. The other two figures in that first column also record Irish catch-up, even on the United States. The remaining counterfactual entries tell us what would happened to those wage ratios—home versus abroad—had the Irish post-famine emigration never taken place. In three cases, the gaps would have *widened* in the absence of emigration: all three are in the "upper" and capital-immobile category, where the counterfactual conditions assumed are most extreme. In the other six cases, emigration still matters a great deal. Take the "lower" cases: here, emigration accounts for perhaps

Table 9.4 Changes in Irish Real Wage Ratios, Home versus Abroad, 1851–1911

		Counterfactual			
		Capital immobile		Capital mobile	
	Actual	lower	upper	lower	upper
Ireland/Great Britain					
Agricultural real wage	0.11	0.00	−0.09	0.07	0.04
Nonagricultural real wage	0.28	0.11	−0.02	0.23	0.19
Ireland/United States					
Nonagricultural real wage	0.16	0.06	−0.03	0.13	0.10

Note: Changes in wage ratios are derived using counterfactuals in table 9.2.

20 to 60 percent of the Irish convergence on both Britain and the United States.[19] The effects in the "upper" cases are even bigger: emigration accounts for a third of Irish convergence on the leaders even if capital is assumed mobile.

Irish emigration by itself made a powerful contribution to Irish real wage and living standards convergence on Britain and the United States. What happens when United States immigration is added to the story? Can an even larger share of the Irish-American convergence be explained by mass migrations involving both countries? Chapter 10 applies the same CGE analysis to Britain and the United States. In the absence of immigration after 1870, the United States population might have been around 17 percent smaller in 1910, and the labor force around 24 percent smaller (table 10.1). The CGE counterfactual analysis suggests that unskilled urban real wages would have been 9.2 percent higher in the capital-mobile case and 34 percent higher in the capital-immobile case, in which case *all* of the postfamine Irish convergence on the United States was due to mass migration. The same was not true for Anglo-Ireland since Britain recorded high emigration rates too: in the absence of emigration, British wages would have been 6 to 12 percent lower. Thus, allowing for the impact of migrations on the two leaders strengthens migration's contribution to Irish real wage convergence on the United States but weakens it on Britain.

Sweden and the Scandinavian Late-Nineteenth-Century Catch-Up

From the Great Famine to the Great War, Ireland, the Scandinavian countries, and even Italy underwent catch-up. The performance of the Scandinavian countries was particularly impressive: per capita income, real wages, and average labor productivity grew faster in Denmark, Norway, Sweden, and even Finland than in the rest of northwestern Europe. Thus, the gap between the Scandinavian latecomers and Britain narrowed considerably. To offer just two examples: between 1870 and 1910, Swedish labor productivity rose from 39 to 53 percent of Britain's; over the same 40 years, Danish unskilled urban real wages rose from 52 to 96 percent of Britain's. Indeed, real wages in Scandinavia even rose relative to those of fast-growing America: Norwegian urban unskilled real wages rose from 25 to 43 percent of the United States', while those in Sweden rose from 30 to 59 percent of the United States' (Williamson 1995, table A2.1, 3-year averages centered on 1870 and 1910).

This rapid Scandinavian catch-up is now well documented, but it was apparent to Swedish economists writing in the middle or at the end of the period—like Knut Wicksell, Eli Heckscher, and Bertil Ohlin. The amazing aspect of the literature on the Scandinavian catch-up is that no one has tried to assess its sources. There is no shortage of assertion, of course, ranging from schooling advantages, favorable price shocks, the right natural resource endowment, trade creation, mass emigration, and elastic foreign capital inflows. Assertion is one thing; however, empirical assessment guided by explicit economic argument is another.

The remainder of this chapter offers that empirical assessment, but it has its limits. It deals only with Sweden and emigration.[20] We start with the catch-up itself.

Four independent sources of evidence can be used to gauge Scandinavian late-nineteenth-century catch-up. The first uses the PPP-adjusted real wages for the urban unskilled in 16 countries that have appeared so often in this book (Williamson 1995: includes Denmark, Norway, and Sweden). The second documents trends in the wage-rental ratio, the ratio of unskilled urban wages to farm land values for 10 of the 16-country sample (O'Rourke, Taylor, and Williamson 1996: includes Denmark and Sweden). The third contains some older constant-price GNP per capita estimates, which overlap with the European portion of the 16-country sample, except for the omission of Ireland and Portugal (Bairoch 1976: includes all four Scandinavian countries). Finally, the fourth contains modern GDP per worker-hour estimates, which have a more limited overlap with the 16-country sample (Maddison 1991: includes all four Scandinavian countries).

Data constructed from different sources and by different scholars, are likely to yield different convergence stories, but the differences here go even deeper. Per capita and per worker-hour convergence may differ according to trends in labor participation rates and length of the working day. If the forces of demographic transition are strongest for the richer countries (higher fertility and lower infant mortality, causing population growth to exceed labor force growth) and if these forces are reinforced by a legislated shortening in the length of the work week first in labor-scarce rich countries (who could best afford it), it follows that per capita convergence will be faster than per worker-hour convergence. If the forces of international migration dominate instead, the opposite would be true since migrants are mainly young adults. Second, GDP per worker-hour is, after all, nothing more than average labor productivity, and convergence of it and real wages may differ for various reasons. The real wage deflator may behave differently than the GDP deflator, especially true in the late nineteenth century when the price of foodstuffs fell sharply in the labor-abundant Old World, which imported these key wage goods, relative to the labor-scarce New World, which exported them. Thus, real wage convergence should have been more dramatic than GDP per-worker convergence on

Table 9.5 Relative Economic Performance of Scandinavia in the Late Nineteenth Century: Growth per Annum (%)

Country	Real wage per urban worker 1870–1913 (1)	Wage-rental ratio 1870–1910 (2)	Real GNP per capita 1870–1913 (3)	Real GDP per worker-hour 1870–1913 (4)
Denmark	2.41	2.85	2.19	1.90
Finland	NA	NA	1.19	1.80
Norway	2.46	NA	1.35	1.65
Sweden	2.92	2.45	2.39	1.74
Scandinavian average	*2.60*	*2.65*	*1.78*	*1.77*
Austria	NA	NA	1.15	1.76
Belgium	1.04	NA	1.05	1.24
France	0.65	1.80	1.06	1.58
Germany	1.05	0.87	1.30	1.88
Great Britain	0.89	2.54	1.00	1.23
Ireland	1.39	4.39	NA	NA
Italy	1.71	NA	0.81	1.33
The Netherlands	0.75	NA	0.93	1.34
Portugal	0.65	NA	0.18	1.10
Spain	0.01	−1.04	0.25	1.52
Switzerland	NA	NA	1.32	1.46
Non-Scandinavian Europe average	*0.90*	*1.71*	*0.91*	*1.44*
Argentina	0.94	−4.06	NA	NA
Australia	0.01	−3.30	NA	1.08
Canada	1.84	NA	NA	2.31
United States	0.90	−1.72	NA	1.93
New World average	*0.92*	*−3.03*	*NA*	*1.77*

Notes and Sources: All averages are unweighted. Col. 1: real wage rate for unskilled urban workers, from Williamson (1995: table A2.1), Great Britain revised. Col. 2: ratio of Williamson's wage to land values per unit of farmland, from O'Rourke, Taylor, and Williamson (1996: table 3). Col. 3: gross national product in constant prices, per capita, from Bairoch (1976: table 6). Col. 4: gross domestic product in constant prices, per worker-hour, from Maddison (1991: table c. 11; 1994: table 2–1), except for Italy, Portugal, and Spain, which are based on Bardini, Carreras, and Lains (1995: table 1), and the assumptions that worker-hours per capita evolved the same way in Iberia as in Italy. NA = not available.

that score alone. This prediction is reinforced to the extent that marginal labor productivity (e.g., the real wage) rose faster than average labor productivity (e.g., GDP per worker-hour) in land-scarce, labor-abundant poor countries than in land-abundant, labor-scarce rich countries. After all, farm land prices and rents collapsed in poor late-nineteenth-century Europe while they surged in the rich New World. Third, it follows from this argument that wage-rental ratio convergence should have been even more dramatic than real wage convergence because both wages and farm rents converge but in opposite directions, thus making wage-rental convergence faster than wages alone and certainly faster than some aggregate GDP measure that, among other things, aggregates up across rents and wages. As we shall see, the late-nineteenth-century annual growth rates implied by all four indicators seem to accord well with these predictions.

Consistent with qualitative accounts (Heckscher 1954; Jorberg 1970; Lieberman 1970; Hildebrand 1978; Persson 1993) and the pioneering comparative national product estimates of Olle Krantz and Carl-Axle Nilsson (1974), the evidence in table 9.5 confirms that Sweden and Denmark tended to outperform Norway and Finland, but only Paul Bairoch's data (column 3) show a wide spread in the performance between the Scandinavian four. Whereas Bairoch's GNP per capita figures show Sweden growing at twice the rate of Finland and almost twice the rate of Norway, Maddison's GDP per worker-hour figures (column 4) reveal only modest differences between them. The same is true of the real wage data (column 1), which show Sweden growing only a little faster than the Scandinavian average (2.92 versus 2.6 percent per annum). In short, recent evidence suggests that rapid catching up was common to all four Scandinavian countries.

The Scandinavian catch-up is certainly confirmed by the evidence in table 9.5. Real wages grew at rates almost three times those prevailing elsewhere in Europe; Swedish workers enjoyed real wage growth rates more than three times that of British workers; and Danish workers enjoyed real wage growth rates almost two and a half times that of German workers. In fact, there was no country elsewhere in our European sample that underwent real wage growth even close to that of Sweden or Denmark. What was true for real wages was also true for the wage-rental ratio. Although the ratio of wage rates per worker to farm land values per acre fell everywhere in the New World, it rose everywhere in Europe (with the exception of Spain). While the Scandinavian wage-rental ratio seems to have tracked the British ratio very closely (2.65 versus 2.54 percent per annum growth), the ratio rose half again faster in Scandinavia than elsewhere in Europe. Once again, factor prices converged more dramatically in Scandinavia. Bairoch's per capita income figures document Scandinavian growth rates almost two times those in the rest of Europe. Consistent with our predictions, Maddison's product per worker-hour estimates document a less spectacular Scandinavian catch-up, but even his data confirm a relatively impressive growth performance among the Nordic countries.

Undoubtedly, Scandinavia outperformed the rest of the greater Atlantic economy (and probably the rest of the world) in the late nineteenth century. However, we have come to expect this kind of performance: poor countries tend to grow faster than rich countries, the economic differences between them tends to erode with time, and economic convergence takes place. Three prominent explanations describe such convergence. The first is central to this chapter and to this book: it appeals to Nobel laureate Robert Solow and his Solovian forces of accumulation and capital deepening. Capital is scarce in poor countries, so accumulation rates should be fast there, whereas capital is abundant in rich countries, so accumulation should be slow there. Labor is abundant in poor countries, so population and labor force growth should be slow there—because of late marriage, low fertility within marriage and high infant mortality, while the opposite should be true of labor-scarce rich countries. Capital deepening should, therefore, favor poor

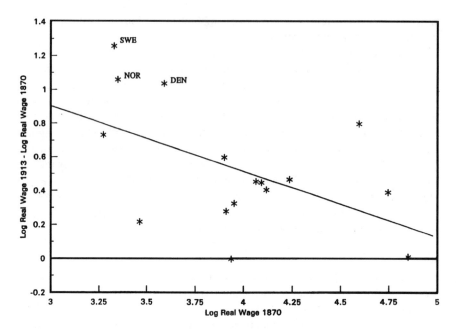

Figure 9.4 "Unconditional" Real Wage Convergence, 1870–1913

countries. Mass migrations and well-functioning world capital markets should help this process along: mass migration from poor countries to rich countries and capital export from rich countries to poor countries should help contribute to catching up. The second appeals to Alexander Gerschenkron (1952) and the forces of technology diffusion: in the poorest countries, the productivity gap between best technological practice prevailing among the industrial leaders abroad and the traditional technological practice prevailing at home is enormous; thus, a catch-up growth potential among the poorest is also enormous. Convergence is assured (if "social capability" conditions are satisfied: Abramovitz 1986). The third gets its inspiration from Eli Heckscher and Bertil Ohlin who, after the Great War, offered the factor-price-equalization theorem to help account for the Scandinavian catch-up they had been observing. For them, trade can be a partial substitute for factor mobility or even the diffusion of technology.

Scandinavia was central to convergence in the Atlantic economy up to the Great War, but did it grow as fast as convergence models predict? Or did it grow faster? Figure 9.4 supplies two answers using real wages. There we plot the results of the unconditional convergence regressions reported in table 9.6.[21] The equation estimated is widely used in the convergence literature (Barro 1991; Barro and Sala-i-Martin 1991, 1992; Mankiw, Romer, and Weil 1992; Prados, Sanchez, and Oliva 1993). Thus, in the first row of table 9.6 a measure of late-nineteenth-century real wage growth (the difference in the logarithms of real wages, 1913 versus 1870) is simply regressed on the logarithm of the real wage in 1870. Each row confirms

Table 9.6 Unconditional Convergence Regressions for the Late Nineteenth Century

Sample	$\hat{\beta}$ on log 1870 value	R^2	n	λ
1870–1913, real wage (figure 9.4)	−0.390 (2.290)	0.27	16	0.011
1850–1870, real wage	−0.174 (1.718)	0.25	11	0.010
1870–1890, real wage	−0.188 (1.849)	0.20	16	0.010
1890–1913, real wage	−0.151 (1.136)	0.08	16	0.007
1870–1913, GNP per capita	−0.126 (0.398)	0.16	11	0.003

Source: See text. *t* statistics are in parentheses.

"unconditional" convergence, although the real wages underlying row 1 converged faster than GNP per capita (row 5), just as theory would predict.[22] Furthermore, the rate of convergence (λ) underlying the real wage data in figure 9.4 is very close to that estimated recently by Leandro Prados and his collaborators; the λ implied by figure 9.4 is 0.011 (table 9.6, row 1) while Prados and his collaborators (1993: 9, table 4) report λ ranging between 0.009 and 0.010 for what they call the pre–World War I European "core" (Belgium, Denmark, France, Germany, the Netherlands, Sweden, Switzerland, and the United Kingdom). In any case, the slope coefficient in these regressions imply a rate of convergence that accords fairly well with post–World War II experience: a late-nineteenth-century rate of convergence of 1.1 percent per annum (e.g., $\lambda = 0.011$) is a little more than half the estimates typically found for post–World War II, about 2 percent per annum (Mankiw et al. 1992; Barro and Sala-i-Martin 1992).

Rows 2 through 4 in table 9.6 confirm that convergence took place throughout the late nineteenth century: that is, it proceeded at exactly the same rate between 1850 and 1870 as between 1870 and 1890 ($\lambda = 0.010$), falling off a bit only after 1890 ($\lambda = 0.007$). It should be noted, however, that while Norway and Sweden grew faster than average between 1850 and 1870, they still exhibited predictable rates of catch-up. The Scandinavian countries began to deviate on the up side of the convergence path in the 1870s and 1880s, although Sweden was the main overachiever. From the 1890s to World War I, Norway and Denmark joined Sweden as overachievers (O'Rourke and Williamson 1996: figures 2–4; 1997).

Scandinavia was clearly part of the catch-up process in the late nineteenth century that started as early as 1850. In fact, Scandinavia, led by Sweden, was an overachiever, growing even faster than an estimated European unconditional catch-up relationship predicts. Even though Scandinavian catching up started as early as 1850, the impressive overachievement did not appear until after 1870. This evidence raises a number of questions: What explains the late-nineteenth-century Scandinavian catch-up? What explains Scandinavian overachievement after 1870?

Does the appearance of overachievement after 1870 relate to high emigration numbers then? How important was emigration to the spectacular Scandinavian catch-up, or at least to Sweden's part in it?

Making Wicksell's Assertion Testable with a Model of the Swedish Economy

As we pointed out at the start of this chapter, Knut Wicksell asserted a century ago that emigration would solve the pauper problem that blighted labor-abundant and land-scarce Swedish agriculture (Wicksell 1882, cited in Karlstrom 1985: 1). His pro-emigration agitation was followed by other voices in the 1890s, including Adrian Molin's and Gustav Sundbarg's. Tests of Wicksell's assertion were very slow to come despite the intensity of the debate on the economic impact of the late-nineteenth-century mass migrations. The quantitative literature has always been thick on the determinants of Swedish emigration (Wilkinson 1970; Quigley 1972; Williamson 1974a, b; Rundblom and Norman 1976; Carlsson 1976; Moe 1970), but thin on the impact of emigration. Indeed, older surveys by Semmingsen (1960, 1972) and Hvidt (1966) had almost nothing to say about labor market impact.[23]

One can pose two questions about the late-nineteenth-century mass migrations. How much of Swedish (Norwegian or Danish) real wage and labor productivity growth can be assigned to emigration, the out-migrations having created more labor scarcity at home? How much of the Swedish (Norwegian or Danish) catch-up can be assigned more generally to mass migration, *both* the emigrations from poor Sweden *and* the immigrations (of Swedes and non-Swedes) into the rich New World, like the United States (where most of the Swedes and the rest of the Scandinavian emigrants went)? What about Swedish catch-up on Britain, itself an emigrant country? Our interest is in the last two catching-up questions, but as we saw in the Irish analysis each of these questions employs the same methodology to get answers: estimate the labor force in a counterfactual no-migration environment for both the rich and poor country; with the counterfactual labor force estimate in hand, assess the impact of the altered labor force on living standards and productivity by the application of a model of the rich and poor economies; finally, compute the share of the measured living standards and productivity catch-up explained by the mass migrations.

Irish experience has illustrated how a CGE model can be applied to the problem, but a pioneering application by Urban Karlstrom (1985) did the same for Sweden about a decade ago. He estimated that the Swedish emigrations in the 1870s and 1880s served to raise real wages there by 4.9 percent per decade. Karlstrom's result suggests that the mass migrations might have accounted for about a quarter of the impressive contraction of the American-Swedish wage gap between 1870 and 1910 (O'Rourke, Williamson, and Hatton 1994). Karlstrom's pioneering work stimulated the construction of what is (hopefully) a better Swedish CGE model in an effort to sharpen our answers to Wicksell's question (O'Rourke and Williamson 1995). The reader can find the details in the appendix. We offer only a brief description here and stress the differences with the Irish 1907–1908 CGE model already seen.

Karlstrom's model had five sectors: agriculture (including forestry and fishing), an export-oriented industry (mining and metals, wood products, pulp, paper, and printing), a home market–oriented industry (textiles and clothing, leather and rubber goods, chemicals, utilities, stone, clay, glass, and food products), services, and construction. Because the Swedish model used here has also been applied to trade issues (O'Rourke and Williamson 1995) and the international price experience was so different within Swedish "agriculture," we split Karlstrom's agricultural sector into tillage (T), pasture (P), and forestry plus fishing (FF). Karlstrom's export-oriented (X) and home market–oriented (H) industrial sectors have been retained, but his services and construction sectors have been collapsed into a single nontraded sector (NT). There are thus six sectors in our Swedish CGE model, as opposed to five in Karlstrom's and three for Ireland.

Two goods are imported that are not produced at home, foreign vegetable (TF) and foreign animal (PF) products. There are four primary factors of production: raw labor (L_R), capital (K), land specific to pasture (R_P), and land specific to tillage (R_T). As with Ireland, Swedish production functions are taken to be CES, and there are detailed intermediate input-output relationships:

[9.5]
$$T = T\left(L_{AT}, K_T, R_T, T_T, X_T, H_T, S_T\right)$$

[9.6]
$$P = P\left(L_{AP}, K_P, R_P, T_P, P_P, TF_P, X_P, H_P, S_P\right)$$

[9.7]
$$FF = FF\left(L_{FF}, K_{FF}, X_{FF}, H_{FF}, S_{FF}\right)$$

[9.8]
$$X = X\left(L_{NAX}, K_X, T_X, P_X, TF_X, PF_X, FF_X, X_X, H_X, S_X\right)$$

[9.9]
$$H = H\left(L_{NAH}, K_H, T_H, P_H, TF_H, PF_H, FF_H, X_H, H_H, S_H\right)$$

[9.10]
$$S = S\left(L_{NAS}, K_S, X_S, H_S, S_S\right)$$

The rest of the Swedish model is similar to the Irish model. Capital is mobile across sectors; land is specific to agriculture and immobile between tillage and pasture; labor is imperfectly mobile between agriculture, forestry and fishing, and the rest of the economy. We treat that imperfect mobility exactly as we did for Ireland. Like Ireland, Sweden is viewed as a small country that takes prices of tradables as determined in world markets. The Swedish CGE model is estimated for 1871, and the Swedish trade deficit at that time is taken to be exogenous and unchanged.

Was Wicksell Right? Swedish Emigration and Real Wages

Did emigration have an important impact on the labor force at home? Scandinavian emigration rates reached their peak in the 1880s; at that time they were among the

Table 9.7 Computable General Equilibrium Analysis of
Swedish Emigration

	1870–1910 total impact
Labor force decrease due to emigration	−18.1%
Impact on	
Farm real wage	+11.8
Non-farm real wage	+12.3
Output in tillage	−14.2
Output in pasture	+14.7
Output in forestry	−22.6
Output in export industries	−18.5
Output in home-market industries	−7.6
Output in services	−5.5
Real rental rates on land, tillage	−11.2
Real rental rates on land, pasture	+24.5
Real rental rates on capital	−12.9

Source: O'Rourke and Williamson (1995, appendix 2).

highest in Europe, exceeded only by Ireland and the rest of the United Kingdom. The rate for the decade was 95.2 per thousand of the population in Norway, 70.1 per thousand in Sweden, and 39.4 per thousand in Denmark (table 1.1): Sweden lay in the middle of the Scandinavian range. Emigration went through booms and busts, but by 1910 the Danish population was 11 percent below what it would have been in the absence of the emigrations over the four decades following 1870, the Swedish population was 15 percent lower, and Norwegian population 19 percent lower (Taylor and Williamson 1997: table 1). Since emigration favored young adults with high labor participation rates, the impact on the home labor force exceeded that on the home population. The bottom line is that the Swedish labor force was 18.1 percent smaller in 1910 than it would have been in the absence of emigration (table 9.7, first row).[24] Thus, the influence of emigration on Sweden and the rest of Scandinavia was not trivial.

O'Rourke and Williamson (1995: appendix 2) report the cumulative impact of Swedish 1870–1910 emigration on Swedish real wages in 1910, which is summarized in table 9.7. In contrast with the Irish analysis in table 9.2, table 9.7 does not report separate (foreign) capital-immobile and capital-mobile cases: capital inflows into Sweden over these four decades were very large *in spite of* the Swedish emigration; it is hard to imagine that it would have been even larger in the absence of emigration, so we ignore the possibility. Again in contrast with the Irish analysis in table 9.2, table 9.7 reports the direct contribution of Swedish emigration from 1870 to 1910 to observed historical performance. The emigration served to make labor scarcer in Sweden, so the model predicts that labor-intensive activities declined (*ceteris paribus*) as a consequence. Thus, output in tillage activities, forestry, and export industries all decline sharply, activities where abundant Swedish labor had been used extensively to exploit comparative advantage. Output in pasture increased as comparative advantage shifted in that direction in the wake of emigration. Consistent with these effects, Swedish emigration served to raise land rents and land values in pasture while lowering them in tillage. As it turns out, the "grain invasion" from the New World reinforced all of these effects, including the distributional effects that influenced the tariff response in the 1880s (O'Rourke and Williamson 1995), but here we focus on the independent impact of emigration.

Table 9.7 reports the bottom line in terms of labor market impact and Wicksell's prediction: emigration between 1870 and 1910 raised urban wages in Sweden by 12.3 percent above what they would have been in its absence. Urban unskilled wages in Sweden actually increased by 191 percent (34.3 to 99.7) over the four decades. The 12.3 percent looks small by comparison. Granted, Wicksell was talking about agricultural poverty, but the impact of emigration on farm wages was still "only" 11.8 percent, hardly enough to confirm Wicksell's optimism that emigration would solve the pauper problem in Swedish agriculture. Other events mattered far more, it seems.

Wicksell, Swedish Emigration, and Catch-Up

What about migration as a share of the catch-up with Britain or the United States?[25] The impact of the mass migrations on the rapidly contracting wage gap between Britain and Sweden was small, perhaps a tenth of the catch-up. The reason for the small contribution is clear: Britain recorded an emigration rate not too far below Sweden (and the rest of Scandinavia). Once again, Wicksell seems to have been wrong: emigration did not make a significant contribution to Anglo-Swedish catch-up. But what about Swedish catch-up with the United States, the country that absorbed 98 percent of the Swedish overseas emigrants?[26] As we shall see in chapter 10, the immigration rate in the late-nineteenth-century United States was enormous, and its cumulative impact from 1870, according to one estimate, increased the 1910 labor force 24 percent higher than it would have been in its absence (table 10.3), making urban wages 15 percent lower than they would have been without the immigration (table 10.6). The impact of the mass migrations on the rapidly contracting wage gap between the United States and Sweden was significant, about half of the Swedish catch-up on the United States.

Wicksell was only half right.

Appendix. CGE Models of Ireland and Sweden

Both of these models were constructed by Kevin O'Rourke in collaboration with us on two separate but related projects (Boyer, Hatton, and O'Rourke 1994; O'Rourke and Williamson 1995, 1996). We start with the Swedish model and finish with the Irish model.

The Swedish CGE Model for 1871

This is a standard neoclassical model, in which there is no unemployment and prices play an important role. The assumptions of such models (with their ancestral roots leading back to Heckscher, Ohlin, and Wicksell) may be questioned, but they have the best chance of holding when looking at a period as long as four decades.

There are four components to any neoclassical CGE model. Sectors are characterized by production functions; to each sector there corresponds an activity level that is endogenously determined. Each commodity has a price that may or may not be endogenous depending on whether the price is determined in world markets. Consumers have endowments and utility functions; their incomes and utilities are endogenous. Finally, a model may also incorporate side constraints (e.g., a minimum wage), to which there correspond "rationing variables" that move so as to ensure that the constraint is fulfilled (e.g., unemployment or underemployment).

The computer package used here, called MPS/GE, exploits this standard neoclassical framework (Rutherford 1988). Production and utility functions are specified; the package then calculates cost, factor demand, and demand functions for all sectors and commodities. Equilibrium is defined by a set of prices, activity levels, and incomes so that no sector earns a positive profit, supply (home plus foreign) minus demand (home plus foreign) for each commodity is nonnegative, and income from factor endowments is fully distributed.

Production

Tillage (T) and pasture (P) are taken as agricultural (A) while the export-oriented industry (X), the home-oriented industry (H), and the nontraded service sector (NT) are, of course, taken as nonagricultural (NA). The six commodities produced satisfy both final and intermediate demand. There are four primary factors of production—land specific to pasture (R_P), land specific to tillage (R_T), raw labor (L_R), and capital (K); three "produced" factors of production—agricultural labor (L_A), forestry plus fishing labor (L_{FF}), and urban labor (L_{NA}); and two imported goods—foreign vegetable products (TF) and foreign animal products (PF). An artificial good, "foreign exchange," is used in modeling trade flows and serves as the *numeraire*.

MPS/GE constrains production functions to be CES, of which the Cobb-Douglas and Leontief cases are special. Given the elasticity of substitution, this makes estimating all the parameters of such production functions from a consistent data set possible.

Nested production functions are used throughout. First, capital and labor are combined in a CES production function to produce an artificial good (J) (sector subscripts are omitted):

[1]
$$J = \left[a_L L_i^\tau + a_K K^\tau \right]^{1/\tau}$$

where i = A, FF, or NA depending on the sector. The a_i's are constants; and

[2]
$$\tau = (\sigma - 1)/\sigma$$

where σ is the elasticity of substitution between capital and labor.

In the nonagricultural sectors as well as forestry plus fishing, labor and capital are the only primary factors of production. Thus, value added (VA) is simply J:

[3]
$$VA = J$$

In the tillage and pasture sectors, J is combined with land in a Cobb-Douglas manner to produce value added

[4]
$$VA = J^\Theta R^{1-\Theta}$$

where Θ is a constant. In all sectors, value added is combined with intermediate inputs in (Leontief) fixed proportions to produce final output:

[5]
$$Q = \min_i \left[VA, Q_i/a_i \right]$$

where Q is the input of good i, and the a_i's are constants.

Firms in all sectors minimize costs, which generates factor demand and cost functions. It is a standard problem to generate these functions in the Cobb-Douglas, Leontief, and CES cases. In the Cobb-Douglas case, where Q is output, X_i is the input of factor i, w_i is the price of factor i, and production is described by

[6]
$$Q = \Pi_i X_i^{\Theta i}$$

the demand for factor i equals

[7]
$$X_i \left(\{w_j\}, Q \right) = Q(\Theta_i/w_i) \Pi_j \left(w_j/\Theta_j \right)^{\Theta j}$$

and the cost function is given by

[8]
$$c \left(\{w_i\}, Q \right) = Q \Pi_i \left(w_i/\Theta_i \right)^{\Theta i}$$

In the more general CES case, where $\tau = (\sigma - 1)/\sigma$ production is given by

[9]
$$Q = \left[\Sigma_i a_i X_i^\tau \right]^{1/\tau}$$

and factor demands are given by

[10]
$$X_i \left(\{w_j\}, Q \right) = Q \left[(a_i/w_i) \left\{ \Sigma_j \left(a_j^\sigma w_j^{1-\sigma} \right) \right\}^{1/1-\sigma} \right]^\sigma$$

and the cost function is

[11]
$$c(\{w_i\}, Q) = Q\left[\Sigma_i (w_i/a_i)^{1-\sigma}\right]^{1/1-\sigma}$$

In the Leontief case, where production is given by

[12]
$$Q = \min_i \left[X_i/a_i\right]$$

where again the a_i's are constants, factor demands are given by

[13]
$$X_i(\{w_j\}, Q) = a_i Q$$

and the cost function is

[14]
$$c(\{w_i\}, Q) = \Sigma_i w_i a_i Q$$

The model assumes perfect competition; thus, in each sector price equals unit cost (which depends uniquely on factor prices, given constant returns to scale).

Intersectoral Migration

Labor is assumed to be less than perfectly mobile, so the model determines inter-sectoral wage gaps endogenously. The economy is endowed with "raw" labor, which is then transformed into agricultural, forestry plus fishing, and urban labor via a pseudo-production function. The migration "sector" solves (or potential migrants solve) the following problem:

$$\text{maximize}\left[w_A L_A + w_{FF} L_{FF} + w_{NA} L_{NA}\right] \text{ s.t.}$$

$$\left[\delta_A L_A^{(\mu-1)/\mu} + \delta_{FF} L_{FF}^{(\mu-1)/\mu} + \delta_{NA} L_{NA}^{(\mu-1)/\mu}\right]^{\mu/\mu-1} = L_R$$

where w_i is the wage in sector i, L_R is the fixed endowment of raw labor, and μ is the constant elasticity of transformation of this joint production function, which describes how sensitive the intersectoral allocation of labor is to changes in inter-sectoral wage gaps. The solution to this problem is:

[15] $L_A = L_R\left[w_A/\delta_A \Gamma\right]^\mu$; $L_{FF} = L_R\left[w_{FF}/\delta_{FF}\Gamma\right]^\mu$; $L_{NA} = L_R\left[w_{NA}/\delta_{NA}\Gamma\right]^\mu$

where $\Gamma = [\delta_A^\mu w_A^{1-\mu} + \delta_{NA}^\mu w_{NA}^{1-\mu}]^{1/1-\mu}$.

Since the economy is endowed with raw labor, we need to determine its price, w_R; given w_A, w_{FF}, and w_{NA} (and hence, via equation 15, L_A, L_{FF}, and L_{NA}), we can cal-culate it from the zero-profit condition in the migration sector (in other words, a weighted average):

[16]
$$w_R L_R = w_A L_A + w_{FF} L_{FF} + w_{NA} L_{NA}$$

Trade Flows

Exports are converted into foreign exchange and imports are converted into foreign exchange requirements. In the benchmark equilibrium (1871), Sweden ran a trade deficit. Sweden is therefore endowed with enough foreign exchange to finance the deficit. This (together with the assumption that "foreign exchange" is the *numeraire*) amounts to assuming that the nominal trade deficit is exogenous.

Sweden is assumed to be "small" in world markets for all traded goods; prices for all tradables are exogenous. This is modeled by allowing exports or imports of these goods to swap for foreign exchange at a fixed ratio. Let E_i and I_i stand for exports and imports of good i, and let F_i denote the amount of foreign exchange used as an input to, or derived as an output from, the relevant trade sector:

Sector	Output		Input
Tillage exports	F_T	=	$p_T E_T$
Pasture exports	F_P	=	$p_P E_P$
Forestry exports	F_{FF}	=	$p_{FF} E_{FF}$
X-sector exports	F_X	=	$p_X E_X$
H-sector imports	I_H	=	F_H / p_H
TF imports	I_{TF}	=	F_{TF} / p_{TF}
PF imports	I_{PF}	=	F_{PF} / p_{PF}

The price-cost equations for these sectors tie down the exogenous prices of these goods; it remains to determine the level of exports or imports of the goods.

Demand

There is only one consumer in the model, but the exposition will sound more familiar if we pluralize. Thus, Swedish consumers are endowed with all the raw labor, capital, and land in the economy. In addition, as mentioned, they are endowed with enough foreign exchange to run the exogenous trade deficit. Sweden consumes two kinds of manufactured goods (X and H), domestic and foreign animal and vegetable products, fish and timber, and nontraded services. Consumers maximize a Cobb-Douglas utility function subject to the normal budget constraint. As is well known, Cobb-Douglas utility implies constant expenditure shares. Thus

$$[17] \qquad\qquad C_i = \Theta_i Y / p_i$$

where C_i is the consumption good i, Y is consumer income, Θ_i is a constant, the Θ_i's sum to 1, and p_i is the price of good i.

Equilibrium

Equilibrium is defined by the following conditions: for every sector, price equals cost; for every commodity, demand equals supply; consumer income equals the annual yield from endowments. If there are n sectors and m commodities, this implies $n + m + 1$ equations (and, owing to Walras's Law, $n + m$ *independent* equations), to solve for $n + m + 1$ unknowns (n activity levels, m prices and consumer income). Sectors here include those that transform goods into foreign exchange or vice versa, and the "sector" that transforms raw labor into agricultural and nonagricultural labor.

Data

The model is estimated on data from 1871, and the full details can be found in O'Rourke and Williamson (1995, appendix 1).

The Irish CGE Model for 1907–1908

The remainder of this appendix will point out only those features of the Irish model different from the Swedish model.

Instead of six, there are only three producing sectors in the Irish model: agriculture (A), manufacturing (M), and services (S). Agriculture produces food by using as inputs agricultural labor (L_A), capital (K), land (R), and imported manufactures (M_{FA}, denoting imported fertilizers). Manufacturing produces output by using as inputs nonagricultural labor (L_{NA}), capital, agricultural goods (food processing was an important industrial activity in nineteenth-century Ireland), imported manufactures (M_{FM}, denoting, for example, cotton yarns) and "exotic imports" (F, goods for which no (or almost no) domestic substitutes were produced at home, such as raw cotton and coal). Services are produced by using nonagricultural labor, capital, and agricultural goods (horses and horsefeed sold to the transport part of the sector). These production functions can be written formally as:

[18] $$A = A\left(L_A, K_A, R, M_{FA}\right)$$

[19] $$M = M\left(L_{NAM}, K_M, A_M, M_{FM}, F_M\right)$$

[20] $$S = S\left(L_{NAS}, K_S, A_S\right)$$

Food and manufactures are internationally traded: Ireland exports domestic manufactures (linen) and food (cheese and meat), and imports foreign manufactures (cotton textiles and machines) and the "exotic" intermediate inputs. With one exception, we view Ireland as fulfilling the so-called small-country case: prices of all tradables but one are taken as exogenous, determined in world markets, and over which Ireland has no control. The exceptions are those domestically produced manufactures: Irish manufactures face a constant elasticity demand function abroad, a standard treatment in the trade literature. Ireland is allowed to run the (tiny) trade deficit observed in 1908, but it is exogenous.

Data

The Irish model is estimated on data from 1907–1908 and the full details can be found in Boyer, Hatton and O'Rourke (1993).

Labor Market Impact Abroad and Convergence

Introduction

The rest of this book has established that the mass migration was driven in large measure by market forces at origin and destination. The previous chapter has also established that European emigration had a significant impact on labor markets at home: the departure of the movers improved economic conditions of the stayers faster than would have been true without emigration—raising real wages, lowering unemployment and eroding poverty. By glutting labor markets abroad, the mass migrations must also have reduced the pace of real wage growth in immigrating countries. Thus, mass migration must have tended to create economic convergence among the participating countries; living standards in the poor emigrating countries tended, as a consequence, to catch up with living standards in rich immigrating countries. Not all countries participated, some had offsetting influences, and some had more induced catch-up than others, but the underlying tendencies must have been pervasive. These are qualitative statements, however. We want to give them more quantitative muscle. So far, chapter 9 has offered that muscle for two important emigrating countries that exhibited impressive catch-up—Ireland and Sweden. What about all the rest, especially the immigrating countries in the New World? How important *was* the impact of the mass migrations?

This chapter identifies the contribution of the mass migrations to late-nineteenth-century economic convergence in two ways.[1] The first offers an assessment for the two most important economies in the Old and New World—Britain and the United States. It makes the assessment using the same kind of CGE models applied already to Ireland and Sweden in the previous chapter, constructed and implemented in collaboration once again with Kevin O'Rourke (O'Rourke, Williamson, and Hatton, 1994). The second uses econometrics and expands the sample from two to 17, a project implemented by one of us and Alan Taylor (Taylor and Williamson 1997). The 17-country econometric analysis confirms the Anglo-American CGE experiment: indeed, it appears that mass migrations explain an even larger share of the Atlantic economy convergence up to World War I than of Anglo-America alone. The estimated contribution of the mass migrations is so large, in fact, that its impact on convergence must have been offset (on net) by a variety of countervailing forces: independent disequilibrating forces of technical change (faster in rich countries, and confirmed for the United States in the Anglo-American comparison) and dependent offsetting forces of capital-accumulation (international capital chasing after the migrants or native capital accumulation stimulated by the presence of immigrants), of natural resource exploitation (land settlement by migrants or by natives who the migrants displaced in settled areas), of trade (migrant labor favoring the expansion of labor-intensive activities in rich countries), or of productivity gains (migrant labor–induced scale economies). While these interactions were rich and subtle, the chapter shows unambiguously that the mass migrations contributed profoundly to economic convergence and to global labor market integration prior to World War I.

The Impact of Migration on Anglo-American Labor Markets: Maintaining Wicksell's Classical Assumptions

International migration certainly improves the living standards of those who move, and chapters 2 through 7 offered abundant evidence confirming that the gains from moving were typically very significant, even if assimilation sometimes was a problem in the new country. Chapter 9 showed how such migrations also improved the living standards for those who stayed behind, at least for the Irish and Swedes, stayers who witnessed two of the fastest catch-up performances in the late-nineteenth-century. But what did the mass migrations do for the natives (and old immigrants) who competed with the new immigrants abroad?

As we have already stressed, debate on this question is at least as old as the Industrial Revolution in Europe, which sent so many emigrants to the New World in the nineteenth century. The debate also has a long history in the United States, the New World country that absorbed the majority of the emigrants leaving Europe. It reached a crescendo in 1911 after the Immigration Commission had pondered the problem for four years. As we have seen, the Commission concluded that immigration was not advantageous and contributed to poor working conditions, findings that helped create the quota legislation implemented in the 1920s.

Since the Immigration Commission had no model that could be used to assess a counterfactual world without immigrants, it's hard to imagine how it reached its conclusion. In chapter 8 we began to shape our own conclusion but stopped short of a full general equilibrium assessment. Now we finish the task.

There is no doubt that population and labor shifted their center of gravity away from Europe in the nineteenth century. After all, scarce labor in the New World encouraged exactly that kind of supply response. Part of the supply response took the form of high fertility and low mortality, and part of it took the form of

Table 10.1 Summary Data: Net Migration Rates and Cumulative Impact, 1870–1910

	Persons-adjusted net migration rate, 1870–1910	Persons-adjusted cumulative population impact, 1910	Labor force-adjusted net migration rate, 1870–1910	Labor force-adjusted cumulative labor force impact, 1910
Argentina	11.74	60%	15.50	86%
Australia	6.61	30%	8.73	42%
Belgium	1.67	7%	2.20	9%
Brazil	0.74	3%	0.98	4%
Canada	6.92	32%	9.14	44%
Denmark	−2.78	−11%	−3.67	−14%
France	−0.10	0%	−0.13	−1%
Germany	−0.73	−3%	−0.96	−4%
Great Britain	−2.25	−9%	−2.97	−11%
Ireland	−11.24	−36%	−14.84	−45%
Italy	−9.25	−31%	−12.21	−39%
Netherlands	−0.59	−2%	−0.78	−3%
Norway	−5.25	−19%	−6.93	−24%
Portugal	−1.06	−4%	−1.40	−5%
Spain	−1.16	−5%	−1.53	−6%
Sweden	−4.20	−15%	−5.55	−20%
United States	4.03	17%	5.31	24%
New World	6.01	29%	7.93	40%
Old World	−3.08	−11%	−4.06	−13%

Notes: Rates per thousand per annum. Minus denotes emigration. See text and appendix 10.2.

Source: Taylor and Williamson (1997, table 1).

migration. Earlier estimates abound: up to 1913, immigration accounted for 50 percent of Argentina's and 30 percent of Australia's population increase (Taylor 1992a: table 1.1). Between 1870 and 1910, immigration accounted for 28 percent of population increase in the United States (Easterlin 1968: 189). Between 1871 and 1890, emigration reduced Swedish population increase by 44 percent (Karlstrom 1985: 155, 181); between 1870 and 1910, it reduced British population increase by 21 percent (Mitchell and Deane 1962: 9–10). Based on the discussion in chapters 6 and 9, even bigger shares characterized Ireland in midcentury and Italy after the 1890s, and based on emigration rates, the shares were probably even higher for Norway. Because the migrations selected young adult men with high labor participation rates, the impact was even greater on the labor force in sending and receiving countries.

Table 10.1 reports an up-to-date, comprehensive assessment of the mass migrations. These estimates have the advantage of using the same method in all countries, but elsewhere in this book we may adjust them where it seems appropriate (e.g., Sweden 20 percent here, but 18.1 percent elsewhere). In any case, table 10.1 shows that the mass migrations served to raise Argentina's labor force in 1910 by 86 percent, 44 percent in Canada, 42 percent in Australia, and 24 percent in the

United States. These same migrations served to lower the labor force in 1910 in Ireland by 45 percent, in Italy by 39 percent, in Sweden by 20 percent, and in Britain by 11 percent.

So, how significant were these mass migrations in causing real wages and living standards in the labor-abundant Old World to catch up with the labor-scarce New World? Did these mass migrations cause economic convergence more generally among participating countries? While the U.S. Immigration Commission was dealing with the New World side of the process, what about the Old World side? Chapter 9 noted that Sweden in the early 1880s was in the midst of lively protection and emigration debates, generated by two decades of massive out-migration to the New World and an "invasion of grains" from the same source. Knut Wicksell (1882) concluded that Swedish emigration should have been encouraged because he thought it would solve the farm pauper problem. Chapter 9 also noted that the 1954 Irish Commission on Emigration shared Wicksell's view, at least as it applied to Ireland.

Despite the visibility of these assertions and their authority, they had never been tested either for emigrating or for immigrating countries until recently.

Furthermore, the available literature typically asks about the impact on the receiving (or less frequently, the sending) region alone, rather than about convergence between them. The difference matters. After all, if real wages were growing at 2 percent per annum in the labor-scarce country and 3 percent in the labor-abundant country, and if the 1 percent difference were attributable entirely to external migration, we might correctly conclude that migration accounted for "only" one quarter of real wage growth in the labor-scarce immigrating country (say, half of the 1 percent, 0.5 percent, divided by 2 percent) and for "only" one sixth in the labor-abundant emigrating country (0.5 percent divided by 3 percent), incorrectly concluding that migration didn't contribute much to the (significant) convergence although in fact it accounted for *all* of it. The moral of the story is that we must explore the two regions simultaneously.

The standard way of presenting the problem on the blackboard is illustrated in figure 10.1. New World wages and labor's marginal product are on the left-hand side and Old World wages and labor's marginal product are on the right-hand side. The world labor supply is measured along the horizontal axis. An equilibrium distribution of labor, of course, occurs at the intersection of the two derived labor demand schedules (O and N). Instead, we start at L^1 where labor is scarce in the New World, and thus where the wage gap between the two regions is very large, $w_n^1 - w_o^1$. If "mass" migrations redistribute labor towards the New World, say to L^2, the wage gap collapses to $w_n^2 - w_o^2$, and all the observed convergence would be attributable to migration. However, the same kind of convergence could have been achieved by a relative demand shift: a shift in O to O^1, an event driven perhaps by relative price shocks favoring labor in the Old World or by faster accumulation and technological "catching up" there. Figure 10.1 is certainly an elegant statement of the question, but how do we implement the answer empirically?

The only way to proceed, of course, is to develop a model in which the long-run impact of the mass migrations can be assessed. But which model? Chapter 9 applied

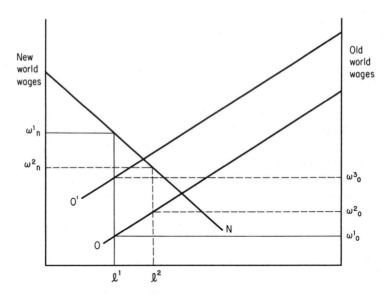

Figure 10.1 World Labor Supply: A Two Region World Labor Market

CGE models to both Ireland and Sweden to assess the impact at home, and the first part of this chapter will do the same for Anglo-America combined. We are well aware, however, of the debatable assumptions that may drive the results. That the models focus on long-run supply-side forces seems appropriate, but, following Wicksell, we also assume the absence of scale economies, accumulation responses, and influences on the rate of technological change. It seems to us sensible to ask first whether those migrations would have mattered to the evolution of international wage gaps if standard classical, comparative static assumptions were approximated by reality. With first-order impacts estimated, we can then explore whether the relaxation of Wicksell's classical assumptions would overturn our interpretation of history.

We start with wage gaps themselves. As before, we use the PPP-adjusted urban unskilled real wage database (Williamson 1995). The 1870–1913 evidence for 15 of these countries is summarized in figure 10.2 by a coefficient of variation, C(15), which documents considerable convergence. Furthermore, the late-nineteenth-century real wage convergence is similar in magnitude to the better-known convergence after World War II. Perhaps most interesting, however, is the finding that most of the late-nineteenth-century real wage convergence can be attributed to an erosion in the real wage gap between the Old and New World (Dno in figure 10.2), not to any significant convergence within the Old World (Do) or within the New (Dn). Around 1870, real wages in the labor-scarce New World (Argentina, Australia, Canada, and the United States) were much higher than in the labor-abundant Old World (Ireland, Great Britain; Denmark, Norway, Sweden; Germany; Belgium, Netherlands, France; Italy and Spain), 136 percent higher. By 1895, real wages in the

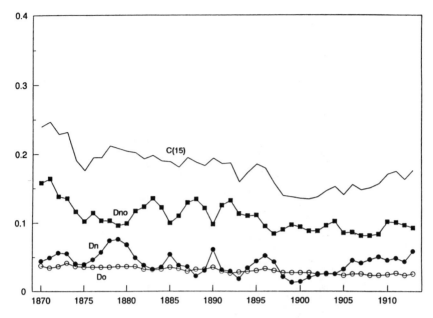

Figure 10.2 International Real Wage Dispersion, 1870–1913. *Source*: Williamson (1994)

New World were "only" 100 percent higher, and in 1913 they were "only" about 87 percent higher. In short, the real wage gap between Old World and New fell 36 percentage points over the 25 years up to 1895, and by 49 percentage points over the 43 years up to 1913. The Old World caught up quite a bit with the New. Although the magnitudes were less dramatic, what was true of the Old and New Worlds was also true of two of the most important members in each: in 1870, real wages in the United States were 66.7 percent higher than in Britain whereas in 1890 they were "only" 49.5 percent higher, in 1895 44 percent higher, in 1910 61.9 percent higher, and in 1913 54 percent higher. Thus, the Anglo-American real wage gap fell by 17.2 percentage points over the 20 years up to 1890, by 4.8 percentage points over the 40 years up to 1910, and by 13 percentage points over the 43 years up to 1913. Britain caught up a bit with the United States, a surprising finding given all that has been said about Britain losing its leadership to America. It must be said, however, that *all* of the British catch-up took place before 1895, not afterward, when American industrial ascendancy was most dramatic. Furthermore, we focus on real wages rather than labor productivity. These two concepts use very different deflators, a distinction that mattered considerably in the late-nineteenth-century. We shall have more to say about these pre-1890 and post-1890 regimes.

We now ask: how much of the Anglo-American real wage convergence after 1870 can be explained by total British net emigration and total American net immigration? The open, multisector British and American CGEs (like the Irish and Swedish

Table 10.2 Counterfactual: What Would Have Been the Impact on Britain and the United States without International Migration? (in percentages)

Variable	United States		Great Britain		United States less Great Britain	
	1870–1890 flows on 1890 economy	1870–1910 flows on 1910 economy	1870–1890 flows on 1890 economy	1870–1910 flows on 1910 economy	1870–1890 flows on 1890 economy	1870–1910 flows on 1910 economy
Panel A: labor migration only, with no capital flow response: capital does not chase after labor						
Urban real wage	+14.4	+34.0	-8.8	-12.2	+23.2	+46.2
Return to capital	-14.5	-23.8	+8.4	+12.7	-22.9	-36.5
Panel B: labor migration with elastic capital flow response: capital chases after labor						
Urban real wage	+3.7	+9.2	-4.7	-6.6	+8.4	+15.8
Return to capital	0	0	0	0	0	0

Source: Entries refer to percentage change in variables' levels. See text. The estimated CGEs underlying the experiments are discussed in O'Rourke and Williamson (1994), while the results are reported in O'Rourke, Williamson, and Hatton (1994, table 10.1).

CGEs in the previous chapter) are in the classical, comparative static tradition: in the counterfactual experiment, land, capital, and technologies are, at least initially, fixed; only labor varies in the no-American-immigration and no-British-emigration counterfactuals. The U.S. labor force would have been about 13 percent smaller in 1890 without the 1870–1890 net immigrations, and about 27 percent smaller in 1910 without the 1870–1910 net immigrations. The British labor force would have been about 11 percent larger in 1891 without the 1871–1891 net emigrations, and about 16 percent larger in 1911 without the 1871–1911 net emigrations. (All of these calculations include the influence of migrant children born after the move. As table 10.1 shows, if the children of the migrants are ignored and some other adjustments are made, the 1910 U.S. labor force would have been about 24 percent smaller in the absence of immigration, not 27 percent. Similarly, the 1911 British labor force would have been 11 percent larger in the absence of emigration, not 16 percent, after making these adjustments.)[2]

What would have been the impact on these two economies had these migrations not taken place? The results are presented in panel A of table 10.2 and the impacts are very big. In 1910, real wages would have been 34 percent higher in the United States and 12.2 percent lower in Britain. American real wage rates were actually about 61.9 percent higher than British in 1910; without the late-nineteenth-century migrations they would have been about 147 percent higher. The Anglo-American real wage gap fell between 1870 and 1910; without the late-nineteenth-century migrations it would have more than doubled!

There would have been no Anglo-American convergence without the mass migrations.

Relaxing Wicksell's Classical Assumptions for Anglo-America

One could argue that the classical assumptions made thus far overstate the impact of the mass migrations on Anglo-American labor markets.

First, we have assumed that labor is homogeneous: natives and migrants are taken to be unskilled, and they compete for the same jobs. In contrast, economists assessing postwar American experience with immigration tend to view migrants and natives more as complements (see the summaries in Simon 1989 and Borjas 1990). Chapter 7 argued that the modern complementarity position should be viewed with skepticism (Hatton and Williamson 1994c). More recent research on post–World War II American experience confirms that skepticism (Borjas and Freeman 1992), but there is reason in any case to think that conditions were quite different a century ago. After all, skilled labor was a much smaller share of the labor force in both sending and receiving regions in the late-nineteenth-century than it is now; skills (post-literacy formal education in particular) were much less important to 1895 technologies than they are to 1995 technologies. Furthermore, human capital gaps between migrants and native-born were much smaller than they are today (especially in the 1980s: Borjas 1991). And finally, chapter 8 has shown that there is very little evidence to suggest that foreign labor entered segmented occupations or lacked mobility. Substitutability far more likely characterized labor markets in the late-nineteenth-century than complementarity: new emigrants competed directly with the native-born and old emigrants at the bottom end of the labor market.

Second, we have stressed the supply side and ignored aggregate demand. The latter view was certainly dominant in the historical literature of the 1950s and 1960s when Keynesian thinking was in vogue (Thomas 1954; Easterlin 1968; Abramovitz 1961, 1968), and a modern version has recently been offered to account for the view that immigrants never robbed jobs from Australians in the past (Pope and Withers 1993). This argument might be credible for the short run, but not for periods spanning as much as 40 years.

Third, we have ignored the possibility of increasing returns, even though it is now firmly embedded in the new growth theory (Romer 1986; Krugman 1991). The reason is simple: even though it may have been present in the late-nineteenth-century, no persuasive evidence has confirmed it or its alleged magnitude.

Finally, there are the more conventional accumulation, land settlement, and comparative advantage responses to consider. Might immigrant-induced long-run supply-side responses have simultaneously shifted the labor demand curve to the right just when immigrant-induced rightward shifts in labor supply were taking place? We find these arguments more compelling, and we now explore them at length. We start with the most important: foreign capital chasing after migrating labor.

Did Capital Chase After Labor and Affect the Impact of the Mass Migrations on Anglo-America?

In the simple two-factor model, labor should migrate from the low-wage to the high-wage country, and capital should migrate from the high-wage (low returns) to the low-wage (high returns) country. The better integrated are world capital markets, the faster the real wage convergence. If world capital markets become better integrated over time, the rate of convergence should accelerate, and if world capital markets break down, convergence should slow down.

Crude correlations would appear consistent with these predictions. After all, there was dramatic real wage convergence during the second half of the nineteenth century, trends that appear to track evolving world capital market integration. The size of the international capital flows was very large, with Britain at the center (Edelstein 1982). Furthermore, there is evidence that world capital markets were at least as well integrated around 1890 as they were around 1980 (Zevin 1992; Obsfeldt 1994). In addition, real wage convergence ceased from the start of World War I to the end of World War II, three decades during which global capital markets collapsed.

Crude correlations may be misleading, however, since the two-factor model is an inadequate characterization of late-nineteenth-century history. What really distinguished the Old World from the New was natural resource endowment, and that fact motivates the concept of New World "dual scarcity" (Temin 1966). Although resources were abundant there, both capital and labor were scarce. And there is plenty of evidence that capital and labor moved together as a consequence: that is, labor emigrated from capital-exporting Old World countries (like Britain, Germany, and France) and labor immigrated into capital-importing New World countries (like Argentina, Australia, Canada, and the United States).

If capital and labor moved together, can it still be said that the overseas mass migrations really contributed to Anglo-American real wage convergence? We need to know whether the international flow of labor dominated the flow of capital. If it did, it served to lower the capital-labor ratio in America compared with Britain, thus contributing to wage convergence. Capital deepening over time can be written as $d(K/L) = (K/L)\{[dK_d/K - dL_d/L] + [NFI/K - MIG/L]\}$. The first term on the right-hand side of this expression refers to domestic capital and labor (K_d, L_d) growth and the second to foreign sources of capital deepening (NFI is equal to the current account balance and MIG is equal to net migration). The second term interests us.[3]

Labor migration clearly dominated capital migration in the United States between 1870 and 1910: while foreign capital imports served on average to raise the rate of accumulation by a trivial amount over the four decades as a whole, 0.03 percent per annum, foreign immigration tended to raise the rate of labor force growth more dramatically, 0.82 percent per annum. In combination, international factor flows served to lower the rate of capital deepening in the United States by 0.79 percentage points per annum: external factor flows into the United States cut the rate of capital deepening by more than a quarter.

Britain, however, appears to offer a different story. British capital moved with labor in such massive amounts that international factor migration must have inhibited convergence: emigration served to lower the rate of labor force growth in Britain by about 0.4 per annum between 1870 and 1910, but capital exports served to lower the rate of accumulation by far more, 2.15 percent per annum. External factor flows did not raise the rate of capital deepening in Britain, but rather lowered it by about 1.8 percent per annum: according to this calculation, British export of capital and labor cut the rate of capital deepening by almost three quarters. Thus, it appears that British factor exports could not have contributed to Anglo-American real wage convergence in the late-nineteenth-century.

Yet, while capital was exiting Britain faster than labor, how much of it was actually *chasing after labor*? The answer is elusive, but we can take a crude cut at the problem by identifying the direction of the flows. Almost all British emigrants went to North America, Australia, and New Zealand, but only 45 percent of British capital exports went to the same regions (Simon 1967). Thus, the "chasing" component of British capital exports cannot have reduced the rate of capital accumulation by more than about 1 percentage point per annum, thus reducing the measured impact on capital deepening to about 0.6 percent per annum. Even then, we do not know how much of the British capital exports to North America, Australia, and New Zealand was actually chasing after that labor and how much of it was responding to third factors.

To estimate the impact of labor migration on real wage convergence, we need to identify that share of British capital flowing to the New World that was chasing after labor. We cannot. But we can place an upper bound on the estimate by exploring a second question: what happens in the no-migration counterfactual reported in table 10.2 when capital is allowed to chase after labor, that is, when world capital markets are treated as perfectly integrated? Panel B supplies the answer. But before we look at panel B, note in panel A the impact on the return to capital in the no-migration counterfactual when international capital is assumed immobile. The capital-labor ratio rises in the United States and falls in Britain, so the return to capital falls in the United States and rises in Britain. Thus, if capital is now allowed to be perfectly mobile, some of it will retreat from America and stay home in Britain, muting migration's impact on convergence. Now look at panel B: in this no-migration counterfactual, 1910 real wages would have been 9.2 percent higher in the United States and 6.6 percent lower in Britain. American real wages were 61.9 percent higher than in Britain in 1910; without the late-nineteenth-century migrations, *and* without that part of the capital flows that chased after the migrants, the American real wage advantage would have been even higher, 89.3 percent; furthermore, there would have been no Anglo-American real wage convergence at all, since the 1870 American real wage advantage of 66.7 percent would have risen to 89.3 percent by the end of the period.

The moral of the story is that international migration contributed to Anglo-American real wage convergence even if we allow for perfect capital market integration and thus for an elastic accumulation response. But the convergence induced by migration is much smaller when capital is allowed to chase after labor, although the assumed elastic response in panel B in table 10.2 is extreme. The impact would, of course, be even smaller if we allowed immigration to augment natural resource endowment, through, for example, land settlement (Findlay 1995: ch. 5). We might therefore view panel A in table 10.2 as an upper bound and panel B as a lower bound. The econometric results reported later in this chapter are much closer to the lower-bound figures, which we use to identify the sources of Anglo-American convergence in the next section.

What Explains Late-Nineteenth-Century Anglo-American Convergence?

Real wages and living standards converged among the currently industrialized Organization for Economic Cooperation and Development (OECD) countries between 1870 and World War I. The convergence was driven primarily by the erosion of the average wage gap between the New World and the Old, rather than by convergence within either of the two regions. Although the real wage convergence between the resource-rich and labor-scarce United States and resource-poor and labor-abundant Britain was far less spectacular than was true for the rest of the OECD sample, and although it was far greater in the first half than in the second half of the period, some Anglo-American convergence did take place.

How much of this Anglo-American convergence was due to the mass migrations? How much of it was due to other forces such as trade-induced factor-price

Table 10.3 The Sources of Late-Nineteenth-Century Anglo-American Real Wage
Convergence: Wage Gap (in percentages)

Source	1870	1890	1910
1. Wage gap trend observed	66.7	49.5	61.9
Due to			
2. Post-1870 labor migration, with capital flow response	66.7	53.2	42.6
3. Residual: due to post-1870 productivity	66.7	62.7	89.2
advance and resource accumulation favoring			
the United States, plus trade forces			

Notes: **Row 1** reports the percentage by which real wage rates in the United States exceeded Britain in 1870, 1890, and 1910.

    Row 2 can be illustrated by the 1890 calculation: table 10.2, panel B, reports that the U.S. wage would have increased 3.7 percent in the absence of immigration (to 172.9 = 1.037 × 166.7), so it follows that immigration by itself served to reduce the U.S. wage 3.6 percent ([166.7 − 172.9]/172.9 = − 0.036), that is from 166.7 (Britain = 100) in 1870 to 160.7 in 1890 (= 0.964 × 166.7); table 10.2, panel B, reports that the British wage would have decreased 4.7 percent in the absence of emigration (to 95.3 = 0.953 × 100), so it follows that emigration by itself served to raise the British wage 4.9 percent ([100 − 95.3]/95.3 = + 0.049), that is from 100 in 1870 to 104.9 in 1890; thus, migration by itself served to reduce the wage gap from 66.7 percent in 1870 to 53.2 percent in 1890 ([160.7 − 104.9]/104.9 = 0.532).

    Row 3 calculates the residual: migration alone implies a 1890 wage ratio of 1.532 (row 2). All forces combined to produce the actual 1890 wage ratio of 1.495 (row 1). Thus, residual forces joined migration forces in lowering the wage ratio still more, by [1.495 − 1.532]/1.532 = −2.4%. Residual forces on their own would have implied a 1890 wage ratio of [0.976 × 1.667] = 1.627 or a gap of 62.7%. Mass migration was clearly the dominant force at work between 1870 and 1890. Migration alone implies a 1910 wage ratio of 1.426 (row 2). All forces combined to produce the 1910 actual wage ratio of 1.619 (row 1). Thus, residual forces on their own *raised* the wage ratio by [1.619 − 1.426]/1.426 = 13.5%. The residual forces on their own would have implied a 1910 wage ratio of [1.135*1.667] = 189.2, or a gap of 89.2%.

    Source: O'Rourke, Williamson, and Hatton (1994, table 10.3).

convergence, resource accumulation, and productivity advance? Table 10.3 offers some tentative answers. The first row reports the observed real wage convergence, the United States losing some of its real wage advantage between 1870 and 1890, while recovering most of that lost ground between 1890 and 1910. The second row reports the independent impact of United States immigrations and British emigrations on the Anglo-American wage gap, netting out the possibility that capital chased after labor (from table 10.2, panel B). Row 2 offers a lower bound of the impact of the mass migrations since it makes the extreme assumption of perfectly elastic capital flow responses to rate of return differentials in the two economies. The third row reports the residual: it estimates what would have happened to the Anglo-American wage gap in the absence of the convergence forces associated with mass migration. As an upper bound, it includes the impact of resource deepening and productivity advance favoring the United States, all stressed by Gerschenkron (1952), Abramovitz (1986), and Wright (1990).

    What did we find? The story is written in two parts, and we start with the first part, the 1870s and 1880s.

    Between 1870 and 1890, what might be called open economy or globalization forces were working hard to erase America's real wage advantage over Britain. In the absence of any other influences, these combined globalization forces—commodity trade and mass migration—by themselves would have cut the Anglo-

American wage gap by about a third, from 66.7 percent to 44.7 percent (not reported in table 10.3). Furthermore, international migration and commodity trade had roughly equal influence, so Wicksell and Heckscher and Ohlin were about equally right. Nonetheless, these globalization convergence forces were partially offset by the combined influence of more rapid productivity advance and resource accumulation in America. We have no way of knowing which of these residual forces was most important, although a recent article involving one of us suggests that it was productivity advance (O'Rourke, Taylor, and Williamson 1996). The globalization convergence forces dominated the residual divergence forces in the 1870s and 1880s, however, so the observed Anglo-American wage gap declined from 66.7 to 49.5 percent. Had those convergence forces been absent, the Anglo-American wage gap would have *increased* from 66.7 percent in 1870 to 72.5 percent in 1890.

Between 1890 and 1910, the story seems quite different. Looks, however, can often be deceiving. Globalization forces were working just as hard to erase the wage gap. In the absence of other influences, these combined convergence forces by themselves would have cut the Anglo-American wage gap still further, down to 25.6 percent by 1910 (not reported in table 10.3). And, once again, international migrations and commodity trade contributed about equally to the further erosion in the wage gap. What is different after 1890 is the residual: rapid productivity advance and resource accumulation favoring America were so spectacular that the globalization forces fostering convergence were swamped by these residual divergence forces, thus allowing the United States to regain most of real wage advantage lost in the 1870s and 1880s. Indeed, in the absence of the combined globalization forces, the Anglo-American wage gap would have *risen* over these four decades from 66.7 percent to 114.9 percent, and the vast majority of the rise would have occurred after 1890. To put it another way, a rapidly industrializing United States bucked the convergence tide after 1890 (and up to 1940: Wright 1990), but the tide was still running strong and still being pushed by globalization forces associated with migration and commodity price convergence.

These Anglo-American findings are directly relevant to debates about convergence, but can they be generalized for the late-nineteenth-century Atlantic economy? In some ways yes, in some ways no: (1) "no" in the sense that the factor-price-equalization forces from commodity trade were weaker for many other European trading partners (due, of course, to protection: O'Rourke, Taylor, and Williamson 1996); (2) "yes" in the sense that Old World mass emigrations were even bigger in Ireland, Italy, and Norway than in Britain, and in the sense that New World mass immigrations were even bigger in Argentina and Canada than in the United States; (3) "maybe" in the sense that those residual factors likely favored convergence for other pairs of countries, poor countries catching up technologically with the rich. Of course, we need more studies like this one to find out whether the late-nineteenth-century Anglo-American convergence forces were replicated at the global level. The remainder of this chapter moves in that direction.

The Late-Nineteenth-Century Atlantic Economy Facts

Table 10.1 reports late-nineteenth-century net migration rates for five New World and 12 Old World countries. It also reports consistent estimates of the impact of these migrations on the 1910 labor force in each country. The labor force impact varied greatly. Britain and the United States were a bit below average: Argentina's labor force was augmented most by immigration (86 percent), Brazil's the least (4 percent), and the United States' in between (24 percent), but below the New World average of 40 percent; Ireland's labor force was diminished most by emigration (45 percent), France and the Netherlands the least (1 and 3 percent), and Britain in between (11 percent), slightly below the Old World average of 13 percent. These, then, are the mass migrations whose labor market impact we wish to assess.[4]

Table 10.4 shows exactly what we wish to explain. There we offer four measures of convergence across the late-nineteenth-century: as with figure 10.2, the last column is based on Williamson's (1995) 17-country sample that includes the 12 Old World countries listed in table 10.5 plus three New World OECD members, Australia, Canada, and the United States, and two New World nonmembers, Argentina and Brazil. The first three columns include Ireland as part of the United Kingdom. The 1870–1913 rate of convergence in the first column of table 10.4 is based on Maddison's GDP data originally used by Abramovitz (1986): it was about 1 percent per annum, roughly equal to the long-run convergence rate over the past century or so. The degree of convergence depends greatly, however, on the measure

Table 10.4 Summary Data: Convergence, 1870–1980s

Variable: references:	GDP/work hour, Abramovitz, Maddison (1982) ($n = 16$) (1)	GDP/capita, this study, Maddison (1991) ($n = 16$) (2)	GDP/work hour, this study, Maddison (1991) ($n = 16$) (3)	Real wages, this study, Williamson (1995) ($n = 17$) (4)
A. Coefficient of variation (cv)				
1870	0.51	0.38	0.44	0.50
1913	0.33	0.33	0.37	0.43
1950	0.36	0.36	0.43	0.45
1987	0.15*	0.11†	0.13	0.33
B. Implied convergence speed per annum (in %)				
1870–1913	1.01	0.34	0.36	0.35
1913–1950	−0.24	−0.23	−0.37	−0.07
1950–1987	3.02*	2.91†	3.14	0.79
Overall	1.12*	1.00†	1.01	0.36

Notes: In this table the coefficient of variation (CV) is standard deviation divided by the mean. Implied convergence speed is rate of decline of ln(CV). * = 1979 alternate terminal date. † = 1989 alternate terminal date.

Sources: Taylor and Williamson (1997, table 2). Original data from Abramovitz (1986); Maddison (1982; 1991); Williamson (1995).

used and on the PPP comparison adopted. All three newer estimates in columns 2 through 4 record lower rates of convergence in the 1870–1913 period. Note also the extent to which late-nineteenth-century convergence is diminished by the switch from Maddison's 1982 data (table 10.4, column 1, the same data used by Abramovitz) to Maddison's 1991 revised data (table 10.4, column 2). The sensitivity stems from the estimation methodology: using individual-country growth rates, Maddison projects backwards from the 1970s or 1980s GDP benchmarks constructed from PPP comparisons, an approach that, of course, invites concern about long-run index-number problems and doubts about the accuracy of the implicit back-projected PPPs assumed stable over the past century and even longer. Thus, the availability of new data based on real wages, and use of additional PPP benchmarks from the 1920s and 1900–1913, provides a welcome consistency check on Maddison's aggregates. In short, the remainder of this chapter uses three measures of convergence performance: Maddison's newest GDP per capita data, Maddison's newest GDP per worker data, and Williamson's real wage data.

Measuring the Impact of Mass Migration in the Atlantic Economy

Like the CGE analysis earlier in this chapter, what follows also uses a counterfactual simulation approach. However, the model, though much simpler, is now estimated econometrically. As before, our purpose is to assess migration's role in accounting for convergence, here measured by the decline in dispersion between 1870 and 1910. The relevant data are summarized in the middle panel of table 10.5: real wage dispersion declined by 28 percent over the period, GDP per capita dispersion by 18 percent, and GDP per worker dispersion by 29 percent.[5] What contribution did international migration make to that measured convergence? To answer the question, we ask another: what would have been the measured 1870–1910 convergence had there been no (net) migration? The no-migration counterfactual invokes the *ceteris paribus* assumption: in each country, we adjust population and labor force according to the average net migration (and labor participation) rate observed during the period and assume that technology, capital stocks, prices, and all else remain constant. The Anglo-American discussion argued that such assumptions impart an upward bias on the measured impact of mass migration, but let's see whether the magnitudes for the Atlantic economy as a whole are large enough to warrant further debate over bias.

A country with an observed cumulative net migration rate M, will be assumed to experience a counterfactual population change of $POP^* = M(1 - \rho)$ in the terminal year, where we use X^* to denote dX/X, and where ρ is a return rate correction factor introduced to allow for the well-known fact that return migration was underenumerated.[6] Migration affects long-run equilibrium output and wages to the extent that it influences aggregate labor supply L^*. If we assume a standard aggregate production function where output $Y = F(L, . . .)$, a labor market where competitive wages equal labor's marginal product, and inelastic labor supplies, then it

Table 10.5 Summary Data: Convergence, 1870–1910

	Real wages		GDP per capita		GDP per worker	
	1870	1910	1870	1910	1870	1910
Levels						
Argentina	61	95	915	2,226	1,946	5,317
Australia	127	135	3,123	4,586	7,811	10,573
Belgium	60	87	2,104	3,171	4,836	7,059
Brazil	39	85	425	549	1,101	1,422
Canada	99	205	1,365	3,263	3,781	7,876
Denmark	36	99	1,624	3,005	2,943	5,900
France	50	71	1,638	2,503	3,336	5,031
Germany	58	87	772	1,424	2,996	5,510
Great Britain	69	105	3,055	4,026	7,132	9,448
Ireland	49	91	—	—	—	—
Italy	26	50	1,244	1,933	2,309	3,920
Netherlands	52	70	2,064	2,964	5,322	7,795
Norway	28	70	1,190	1,875	2,800	4,719
Portugal	32	42	612	901	1,346	2,024
Spain	51	52	1,308	1,962	3,194	4,919
Sweden	28	100	1,316	2,358	2,814	5,019
United States	115	170	2,254	4,559	5,925	10,681
Dispersion (1870 = 100)						
All	100	72	100	82	100	71
New World	100	76	100	71	100	65
Old World	100	73	100	70	100	61
New World/Old World						
Gap (parity = 100)	196	179	109	128	116	129

Notes: Dispersion measure is variance divided by the square of the mean (or CV squared), using an index with 1870 = 100. See text and appendix 10.2.

Source: Taylor and Williamson (1997, table 3).

follows that $Y^* = (wL/Y)L^* = \theta L^*$, where θ is labor's share in output, and that $(w/P)^* = \eta^{-1}L^*$, where η is the elasticity of labor demand with respect to the wage, holding all other inputs fixed. Under the *ceteris paribus* assumption, the structure of prices is invariant under the counterfactual so that the impact of migration on the producer wage and consumer wage is identical: $(w/P)^* = (w/CPI)^*$, where CPI is the consumer price index.

Thus, the long-run migration impact on wages and output can be derived as long as migrant population streams can be converted into labor supply effects. Suppose, therefore, that α_M of a given migrant stream is active in the labor force, while the share of the total population active is α_{POP}. Moreover, assume that migrants have an effective-worker or worker-quality ratio with respect to the total labor force equal to μ (reflected, presumably, by an average wage gap between working migrants and native born: see chapter 7). Hence, the labor content of the population is $L = \alpha_{POP}POP$, and the labor content of the migrant flow is $dL = \mu(\alpha_M)M(1 - \rho)POP$. Defining $\gamma = \alpha_M/\alpha_{POP}$ (the migrant-to-population ratio of labor participation rates), we emerge with the expression $L^* = \mu\gamma M(1 - \rho)$.

Given all these terms, we can now define the impact of migration on GDP per capita (Y/POP), GDP per worker (Y/L), and real wages (w/CPI):

[10.1]
$$(w/CPI)^* = (\eta^{-1})L^* = \mu\gamma(\eta^{-1})M(1-\rho)$$

[10.2]
$$(Y/POP)^* = Y^* - POP^* = \theta L^* - M(1-\rho) = (\mu\gamma\alpha - 1)M(1-\rho)$$

[10.3]
$$(Y/L)^* = Y^* - L^* = \theta L^* - \mu\gamma M(1-\rho) = \mu\rho(\theta-1)M(1-\rho)$$

The simulations use the above equations to assess the impact of the mass migrations on 1870–1910 convergence in our Atlantic economy sample of 17 countries.

The data requirements for the counterfactuals are spelled out elsewhere (Taylor and Williamson, 1997, appendix 2) but we offer a brief summary here. The real GDP, population, and labor force estimates are taken primarily from Maddison's (1991) latest study, with extensions, adjustments, and modifications to bring Argentina, Brazil, Portugal, and Spain into our sample and to separate the United Kingdom into Great Britain and Ireland. For real wages we use Williamson's long-run database on internationally comparable real wages (1995). The migration data are collected from standard sources, again with modifications, especially for Australia and Portugal (Ferenczi and Willcox 1931; Hatton and Williamson, 1994b; Taylor and Williamson 1997).

We know far more about some parameters than others. The return migration rate is documented hardly at all in the official data, but we know that it ranged from very high for Italians to almost zero for the Irish and the Scandinavians. The base-line assumption invoked here is that the appropriate correction for underenumeration of return migration implies $\rho = 0.1$. Migrant quality is also poorly documented, and the same movers may have exhibited different quality relative to stayers in the sending and receiving countries. The baseline assumption has been to set the effective worker ratio $\mu = 0.8$ because, although we have little evidence relating to the size of mover versus stayer wage or productivity gaps, we know that immigrants were considered low-quality in the United States and that they typically entered at the bottom of the job ladder (see chapter 7).[7]

The parameter γ (relative labor participation rates) is based on detailed studies of Anglo-American experience used earlier in this chapter (Kuznets 1952; O'Rourke, Williamson, and Hatton 1994). A priori, we expect γ to exceed unity, since migrant streams self-select and have a relatively high proportion of young adult men. Thus, the labor content of the migrant stream will be skewed by the presence of an overrepresentation of working-age adults, and by the overrepresentation of men also with high labor participation rates. Guided by activity rates alone, we might guess α_M to have been around 90 percent, α_{POP} around 60 percent, and, hence, γ around 1.5 for most countries. Estimates of γ from the United States and Britain in fact document a tight range of 1.53–1.78 for the late-nineteenth-century, and a midpoint estimate of 1.65 was chosen as the baseline parameter subject to sensitivity analysis in the range 1.55–1.75.[8] Labor's share is documented in various country factor-distribution studies, most of which were done in the 1960s. These estimates of θ are described in detail elsewhere (Taylor and Williamson 1997) and were supplemented by constructing alternative estimates of θ = wL/Y from a database on average nominal wages, nominal output, and labor force. Independent estimates of θ were thus derived for almost all countries, the remainder covered by contiguous-country estimates (for example, Brazil uses Argentina's θ estimate).

Last, an estimate of η was obtained using standard aggregate labor demand estimation techniques (e.g., Hammermesh 1993). The estimation of η is discussed in detail elsewhere (Taylor and Williamson 1997). For any (degree one) homogeneous two-factor production function, it can be shown that $\eta = -\sigma/(1 - \theta)$. The elasticity of substitution σ was estimated econometrically with a late-nineteenth-century panel of 14 countries, with four decade observations for each country. Under a CES production function, $Y = (aL^e + bK^e)^{1/e}$, it can be shown that producer wages are related to aggregate output per worker according to $\ln(Y/L) = \sigma\ln(w/P)$, where $\sigma = 1/(1 - e)$ is the elasticity of substitution. In fact, estimates of σ can be derived from a number of estimating equations (Hammermesh 1993; Arrow et al. 1961):

[10.4] $$\ln\left(Y/L\right) = \sigma\ln\left(w/P\right)$$

[10.5] $$\ln\left(w/P\right) = \left(1/\sigma\right)\ln\left(Y/L\right)$$

[10.6] $$\ln\left(L\right) = \tau\ln\left(Y\right) - \sigma\ln\left(w/P\right), \text{ testing the restriction } \tau = 1.$$

These equations were estimated by using panel fixed-effect econometric techniques on a 14-country subsample over four decades, 1870–1910 (Taylor and Williamson 1997, appendix 2). The point estimate σ = 0.62 was used to derive η,[9] an estimate very close to a modern 70-country average of 0.75 reported recently by Hammermesh (1993).

The Impact of Mass Migration on Convergence

Table 10.6 presents the baseline results. The upper panel shows counterfactual real wages, GDP per capita, and GDP per worker in 1910 had there been zero net migration after 1870 in all countries. The second panel indicates the proportionate impact with respect to the actual country levels in table 10.5. The third panel reports counterfactual convergence or divergence.

The results certainly accord with intuition: in the absence of the mass migrations, wages and labor productivity would have been much higher in the New World and much lower in the Old; and in the absence of the mass migrations,

Table 10.6 Counterfactual Convergence, 1870–1910, with Zero Net Migration

	Real wages		GDP per capita		GDP per worker	
	1870	1910	1870	1910	1870	1910
Levels						
Argentina	61	139	915	2,424	1,946	6,730
Australia	127	173	3,123	4,920	7,811	12,346
Belgium	60	95	2,104	3,272	4,836	7,442
Brazil	39	87	425	552	1,101	1,444
Canada	99	269	1,365	3,533	3,781	9,318
Denmark	36	88	1,624	2,898	2,943	5,491
France	50	71	1,638	2,499	3,336	5,017
Germany	58	84	772	1,406	2,996	5,390
Great Britain	69	96	3,055	3,918	7,132	8,934
Ireland	49	58	—	—	—	—
Italy	26	33	1,244	1,692	2,309	3,048
Netherlands	52	68	2,064	2,931	5,322	7,649
Norway	28	60	1,190	1,818	2,800	4,276
Portugal	32	40	612	901	1,346	2,024
Spain	51	49	1,308	1,962	3,194	4,919
Sweden	28	88	1,316	2,300	2,814	4,639
United States	115	195	2,254	4,714	5,925	11,628
Change (counterfactual versus actual)						
Argentina		46%		9%		27%
Australia		28%		7%		17%
Belgium		9%		3%		5%
Brazil		2%		1%		2%
Canada		31%		8%		18%
Denmark		−11%		−4%		−7%
France		0%		0%		0%
Germany		−3%		−1%		−2%
Great Britain		−9%		−3%		−5%
Ireland		−36%		−13%		−24%
Italy		−33%		−12%		−22%
Netherlands		−3%		−1%		−2%
Norway		−15%		−3%		−9%
Portugal		−5%		−2%		−3%
Spain		−5%		−2%		−3%
Sweden		−12%		−2%		−8%
United States		15%		3%		9%
Dispersion(1870 = 100)						
All	100	142	100	91	100	91
New World	100	86	100	70	100	62
Old World	100	93	100	73	100	69
New World/Old World						
Gap (parity = 100)	196	250	105	139	116	155

Notes: Dispersion measure and actual data are as in table 10.5. On counterfactual, see text.

Source: Taylor and Williamson (1997, table 4).

income per capita would typically (but not always) have been marginally higher in the New World and typically (but not always) marginally lower in the Old World. Not surprisingly, the biggest counterfactual impact is reported for those countries that experienced the biggest migrations: by 1910, Irish wages would have been lower by 36 percent, Italian by 33 percent, and Swedish by 12 percent; and Argentine wages would have been higher by 46 percent, Australian by 28 percent, Canadian by 31 percent, and American by 15 percent. Although the partial equilibrium figures for Britain and the United States in table 10.6 are (predictably) higher than the general equilibrium figures in table 10.3 (panel B), they are remarkably close: for Britain, −9 versus −6.6 percent; for the United States, +15 versus +9.2 percent.

Table 10.6 certainly lends strong support to the hypothesis that mass migration made an important contribution to late-nineteenth-century convergence. Starting first with the third panel, we observe that in the absence of the mass migrations real wage dispersion would have *increased* by 42 percent from 1870 to 1910, rather than decreased by 28 percent as it did in fact (table 10.5). Actually, GDP per worker dispersion would have decreased by only 9 percent rather than by 29 percent as it did in fact. And GDP per capita dispersion would also have decreased by only 9 percent rather than by 18 percent as it did in fact. Wage gaps between New World and Old in fact declined from 96 to 79 percent, but in the absence of the mass migrations they would have *risen* to 150 percent in 1910.

Pairwise comparisons are also easily constructed using table 10.6 and compounding the percentages. Wage gaps between many Old World countries and the United States fell dramatically as a result of mass migration: without Irish emigration (some of whom went to America) and United States immigration (some of whom were Irish), the American-Irish wage gap would have risen by 102 percentage points (from 134 to 236 percent: table 10.6), while in fact it fell by 48 (from 135 to 87 percent: table 10.5); without Italian emigration (a large share of whom went to America) and United States immigration (many of whom were Italian), the American-Italian wage gap would have risen by 149 percentage points, while in fact it fell by 102; without British emigration and Australian immigration, the Australian-British wage gap would have fallen by only 4 percentage points, while in fact it fell by 55; and without Italian emigration and Argentine immigration, the Argentine-Italian wage gap would have risen by 186 percentage points, while in fact it fell by 45. Furthermore, the mass migrations to the New World had an impact on economic convergence within the Old World: without the Norwegian emigration flood and the German emigration trickle, the German-Norwegian wage gap would have fallen by 112 percentage points, while in fact it fell by 122; and without the fact that Irish emigration exceeded British emigration by far, the British-Irish wage gap would have risen by 24 percentage points, while in fact it fell by 26. Although the impact of mass migration *within* the Old World was much smaller than between the Old and New Worlds, remember the caveat that migrations within Europe were underenumerated.

A summary of results appears in table 10.7. Notably, GDP per capita dispersion is least affected. In terms of the convergence accounted for by migration, these

Table 10.7 Summary: Counterfactual Convergence, 1870–1910, with Zero Net Migration

Dispersion (1870 = 100)	Actual 1910	Counterfactual 1910	Percentage of convergence explained, 1870–1910 (change in ln[dispersion])
Real wages			
All	72	142	208
New World	76	86	48
Old World	73	93	78
GDP per capita			
All	82	91	50
New World	71	70	−4
Old World	70	73	12
GDP per worker			
All	71	91	72
New World	65	62	−10
Old World	61	69	25

Notes: See text and table 10.5. Percentage convergence explained is counterfactual-actual ratio of change in ln[dispersion].

Source: Taylor and Williamson (1997, table 5).

counterfactuals suggest that more than all (208 percent) of the 1870–1910 real wage convergence (log measure of dispersion) was attributable to migration, and almost three quarters (72 percent) of the GDP per worker convergence. In contrast, perhaps one half (50 percent) of the GDP per capita convergence might have been due to migration.

The contribution of mass migration to convergence in the full sample and in the New and Old Worlds differs, the latter being smaller and, in two out of three New World cases, even negative. Although those negative numbers may at first appear bizzare, further thought will confirm that they are consistent with intuition. Given the evidence of segmentation in the Atlantic labor market presented in chapters 3 and 6, it should, in fact, come as no surprise that New World impacts are minimal or even negative by some measures. Immigrant flows were not everywhere efficiently distributed, since barriers to entry limited destination choices for many southern Europeans, a point central to discussions of Latin migration experience and invoked as an important determinant of Argentine economic performance (Diaz-Alejandro 1970; Taylor 1992b, 1994; Hatton and Williamson 1994b; and see chapters 2, 3, and 6). Thus, migrants did not always obey some simple market-wage calculus; kept out of the best high-wage destinations, or having alternative cultural preferences, many went to the "wrong" countries. The south-south flows from Italy, Spain, and Portugal to Brazil and Argentina were a strong force for local (Latin), not global, convergence. Furthermore, while barriers to exit were virtually absent in most of the Old World, policy (like assisted passage) still played a part in violating any simple market-wage calculus.[10] However, the minimal contribution of migration to convergence in each region illustrates our opening point: the major contribution of mass migration to late-nineteenth-century convergence was the enormous movement of about 55 million Europeans to the New World and the impact of this movement on convergence between the two regions. The New World-Old World story stands in contrast to the quantitatively less important convergence within each region, an effect only further obscured by the imperfect market-wage correlation.

The relative insensitivity of GDP per capita convergence to migration is a result of countervailing effects inherent in the algebra. For real wages or GDP per worker, high migrant-to-population ratios of labor participation rates amplify the impact of migration, but with GDP per capita the impact is muted. Why? In the former two cases, migration has a bigger impact on the labor force, GDP, and wages, the bigger is the labor content of the migrations. In the case of GDP per capita, things are less clear. For example, with emigration, population outflow generally offsets diminishing returns in production for a net positive impact on output per capita, but selectivity assures that emigration will subtract a disproportionate share of the labor force, lowering output via labor supply losses, a negative impact on output per capita. The latter effect dominated in the late-nineteenth-century Atlantic economy (Taylor and Williamson 1997), so muted GDP per capita effects are no surprise. By our calculation, four decades of migration lowered New World GDP per capita never by more than 9 percent anywhere in the New World, and by as little as 3 percent in the United States, to be contrasted with per worker impacts of 27 and 9 percent, respectively. This labor-supply compensation effect operated in addition to the usual human-capital transfer influences invoked to describe the net benefit to the United States of the millions received before World War I (Uselding 1971; Neal and Uselding 1972). Similar reasoning applies to the Old World: Swedish emigration after 1870 may have raised wages in 1910 by about 12 percent, but it raised GDP per capita by only 2 percent.

The sensitivity of these results to various parameter values is reported at length by Taylor and Williamson (1997). The results seem robust for real wages and GDP per worker: for most parameter combinations, actual convergence is more than half explained by migration, and frequently overexplained. Mass migration accounted for all of the real wage convergence and at least half of the GDP per worker convergence, even assuming an adjustment for return rate underenumeration of about 0.3, which seems implausibly high except for one or two countries (for example, Italy). With a more moderate return rate correction of 0.1, migration accounted for all (or more than all) of the real wage convergence and for at least 70 percent of the GDP per worker convergence.

Qualifying the Bottom Line

The previous analysis suggests that mass migration accounted for 208 percent of the real wage convergence observed in the Atlantic economy between 1870 and 1910. In our zealousness, haven't we overexplained late-nineteenth-century convergence? Perhaps, but the fact is hardly surprising given that there were *other* powerful pro-convergence and anti-convergence forces at work. Although we have discussed them before—especially foreign capital chasing after the migrants—four of these deserve repetition. First, what about capital accumulation forces? We know that capital accumulation was faster in the New World, so much so that the rate of capital deepening was faster in the United States than in any of her competitors (Wolff 1991), and the same was probably true of other rich New World countries. There is evidence therefore that the mass migrations may have been at least partially offset by capital accumulation, and a large part of that capital widening was being carried by international capital flows that reached magnitudes unsurpassed before or since (Edelstein 1982; Zevin 1992). Second, what about the forces of trade emphasized by Eli Heckscher in 1919 and Bertil Ohlin in 1924 (Flam and Flanders 1991)? Their idea was that spectacular transport innovations in the late nineteenth century caused commodity prices to converge and trade to boom. As exports expanded among trading partners, the derived demand for their abundant factors boomed while that for their scarce factors slumped. Factor prices (like real wages) tended to converge as a result. Samuelson (1948) got us thinking about the strong assumptions needed for factor price *equalization*, but factor price *convergence* requires weaker assumptions supported by the late-nineteenth-century evidence (O'Rourke and Williamson 1994, 1995; O'Rourke, Taylor, and Williamson 1996; Williamson 1996). Third, what about the forces of technological catch-up stressed by Gerschenkron (1962) and Abramovitz (1986), but documented only poorly for the late-nineteenth-century (Wolff 1991)? Finally, what about the forces of human capital accumulation debated in the new growth theory and suggested as an important force for convergence in the late-nineteenth-century (Sandberg 1979; Easterlin 1981)?

To the extent that schooling can be taken as a fair proxy for human capital accumulation, we can reject at least one of these four forces quickly: schooling was not an important force accounting for real wage or labor productivity convergence in the late-nineteenth-century (Prados, Sanchez, and Oliva 1993; O'Rourke and Williamson 1996, 1997). But what about the other three forces? Although the evidence is still incomplete, we do know something about the relative importance of Heckscher-Ohlin trade-related forces: they may have accounted for as much as a third of the real wage convergence in the late-nineteenth-century, at last for Anglo-America (O'Rourke and Williamson 1994; Williamson 1996; O'Rourke, Taylor, and Williamson 1996; O'Rourke, Williamson, and Hatton 1994).[11]

The evidence on the role of global capital market responses to migration is even more tentative, but recall earlier in this chapter where the CGE model was allowed to accommodate a capital market response; panel B in table 10.1 shows much smaller migration effects as a consequence. Taylor and Williamson (1997) make the same kind of adjustments in their work. They implement the zero-net-migration counterfactual in a model in which the labor supply shocks generate capital inflows or outflows in order to maintain a constant rate of return on capital in each country. The capital-chasing-labor offsets are very large. Whereas mass migration overexplained 208 percent of the observed real wage convergence using the model without capital chasing labor, it explains about 70 percent of the convergence using the model with capital chasing labor, leaving approximately 30

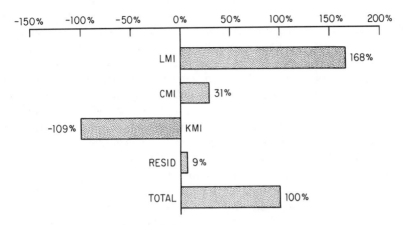

Figure 10.3 Explaining Convergence: An Example, 1870–1910. *Source*: Taylor and Williamson (1994)

percent to trade-induced effects and other forces. The findings for labor productivity are similar.[12]

Figure 10.3 offers a stylized treatment of these informed guesses. Several forces contributed to convergence in the late-nineteenth-century, not only mass migration (labor market integration forces, labeled LMI), but also commodity price convergence and trade expansion (commodity market integration forces, labeled CMI), and any number of residual forces (RESID) such as technological catch-up, unmeasured intra-European migration, human capital accumulation, and the like. Conversely, as noted above, the capital flows of the late nineteenth century were mainly an anticonvergence force (Scandinavia being an outstanding exception), in that they raised wages and labor productivity in the rich New World, while lowering them in the poor Old World (capital market integration, KMI). In a striking corollary, if the previously cited 30 percent CMI figure is plausible, relatively little of the late-nineteenth-century convergence may have been the result of technological catch-up or human capital accumulation, the central elements of modern convergence models.

Conclusions

This chapter suggests that the convergence literature has missed two crucial features of the late-nineteenth-century world economy. First, the key axis around which convergence centered was between Old World and New: along that axis hangs most of the convergence story for 1870–1913 real wages (Williamson 1995). Second, the conventional closed-economy assumption is simply inappropriate given the degree of integration in the world economy at that time, whether in goods markets, labor markets, or capital markets. These insights have been applied elsewhere. In other research, Kevin O'Rourke, Alan Taylor, and we have shown that integration in product markets arising from spectacular ocean and railroad freight declines could account for a significant share of the Anglo-American real wage convergence (O'Rourke and Williamson 1994; O'Rourke, Williamson, and Hatton 1994) and even for some of the Scandinavian catch-up on the leaders (O'Rourke and Williamson 1995, 1996); and for a broader group of countries, terms-of-trade effects and endowment changes could account for a large share of the convergence in the wage-rental ratio (O'Rourke, Taylor, and Williamson 1996; O'Rourke and Williamson 1997). In short, an open-economy perspective is vital to understanding late-nineteenth-century comparative growth: globalization was the most important force driving late-nineteenth-century convergence.

Will this interpretation of mass migration's impact in the past hold up to closer scrutiny? It certainly will need more sophisticated analysis to help confirm it: capital chasing and endogenous frontier effects could offset more of the mass migration impact than we have allowed, in which case technological catch-up might claim more than the residual role history appears to have assigned it.

Does this important impact for globalization—migration and trade—on convergence in the late-nineteenth-century necessarily imply the same for the late twentieth century? Probably not. After all, we are not living in an age of mass migration any more, but rather in one of quotas and restrictions. Perhaps only the United States is absorbing significant immigrant flows today, and even here less so than the late-nineteenth-century. Furthermore, trade was not the main carrier of convergence even in the late-nineteenth-century. And in the late twentieth century, education and technology catch-up have played a much more important role. One must treat lessons of history with care.

Still, we expect these results to offer a new perspective on the convergence debate, one relevant for both economic historians and macroeconomists. The convergence power of free migration, when it is tolerated, can be substantial given the late-nineteenth-century evidence. Convergence explanations based on technological or accumulation catch-up in closed-economy models miss this point. The millions on the move in the late-nineteenth-century did not.

Mass Migration and Inequality Trends Within Countries

Setting the Stage

There were three epochs of growth experience after the middle of the nineteenth century among what are now called the OECD countries: the late nineteenth century, the middle years between 1914 and 1950, and the late twentieth century. The first and last epochs experienced overall fast growth, globalization, and convergence. The middle years experienced overall slow growth, deglobalization, and divergence. Thus, history offers an unambiguous positive correlation between globalization and convergence. When the pre–World War I years are examined in detail, the correlation turns out to be causal: globalization played *the* critical role in contributing to convergence; and, as chapter 10 and other work (Williamson 1996) have argued, it took the form of mass migration and trade.

Since contemporary economists are now hotly debating the impact of these globalization forces on wage inequality in the United States and Europe, the Latin American recently economically liberated regimes, and the open Asian tigers, it seems timely to ask whether the same distributional forces were at work during the late nineteenth century.[1] Chapter 8 reported a literature almost a century old that argues that immigration hurt American labor, especially unskilled, and accounted for much of the rise in inequality from the 1890s to World War I, so much so that a labor-sympathetic Congress passed immigration quotas. Chapter 9 reported a literature just as old that argues that while the New World grain invasion was eroding land rents in Europe, the emigrations were raising unskilled labor scarcity, so much so that landowner-dominated continental parliaments raised tariffs to help protect them from the impact of globalization. But nowhere in this historical literature has anyone constructed a panel dataset across countries and over time that could be used to test two fundamental and contentious hypotheses:

Hypothesis 1: Inequality rose in rich, labor-scarce New World countries such as Argentina, Australia, Canada, and, most importantly, the United States. Inequality fell in poor, labor-abundant, agrarian countries around the Old World periphery such as Italy, the Iberian Peninsula, Ireland, and Scandinavia. Inequality was more stable for the European industrial leaders such as Britain, France, Germany, and the Lowlands, all of whom fell somewhere in the middle between the rich New World and poor agrarian Old World.

Hypothesis 2: If the first hypothesis survives test, a second follows: much of these inequality patterns can be explained by globalization. If so, how much by mass migration?

The next two sections review the theory and tie historical debate about the first globalization boom in the late nineteenth century to current debate about the second globalization boom in the late twentieth century. There is a striking similarity between the two debates. There is also a shared shortcoming to the empirical analysis: nobody has yet explored this issue with late-nineteenth-century panel data across poor and rich countries, and, with the important exception of Adrian Wood (1994), nobody has done so for the late-twentieth-century debate either. Indeed, most economists focus solely on America. This chapter contributes a late-nineteenth-century panel database that includes rich and poor countries, or, in the modern vernacular, north and south. We use this new database to establish the late-nineteenth-century facts: Hypothesis 1 and Hypothesis 2 both survive.

It appears that globalization did drive inequality before the interwar age of autarky. While we don't yet know exactly how much, that fact must have contributed to the implosion, deglobalization, and autarkic policies that characterized the years between 1914 and 1950. Indeed, during this period of trade suppression and migration quotas, the old globalization-inequality connection completely disappeared. It took the globalization events after the early 1970s to renew this old inequality debate.

Globalization and Inequality:
The Late-Twentieth-Century Debate

After 1973 and especially in the 1980s, the United States experienced a dismal real wage performance for the less skilled, mostly due to declining productivity growth coupled with increasing wage inequality between skills. This inequality was manifested primarily by increasing wage premia for workers with advanced schooling and age-related skills. Although the same inequality trends were apparent in Europe, the increase was typically far smaller and centered on the 1980s. Most of the current debate has focused on explaining these inequality facts. Since these developments coincided with convergence, globalization,[2] and a shift in United States spending patterns that resulted in large trade deficits, economists have quite naturally explored the linkages between trade and immigration, on the one hand, and wage inequality, on the other. They have also explored the role of technological change on labor demand by skill. Economists remain divided between globalization and technology explanations, with no resolution in sight.

Robert Lawrence and Matthew Slaughter (1993) studied wage inequality using the standard Heckscher-Ohlin model and concluded that there is little evidence that Stolper-Samuelson effects can explain increasing wage inequality because a lower relative wage for unskilled labor must be coupled with a lower skilled-to-unskilled worker ratio in all industries for such an effect to be present. That is, a trade shock that serves to diminish the relative demand for unskilled labor (following a boom in skill-intensive export industries and a slump in unskilled labor–intensive import-competing industries) should lower the unskilled wage, thus augmenting unskilled employment in all sectors. However, they find that only 10 percent of the United States manufacturing industry in the 1980s moved in this manner. The rest saw an increase in the ratio of skilled-to-unskilled workers. Lawrence and Slaughter then go on to examine the effect of Hicks-neutral technological change occurring more rapidly in goods that are relatively intensive in skilled labor. They conclude that technological change has been an important source of wage inequality trends and find no evidence of a relative price decline of goods that use unskilled labor intensively.

Lawrence and Slaughter stress the evolution of labor demand by skill, ignoring the potential influence of supply. George Borjas (1994) and his collaborators (Borjas, Freeman, and Katz 1992) take a different approach, emphasizing the contribution of trade and immigration to the United States labor force. They first estimate the implicit labor supply embodied in trade flows. Imports embody labor, thus serving to augment effective domestic labor supply. Likewise, exports imply a decrease in the effective domestic labor supply. In this way, Borjas calculates that the huge United States trade deficit of the 1980s implied a 1.5 percent increase in the United States labor supply and, since most of the imports were in goods that used unskilled labor relatively intensively, it also implied an increasing ratio of unskilled-to-skilled effective labor supplies. In addition, there was a shift in national origin of immigrants from the 1960s to the 1980s so that an increasing proportion of immigrants were from the less developed nations (e.g., Mexico and countries in Asia) and thus more unskilled, which in turn meant a far higher fraction of immigrants were relatively unskilled just when there were more of them. It follows that both trade and immigration increased the supply of unskilled relative to skilled workers in the 1980s.

These relative supply shifts give us the desired qualitative result—wage inequality between skill types. The quantitative result, at least in Borjas's hands, also seems big. Borjas estimates that 30 to 50 percent of the decline in wage of high school dropouts relative to all other workers is due to globalization forces, one third of which was due to trade and two thirds to immigration. Even though Borjas's figures are among the largest estimates of the globalization impact on recent earnings inequality trends, they are clearly consistent with our own views of the late nineteenth century reported in chapter 8. Furthermore, Borjas argues that migration was the more important globalization force producing United States inequality trends in the 1980s.

Thus far, we have been talking about only one country, the United States, perhaps because this is where rising inequality and immigration have been greatest. But even shifting the attention to Europe defines the question too narrowly. We are more likely to find an answer if, in addition, we ask whether the same factors were *stimulating* the relative demand for low-skill labor in the poor Third World. This book certainly does not take the narrow approach when viewing the late nineteenth century, and Adrian Wood (1994: ch. 6; 1995b) doesn't either for the late twentieth century. Wood was one of the first economists to examine inequality trends systematically across countries, *including* the poor south.

Wood distinguishes three skill types: uneducated, labor with basic education, and the highly educated. The poor south is richly endowed with uneducated labor, but the supply of labor with basic skills is growing fast. The rich north is, of course, abundant in highly educated labor with a slow-growing supply of labor with basic skills. Wood assumes capital is fairly mobile and that technology is freely available. As the south improves its skills through the expansion of basic education and as trade barriers fall, it produces more manufactures that require only basic skills, whereas the north produces more of the high-skill goods. It follows that the ratio of the unskilled to the skilled wage should rise in the south and fall in the north. The tendency towards relative factor price convergence raises the relative wage of workers with a basic education in the south and lowers it in the north, producing, *ceteris paribus*, rising inequality in the north and falling inequality in the south. Complete factor price equalization is, of course, not necessary to get such relative factor price convergence. Eli Heckscher and Bertil Ohlin understood that fact: it was the late-nineteenth-century *relative* factor price convergence that attracted Heckscher's and Ohlin's attention when they were writing in 1919 and 1924, immediately following the pre–World War I globalization experience (Flam and Flanders 1991).

Basing his results on insights derived from classical Heckscher-Ohlin theory, Wood concludes that the decline in the relative wage of less-skilled northern workers is due to the elimination of trade barriers and increasing relative abundance of southern workers with a basic education. He dismisses biased technological change as a potential explanation.

Wood's research has met with stiff academic resistance.[3] Since his book appeared, we have learned more about the inequality and globalization connection in the Third World. The standard Stolper-Samuelson prediction would be that unskilled labor-abundant poor countries should undergo egalitarian trends in the face of globalization forces, unless they are overwhelmed by industrial revolutionary labor-saving events on the upswing of the Kuznets Curve (Kuznets 1955) or by Malthusian gluts generated by the demographic transition. A recent review by Donald Davis (1996) reports the contrary. This is true of a study of seven countries in Latin America and East Asia that typically show that wage inequality did not fall after trade liberalization, but rather *rose* (Robbins 1996). This apparent anomaly has been strengthened by other studies, some of which have been rediscovered since Adrian Wood's book appeared. For example, almost 20 years ago Anne Krueger (1978) studied 10 developing countries covering the period through 1972, and her findings were not favorable to the simple distribution predictions of standard trade theory. Recent work on the impact of Mexican liberalization on wage inequality (Feenstra and Hanson 1995; Feliciano 1995) confirms Krueger's position. Of course, none of these studies is very attentive to the simultaneous role of emigration from these developing countries.

Clearly, the debate on the late-twentieth-century globalization and inequality connection is far from resolved. What about the late nineteenth century?

Globalization and Inequality: The Late-Nineteenth-Century Debate

Figure 10.1 documented a real wage convergence in the late nineteenth century, and it appears that most of it, and the convergence of GDP per worker-hour, was the combined result of a trade boom and the mass migrations (chapter 10; O'Rourke and Williamson 1994, 1995, 1996, 1997; Taylor and Williamson 1997; Williamson 1996).

Consider the trade boom first. The late nineteenth century was a period of dramatic commodity market integration: railways and steamships lowered transport costs, and Europe moved towards free trade in the wake of the 1860 Cobden-Chevalier treaty. These developments implied large trade-creating price shocks that affected every European participant, the canonical case being the drop in European grain prices: for example, while Liverpool wheat prices were 60 percent higher than Chicago prices in 1870, they were less than 15 percent higher in 1912, implying a decline of 45 percent. The commodity price convergence is even bigger if the price gradient is pushed into the wheat-growing interior west of Chicago. Furthermore, it applied to all tradables, not just grain. We stress that these globalization price shocks were bigger than the decline in OECD tariff barriers in the three decades following the 1940s, events that triggered the globalization boom we have witnessed over the last quarter century. The World Bank reports that tariffs on manufactures entering developed countries fell from 40 percent in the late 1940s to 7 percent in the late 1970s, for a 30-year fall of 33 percentage points. Wood (1994: 173) uses this example to advertise just how revolutionary world commodity market integration has been in the late twentieth century, but this spectacular postwar reclamation of "free trade" from interwar autarky is still smaller than the 45 percent fall in trade barriers between 1870 and 1913 as a result of transport improvements.

Eli Heckscher and Bertil Ohlin argued that such commodity market integration should have led to international factor price convergence, as countries everywhere expanded the production and export of commodities that used their abundant (and cheap) factors relatively intensively. Thus, the late-nineteenth-century trade boom implied convergence in GDP per worker-hour and in the real wage.[4] It also had distributional implications. For poor labor-abundant and land-scarce countries, it meant rising unskilled wages relative to rents and skilled wages. For rich labor-scarce and land-abundant countries, it meant falling unskilled wages relative to rents and skilled wages.

What about mass migration? As chapter 3 showed, the poorest Old World countries tended to have the highest emigration rates while the richest New World countries tended to have the highest immigration rates. Furthermore, the average labor force impact of the mass migrations was very big. Immigration augmented the labor force by about 32 percent in the three New World immigrant countries for which we have the inequality data—Australia, Canada, and the United States—and diminished the labor force by about 15 percent among the six Old World emigrant countries around the European periphery for which we have inequality data—Denmark, Italy, Norway, Portugal, Spain, and Sweden (table 10.1). These figures are much bigger than those for U.S. experience in the 1980s. In any case, one estimate reported in chapter 10 has it that the mass migrations explain about 70 percent of the real wage convergence in the late nineteenth century (Taylor and Williamson 1997). Note that this estimate, in contrast with contemporary debate about the United States in the 1980s, includes the total impact on *both* rich receiving countries *and* poor sending countries.

Because the migrants tended to be increasingly unskilled as the late nineteenth century unfolded (much like in the late twentieth century), they flooded the immigrant-country labor markets at the bottom, thus lowering the unskilled wage relative to skilled wages, white-collar incomes, and rents. Immigration implied rising inequality in rich countries. Emigration implied falling inequality in poor countries.

So much for plausible assertions. What were the nineteenth-century facts?

Establishing the Inequality Facts, 1870–1913

Full-size distributions at various benchmarks between the middle of the nineteenth century and World War I are unavailable except for a few countries and dates,[5] but even if they were, it is not obvious that we would want them to test the mass migration impact. Like economists involved in the late-twentieth-century debate, our interest here is on factor prices, rents, and the structure of pay. In particular, how did the typical unskilled worker near the bottom of the distribution do relative to the typical landowner or capitalist near the top, or even relative to the typical skilled blue-collar worker and educated white-collar employee in the middle of the distribution? Late-twentieth-century debate has a fixation on wage inequality, but since land and landed interests were far more important to late-nineteenth-century inequality events, we need to add them to our distribution inquiry. Two kinds of evidence are available to document inequality trends so defined: the ratio of the unskilled wage to farm rents per acre, and the ratio of the unskilled wage to GDP per worker-hour. Consider each in turn.[6]

Recently, a panel database was constructed documenting wage-rental convergence among 11 late-nineteenth-century countries (O'Rourke, Taylor, and Williamson 1996): four New World countries plotted in figure 11.1 (Argentina, Australia, Canada, and the United States); four free trade Old World countries plotted in figure 11.2 (Denmark, Great Britain, Ireland, and Sweden); and three

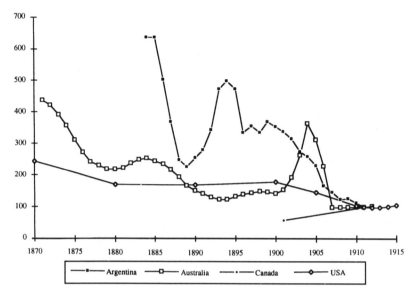

Figure 11.1 Ratio of Unskilled Wages to Land Values, 1870–1910, New World (1911 = 100).
Source: O'Rourke, Taylor, and Williamson (1996), figure 1

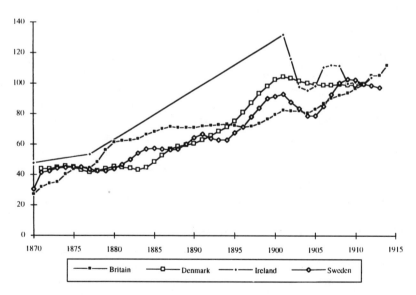

Figure 11.2 Ratio of Unskilled Wages to Land Values, 1870–1910, Old World "Free Trade"
(1911 = 100). *Source*: O'Rourke, Taylor, and Williamson (1996), figure 2

Figure 11.3 Ratio of Unskilled Wages to Land Values, 1870–1910, Old World "Protected" (1911 = 100). *Source*: O'Rourke, Taylor, and Williamson (1996), figure 3

protectionist Old World countries plotted in figure 11.3 (France, Germany, and Spain).

We know that farm land was abundant and cheap in the New World while scarce and expensive in the Old World. And we know that labor was scarce and expensive in the New World while abundant and cheap in the Old World. Thus, we know that the wage-rental ratio was high in the New World and low in the Old. What we *really* want to know, however, is how the ratio evolved over time: are the trends consistent with the predictions of the globalization and inequality literature? Was there relative factor price convergence in the late nineteenth century, implying rising inequality in rich countries and declining inequality in poor countries? Figures 11.1–11.3 supply some affirmative answers.[7] But first, a word about the Old World labels on figures 11.2 and 11.3—"free trade" and "protectionist."

The impact of the New World grain invasion on Old World wage-rental ratios must have been muted where tariffs were raised in defense. As Charles Kindleberger (1951) pointed out long ago, and as the new theories of endogenous tariffs predict, the response was especially strong on the Continent. Comparative measures of late-nineteenth-century protection are hard to construct, but Paul Bairoch (1989) recently offered some comparative crude measures of protection that should serve the purpose here. Based on his evidence for 1913, the protectionist label applied to France, Germany, and Spain, where in addition emigration rates were low. And the free trade label applied to Britain, Denmark, and Ireland, where in addition the emigration rates were high. Sweden lay somewhere in between, but since protectionist policy was implemented there relatively late in the period, Sweden is put into the free trade group. While these categories could be, and have been, debated, they serve well enough to motivate the following discussion.

Relative factor price convergence certainly characterized these four decades, and it implied rising inequality in rich New World countries and declining inequality in poor Old World countries. In the New World, the wage-rental ratio plunged. By 1913, the Australian ratio had fallen to one quarter of its 1870 level, the Argentine ratio had fallen to one fifth of its mid-1880 level, and the United States ratio had fallen to less than half of its 1870 level. In the Old World, the wage-rental ratio surged. The British ratio in 1910 had increased by a factor of 2.7 over its 1870 level, while the Irish ratio had increased even more, by a factor of 5.5. The Swedish and Danish ratios had both increased by a factor of 2.3. The surge was less pronounced in the protectionist-cum-low-emigration group than in the free-trade-cum-high-emigration group. The ratio had increased by a factor of 1.8 in France, 1.4 in Germany, and not at all in Spain.

Since landowners tended to be near the top of the distribution,[8] this evidence seems to confirm Hypothesis 1: inequality rose in the rich, labor-scarce New World; inequality fell in the poor, labor-abundant Old World. There is also some evidence that globalization mattered: Old World countries staying open and sending out the most emigrants absorbed the biggest distributional hit; Old World countries retreating behind tariff walls and sending out the fewest emigrants absorbed the smallest distributional hit.

So much for wage-rental ratios. What about the ratio of the unskilled worker's wage to the returns on *all* factors per laborer (including farm rents)? The details on the construction of this second distribution index, w/y, where w is the unskilled daily or weekly wage rate and y is GDP per worker-hour,[9] can be found elsewhere (Williamson 1997: appendix). Changes in w/y measure changes in the economic distance between the working poor near the bottom of the distribution and the average income recipient in the middle of the distribution.[10] Ideally, and to be most consistent with the evidence used in the late-twentieth-century debate, we would have preferred a distribution index w/z, where $z = y - w$ is the income (per laborer) accruing to all factors other than unskilled labor, including the premium on skills. It turns out that z is hard to construct for our late-nineteenth-century panel, so we stick with w/y.

Figure 11.4 summarizes the wide variance across the 14 countries in the sample. The distribution index is normalized by setting w/y 1870 = 100: Norwegian equality trends establish the upper bound, 1913 = 244; Spanish and United States inequality trends establish the lower bound, 1913 = 53.

An alternative way to standardize these distribution trends is simply to compute the percentage change in the index, $e = d(w/y)/(w/y)$. We will use e in everything that follows, and it ranges from +144 percent for Norway to −47 percent for Spain and the United States. It is plotted in figure 11.5 against 1870 real wage, where the wealth of nations is measured by initial level of labor scarcity.

Figures 11.5 and 11.6 offer a stunning confirmation of Hypothesis 1: between 1870 and 1913, inequality rose dramatically in rich, land-abundant, labor-scarce New World countries such as Australia, Canada, and the United States; inequality

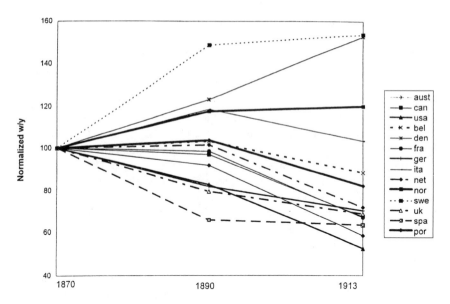

Figure 11.4 Normalized Inequality Levels, 1870–1913 (1870 = 100)

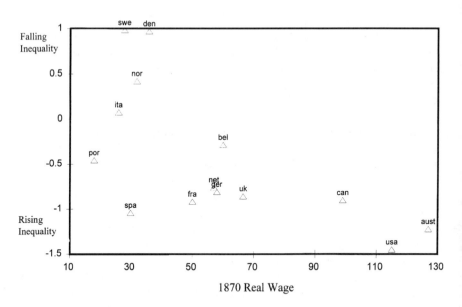

Figure 11.5 Initial Real Wage versus Inequality Trends, 1870–1913

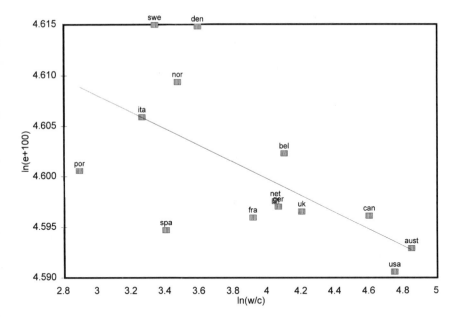

Figure 11.6 Initial Real Wage versus Inequality Trends, Double-log, 1870–1913

fell dramatically in poor, land-scarce, labor-abundant, pre-industrial countries such as Norway, Sweden, Denmark, and Italy; income distribution changed only modestly in middle-income, land-scarce, labor-abundant, industrial economies such as Belgium, France, Germany, the Netherlands, and the United Kingdom.[11]

A key stylized fact has emerged from the late nineteenth century: labor-scarce countries underwent rising inequality, and labor-abundant countries underwent falling inequality.

The Impact of Mass Migration on Late-Nineteenth-Century Inequality Trends

Theory suggests that globalization can account for this key stylized fact: in an age of unrestricted international migration, poor countries should have had the highest emigration rates and rich countries should have had the highest immigration rates; in an age of trade liberalism, poor countries should have exported labor-intensive products and rich countries should have imported labor-intensive products. Theory is one thing: fact is another. What is the evidence that supports the (apparently plausible) globalization hypothesis?

We start with trade effects. We know that there was a retreat from trade liberalism from the 1880s onward, and we know that the retreat included Italy, Portugal, Spain, France, and Germany (Estevadeordal 1993; O'Rourke and Williamson

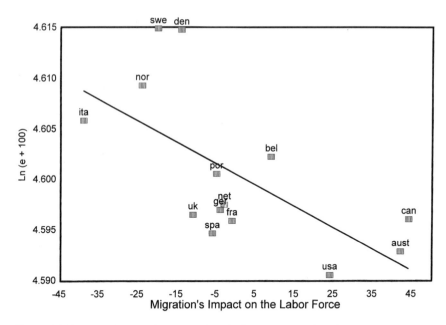

Figure 11.7 Inequality Trends versus Migration's Impact on Labor Force, 1870–1913

1997). In the absence of globalization forces, poor labor-abundant countries who protect should raise the returns to their scarce factors, such as land, relative to their abundant factors, such as unskilled labor; in the face of globalization forces, the same countries should at least mute the rise in unskilled labor's relative scarcity and thus the fall in inequality. The evidence appears to be consistent with these Stolper-Samuelson predictions, supporting the inequality-trade connection (Williamson 1997: figures 9 and 10). That is, the correlation between rising inequality and initial labor scarcity is better for 1870–1890—an environment of shared liberal trade polices—than for 1890–1913—an environment of rising protection on the Continent. In addition, the slope on the inequality-real-wage regression line is far steeper 1890–1913 without the protected five (Italy, Portugal, Spain, France, and Germany) than with them. We saw the same contrast when comparing wage-rental ratio trends in figure 11.2 with figure 11.3.

We turn next to the impact of mass migration. Since we know that migration's impact on the labor force is highly correlated with initial labor scarcity, the former is therefore a prime candidate in accounting for the inequality trends. Figure 11.7 plots the result: where immigration had a large positive impact on the labor force, inequality undertook a steep rise; where emigration had a large negative impact on the labor force, inequality undertook a steep fall.[12]

Unfortunately, it is impossible to decompose globalization effects into trade and migration using this time series information because the correlation between migration's impact and initial labor scarcity is so high. Yet an effort is made by constructing a trade-globalization-impact variable as the interaction of initial labor scarcity and "openness." The former is proxied by dummies for the labor scarce New World (d1 = 1: Australia, Canada, the United States), the labor-abundant Old World periphery (d2 = 1: Denmark, Italy, Norway, Sweden, Spain, Portugal) and the core Old World industrial leaders (Belgium, France, Germany, the Netherlands, United Kingdom). The latter is proxied by the trade shares given in table 1 ("trade"), and the inequality variable is now taken simply as e (R^2 = 0.722):

$$e = -52.072 - 0.313\text{mig} + 0.253\text{trade} + 0.545(\text{d1} \times \text{trade}) + 2.416(\text{d2} \times \text{trade})$$
$$\quad (2.563) \quad\quad (0.995) \quad\quad\quad (0.359) \quad\quad\quad\quad\quad (3.382)$$

The impact of migration is still powerful, significant, and of the right sign: when immigration rates were small (+mig was small), e was big and thus inegalitarian trends were weak; when emigration rates were big (−mig was big), e was even bigger and thus egalitarian trends were strong; when countries had to accommodate heavy immigration, inegalitarian trends were strong. In the Old World periphery, where labor was most abundant, the more open economies had more egalitarian trends (0.253 + 2.416 = +2.669), just as Heckscher and Ohlin would have predicted. It appears that the open-economy tigers of that time enjoyed benign egalitarian effects while those among them opting for autarky did not. Furthermore, the coefficient passes most significance tests. In the Old World industrial core, this effect was far less powerful (+0.253), and the coefficient does not pass any significance test. It appears that open-economy effects on income distribution were ambiguous among the land-scarce industrial leaders in Europe where the farm sector was relatively small. Heckscher and Ohlin would have predicted this result too. In the labor-scarce New World, however, the more open economies also had more egalitarian trends (0.253 + 0.545 = +0.798), which is certainly *not* what Heckscher and Ohlin would have predicted. The result is not significant, however.

Overall, we read this evidence as strong support for the impact of mass migration on distribution trends and weak support for the role of trade. There is, however, at least one qualification for that conclusion.

Perhaps we have *overstated* the impact of mass migration. After all, we have ignored the possibility that capital might chase after labor so that the stayer in Europe would have no more capital per worker than prior to the mass emigration, while the mover in the New World would have no less capital per worker than prior to the mass immigration. We know from chapters 9 and 10 that these capital-chasing forces had an important influence on real wage convergence, but what about distribution trends? One would have to show that capital and labor were closer complements than capital and skills or capital and land and that capital did not chase after labor into sectors where land and skills were used intensively. Whereas such general equilibrium thinking is uncommon to both late-nineteenth- and late-twentieth-century debates, and whereas it is to be applauded, the evidence does not appear to support this particular view of factor complementarity (e.g., Wright 1990). Our strong prior, therefore, is that the overstatement of mass migration's impact on inequality trends is not worth worrying about, as we shall see in a moment.

So far, we have been able to explain two thirds of the variance in distributional trends across the late nineteenth century. While globalization appears to have been the dominant force, and while migration was the dominant globalization force, other forces were at work raising inequality in rich countries and lowering it in poor. What force could possibly account for the remaining third that was also highly correlated with initial labor scarcity (w/c)? Critics of the late-twentieth-century globalization thesis have argued that the answer lies with factor-demand generated by technological change. For example, Lawrence and Slaughter argue that a skill-using bias in America has been driving rising inequality. Wood counters that it cannot be so since United States (and OECD) inequality was on the rise just when productivity slowdown was in full swing. Whichever the case, we must remember that we are searching for an explanation that can account simultaneously for falling inequality in the poor European periphery, rising inequality in the rich New World, and some mixture among the industrialized Europeans in the middle. So, is there any reason to believe that technological change should save unskilled labor in rich countries and use unskilled labor in poor countries?

This issue has already been explored at length using a subsample of the countries offering the wage-rental data plotted in figures 11.1–11.3.[13] Along with Heckscher-Ohlin, capital-deepening, and land-labor ratio forces, a factor-saving impact was estimated. Almost by definition, industrial revolutions typically embody productivity growth that favors industry. Since industrial output makes little use of farmland, industrialization tends to save land, raising instead the relative demands for labor and capital. Such industrial revolutionary events should, therefore, tend to raise the wage-rental ratio. According to this prediction, more rapid industrialization in Europe compared to the New World should also have served to raise the wage-rental ratio by more in Europe. Such events should have contributed to factor-price convergence, including the rise of real wages in the labor abundant Old World relative to the labor-scarce New World. This prediction would be reinforced if productivity advance in the late-nineteenth-century New World saved labor and used land, as an induced-innovation hypothesis would suggest and as economic historians generally believe (Habakkuk 1962; di Tella 1982). The prediction would be further reinforced if productivity advance in the Old World saved land and used labor, as we also generally believe.

The results are striking (O'Rourke, Taylor, and Williamson 1996: table 4, panel C). Changing land-labor ratios and capital deepening in combination accounted for about 26 percent of the fall in the wage-rental ratio in the New World, but for none of its rise in the Old World. Commodity price convergence and Heckscher-Ohlin effects accounted for about 30 percent of the fall in the New World wage-rental ratio and for about 23 percent of its rise in the Old World. Productivity advance, as predicted, saved labor in the labor-scarce New World and used labor in the labor-abundant Old World. Labor-saving technological change appears to have accounted for about 39 percent of the fall in the New World wage-rental ratio whereas labor-using accounted for about 51 percent of its rise in the Old World, powerful technological forces indeed.[14]

Globalization, according to these results, accounted for more than half of the rising inequality in rich, labor-scarce countries, and labor-saving technological change for another four tenths. Globalization accounted for a little more than a quarter of the falling inequality in poor, labor-abundant countries, and labor-using technological change another half.

Establishing the Inequality Facts, 1921–1938

What happened after World War I when quotas were imposed in immigrating countries, when capital markets collapsed, and when trade barriers rose—that is, under conditions of de-globalization?

First, convergence ceased. Figure 11.8 documents what macroeconomists call σ-divergence for real wages between 1914 and 1939. Some of the divergence was war-related, and some of it was Great Depression–related, but even during the 1920s late-nineteenth-century σ-convergence had ceased.

Second, the globalization-inequality connection was broken. Figure 11.9 shows the correlation between e and the 1921 real wage. The late-nineteenth-century inverse correlation has disappeared from the figure, replaced by a positive correlation. In the interwar period of deglobalization, the poorer countries underwent sharply increasing inequality while the richer countries underwent more moderate increases, or, in four cases, egalitarian trends.

The Political Economy of Migration Policy

Chapter 8 reported a consensus that immigration policy has always been sensitive to labor market conditions. Claudia Goldin (1994) noted that the mid–late 1890s started a new push toward American immigration restrictions, this during years of low immigration but high unemployment. Indeed, United States immigration hit a trough in 1897, the very year when the House of Representatives first voted on generalized immigration restrictions. The same was true of Australia: when immigration hit a low in the 1890s, the domestic economy was in deep recession and immigrant transport subsidies had dried up. Brazil revealed the same correlation, driven by the state of the coffee market.

Such correlations suggest that immigration restrictions have been driven more by domestic market demand than by immigrant supply. These correlations, however, say far more about the short-run timing of immigration policy than about its long-run evolution. In fact, chapter 8 was able to report that the U.S. Immigration Commission was right when, in 1911, it concluded that immigrants were eroding the economic position of unskilled workers in America. Was it an erosion in their relative or absolute incomes that mattered to the formation of policy? Was it the living standards of unskilled workers that mattered, or was it the gap between them and the rich that mattered? Was it rising inequality or falling wages?

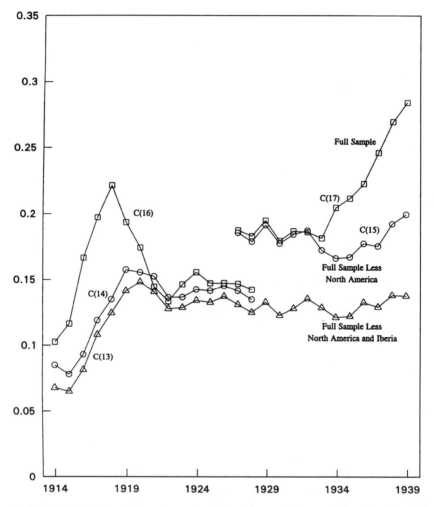

Figure 11.8 Real Wage Dispersion, 1914–1939. *Source*: Williamson (1995a), table A2.2.
C(14) and C(16) exclude Portugal, which enters in 1927, giving rise to series C(15) and C(17)

The political economy of immigration policy is important, but with the exception of James Foreman-Peck (1992), Jess Benhabib (1996), and William Shughart, Robert Tollison, and Mwangi Kimenyi (1996), there has been little effort to use models to predict immigration policy. Furthermore, empirical work has been confined to the United States, best illustrated by Shughart et al. (1986) and Goldin (1994). A recent project has had some success filling this gap by exploring the determinants of immigration policy in five major immigrating countries between 1860 and 1930 (Timmer and Williamson 1996).

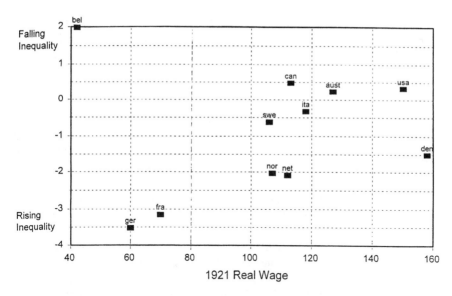

Figure 11.9 Initial Real Wage versus Inequality Trends, 1921–1938

The naive view is that the United States pursued an open or "free" immigration policy until the quotas were implemented in the 1920s, and thus that the decade between the Immigration Commission Report in 1911 and the quotas in 1921 was one of abrupt regime switch. The facts are different. From the mid-1870s to the eve of the Literacy Act in 1917, America slowly adopted an increasingly hostile immigration policy. On a 10-point scale, policy fell from a score of 0 in the early 1870s (neutral policy, without subsidy or interference), to –1.5 by the late 1880s (Chinese exclusion, tougher anticontract labor policy, excluding likely public charges, rising head tax), to –3 with the Literacy Act in 1917, and finally to –4.5 with the 1921 quotas. Thus, there was considerable variability in United States immigration policy and a slow evolution from benign neutrality to tight restriction. The same was true for the other four immigrant New World countries. Indeed, in some cases there was even *more* variability than in the United States since immigrant countries like Australia and Brazil often went from high subsidies to no subsidies *plus* restrictions.

What were the underlying fundamentals driving policy changes over those 70 years? Timmer and Williamson (1996) are able to conclude the following about the long-run fundamentals: xenophobia did not matter, but markets did; trade was never viewed as a substitute for immigration since more restrictive trade policies were never associated with more open immigration policies; the immigration rate by itself never mattered, but the combined "threat" of a glut of low-skilled immigrants did (immigration rates adjusted by quality). What changed immigration policy most, however, were changes in inequality. Rising inequality, manifested by an increasing gap between unskilled workers and the average citizen, caused more restrictive immigration policy. Rising equality, manifested by a declining gap between unskilled workers and the average citizen, created more open immigration policy.

Some Things Never Change

It appears that the late nineteenth and the late twentieth centuries shared more than simply globalization and convergence. Globalization also seems to have had the same impact on income distribution: in the late nineteenth century, inequality rose in rich countries and fell in poor countries; according to Adrian Wood, the same seems to have been true of the late twentieth century. Furthermore, whereas Borjas and Wood seem to think that globalization accounted for something like a third to a half of the rise in inequality in America and other OECD countries since the 1970s, the late-nineteenth-century evidence suggests much the same. In addition, it appears that mass migration accounted for most of the globalization-inequality connection, as in the United States since the 1970s. However, those modern economists who favor an explanation of rising inequality coming from labor-saving technological change will be pleased to hear that it probably accounted for more than a third of the rising inequality in the rich New World between 1870 and 1910. And factor saving accounted for even more of falling inequality in the Old World, more than half.

Some things never change, and that fact implies a warning. Globalization and convergence ceased between 1913 and 1950. It appears that the inequality trends that globalization produced are at least partly responsible for the interwar retreat from globalization manifested by immigration quotas, tariffs, restrictions on international capital flows, competitive devaluations, and other autarkic policy interventions. That fact should make us look to the next century with some anxiety: will the world economy retreat once again from its commitment to globalization?

Coda

The Evolution of a Global Labor Market

The time has come to take stock: what does history tell us about the evolution of a global labor market?

The process was immensely complicated by cyclical instability, unpredictable policy intervention, racial discrimination in receiving regions, ecological disaster in sending regions, and the sociology of networks, but fundamental economic and demographic tides were at work underneath those choppy waves. The evolution of a global labor market was slow, and the final steady state did not imply equal wages for the same jobs everywhere. However, this book has shown that those economic and demographic fundamentals were at work for the century of relatively free migration that ended around World War I.

The global labor market this book has been talking about excludes what is now known as the Third World (and much of poorly documented eastern Europe). It includes Europe and the overseas European-settled areas, what might now be called the OECD plus Latin American late-nineteenth-century participants like southern Brazil, Uruguay, Argentina, and Chile. There is little mention in this book of Asia, Africa, the Carribean, and those Latin American regions that had a long history with colonial plantations, slavery, and sugar. The justification is simple: these two labor markets—the Third World and the rest—were segmented by racial discrimination, language, and custom. They were segmented by long distance and high migration cost. They were segmented by the poverty of the Third World labor-surplus areas, areas so poor that potential emigrants would have found it impossible to finance the move to the booming OECD labor markets anyway. Slavery was one coercive device that had been used to facilitate the labor transfer, but it was erased politically as the nineteenth century progressed. Indentured or contract labor was another such device, but it got such a bad reputation that it too was erased for three crucial decades in the late nineteenth century. Indian and Chinese emigration had, of course, reached enormous proportions by the middle of the nineteenth century, but the vast majority of it failed to reach what we call the OECD labor market. Rather, those Asian mass migrations took place within the Third World itself. Indians went to East and South Africa, Ceylon, Burma, the Caribbean, the islands of the Pacific, and the islands of the Indian Ocean. The Chinese went to Manchuria, Southeast Asia, the Caribbean, and Peru. An interesting question for future research is the extent to which migration's laws of motion were roughly the same in the nineteenth-century Third World as they were in the OECD. But until they were legislated away, the areas of overlap were modest (e.g., the North American west coast, Hawaii, and Australia's Queensland), and they were a small part of the story.

The story begins with two economic shocks of enormous proportions: a resource discovery in the New World and an industrial revolution in the Old World. Neither of these two shocks was a discrete event, of course, since both gained momentum as the nineteenth century progressed. Furthermore, both shocks were technological. This was certainly true of resource discovery because the event was driven by the extent to which declining transport costs between Europe and the New World raised the price of resource-intensive products in the New World while lowering the cost of migration between them. That decline in transport costs was driven, at least in part, by technological change and scale. It was also true of the industrial revolution because technological change, in combination with capital accumulation and labor-supply responses, drove industrialization in Europe.

These two shocks produced a profound labor market disequilibrium early in the century. Wage gaps between the labor-scarce New World and the labor-abundant Old World reached huge dimensions. By 1870, real wages in the United States were more than 4 times what they were in Sweden, Australian wages were more than 2.5 times the Irish, Argentine wages were more than 2.3 times the Italian, and Canadian wages were almost 1.5 times the British. By 1870, wage gaps had also become large within Europe: British wages were almost 1.5 times what they were in Ireland, German wages were more than 2.2 times the Italian, and French wages had, no doubt, similar advantages over the Polish. These wage gaps seem to have been even bigger around midcentury: United States wages in 1850 were almost 4.3 times those in Sweden, while Australian wages were almost 3.2 times those in Ireland.

But these two shocks also produced the means by which global labor market integration could, at least eventually, be achieved. First, trade itself offered a partial and indirect solution to the disequilibrium. As transport costs declined, trade boomed and commodity prices converged. Most countries chose to participate in this globalization process and thus enjoyed a surge in exports that exploited their abundant factor. The demand for land boomed in high-wage areas and the demand for labor boomed in low-wage areas. As a result, land rents, wages, and even GDP per worker tended to converge. But these indirect forces of global labor market evolution were too weak to have played a very big role in the process. Mass migration offered the second and more direct solution to the disequilibrium.

The migrations were modest early in the century. Whereas they rose thereafter, they had not yet grown large enough by mid-century to overcome the effects of the two shocks. By the last third of the nineteenth century, they had. The labor supply responses had two mutually reinforcing parts: local demographic adjustments and foreign migration. High wages and labor scarcity encouraged early marriage, high fertility, low infant mortality, and, two decades later, high rates of labor force growth. Low wages and labor abundance encouraged late marriage, low fertility, high infant mortality, and, two decades later, low rates of labor force growth. This local labor supply adjustment to the global labor market disequilibrium was slow, not only because of the two-decade lag, but also because it took time for attitudes towards marriage and fertility to adjust to labor market conditions, especially in the Old World where demographic adjustment to exogenous improvements in the mortality environment was slow enough to generate Malthusian panic. Migration thus offered a quicker solution since the movers overwhelmingly were young adults.

But even the emigrations from low-wage European regions were slow in coming. While immigration rates were certainly biggest in high-wage countries, emigration rates were rarely highest among the poorest countries, or among the poorest regions in any poor country, or among the poorest workers in any poor country. Why didn't the poorest, for whom the gains from migration were the greatest, exploit those wage gaps earliest and most? The answer was simple enough: potential migrants were income-constrained. Mass migrations over long distances were expensive early in the century, and capital markets have always been notoriously imperfect when human capital is the only collateral available. It took time to release that income constraint. First, the financial and time cost of the migrant's journey fell, especially in the middle third of the nineteenth century at the start of the mass migrations. These migrant transport costs had fallen enough by 1848 so that poor Irish peasants could find the resources to flee the potato famine in great numbers. The rate of fall slowed thereafter, but migrant transport costs had fallen enough by 1900—in part because per unit costs between ports were driven down by scale economies achieved by the earlier rise in the mass migrations—so that temporary migration had become common and Italian workers could be called birds of passage. Second, the pioneer emigrants sent remittances home to finance the move of the next sibling. As the stock of past emigrants abroad rose, so too did the remittances, and so did the flow of current emigrants. Furthermore, the dynamic was one of trend acceleration, rising stocks of past emigrants abroad contributing to acceleration in the current emigration rate. Third, the Industrial Revolution spread from European leaders to followers, and by increasing the living standards of those who stayed home, augmented the family resources for investing in the move. Since the Industrial Revolution was carried on a path of trend acceleration, the income constraint on emigration was also released at an increasing rate. Although the last of these three forces was probably the weakest, all three tended in concert to translate a potential mass migration into a veritable flood as the century progressed.

Much of the income constraint on mass migration had been released by 1850 or 1870, so that disequilibrium wage gaps could do their work, pulling immigrants into high-wage countries, pushing emigrants out of low-wage countries, and redistributing the global labor force from labor-abundant to labor-scarce areas. This redistribution was effective since wage gaps shrank and living standards began to converge. Had the mass migrations continued at the high rates achieved by 1910, wage gaps might have almost disappeared by 1950. Even without interruption, those wage gaps would not have disappeared totally since individuals were willing to sacrifice some nominal income for the qualitative attraction of home. Nonetheless, without interruption, stable wage differentials might have been achieved by 1950, and the global OECD labor market might have arrived at a fully integrated equilibrium.

But the process *was* interrupted. Although we tend to think of the two wars, the Great Depression, and the quotas as the only interruptions in the process of global labor market integration, in fact there were far more fundamental forces at work slowing the process. After all, as the poorest countries in northwestern Europe caught up with the richest, the wage gap closed, the incentive to emigrate diminished, and the emigration rate fell off. True, other, even poorer, European countries to the east and south joined in, but even those sources would have dried up as the twentieth century progressed, and for the same reasons.

Thus, the process of global labor market integration in the OECD would have slowed by its own doing after 1914 and in the absence of wars and quotas. But were those quotas and other restrictions on international migration really exogenous to the process of global labor market integration? We doubt it. The rise of quotas and other immigrant policy restrictions everywhere in the New World were an integral part of the process. The alarming growth in the immigrant numbers (especially from the poorer European countries), and the fact that they competed on almost equal terms with previous immigrant and native-born labor, led to a glut in unskilled labor markets and to increasing inequality in the receiving countries. Those events provoked intense political debate and, eventually, led to the restrictive legislation that sharply constrained global labor market integration. Trade restrictions reinforced the migration policies.

The process of global labor market integration fell short of its equilibrium steady-state. It had to await the technological catch-up events of the post–World War II era to complete the process that had been underway for a century. But it had already come a good portion of the way by 1914.

Notes

Chapter 2. The Issues

1. These statistics were derived mainly from official government emigration records. They cover a limited number of countries, and the records are often limited to those leaving from ports, but the number of countries offering such data increases as the century unfolds. The countries included in the lower series plotted on the graph are Austria-Hungary, Poland, Russia, Italy, Portugal, Spain, and Malta.

2. Immigration statistics tend to yield larger totals than emigration statistics. Hence, immigration totals recorded for the Americas are very similar to those for all European intercontinental emigration despite the fact that the latter include such destinations as Australia, New Zealand, and South Africa.

3. Table 3.1 reports the same information, but the rates are annual and the decades are defined a little differently.

4. These findings are based on the examination of the passenger lists from emigrant ships. There has some debate about the proportion who were unskilled and from farms.

5. A number of studies have examined the composition of European emigrant flows by country. What follows in the text draws on Carlsson (1976) for Sweden, Erickson (1972) for Great Britain, Fitzpatrick (1984) for Ireland, Hvidt (1975) for Denmark, and Swierenga (1976) for Holland.

6. Women constituted a higher share of emigrants from a few countries like Ireland, where they accounted for 48 percent between 1851 and 1913. These were, however, the exceptions to the rule.

7. This insight is often attributed to Sjaastad (1962), who was one of the first to suggest that migration could be analyzed using a human capital framework.

8. Cohn (1984: 297) estimates emigrant deaths on the passage to New York at 1.36 percent during 1836 to 1853, a large number for such a short trip and for a group dominated by adults. McDonald and Schlomowitz (1990: 90) estimate deaths on the longer passage to Australia at 1.45 percent between 1838 and 1892.

9. Australia and Brazil offer good counterexamples. Both went through periods when they used extensive subsidies to encourage immigration.

10. In their recent survey of the theory relevant to contemporary migration, Massey et al. (1993: 455) reach a similar conclusion.

11. Important recent studies that use a multivariate approach in explaining interregional emigration rates are Lowell (1987) for Norway and Sweden and Sanchez-Alonso (1995) for Spain.

12. Easterlin disagreed: "There seems to be little . . . to support the view that a *general* influence among European countries giving rise to swings in emigration was a common swing in natural increase" (1961: 345; see also 1968: 33).

13. For this debate as it relates to American unemployment rates, see Romer (1986a, 1986b), Weir (1986, 1992).

Chapter 3. Why Did Europeans Emigrate?

1. This chapter is based on a reworking of the material in Hatton and Williamson (1994b and 1994d).

2. It is worth stressing that intra-European migration was confined mainly to Europe's low wage countries, as with the Latin countries. The exceptions were those with close cultural affinities over the border, as with Belgium.

3. The time trend took a positive coefficient consistent with falling transport costs but its t statistic was 0.75.

4. When the linear term alone was included, it also gave a very insignificant coefficient, with a t statistic of 0.05.

5. Assuming that the "correct" home wage is a weighted average of the agricultural and nonagricultural wage with weights reflected in the agricultural share variable, our urban real wage rates are too high—the more so the higher the agricultural share. If the higher agricultural share reflects a lower average wage relative to our urban wage, it would therefore have a positive effect on emigration, partially offsetting the negative effect of lower mobility among the agricultural population.

6. Recall that the return migration rate was far higher in the Latin countries, especially Italy. This may be attributable to the fact that lower transportation costs made temporary migration more feasible as the late nineteenth century wore on. In any case, the relatively high gross migration rates for the Latin latecomers might disappear if we had really good *net* migration data. Alas, we do not, but what we do have is reported in the appendix B table where the coefficients on the Latin dummy in the net emigration regressions are still positive and significant, although smaller.

7. And, once again, a chi-squared test implies that all three countries—Italy, Portugal, and Spain—can be pooled together as "Latin."

8. On the so-called Edwardian failure in Britain, see McCloskey (1970).

9. This is based on regressions on a quadratic in "emigration time" that again include country dummies, although they are not reported in table 3.7.

Chapter 4. Cycles, Swings, and Shocks: Waiting to Make the Move

1. This chapter is based on a reworking of the material in Hatton (1995a and 1995b).

2. Other studies, some of which are referred to in the following discussion, include Moe (1970), Williamson (1974a, b), Pope (1976a, b; 1981a, b; 1985), Gandar (1982), Larsen (1982), and Norstrom (1988).

3. A similar approach has been used in the context of rural-urban migration by Banerjee and Kanbur (1981).

4. Interest in this topic was very active in the 1950s and 1960s. Apart from Simon Kuznets himself, the pioneers were Moses Abramovitz (1961, 1968), Richard Easterlin (1966, 1968) and Brinley Thomas (1954, 1972).

5. There is a positive correlation coefficient of 0.54 between inward and outward flows.

6. This is a geometric weighted average with weights of 0.5 for the United States and 0.25 each for Canada and Australia. Recall that 53.8 percent of the emigrants from the United Kingdom went to the United States, 25.4 percent went to Canada, and 16.5 percent went to Australia and New Zealand combined.

7. The variable was constructed by regressing a nonlinear transformation of the employment rate on the deviation of real GNP per capita from logarithmic trend between 1916 and 1939, and then extrapolating backwards. The employment rate was taken from Galenson and Zellner (1957: 455) and real GNP per capita from Urquhart (1986: 30–31).

8. Before estimating the full model, the time series properties of the data were explored and tested for cointegration to see whether the model needed modification. The individual time series appears, for the most part, to be integrated of order 1. The cointegration tests generally support the hypothesis that the explanatory variables represent a cointegrated set. The test statistics for gross and net emigration, respectively, were: Cointegrating Regression Durbin Watson Statistic: 1.09, 1.02; Dickey-Fuller: −4.45, −4.15; Augmented Dickey-Fuller: −3.90, −3.88.

9. The computed chi-squared statistics for the restrictions in columns 3 and 4 are 1.82 and 7.19, respectively, compared with the critical 5 percent value of 3.84.

10. Detailed descriptions of the emigrant composition are given in Jensen (1931), Hvidt (1975) and Carlsson (1976).

11. To the extent that per capita income measures contain a cyclical component, they tend to conflate the two elements of the expected income approach—the wage rate and the employment probability. More importantly, only the wage component of national income was relevant to potential migrants, and for most it was the unskilled wage at that.

12. Real GDP and population for the Scandinavian countries were taken from Maddison (1991). Romer's (1989) real GDP series was used for the United States.

13. Examination of the time series properties of the explanatory variables indicates that they are generally integrated of order 1. Cointegrating regressions were run for each of the three countries of the emigration rate on the log wage ratio, domestic and United States economic activity, and the migrant stock. The tests gave the following results:

	Sweden	Norway	Denmark
Cointegrating regression D.W.	1.30	1.12	0.68
Dickey-Fuller	−4.45	−4.34	−3.92
Augmented Dickey-Fuller	−4.35	−5.55	−3.92

Although the test statistics are close to the 5 percent significance level for Denmark, they generally indicate that these variables form cointegrated sets and thus that legitimate regression models can be estimated.

14. The relevant computed chi-squared(1) statistics for this restriction for the three countries respectively were 0.88, 1.42, and 0.35, critical 5 percent value = 3.84.

Chapter 5. After the Famine: Irish Experience

1. This chapter is based on Hatton and Williamson (1993).

2. Since the country of destination was not distinguished in the emigration statistics until 1876, Ó Gráda (1975) estimated the flow to Britain over the whole period from 1852

to 1911 by subtracting an estimate of total extra-European emigration (based on immigration reports abroad) from the recorded total emigration. This yielded an Irish flow to Britain slightly above half a million. Applying standard survival rate techniques, Ó Gráda then calculated that over a million must have emigrated to Britain to achieve the total Irish-born recorded as living in Britain at the time of the 1911 census. This, then, is the source of the estimated half million Irish who migrated to Britain but were "missed" in the official emigration counts.

3. Statistics on United States immigrant arrivals are available by country of origin starting in 1820. They relate to "alien passengers" up to 1868, and to "alien immigrants" thereafter. A considerable number arriving from the United Kingdom before 1872 were not allocated to the four sources—England, Scotland, Wales, and Ireland. Hence, until this date the officially record of Irish immigrants to the United States clearly understates the true total.

4. The correlation coefficient between the two series is 0.945 and a regression of the emigration series on the immigration series yields the following result (t statistics in parentheses):

$$EM(US) = -406.58 + 0.93\ IM(US)\quad R^2 = 0.89$$
$$(0.16)\ (17.34)$$

Since the emigration series is for calendar years while the immigration series is for fiscal years, a more exact alignment of the data would likely give an even closer fit.

5. Take as a starting point the emigration rate of 15 per thousand population in 1861. If the numerator is divided instead by the population aged 15–34, the revised emigration rate (for those at "risk") is 42.5 per thousand. Applying this 42.5 rate to the 1911 population aged 15–34 implies an emigration rate per thousand population of 13.9 in that year, compared with the true rate of 8 per thousand. In short, the shift in the age structure of the Irish population cannot have accounted for more than a 1.1 per thousand fall in the emigration rate (e.g., 15 minus 13.9), or for a little more than a seventh of the total fall (e.g., 1.1 divided by 7). This number is not trivial, and it is consistent with the *direct* Easterlin effect documented in chapter 3. However, other factors were clearly more important.

6. [Irish] *Commission on Emigration and other Population Problems* (1954: 126).

7. The weights are United States, 0.7; Great Britain, 0.2; Canada and Australia, each 0.05. In the estimates presented below for intercontinental emigration, the weights are United States, 0.875; Canada and Australia, each 0.0625.

8. The agricultural output data was taken from Drescher (1955).

9. We also experimented with separate regressions for the comparatively small flows to Canada and Australia. Although these provided some support for the model, the equations did not perform as well as for aggregate emigration or for United States emigration alone. We suspect that these poorer results can be explained largely by competing labor market conditions in the United States and Britain. We have not been able to test this assertion, however, because high collinearity exists between the country-specific labor market variables. The fact that national labor market variables were so highly correlated implies, of course, fairly well-integrated labor markets in the Atlantic economy.

10. This is especially true by county of origin. The authorities improved the enumeration significantly after the so-called great depression of the 1870s (Fitzpatrick 1980a: 28).

11. This result does not depend on our selection of these specific years. If we take average emigration rates for intercensal periods, the coefficients of variation are 0.25 for the 1870s, 0.31 for the 1880s, 0.60 for the 1900s, and 0.46 for the 1910s.

12. Deviations from a linear trend 1880–1913 for the aggregate emigration rate were (in emigrants per thousand) −1.15 in 1881, +0.07 in 1891, −0.33 in 1901, and +1.31 in 1911.

13. The county wage data were taken from Bowley (1899: 401) for 1880–1881, and from Fitzpatrick (1980b: 90) for 1893 and 1911, with estimates for 1901 obtained by linear interpolation. For each census year, the wage ratios between county and destinations abroad were adjusted so that the mean of the counties relative to the wage overseas would be the same as that for unskilled in the building trades used in the time series analysis.

14. This variable includes both indoor and outdoor relief. In preliminary tests, we attempted to adjust for differences in county poor law policy in the manner suggested by Mackinnon (1987), using the ratio of the number relieved indoors to total relieved as an indicator of policy stance. The results were very similar to those using the unadjusted relief variable, so we retain the latter in the analysis reported in table 5.4.

15. As with the time series analysis, a regression was also run for adjusted total emigration where the recorded number emigrating to Britain was doubled. The main difference (not shown in table 5.4) was that the coefficient on the Catholic variable became even more negative (−8.7) and even significant ($t = 2.8$)!

16. The unweighted means for each census year are given in the appendix.

17. The result for total emigration is

$$M/P = 0.42 + 19.73 \log\left(W_f/W_h\right) \quad R^2 = 0.18$$
$$\left(0.20\right) \quad \left(5.19\right)$$

The 19.73 should be compared with the long-run coefficient for total emigration estimated in table 5.2 to be 20.1.

Chapter 6. Segmented Markets, Multiple Destinations: Italian Experience

1. Almost all the emigration data used in this chapter were taken from the compilation of statistics in Commisariato Generale Dell'Emigrazione (1926) cited in the appendix.

2. The abrupt upward shift in net and gross emigration between 1912 and 1913 is not a typographical error, although it may be a flaw in the original source.

3. Direct estimates of return migration are unavailable until 1902 when officials began to record return migration at ports of entry. However, even these figures are incomplete since they exclude emigrants returning from European destinations.

4. The year-to-year movements in the net migration series cannot be taken too seriously. The sharp discontinuities in 1900–1901 and 1911–1912 may be explained in part by the fact that the movement between the census benchmarks relies on the series for gross emigration rather than on direct observation of movements in net emigration (see Gould 1980a: 84).

5. Prior to 1904, the gross emigration statistics relate to passports authorized by the *nulla osta* (a certification by the local mayor that there were no legal obstacles to the individual's departure). They relate to passports actually issued after 1904. Passports were normally valid for three years. For discussions of the changes in passport regulations and their effects on the emigration statistics, see Coletti (1911: 10–13), Foerster (1919: 10–17), and Gould (1980a: 87–93).

6. Faini and Venturini (1994b) have elaborated on these themes in the post–World War II context as well.

7. The regional differences in economic development are examined in Eckaus (1961), Williamson (1965) and Zamagni (1993: chs. 1, 2).

8. For the purposes of this chapter, the islands are not distinguished as a separate region: Sardinia is grouped with the center and Sicily is included in the south. The Compartimenti are divided into regions as follows: north—Piedmont, Liguria, Lombardy, Venetia, Emilia; center—Tuscany, Marches, Umbria, Lazio, Sardinia; south—Abruzzi and Molise, Campania, Apulia, Basilicata, Calabria, Sicily.

9. If smaller geographical units were used, the regional composition effect would probably be even greater (Gould 1979: 104).

10. The share of Italian emigrants from agriculture in those reporting occupations was 40 percent. This figure is clearly an understatement given what we know about the Italian employment share in agriculture. Based on American immigration evidence, agricultural migrants always underreported their true occupation, perhaps reflecting their intent to leave it behind.

11. Some of these emigrant characteristics can be found in the published statistics. More detailed analyses of intercontinental emigrant characteristics have been produced from passenger lists of ships arriving in the Americas (Di Comite and Glazier 1982; Glazier and Okeke 1994).

12. See especially Foerster (1919: ch. 2) and Cinel (1982, 1991).

13. Given the nature of Italian passport statistics, seasonal emigration was undoubtedly underrecorded, especially before 1901. This downward bias suggests that many passport applicants after 1901 did not emigrate.

14. For a discussion of seasonality in the United States, see Goldin and Engerman (1993).

15. More accurately, these are constructed from logarithmic deviations from trend in real per capita gross domestic product, using data from Maddison (1991).

16. This is constructed as a five-year moving-average of the rate of natural increase centered on year t-20. Because the vital rates are not available before 1860, the first few observations had to be extrapolated. The data on natural increase are taken from Mitchell (1980).

17. In preliminary estimation, changes in the explanatory variables were found to be unimportant, so only levels are reported in what follows. Both the one- and two-year lags of the dependent variable are included to be consistent with the chapter 4 results for Scandinavia.

18. In addition, the inclusion of this extra variable has a negligible impact on the size and significance of the other coefficients.

19. The time trend itself does not take a significant coefficient unless the real wage is excluded. When the real wage was omitted from the equation in the third column of table 6.3, the coefficient on time took a *t* value of 3.16. When the time trend was added to the specification in the first column of table 6.3, it took a *t* value of 1.33. The migrant stock term was robust to this change, taking a *t* value of 2.99.

20. Of course, if the totals are disaggregated between European and intercontinental emigration, then the variation increases with the former still dominating in the north and the latter in the south.

21. One would have thought that emigration would also have been stimulated to the extent that factory industry displaced more labor-intensive forms of proto industry, either in the immediate hinterland or in the mountain regions farther afield (Ramella 1991). The growing concentration of factory industries, such as textiles in Lombardy and the rest of the northwest, also affected more distant regions like Abruzzi and Basilicata where traditional

craft industries declined (Esposto 1992). In Italy, however, women mainly did this work and thus were displaced, while the men emigrated.

22. The availability of small land parcels was determined largely by various land reforms beginning in 1862 when estates formerly owned by the church or the state were sold off. These "privatizations" had an especially large effect in the south where a quarter of all farm land was sold off. These parcels were too large to be acquired by small farmers who lacked agricultural credit and were therefore acquired by larger landlords (Foerster 1919: 67; Zamagni 1993: 67).

23. Potential emigrants may have been constrained from emigrating from the poorest regions by their inability to raise the necessary funds for a passage, an argument also offered by Faini and Venturini to explain Italian time series, an argument that the evidence seems to reject. And as MacDonald (1963: 437) notes, "even the poorest of them were able to pay for the necessary transportation, sooner or later."

24. Unfortunately, good regional wage data is not available earlier. By 1913 one would have thought that emigration would have diminished regional wage gaps. Thus, the 1913 wage data will understate the true impact of wages on regional emigration in 1902 and perhaps even in 1912, if emigration lagged behind labor market conditions.

25. According to O'Brien and Toniolo (1991: 397), "before 1914 the massive and endemic under-employment which afflicted most men, women, and children employed in Italian agriculture varied region by region and was probably related to the terms upon which families obtained access to land. Involuntary unemployment was certainly more severe among landless labourers (*braccianti*) and their dependents than among farmers and their families who owned or hired their land, regardless of form of tenure."

26. Other demographic measures such as average family size and the share of the population between ages 15 and 29 were also explored, but these were judged less satisfactory since they were significantly influenced by emigration in the very recent past. These variables were dominated by the lagged rate of natural increase when entered into the regression, but the population aged 15–29 gave a negative sign, consistent with previous emigration having depleted the emigration-sensitive cohort.

27. This cutoff was chosen to exclude as far as possible small towns and large villages that were essentially rural communities.

28. Several Italian specialists thought that these agricultural attributes had different implications depending on the region. Thus, in early experiments we interacted the share of owner-occupiers and sharecroppers with the regional dummies, but none of these was significant.

29. Vera Zamagni (1978, tav. 59, 204) reports a similar index constructed by G. Tagliacarne for 1915, as well as one of her own for 1911. In the regressions, the Mortara index did better than either the Tagliacarne or the Zamagni index. Perhaps this was because Mortara constructed his index for 1900–1902 and 1910–1912, and we were able to use them both in the pooled regressions for 1902 and 1912. In any case, only the Mortara index is reported in table 6.6.

30. Literacy rates for those in the prime emigrating age group, 15–30, were also constructed, but this alternative variable changed the results hardly at all.

31. These were not the only, or even the main, emigrant destinations in Europe, but they seem a better compromise than, say, Paris or Marseilles on one hand and Frankfurt or Dortmund on the other. Since these two centers are roughly equidistant from Milan, the measure takes on a roughly equal weight in the northeast and northwest provinces.

32. When the emigration rate is used as the dependent variable, the estimated equations were found to fail badly the test for functional form. Perhaps this is not surprising since there is such a wide spread in the measured emigration rates and since these are bounded below at zero. Hence, they were reestimated using the log of the emigration rate.

33. Such effects are more clearly revealed in the cross section where the variation is greater than in time series where it is more strongly correlated with other variables.

34. One might think that these results are driven largely by the south and north dummies, which are interacted with the agricultural and urban shares, respectively, but, when entered separately, the dummies were both insignificant. The distance variables embody a continuous version of the north-south dichotomy.

35. Because the logarithmic specification imposes nonlinearity, the measurement of these contributions is sensitive to the point of evaluation. Different methods of scaling affect the total explained difference quite markedly. The point of evaluation used here is the weighted mean of the emigration rates for the south and north (excluding the center).

Chapter 7. Assimilating the Immigrant: An American Melting Pot?

1. The history of American nativism is described in full by Higham (1955).

2. The Commission's (and other contemporaries') use of the term "race" is closer to what in today's language we might describe as "ethnicity."

3. While the commission's views seem racist, they were not uncommon at the time. Madison Grant's book, *The Passing of the Great Race*, (1923) is perhaps the best known (and most extreme) example of this literature, but similar sentiments were expressed by other observers such as John R. Commons. According to Commons: "Each race comes from a country lower in the scale than that of the preceding, until finally the ends of the earth have been ransacked in the search for low standards of living compared with patient industriousness" (1920: 152).

4. See, for example, the early review of Handlin by Shlakman (1953).

5. Perhaps the same might be true of native-born Americans immigrating from farm to city, but we expect the differences between American city-born and American rural immigrants to be much smaller. Unfortunately, the historical data rarely distinguished between native-born rural immigrants and city-born natives. To the extent that American cities were also full of native-born rural immigrants, the literature must understate foreign-born assimilation problems in the same American cities.

6. The data were collected, computerized, and made available by the Historical Labor Statistics Project at the University of California (Carter, Ransom, Sutch, and Zhao, 1993a, b). Hannon's earlier study (1982b) was based on a 25 percent sample of the original records.

7. Recent research by Rachael Friedberg (1992, 1993) on 1976 and 1980 data indicates that immigrants who arrived as children assimilated better and had higher earnings than those who arrived as adults. She attributes the advantage of child arrival (in roughly equal parts) to the higher share of schooling received in the United States rather than in the home country, greater English language facility, and greater adaptability compared with adult arrival.

8. Not surprisingly, the regressions underlying the fitted curves massively fail the RESET test for functional form. The computed test statistics for native-born and foreign-born are 42.7 and 36.2, compared to the critical chi-square value of 3.84.

9. A study by Murphy and Welch suggests the same problem exists for earnings functions on post–World War II data. Using CPS surveys for 1964–1987, they find that earnings functions with quadratic terms in experience and experience squared systemmatically underpredict earnings between 7 and 17 years of experience and overpredict between 18 and 35 years of experience (Murphy and Welch 1990: 208).

10. Murphy and Welch (1990) model post–World War II earnings as a quartic function of experience. We experimented with functional forms such as cubic or quartic functions of age, but these produced less satisfactory results for the late-nineteenth-century data. They tend to produce points of inflexion at the upper ages and can produce implausible increases (or declines) in the predicted wage over the age of 55. The reason seems to be that the coefficients are largely determined by the concentration of observations at the lower ages and hence track mean earnings rather poorly at the higher ages. The use of the age-25 variable (for positive values; zero otherwise) creates a spline with the knot point at age 25 and avoids any discontinuity in the earnings function. For the equations in table 7.5 a test of specification was performed against the quartic by adding variables for age^3 and age^4. These always proved insignificant and each equation in table 7.5 is a valid restriction of this more general model. The computed F statistics for the four equations respectively are 0.68, 2.94, 1.15, and 0.19, compared with the 5 percent critical value of 3.0.

11. Hypothesis tests clearly reject the more restrictive quadratic specification (i.e., excluding the shift terms for age-25) against that in table 7.5. The computed F statistics for the four equations respectively are 359.9, 280.5, 44.1, and 137.2, compared with the 5 percent critical value of 3.0.

12. The overall explanatory power of the equation for immigrants who arrived as adults is noticably lower than for the other three, largely for two reasons. As we shall see, immigrants are a more heterogeneous group than natives. But more important, compared with the other groups, a higher proportion of the observations fall on the flat part of the age-earnings profile, so the share of the variance explained is relatively small.

13. Over the whole period, the figure is 1 percent for the native-born of native parents.

14. The data displayed for the Michigan ironworkers in table 7.6 is not quite the same as that used in the regression analysis; in order to obtain a direct comparison with the census categories, it includes 15-year-olds and excludes those over 64.

15. It might be suggested that the steep rise in earnings during early years displayed in figure 7.1 owes something to the fact that those with more years of education appear in the data only at higher ages and with higher incomes. However, this is unlikely to account for the steep rise in earnings up through the midtwenties, since high educational achievement a century ago meant high school completion and thus 18- and 19-year-olds.

16. There was also some decline in the quality of cohorts within individual national groups. This might be attributed to the 1965 Amendments to the Immigration and Nationality Act since it shifted the criteria for admission away from immigrant skills towards family reunification. No such changes characterized the late nineteenth century; hence, erosion in cohort quality within national groups was never important in that debate.

17. The east European group contains workers born in Albania, Austria, Bohemia, Hungary, Poland, and Russia. The few immigrants from Switzerland were included with the German-born.

18. The computed F statistic for this restriction is 1.25, which can be compared with the 5 percent critical value of 1.43.

19. The numbers of observations in the regressions in table 7.7 are slightly lower than for the regressions in table 7.5 because the small number of immigrants from other regions or countries, for instance, southern Europe, were dropped from the dataset.

20. Public Use Manuscript Samples are available from the censuses of 1900 and 1910 but these datasets, although nationally representative, do not contain information on earnings, which is our main focus. Econometric analysis of occupational status scores for immigrants and natives in 1900 has been undertaken by Chiswick (1991) and Hanes (1996).

21. Other studies using the same source are limited to fewer observations: McGouldrick and Tannen (1977) used 151, Blau (1980) used 202, and Chiswick (1992) used 210. This is because information was not reported for some variables in the race/industry cells and because these studies included industry characteristics derived from other sources, which limits the set of industries. We avoid the former problem by using a more restricted set of right-hand-side variables and the latter problem by including the full set of industry dummies in our regressions.

22. The industries from which the data are drawn are bituminous coal, iron and steel, woolen and worsted, cotton, leather, boots and shoes, gloves, silk, clothing, slaughtering and meat packing, agricultural implements, cigars and tobacco, furniture, sugar refining, copper mining, and iron ore mining. These industry summaries appear in volumes 7–16 of the Immigration Commission *Report*.

23. Given that each of the cells used in estimation represents a different number of individuals, one might have expected heteroskedasticity to be a problem. But the Cook-Weisberg test for heteroskedasticity gives a value of 0.28 compared with the chi-squared 5 percent critical value of 3.84. When weighted least squares was used (with the number represented by each cell as the weight), the null hypothesis was rejected.

24. Including industry dummies raises the issue of the self-selection of immigrants among industries and career mobility across industries, which will be captured in the industry dummies rather than the nationality dummies. However, there are other reasons, such as working conditions and hours of labor, why wage rates differ between industries. Eliminating the industry dummies makes little difference to the pattern of coefficients across nationalities.

25. The estimated starting disadvantage of 14 percent for Hebrews is consistent with Chiswick's (1992: 283) finding that they earned significantly more than other southern and eastern European immigrants.

26. We could alternatively use the wage differential after 20 years or the average, say, between the ages of 20 and 60, but these will amount to the same thing since the wage differentials between immigrant groups estimated in table 7.8 do not change with years in the United States.

27. Illiteracy is defined as the proportion of the immigrant group aged 14 and above who either could read but not write or who could not read or write (in any language).

28. Adding further variables such as the proportion of men or the proportion of immigrants who reported a previous occupation did not result in significant coefficients in the presence of the variables already included.

29. When the proportion of farm laborers alone was entered, it took a coefficient of 0.221 (*t* statistic 4.09).

30. The Immigration Bureau classified immigrants by country of origin while after 1899 they were classified by "race or people." Fortunately, the Immigration Bureau provided a cross-tabulation of race by country of origin, so it is possible for later years to map race into country of origin, so we can use the latter throughout. It would have been preferable to work on the basis of the post-1899 classification both because it is a much finer classification and because it is consistent with the disaggregation used by the Immigration Commission. Unfortunately, it is not possible to reclassify immigrants by race or nationality before 1899.

31. The 1893 figure in table 7.10 combines the literacy rates for 1896 (the first year for which they are available) with the adult immigrant weights of 1893.

32. This calculation is based on 1980 characteristics. If, instead, 1940 immigrant characteristics are used, the estimated quality decline is much smaller—18 percent for the unadjusted wage and 2.1 percent for the adjusted wage. The text selects the end period 1980 characteristics for better comparability with our analysis of 1909, the end of the late-nineteenth-century period of mass migration.

33. As Hourwich put it: "while the root of all evil today is now sought in the racial makeup of the new immigration as contrasted with the old, every objection to the immigrant from Southern and Eastern Europe is but an echo of complaints which were made at an earlier day against the then new immigration from Ireland, Germany and even from England" (1922: 2).

Chapter 8. Absorbing the Immigrant: The Impact on Americans

1. The political, legal, and bureaucratic aspects of guestworker policy in postwar western Europe can be found in a number of sources including Power (1979: 10–14), Böhning (1984: 125–33), and Castles and Miller (1993: 66–71).

2. When Stephen Castles (1986) writes an "obituary" for the system, it is by way of noting that host countries were unprepared for those temporary workers who became permanent. For recent accounts of postwar European immigration and immigration policy see Booth (1992), Collinson (1993), and Hollifield (1992).

3. It might appear that our calculations are biased downwards by the assumption that immigrants did not have a significant impact on aggregate demand and thus employment rates, taken here to have been exogenous to the immigrations. David Pope and Glen Withers (1993, 1994) would quarrel with this assumption, based on their analysis of Australia, as, no doubt, would Richard Easterlin (1966, 1968) and Moses Abramovitz (1961, 1968), based on their analysis of the American long swing. On the other hand, we ignore the very real possibility that some of the guestworkers competed directly with secondary members of the work force. These secondary workers helped contribute to the procyclical movement in the labor force of which so much was made by Robert Coen (1973) and Christina Romer (1986a) in their debates with Stanley Lebergott (1964). In short, it's not clear whether the estimates reported in the text are upper or lower bounds.

4. The term comes from Sidney Pollard (1978), who characterized the Irish in early industrializing Britain the same way. Williamson (1986) disagreed. The exchange between Pollard and Williamson over the impact of the Irish immigrants on British workers from the 1820s to the 1850s exactly parallels this later debate in America. The issues are the same, only the names have changed.

5. It would have been interesting to examine this hypothesis at the industry level, but, unfortunately, it was not possible to construct a matching set of variables across the two census dates.

6. The confirmation has emerged in very recent work by William Collins (1997).

7. Both native-born and foreign-born migrants favored city location, but this was especially true of the latter: in 1900, 17.3 percent of the population in cities greater than 25,000 were native interstate migrants and 26 percent were foreign-born (Hill 1906: 277).

8. But as Filer (1992) points out, in the presence of demand shocks driving internal migration, an inverse relationship between native-born and foreign-born migration is sug-

gestive of crowding-out even though it could also be present where there is in-migration of both native-born and foreign-born. The question is whether an influx of immigrants into a local or regional labor market tends to increase the out-migration or lower the in-migration rate of natives.

9. In 1900, for example, the farm real wage was about 70 percent of the urban unskilled real wage (Hatton and Williamson 1992: 269).

10. Foreman-Peck's results are consistent with the earlier observations of McGouldrick and Tannen (1977), who found no differences in the productivity performance of New England and southern textile industries even though the former employed immigrant labor, while the latter did not.

11. Douglas found that the real wages of unskilled workers declined between 1900 and 1914 and remained roughly constant overall between 1890 and 1914. These estimates were questioned by Rees, who found faster growth in manufacturing earnings between 1900 and 1914 but who did not rule out the possibility that immigration during this period may still have retarded real wage growth (1961: 126).

12. There are also other possible sources of bias. For example, if immigrants migrate to high-wage areas, then the (negative) wage effects would be biased towards zero unless a technique like instrumental variables is used (Friedberg and Hunt 1995: 31).

13. As Borjas puts it, "As long as native workers and firms respond to the entry of immigrants by moving to areas offering better opportunities there is no reason to expect a correlation between the wage of natives and the presence of immigrants" (1994: 1699).

14. Although it has rarely been attempted for the United States, a recent study by David Pope and Glen Withers (1994) tried to gauge the impact of immigration on wages in Australia using aggregate time series from 1861 to 1913. They found no negative effect; indeed the effect while small was *positive*. But their study looked only at the impact of current and lagged immigration, not at the total impact of the immigrant-augmented labor force. Labor's marginal product and the wage should be associated with the total labor supply, not with the current addition to that supply; and the current addition should include all sources, not just immigration, since, after all, Australian immigration may have been offset by changes in native labor suply, potential offsets that were ignored by Pope and Withers. In another study, the same authors (Pope and Withers 1993) also found little effect of immigration on the Australian unemployment rate in the long run, concluding that immigrants did not "rob" jobs from Australians. This second finding ought not to surprise any reader since the Australian economy ought to have adjusted back to its long-run equilibrium unemployment rate after an immigration-induced labor supply shock, but with a lower real wage. It is the first finding of no immigration-induced negative wage effects that deserves critical assessment.

15. Sachs (1980), James (1989), Allen (1992), and Hanes (1993) all provide estimates for the pre–World War I period. But they each estimate the equivalent of equation 8.1 rather than combining it with the marginal productivity condition for labor to yield a term for the lagged real wage as in equation 8.3.

16. The negative coefficient on the time trend is not, however, consistent with theory. A possible reason is that the error correction term, which arises from the first-order condition for labor, should, in principle, reflect the producer price index rather than the cost-of-living index. Since the cost-of-living index fell relative to the GNP deflator, this might account for the negative trend component. In initial estimation, the ratio of the cost-of-living to GNP deflator was included as a separate variable, but it never took a significant coefficient.

17. The computed chi-squared statistics for these restrictions are 0.34 and 1.92, respectively, compared with the 5 percent critical values of 3.84 and 5.99.

18. If we simply added up the worker immigration flow to 1910 (appendix), these percentages would be 12.4 and 21.8. But this method does not allow for the death and retirement of immigrants or for the eventual labor force entry of their children.

19. These orders of magnitude are also supported when the marginal productivity condition for labor is estimated on panel data across countries and decades. The results indicate that in the absence of immigration from 1870 to 1910, the United States real wage would have been 12 percent higher in 1910. (See chapter 10.)

20. Robert Coen (1973) also offered a critical assessment of the 1920s and 1930s, but his work falls outside of our period of interest.

Chapter 9. Labor Market Impact at Home: Ireland and Sweden

1. This chapter draws heavily on Boyer, Hatton, and O'Rourke (1994), O'Rourke and Williamson (1995) and Williamson (1994).

2. This and the following sections on Ireland draw heavily on Boyer, Hatton, and O'Rourke (1994), although some of the estimates and calculations have been revised.

3. The agricultural wage data for 1880–1913 were obtained from the U.K. Board of Trade *Seventeenth Abstract of Labour Statistics of the United Kingdom* (1915, p. 67). The series consists of weekly wages on 27 farms. For 1855–1880 a wage series for 10 farms was taken from the Board of Trade *Second Report . . . on Wages, Earnings, and Conditions of Employment of Agricultural Labourers in the United Kingdon* (1905, p. 1370, by A. Wilson Fox). The two series were spliced together in 1880 and deflated by the same cost of living index used for building laborers.

4. Other evidence suggests that wage growth for skilled trades, carpenters, and fitters was somewhat slower between 1860 and 1913 than for unskilled workers. Trends in skilled wage rates closely resemble those in Great Britain, suggesting that the market for skilled labor in Ireland was better integrated with skilled labor markets across the Irish sea than with the Irish unskilled labor market (see Boyer, Hatton, and O'Rourke 1994: 224, 226).

5. The agricultural price index is taken from Turner (1987: 135–36).

6. We do not have annual data for either the farm labor force or the rural male population, so the total male population will have to do.

7. Ó Gráda (1988: ch. 4) points to the diffusion of a number of innovations including the use of new potato varieties, crop spraying, and the diffusion of the milk separator. He estimates that total factor productivity in agriculture grew by 34 percent between 1854 and 1908, or by about 0.5 percent per annum. Michael Turner's (1991) recent evidence suggests that Ó Gráda's earlier estimates need to be reduced; indeed, Turner suggests that there was no increase at all after the late 1860s or the early 1870s!

8. This model is related to that used to estimate the labor force impact on the wage in the United States in chapter 8, table 8.6.

9. Since the agricultural labor force fell faster than the population, the time trend may, however, be compensating for the understated decline in the farm labor force.

10. There are various surveys available in the literature. Kemal Dervis, Jaime DeMelo, and Sherman Robinson (1982) offer one for development. John Shoven and John Whalley (1984) offer another for trade and public finance, as well as a more recent overview (1992). John James (1984) and Mark Thomas (1987) offer others for economic history.

11. The model was constructed by Kevin O'Rourke as part of another collaboration. A

more detailed description of the model is available elsewhere (Boyer, Hatton, and O'Rourke 1993: appendix 2).

12. Wage gaps are common during development, and they have been analyzed over time and across countries (Hatton and Williamson 1991, 1992). The treatment in the text is consistent with these earlier findings.

13. For more detail on the method used for this calculation, see Boyer, Hatton, and O'Rourke (1994: 231–32).

14. For an elaboration of the effect of trade on factor prices and convergence in the greater Atlantic economy, see O'Rourke and Williamson (1994; 1995; 1996; 1997), O'Rourke, Williamson, and Hatton (1994), O'Rourke, Taylor, and Williamson (1996), and Williamson (1996b).

15. By the 1950s at least, the assumption of capital mobility would evidently have been preferred by the Irish Commission on Population, which observed: "Irish capital formed part of the world market and Irish industrial projects had to compete for capital with the opportunities for investment, not only in Great Britain but throughout the world" (1954: 26).

16. There are at least two reasons to have expected different elasticities implied by the CGE and the time series. First, the farm wage deflated by a cost-of-living index (in the CGE) and the farm wage deflated by a farm output price index (in the time series) differed somewhat. Second, the farm labor force (in the CGE) and the total male population (in the time series) differ.

17. Note that the entries in the last row of the capital mobile case in table 9.2 are −2.0 and −2.9, not zero. The *nominal* return to capital is taken to be exogenous and pegged to world markets. But it is the *real* rate—nominal deflated by a cost of living index—that is reported here. It should also be noted that the results are *far* more sensitive to assumptions about international capital mobility than to any other. See Boyer, Hatton, and O'Rourke (1993: appendix 3; 1994: 239).

18. The actual nonfarm wage used in this comparsion is the unskilled building wage.

19. Consider the nonagricultural real wage, Ireland-United States, to illustrate. The no-emigration counterfactual increase in the ratio is 0.06 and 0.13 for the two "lower" cases. Thus, Irish emigration must have accounted for $[0.16 - 0.06]/0.16 = 62.5$ percent or $[0.16 - 0.13]/0.16 = 18.75$ percent.

20. The full details of the sources of the Scandinavian catch-up are offered elsewhere (O'Rourke and Williamson 1995, 1996).

21. The words "conditional" and "unconditional" come from the empirical work of the new growth empiricists like Robert Barro and Xavier Sala-i-Martin (1992), and Gregory Mankiw, David Romer, and David Weil (1992). They refer to convergence conditional on, or after controlling for, schooling and other forces excluded from the standard Solow model. Both Milton Friedman (1992) and Danny Quah (1993) have pointed out that these convergence equations may be plagued by Galton's classical fallacy of regression towards the mean. However, Galton's fallacy is absent when measures of dispersion are also plotted through time: they decline from 1870 to 1913 (Williamson 1995, 1996b).

22. The β underlying figure 9.4 is −0.390 (table 9.6, row 1). The rate of convergence is $\lambda = (1/t)\ln(\beta + 1)$, where t is the time span (43 years) and β is the coefficient for the log of initial real wages (income per capita or labor productivity). Actually, we use the term "speed of convergence" too loosely in this context. Speed of convergence technically is λ times the initial gap. If $\lambda = 0.01$, it would take 70 years to cut the gaps in half. Thus, had the late-nineteenth-century rate of convergence persisted, by 1940 gaps would have been half those of 1870. Eliminating big initial gaps takes a long time, even when fast convergence is at work.

23. An article in an economic history journal on "impact" had no historical content at all (Ekberg 1977). However, a very sophisticated survey by Scott (1960) *did* have things to say about impact, but in the end the author could only account for the absence of such work by the fact that "it is easier to trace the rise in wages than it is to relate it to emigration" (1960: 167).

24. We ignore the possibility that the Swedish natural rate of increase would have been lower in the absence of emigration (by later marriages and lower fertility within marriage), a response that was included for Ireland. Although we think such effects would have been small, the assumption does serve to exaggerate the impact of mass migration.

25. All of the results that follow in this paragraph are taken from O'Rourke and Williamson (1995).

26. The United States absorbed 90 percent of the Danish emigrants and 97 percent of the Norwegian emigrants. See chapter 4.

Chapter 10. Labor Market Impact Abroad and Convergence

1. This chapter is based on material in O'Rourke, Williamson, and Hatton (1994) and Taylor and Williamson (1997).

2. The underlying data and the CGEs for both countries are described in O'Rourke, Williamson, and Hatton (1994). They are similar to the Irish and Swedish CGEs laid out in the appendix to chapter 9.

3. A background working paper to O'Rourke, Williamson, and Hatton (1994) has these figures and is available upon request.

4. Migration rates M = (net flow)/POP shown in table 10.1 are derived from data in Taylor and Williamson (1997) and reflect adjustments for unobserved return migration. It is well known that historical data from the period systematically underenumerate return migration. We cannot know how serious the errors are, but it is not unreasonable to think that underreporting lay somewhere in the 0–30 percent range. Thus, if M is the net migration rate in the raw data for inflows and outflows, we estimate the true net migration rate to be $M(1 - \rho)$ where ρ is a return rate correction factor, taken to be 0.1 (10 percent) in the "baseline" estimates. The labor force migration rates $\gamma M(1 - \rho)$ correct for the relative labor content of the migrant flow relative to the population stock, γ. Cumulative impacts on stocks over 40 years, 1870–1910, are given by the formula $\exp(40 \times$ [average net migration rate 1870–1910]) – 1.

5. The dispersion measure is variance divided by mean squared; cf table 10.4 where the square root of this measure was adopted for consistency with Abramovitz (1986).

6. M equals the raw cumulative population impact, uncorrected by return migration underenumeration and, to repeat, is given by $\exp(40 \times$ [average net migration rate 1870–1910]) – 1. Recall that table 10.1 corrects for underenumerated return migration.

7. Note that the concern here is with migrants' raw productivity, not adjusted for skills, experience, or other characteristics. Still, given that the literature often asserts that Europe suffered a brain drain by the loss of the best and the brightest, Taylor and Williamson (1997) later subject μ to sensitivity analysis in the range 0.8–1.2. Note that an understatement of μ or γ tends to understate the impact on GDP per capita while overstating the impact on the real wage and labor productivity. Thus, sensitivity analysis is especially important for these two parameters given the several measures of convergence being studied.

8. Anglo-American estimates for γ underlying the calculations in the first half of this chapter (from O'Rourke, Williamson, and Hatton 1994) range from 1.57 in 1890 to 1.65 in

1910 for the United Kingdom, and from 1.78 in 1890 to 1.57 in 1910 for the United States. The United States figures are consistent with Kuznets's earlier (1952) study that estimated γ in the 1.53–1.66 range between 1870 and 1910.

9. The three estimates of σ derived by Taylor and Williamson (1997) are 0.22, 0.62, and 0.87. The middle value of 0.62 is used in the analysis to follow in this chapter, but Taylor and Williamson use all three values for sensitivity analysis.

10. Barriers to exit did exist in countries outside our Atlantic economy sample: for example, most emigration from Russia was illegal. On this, and for a more detailed discussion of migration policy, see Foreman-Peck (1992).

11. A related point has been made by Richard Nelson and Gavin Wright with respect to United States industrial leadership since 1870, with an early resource advantage gradually eroded by the increased tradability of oil and minerals, to be replaced by a later advantage built on human capital (Nelson and Wright 1992; Wright 1990).

12. Capital chasing also erases about two thirds of the proconvergence migration forces in the Anglo-American case (table 10.2), not too different from the 66 percent ([208 – 70]/208) estimated in the text for the whole Atlantic economy.

Chapter 11. Mass Migration and Inequality Trends Within Countries

1. This chapter is taken from Williamson (1997).

2. Gross National Product trade shares in the United States increased from 12 to 25 percent between 1970 and 1990 (Lawrence and Slaughter 1993), while the labor force had to accommodate increasing proportions of unskilled immigrant workers (Borjas 1994). Meanwhile, World Bank figures document that the share of output exported from low-income countries rose from 8 to 18 percent between 1965 and 1990. The figures for middle-income countries are 17 and 25 percent. See Richardson (1995: 34).

3. The literature is exploding. Apart from those already cited, see, for example, Krugman and Venables (1995), Leamer (1984, 1995), and Wood (1995a, 1995b). The 1995 *World Development Report* was primarily devoted to the issue.

4. It turns out that estimates of the impact of trade on convergence are significant but modest. Commodity price convergence accounts for about three tenths of real wage convergence between the United States and Britain during the 25 years after 1870, and about a tenth of the convergence between the United States and Sweden over the four decades after 1870; however, Anglo-American commodity price convergence effects were swamped by other forces after 1895, and they made only a modest contribution to Anglo-Swedish real wage convergence over the four decades as a whole (O'Rourke and Williamson 1994, 1995, 1996, 1997). All of these results used computable general equilibrium models. These late-nineteenth-century estimates are not unlike those reported for the contribution of trade to rising U.S. inequality from the 1970s, about 10–15 percent (Richardson 1995: 36).

5. Some evidence on late-nineteenth- and early-twentieth-century inequality trends has been collected by economic historians since Simon Kuznets published his presidential address to the American Economic Assocation in 1955. For surveys, see Brenner et al. (1991) and Williamson (1991: ch. 1). They seem to offer some support for the view that inequality was on the rise in the United States before World War I while it had been falling in Britain since the 1860s. But the coverage is not sufficiently comprehensive to be used in the following analysis.

6. The following five paragraphs draw on O'Rourke, Taylor, and Williamson (1996).

7. Land values were used as proxies for land rents for the late nineteenth century. The

underlying assumptions linking the two should be made explicit. If land is an economic asset with infinite life, and if the land markets of that time simply projected current rents into the future, and if global financial markets were well enough integrated so that interest rates were pretty much the same everywhere across our 11 countries, land values should serve as an effective proxy for land rents. The last two assumptions are clearly violated and in a way that tends to exaggerate wage-rental trends, but our guess is that the exaggeration isn't very big. See O'Rourke, Taylor, and Williamson (1996).

8. This was certainly true of Europe, Argentina, and the American south, but less true for the American midwest and Canada, where the family farm dominated.

9. The wage w is in fact a real wage rate, w/c, where the deflator is a cost-of-living index. Labor productivity y is in fact real GDP per worker-hour, y/p, where the deflator is the implicit GDP price index. Both w/c and y/p have been reflated to nominal levels in computing w/y since we want to isolate the behavior of nominal returns, as opposed to relative prices.

10. The little data we have suggest a strong correlation between w/y and other distribution measures across the late nineteenth century. When Germany, Norway, the United States, and the U.K. c1870–c1913 are pooled, changes in w/y have a negative correlation (−0.798) with changes in the share of income held by the top 10%. See Williamson (1996a, appendix table 3).

11. A fairly tight nonlinear correlation can also be seen in the following simple bivariate regression (whose dependent variable is simply the log values of e plotted on the vertical axis of figure 11.6):

$$\ln(100+e)=6.951 - 0.634\ln(1870\ w/c), \quad R^2 =0.537.$$
$$(10.275) \quad (3.734)$$

t statistics are reported in parentheses.

12. The regression result (migration's impact = mig) is:

$$\ln(100+e)=4.439 - 0.011\ \text{mig}, \quad R^2 =0.356.$$
$$(43.942) \quad (2.578)$$

13. O'Rourke, Taylor, and Williamson (1996). Explanatory variables were available for seven of the countries in figures 11.1–11.3: AUS, USA, UK, FRA, GER, DEN, and SWE. Thus, the sample excludes the relevant cases of Argentina, Canada, Ireland, and Spain.

14. The residual was 5.1 percent for the New World and 27.5 percent for the Old.

References

Abramovitz, M. (1961), "The Nature and Significance of Kuznets Cycles," *Economic Development and Cultural Change* 9: 225–48.

———(1968), "The Passing of the Kuznets Cycle," *Economica* 35: 349–67.

———(1979), "Rapid Growth Potential and Its Realization: The Experience of the Capitalist Economies in the Postwar Period," in E. Malinvaud (ed.), *Economic Growth and Resources*, Vol. 1, London: Macmillan, 1–30.

———(1986), "Catching Up, Forging Ahead, and Falling Behind," *Journal of Economic History* 46: 385–406.

Adams, W. F. (1932), *Ireland and Irish Emigration in the New World from 1815 to the Famine*, New Haven: Yale University Press.

Akerman, S. (1976), "Theories and Methods of Migration Research," in H. Rundblom and H. Norman (eds.), *From Sweden to America; A History of the Migration*, Minneapolis: University of Minnesota Press, 19–75.

Allen, S. (1992), "Changes in the Cyclical Sensitivity of Wages in the United States," *American Economic Review* 82: 122–40.

Altonji, J. G., and D. Card (1991), "The Effects of Immigration on the Labor Market Outcomes of Less-Skilled Natives," in J. M. Abowd and R. B. Freeman (eds.), *Immigration, Trade and the Labor Market*, Chicago: University of Chicago Press, 201–34.

Arcari, P. M. (1936), "Le Variazione dei Salari Agricoli in Italia della Fondazione del Regno al 1933," *Annali di Statistica*, Series 5, 36, Roma: ISTAT.

Arrow, K. J., H. B. Chenery, B. S. Minhas, and R. M. Solao (1961), "Capital-Labor Substitution and Economic Efficiency," *Review of Economics and Statistics* 43: 225–50.

Baganha, M. I. B. (1990), *Portuguese Emigration to the United States, 1820–1930*, New York: Garland.

Bailey, W. B. (1912), "The Bird of Passage," *American Journal of Sociology* 18: 391–7.

Baily, S. L. (1983), "Italian Immigrants in Buenos Aires and New York," *American Historical Review* 88: 281–305.

Baines, D. E. (1986), *Migration in a Mature Economy*, Cambridge: Cambridge University Press.

———(1991), *Emigration from Europe, 1815–1930*, London: Macmillan.

Bairoch, P., et al. (1968), *The Working Population and Its Structure*, Brussels: Institut de Sociologie, Université Libre de Bruxelles.

———(1976), "Europe's Gross National Product: 1800–1975," *Journal of European Economic History* 5: 273–340.

———(1989), "European Trade Policy, 1815–1914," in P. Mathias and S. Pollard (eds.), *The Cambridge Economic History of Europe*, Vol. 3, Cambridge: Cambridge University Press, 1–159.

Banerjee, B., and S. M. R. Kanbur (1981), "On the Specification and Estimation of Macro Rural-Urban Migration Functions, With an Application to Indian Data," *Oxford Bulletin of Economics and Statistics* 43: 7–29.

Bardini, C., A. Carreras, and P. Lains (1995), "The National Accounts for Italy, Spain and Portugal," *Scandinavian Economic History Review* 43: 115–46.

Barro, R. J. (1991), "Economic Growth in a Cross Section of Countries," *Quarterly Journal of Economics* 106: 407–43.

Barro, R. J., and X. Sala-i-Martin (1991), "Convergence across States and Regions," *Brookings Papers on Economic Activity* 1: 107–82.

———(1992), "Convergence," *Journal of Political Economy* 100: 223–52.

———(1995), *Economic Growth*, New York: McGraw Hill.

Barton, J. (1975), *Peasants and Strangers: Italians, Rumanians and Slovaks in an American City, 1890–1950*, Cambridge, Mass.: Harvard University Press.

Baumol, W. J. (1986), "Productivity Growth, Convergence and Welfare: What the Long-Run Data Show," *American Economic Review* 76: 1072–85.

Baumol, W. J., S. Blackman, and E. N. Wolff (1989), *Productivity and American Leadership: The Long View*, Cambridge, Mass.: MIT Press.

Benhabib, J. (1996), "On the Political Economy of Immigration," *European Economic Review* 40: 1737–43.

Berndt, E. R. (1976), "Reconciling Alternative Estimates of the Elasticity of Substitution," *Review of Economics and Statistics* 58: 59–68.

———(1991), *The Practice of Econometrics, Classical and Contemporary*, Reading, Mass.: Addison-Wesley.

Blau, F. D. (1980), "Immigration and Labor Earnings in Early Twentieth Century America," *Research in Population Economics* 2: 21–41.

Blessing, P. L. (1985), "Irish Emigration to the United States, 1800–1920: An Overview," in P. J. Drudy (ed.), *The Irish in America: Emigration Assimilation and Impact*, Cambridge: Cambridge University Press, 11–37.

Bodnar, J. (1985), *The Transplanted: A History of Immigrants in Urban America*, Bloomington: Indiana University Press.

Bodnar, J., R. Simon, and M. P. Weber (1982), *Lives of Their Own: Blacks, Italians and Poles in Pittsburgh, 1900–1960*, Urbana: University of Illinois Press.

Böhning, W. R. (1984), *Studies in International Labour Migration*, London: Macmillan.

Booth, H. (1992), *The Migration Process in Britain and Germany*, Aldershot, England: Avebury.

Borjas, G. J. (1985), "Assimilation, Changes in Cohort Quality and the Earnings of Immigrants," *Journal of Labor Economics* 3: 463–89.

———(1987), "Self-selection and the Earnings of Immigrants," *American Economic Review* 77: 531–53.

———(1990), *Friends or Strangers? The Impact of Immigrants on the U.S. Economy*, New York: Basic Books.

———(1991), "Immigrants in the U.S. Labor Market: 1940–80," *American Economic Review* 81: 287–91.

———(1992), "National Origin and the Skills of Immigrants in the Postwar Period," in G. J. Borjas and R. B. Freeman (eds.), *Immigration and the Workforce: Economic Consequences for the United States and Source Areas*, Chicago: University of Chicago Press, 17–47.

———(1994), "The Economics of Immigration," *Journal of Economic Literature* 32: 1667–717.

———(1995), "Assimilation and Changes in Cohort Quality Revisited: What Happened in the 1980s?" *Journal of Labor Economics* 13: 201–45.

Borjas, G. J., and R. B. Freeman (eds.) (1992), *Immigration and the Workforce*, Chicago: University of Chicago Press.

Borjas, G. J., R. B. Freeman, and L. F. Katz (1992), "On the Labor Market Impacts of Immigration and Trade," in G. J. Borjas and R. B. Freeman (eds.), *Immigration and the Work Force: Economic Consequences for the United States and Source Areas*, Chicago: University of Chicago Press, 213–44.

Bowley, A. L. (1899), "The Statistics of Wages in the United Kingdom During the Last Hundred Years. Part 3, Agricultural Wages," *Journal of the Royal Statistical Society* 62: 395–404.

Boyer, G. R., T. J. Hatton, and K. H. O'Rourke (1993), "The Impact of Emigration on Real Wages in Ireland, 1850–1914," Center for Economic Policy Research Discussion Paper No. 854, London: CEPR.

———(1994), "The Impact of Emigration on Real Wages in Ireland, 1850–1914," in T. J. Hatton and J. G. Williamson (eds.), *Migration and the International Labor Market, 1850–1939*, London: Routledge, 221–39.

Brenner, J., et al. (eds.) (1991), *Income Distribution in Historical Perspective*, Cambridge: Cambridge University Press.

Briggs, J. W. (1978), *An Italian Passage; Immigrants to Three American Cities, 1890–1930*, New Haven, Conn.: Yale University Press.

Briggs, V. M. (1985), "Employment Trends and Contemporary Immigration Policy," in N. Glazer (ed.), *Clamor at the Gates: The New American Immigration*, San Francisco: ICS Press.

Burda, M. C. (1993), "The Determinants of East-West German Migration: Some First Results," *European Economic Review* 37: 452–61.

Butcher, K. F., and D. Card (1991), "Immigration and Wages: Evidence from the 1980s," *American Economic Review* (Papers and Proceedings) 81: 292–6.

Butlin, N. G. (1946), "An Index of Engineering Unemployment, 1852–1943," *Economic Record* 22: 241–60.

Card, D. (1990), "The Impact of the Mariel Boatlift on the Miami Labor Market," *Industrial and Labor Relations Review* 43: 245–57.

Carlsson, S. (1976), "Chronology and Composition of Swedish Emigration to America," in H. Rundblom and H. Norman (eds.), *From Sweden to America; A History of the Migration*, Minneapolis: University of Minnesota Press, 114–48.

Carter, S. B., R. L. Ransom, R. Sutch, and H. Zhao (1993a), "Codebook and User's Manual: A Survey of 3,920 Male Workers in the Agricultural Implement and Iron Industries of Detroit, 1890," Berkeley: Institute of Business and Economic Research.

———(1993b), "Codebook and User's Manual: A Survey of 4,918 Male Workers in the

Agricultural Implement and Iron Industries Outside Detroit, 1890," Berkeley: Institute of Business and Economic Research.

Castles, S. (1986), "The Guest-Worker in Western Europe—An Obituary," *International Migration Review* 20: 761–78.

Castles, S., and M. J. Miller (1993), *The Age of Migration: International Population Movements in the Modern World*, London: Macmillan.

Chiswick, B. R. (1977), "Sons of Immigrants: Are They at an Earnings Disadvantage?" *American Economic Review* 67: 376–80.

———(1978), "The Effect of Americanization on the Earnings of Foreign-Born Men," *Journal of Political Economy* 86: 897–921.

———(1986), "Is The New Immigration Less Skilled than the Old?" *Journal of Labor Economics* 4: 168–92.

———(1991), "Jewish Immigrant Skill and Occupational Attainment at the Turn of the Century," *Explorations in Economic History* 28: 64–86.

———(1992), "Jewish Immigrant Wages in America in 1909: An Analysis of the Dillingham Commission Data," *Explorations in Economic History* 29: 274–89.

Cinel, D. (1982), *From Italy to San Francisco: The Immigrant Experience*, Stanford, Calif.: Stanford University Press.

———(1991), *The National Integration of Italian Return Migration, 1870–1929*, Cambridge: Cambridge University Press.

Coen, R. M. (1973), "Labor Force and Unemployment in the 1920s and 1930s: A Reexamination Based on Postwar Experience," *Review of Economics and Statistics* 55: 46–55.

Cohn, R. L. (1984), "Mortality on Immigrant Voyages to New York, 1836–1853," *Journal of Economic History* 44: 289–300.

———(1992), "The Occupations of English Immigrants to the United States, 1836–1853," *Journal of Economic History* 52: 377–88.

Coletti, F. (1911), "Dell'Emigrazione Italiana," in P. Blaserna (ed.), *Cinquant'Anni di Storia Italiana*, Milan: Ulrico Hoepli.

Collins, W. (1997), "When the Tide Turned: Immigration and the Delay of the Great Migration," *Journal of Economic History* 57: 607–32.

Collinson, S. (1993), *Europe and International Migration*, London: Royal Institute of Economic Affairs.

Commons, J. R. (1920), *Races and Immigrants in America*, 2nd. ed., reprinted 1967, New York: Augustus Kelley.

Cortés Conde, R. (1982), "Income Differentials and Migrations," in C. P. Kindleberger and G. di Tella (eds.), *Economics in the Long View: Essays in Honor of W. W. Rostow*, Vol. 2, London: Macmillan, 132–46.

Cousens, S. H. (1964), "The Regional Variations in Population Changes in Ireland 1861–1881," *Economic History Review* 17: 301–21.

Crafts, N. F. R. (1984), "Patterns of Development in Nineteenth Century Europe," *Oxford Economic Papers* 36: 438–58.

Crafts, N. F. R., and M. Thomas (1986), "Comparative Advantage in UK Manufacturing Trade 1910–35," *Economic Journal* 96: 629–45.

Crotty, D. (1966), *Irish Agricultural Production: Its Volume and Structure*, Cork, Ireland: University College Press.

Davis, D. R. (1996), "Trade Liberalization and Income Distribution," mimeo., Harvard University (June).

Davis, M. R. (1931), "Critique of Official United States Immigration Statistics," in I. Ferenczi and W. F. Willcox, *International Migrations*, Vol. 2, New York: National Bureau of Economic Research, 645–58.

de Long, J. B. (1988), "Productivity Growth, Convergence and Welfare: Comment," *American Economic Review* 78: 1138–54.

———(1992), "Productivity Growth and Machinery Investment: A Long-Run Look, 1870–1980," *Journal of Economic History* 52: 307–24.

de Long, J. B., and L. Summers (1991), "Equipment Investment and Economic Growth," *Quarterly Journal of Economics* 106: 445–502.

de Rosa, L. (1988), "Urbanisation and Industrialisation in Italy (1861–1921)," *Journal of European Economic History* 17: 467–90.

Dervis, K., J. DeMelo, and S. Robinson (1982), *General Equilibrium Models for Development Policy*, Cambridge: Cambridge University Press.

Diaz-Alejandro, C. F. (1970), *Essays on the Economic History of the Argentine Republic*, New Haven, Conn.: Yale University Press.

di Comite, L. (1976), "Aspects of Italian Emigration, 1881–1915," in I. A. Glazier and L. de Rosa (eds.), *Migration Across Time and Nations*, New York: Holmes and Meier, 148–59.

di Comite, L., and I. A. Glazier (1984), "Socio-Demographic Characteristics of Italian Emigration to the United States from Ship Passenger Lists, 1880–1914," *Ethnic Forum* 4: 78–90.

di Tella, G. (1982), "The Economics of the Frontier," in C. P. Kindleberger and G. di Tella (eds.), *Economics in the Long View: Essays in Honor of W. W. Rostow*, Vol. 1, New York: New York University Press, 210–27.

Dore, G. (1968), "Some Special and Historical Aspects of Italian Migration to America," *Journal of Social History* 2: 95–122.

Douglas, P. H. (1919), "Is the New Immigration More Unskilled than the Old?" *Journal of the American Statistical Association* 16: 393–403.

———(1930), *Real Wages in the United States, 1890–1926* (reprinted 1966), New York: Augustus M. Kelley.

Dowrick, S., and D.-T. Nguyen (1989), "OECD Comparative Economic Growth 1950–85: Catch-Up and Convergence," *American Economic Review* 79: 1010–30.

Drazen, A., D. S. Hammermesh, and N. P. Obst (1984), "The Variable Employment Elasticity Hypothesis: Theory and Evidence," in R. G. Ehrenberg (ed.), *Research in Labor Economics*, Vol. 6, Greenwich, Conn.: JAI Press, 286–309.

Drescher, L. (1955), "The Development of Agricultural Production in Great Britain and Ireland from the Early Nineteenth Century," *Manchester School* 23: 153–75.

Dunlevy, J. A. (1980), "Nineteenth Century Immigration to the United States: Intended Versus Lifetime Settlement Patterns," *Economic Development and Cultural Change* 29: 77–90.

———(1983), "Regional Preferences and Migrant Settlement: On the Avoidance of the South by Nineteenth Century Immigrants," *Research in Economic History* 8: 217–51.

Dunlevy, J. A., and H. A. Gemery (1977), "The Role of Migrant Stock and Lagged Migration in the Settlement Patterns of Nineteenth Century Immigrants," *Review of Economics and Statistics* 59: 137–44.

———(1978), "Economic Opportunity and the Responses of Old and New Immigrants in the United States," *Journal of Economic History* 38: 901–17.

Dunlevy, J. A., and R. P. Saba (1992), "The Role of Nationality-Specific Characteristics on the Settlement Patterns of Late Nineteenth Century Immigrants," *Explorations in Economic History* 29: 228–49.

Easterlin, R. A. (1960), "Interregional Differences in Per Capita Income, Population and Total Income, 1840–1950," in *Trends in the American Economy in the Nineteenth Century* (Studies in Income and Wealth, Vol. 24), Princeton, N.J.: Princeton University Press, 73–140.

———(1961), "Influences in European Overseas Emigration before World War I," *Economic Development and Cultural Change* 9: 33–51.

———(1966), "Economic-Demographic Interactions and Long Swings in Economic Growth," *American Economic Review* 56: 1063–104.

———(1968), *Population, Labor Force and Long Swings in Economic Growth*, New York: National Bureau of Economic Research.

———(1981), "Why Isn't the Whole World Developed?" *Journal of Economic History* 41: 1–19.

Eckaus, R. (1961), "The North-South Differential in Italian Economic Development," *Journal of Economic History* 20: 285–317.

Edelstein, M. (1982), *Overseas Investment in the Age of High Imperialism*, New York: Columbia University Press.

Edwards, A. M. (1917), "Social-Economic Groups of the United States," *Journal of the American Statistical Association* 15: 643–61.

Eichengreen, B. J., and H. A. Gemery (1986), "The Earnings of Skilled and Unskilled Immigrants at the End of the Nineteenth Century," *Journal of Economic History* 46: 441–54.

Eichengreen, B. J., and T. J. Hatton (1988), "Interwar Unemployment in International Perspective: An Overview," in B. J. Eichengreen and T. J. Hatton (eds.), *Interwar Unemployment in International Perspective*, Boston: Kluwer, 1–60.

Ekberg, J. (1977), "Long Term Effects of Immigration: A Simulation Approach," *Economy and History* 20: 3–22.

Eldridge, H. T., and D. S. Thomas (1964), *Population and Economic Growth: United States, 1870–1950, Vol. 3, Demographic Analysis and Interrelations*, Philadelphia: American Philosophical Society.

Eltis, D. (1983), "Free and Coerced Transatlantic Migrations: Some Comparisons," *American Historical Review* 88: 251–80.

Erickson, C. (1972), "Who Were the English and Scottish Emigrants in the 1880s?" in D. V. Glass and R. Revelle (eds.), *Population and Social Change*, London: Arnold, 347–81.

———(1990), "Emigration to the U.S.A. from the British Isles in 1841: Part 2. Who were the English Emigrants?" *Population Studies* 44: 21–40.

Esposto, A. G. (1992), "Italian Industrialization and the Gerschenkronian Great Spurt—A Regional Analysis," *Journal of Economic History* 52: 353–75.

Estevadeordal, A. (1993), "Historical Essays on Comparative Advantage: 1913–1938," Ph.D. dissertation, Harvard University.

Faini, R. (1991), "Regional Development and Economic Integration," in J. da Silva Lopes and L. Beleza (eds.), *Portugal and the Internal Market of the EEC*, Lisbon: Banco de Portugal, 151–71.

Faini, R., and A. Venturini (1994a), "Italian Emigration in the Pre-War Period," in T. J. Hatton and J. G. Williamson (eds.), *Migration and International Labor Market 1850–1939*, London: Routledge, 72–90.

———(1994b), "Migration and Growth: The Experience of Southern Europe," Centre for Economic Policy Research Discussion Paper 964, London: CEPR.

Federico, G., and G. Toniolo (1991), "Italy," in R. Sylla and G. Toniolo (eds.), *Patterns of European Industrialization*, London: Routledge, 197–217.

Feenstra, R. C., and G. H. Hanson (1995), "Foreign Investment, Outsourcing and Relative Wages," in R. C. Feenstra, G. M. Grossman, and D. A. Irwin (eds.), *Political Economy of Trade Policy: Essays in Honor of Jagdish Bhagwati*, Cambridge, Mass.: MIT Press. 89–127.

Feinstein, C. H. (1972), *National Income, Expenditure and Output of the United Kingdom 1855–1965*, Cambridge: Cambridge University Press.

Feliciano, Z. (1995), "Workers and Trade Liberalization: The Impact of Trade Reforms in Mexico on Wages and Employment," mimeo., Queens College.

Ferenczi, I., and W. F. Willcox (1929, 1931), *International Migrations*, Vols. 1 and 2, New York: National Bureau of Economic Research.

Ferrie, J. P. (1992), "We Are Yankeys Now: The Economic Mobility of Ante Bellum Immigrants to the US," Ph.D. dissertation, University of Chicago.

———(1994), "The Wealth Accumulation of Antebellum European Immigrants to the U.S., 1840–1860," *Journal of Economic History* 54: 1–33.

Filer, R. K. (1992), "The Effect of Immigrant Arrivals on Migratory Patterns of Native Workers," in G. J. Borjas and R. B. Freeman (eds.), *Immigration and the Workforce: Economic Consequences for the United States and Source Areas*, Chicago: University of Chicago Press, 245–69.

Findlay, R. (1995), *Factor Proportions, Trade, and Growth*, Cambridge, Mass.: MIT Press.

Fitzpatrick, D. (1980a), "Irish Emigration in the Later Nineteenth Century," *Irish Historical Studies* 22: 126–43.

———(1980b), "The Disappearance of the Irish Agricultural Labourer, 1841–1912," *Irish Economic and Social History* 7: 66–92.

———(1983), "Irish Farming Families before the First World War," *Comparative Studies in Society and History* 25: 339–74.

———(1984), *Irish Emigration 1801–1921*, Dublin: Economic and Social History Society of Ireland.

Flam, H., and M. J. Flanders (1991), *Heckscher-Ohlin Trade Theory*, Cambridge, Mass.: MIT Press.

Foerster, R. F. (1919), *The Italian Emigration of Our Times*, Cambridge, Mass.: Harvard Universtiy Press.

Foreman-Peck, J. S. (1992), "A Political Economy of International Migration, 1815–1914," *Manchester School* 60: 359–76.

Freeman, R. B. (1995), "Are Your Wages Set in Beijing?" *Journal of Economic Perspectives* 9: 15–32.

Friedberg, R. M. (1992), "The Labor Market Assimilation of Immigrants in the United States: The Role of Age at Arrival," Brown University, unpublished manuscript.

———(1993), "The Success of Young Immigrants in the US Labor Market: An Evaluation of Competing Explanations," Brown University, unpublished manuscript.

Friedberg, R. M., and J. Hunt (1995), "The Impact of Immigrants on Host Country Wages, Employment and Growth," *Journal of Economic Perspectives* 9: 23–44.

Friedman, M. (1992), "Do Old Fallacies Ever Die?" *Journal of Economic Literature* 30: 2129–32.

Galenson, W., and A. Zellner (1957), "International Comparisons of Unemployment Rates," in National Bureau of Economic Research, *The Measurement and Behavior of Unemployment*, Princeton, N.J.: Princeton University Press, 439–580.

Galenson, D. W. (1984), "The Rise and Fall of Indentured Servitude in the Americas: An Economic Analysis," *Journal of Economic History* 44: 1–26.

Gallaway, L. E., and R. K. Vedder (1971), "Emigration from the United Kingdom to the United States, 1860–1913," *Journal of Economic History* 31: 885–97.

Gallaway, L. E., R. K. Vedder, and V. Shukla (1974), "The Distribution of the Immigrant Population in the United States: An Economic Analysis," *Explorations in Economic History* 11: 213–26.

Gandar, J. (1982), *Economic Causation and British Emigration in the Late Nineteenth Century*, Ph.D. dissertation, University of Missouri-Columbia, Ann Arbor: University Microfilms.

Geary, P. T., and C. Ó Gráda (1985), "Immigration and the Real Wage: Time Series Evidence from the United States, 1820–1977," Discussion Paper No. 71, Centre for Economic Policy Research, London.

Gerschenkron, A. (1952), "Economic Backwardness in Historical Perspective," in B. F. Hoselitz (ed.), *The Progress of Underdeveloped Areas*, Chicago: University of Chicago Press.

———(1962), *Economic Backwardness in Historical Pespective*, Cambridge, Mass.: Harvard University Press.

Gibbon, P., and C. Curtin (1978), "The Stem Family in Ireland," *Comparative Studies in Society and History* 20: 429–53.

Giusti, F. (1965), "Bilanca Demografici della Popolazione Italiana dal 1861 al 1961," *Annali di Statistica*, Series 8, 17, Roma: ISTAT.

Glazier, I. A., and B. Okeke (1994), "Socioeconomic Characteristics of Italian Emigrants From the U.S. Passenger Manifests, 1880–1897," Paper presented to the Eleventh International Economic History Congress, Milan.

Goldin, C. (1994), "The Political Economy of Immigration Restriction in the United States, 1890 to 1921," in C. Goldin and G. D. Libecap (eds.), *The Regulated Economy: A Historical Approach to Political Economy*, Chicago: University of Chicago Press, 223–57.

Goldin, C., and S. Engerman (1993), "Seasonality in Nineteenth Century Labor Markets," in D. Schaefer and T. Weiss (eds.), *Economic Development in Historical Perspective*, Stanford: Stanford University Press.

Goldin, C., and R. A. Margo (1992), "The Great Compression: The Wage Structure in the United States at Mid-Century," *Quarterly Journal of Economics* 107: 1–34.

Gould, J. D. (1979), "European Inter-continental Emigration, 1815–1914: Patterns and Causes," *Journal of European Economic History* 8: 593–679.

———(1980a), "European Inter-continental Emigration. The Road Home: Return Migration from the U.S.A.," *Journal of European Economic History* 9: 41–112.

———(1980b), "European Inter-continental Emigration: The Role of 'Diffusion' and 'Feedback'," *Journal of European Economic History* 9: 267–315.

Grant, M. (1923), *The Passing of the Great Race* (4th ed.), New York: Charles Scribner.

Green, A. G., and D. A. Green (1993), "Balanced Growth and the Geographical Distribution of European Immigrant Arrivals to Canada, 1900–12," *Explorations in Economic History* 30: 31–59.

Green, A. G., and M. C. Urquhart (1976), "Factor and Commodity Flows in the International Economy of 1870–1914: A Multi-Country View," *Journal of Economic History* 36: 217–52.

Greenwood, M. J., and J. M. McDowell (1986), "The Factor Market Consequences of U.S. Immigration," *Journal of Economic Literature* 24: 1738–72.

———(1994), "The National Labor Market Consequences of U.S. Immigration," in H. Giersch (ed.), *Economic Aspects of International Migration*, Berlin: Springer-Verlag, 155–94.

Grubb, F. (1994), "The End of European Servitude in the United States: An Economic Analysis of Market Collapse, 1772–1835," *Journal of Economic History* 54: 794–824.

Guinnane, T. W. (1992a), "Intergenerational Transfers, Emigration, and the Rural Irish Household System," *Explorations in Economic History* 29: 457–76.

———(1992b), "Age of Leaving Home in Ireland 1901–1911," *Journal of Economic History* 52: 651–74.

Habakkuk, H. J. (1962), *American and British Technology in the Nineteenth Century*, Cambridge: Cambridge University Press.

Hammermesh, D. S. (1993), *Labor Demand*, Princeton, N.J.: Princeton University Press.

Hamilton, B., and J. Whalley (1984), "Efficiency and Distributional Implications of Global Restrictions on Labour Mobility," *Journal of Development Economics* 14: 61–75.

Handlin, O. (1951), *The Uprooted*, Cambridge, Mass.: Harvard University Press.

———(1957), *Race and Nationality in American Life*, New York: Doubleday.

———(1959), *Boston's Immigrants: A Study in Acculturation* (2nd ed.), Cambridge, Mass.: Belknap Press.

Hanes, C. (1993), "The Development of Nominal Wage Rigidity in the Late Nineteenth Century," *American Economic Review* 83: 732–56.

———(1996), "Immigrants' Relative Rate of Wage Growth in the Late Nineteenth Century," *Explorations in Economic History* 33: 35–64.

Hannon, J. U. (1982a), "Ethnic Discrimination in a Nineteenth Century Mining District: Michigan Copper Mines, 1888," *Explorations in Economic History* 19: 28–50.

———(1982b), "City Size and Ethnic Discrimination: Michigan Agricultural Implements and Iron Working Industries, 1890," *Journal of Economic History* 42: 825–45.

Harley, C. K. (1988), "Ocean Freight Rates and Productivity, 1740–1913: The Primacy of Mechanical Invention Reaffirmed," *Journal of Economic History* 48: 851–76.

Hatton, T. J. (1995a), "A Model of U.K. Emigration, 1870–1913," *Review of Economics and Statistics* 77: 407–15.

———(1995b), "A Model of Scandinavian Emigration, 1870–1913," *European Economic Review* 39: 557–64.

———(1997), "The Immigrant Assimilation Puzzle in Late Nineteenth-Century America," *Journal of Economic History* 57: 34–62.

Hatton, T. J., and J. G. Williamson (1991), "Integrated and Segmented Labor Markets: Thinking in Two Sectors," *Journal of Economic History* 5: 413–25.

———(1992), "What Explains Wage Gaps between Farm and City? Exploring the Todaro Model with American Evidence, 1890–1941," *Economic Development and Cultural Change* 40: 267–94.

———(1993), "After the Famine: Emigration from Ireland 1850–1913," *Journal of Economic History* 53: 575–600.

———(1994a), "International Migration 1850–1939: An Economic Survey," in T. J. Hatton and J. G. Williamson (eds.), *Migration and the International Labor Market, 1850–1939*, London: Routledge, 3–32.

———(1994b), "Latecomers to Mass Emigration: The Latin Experience," in T. J. Hatton and

J. G. Williamson (eds.), *Migration and the International Labor Market, 1850–1939*, London: Routledge, 55–71.

——(1994c), "International Migration and World Development: A Historical Perspective," in H. Giersch (ed.), *Economic Aspects of International Migration*, Berlin: Springer-Verlag, 3–56.

——(1994d), "What Drove the Mass Migrations from Europe in the Late Nineteenth Century?" *Population and Development Review* 20: 533–59.

Heckscher, E. F. (1954), *An Economic History of Sweden*, Cambridge, Mass.: Harvard University Press.

Higgs, R. (1971), "Race, Skill and Earnings: American Immigrants in 1909," *Journal of Economic History* 31: 420–9.

Higham, J. (1955), *Strangers in the Land: Patterns of American Nativism, 1880–1925*, New Brunswick, N. J.: Rutgers University Press.

Hildebrand, K.-G. (1978), "Labour and Capital in the Scandinavian Countries in the Nineteenth and Twentieth Centuries," in P. Mathias and M. M. Postan (eds.), *The Cambridge Economic History of Europe: Volume 7: The Industrial Economies: Capital, Labour and Enterprise: Part 1*, Cambridge: Cambridge University Press, 590–628.

Hill, J. A. (1906), "Interstate Migrations," in *12th Census of the United States, Special Reports: Supplementary Analysis and Derivative Tables*, Washington, D.C.: US Government Printing Office.

Hill, P. J. (1975), *The Economic Impact of Immigration into the United States*, Chicago: Arno Press.

Hollifield, J. F. (1992), *Immigrants, Markets and States: The Political Economy of Postwar Europe*, Cambridge, Mass.: Harvard University Press.

Hourwich, I. (1922), *Immigration and Labor: The Economic Aspects of European Immigration to the United States*, 2nd ed., New York: Huebsch.

Hvidt, C. (1966), "Danish Emigration Prior to 1914: Trends and Problems," *Scandinavian Economic History Review* 14: 158–78.

——(1975), *Flight to America*, New York: Academic Press.

Hyde, F. E. (1975), *Cunard and the North Atlantic 1840–1973*, Atlantic Highlands, N.J.: Humanities Press.

International Bank for Reconstruction and Development (1995), *The World Development Report*, Washington, D.C.: The World Bank.

[Irish] Commission on Emigration and other Population Problems (1954), *Reports*, Dublin: Eire.

James, J. (1984), "The Use of General Equilibrium Analysis in Economic History," *Explorations in Economic History* 21: 231–53.

——(1989), "The Stability of the 19th-Century Phillips Curve Relationship," *Explorations in Economic History* 26: 117–34.

Jasso, G., and M. R. Rosenzweig (1988), "How Well Do U.S. Immigrants Do? Vintage Effects, Emigration Selectivity and Occupational Mobility," *Research in Population Economics* 6: 229–53.

——(1990), *The New Chosen People: Immigrants in the United States*, New York: Russell Sage Foundation.

Jenks, J. W., and W. J. Lauck (1926), *The Immigration Problem*, 6th ed., New York: Huebsch.

Jensen, A. (1931), "Migration Statistics of Denmark, Norway and Sweden," in I. Ferenczi and W. Willcox (eds.), *International Migrations*, Vol. 2, New York: National Bureau of Economic Research, 283–312.

Jerome, H. (1926), *Migration and Business Cycles*, New York: National Bureau of Economic Research.

Jones, M. A. (1992), *American Immigration* (2nd ed.), Chicago: University of Chicago Press.

Jorberg, L. (1970), "The Industrial Revolution in the Nordic Countries," in C. M. Cipolla (ed.), *The Emergence of Industrial Societies: Part 2*, London: Harvester Press, 375–485.

Kamphoefner, W. D. (1976), "At the Crossroads of Economic Development: Background Factors Affecting Emigration from Nineteenth Century Germany," in I. A. Glazier and L. de Rosa (eds.), *Migration Across Time and Nations*, New York: Holmes and Meier, 174–201.

Karlstrom, U. (1985), *Economic Growth and Migration During the Industrialization of Sweden: A General Equilibrium Approach*, Stockholm: Stockholm School of Economics.

Kayser, B. (1972), *Cyclically-Determined Homeward Flows of Migrant Workers and the Effects of Emigration*, Paris: OECD.

Kelley, A. C. (1965), "International Migration and Economic Growth: Australia, 1865–1935," *Journal of Economic History* 25: 333–54.

Kennedy, L. (1991), "Farm Succession in Modern Ireland: Elements of a Theory of Inheritance," *Economic History Review* 44: 477–99.

Kennedy, R. E. (1973), *The Irish: Emigration, Marriage and Fertility*, Berkeley: University of California Press.

Kenwood, A. G., and A. L. Lougheed (1992), *The Growth of the International Economy, 1820–1990*, 3rd ed., London: Routledge.

Kero, R. (1974), *Migration from Finland to North America in the Years Between the United States Civil War and the First World War*, Turku, Finland: Turun Yliopisto.

———(1991), "Migration Traditions from Finland to North America," in R. J. Vecoli and S. M. Sinke (eds.), *A Century of European Migrations 1830–1930*, Urbana: University of Illinois Press, 111–33.

Kessner, T. (1977), *The Golden Door: Italian and Jewish Immigrant Mobility in New York, 1880–1915*, New York: Oxford University Press.

Keyssar, A. (1986), *Out of Work: The First Century of Unemployment in Massachusetts*, Cambridge: Cambridge University Press.

Kindleberger, C. P. (1951), "Group Behavior and International Trade," *Journal of Political Economy* 59: 30–46.

———(1967), *Europe's Postwar Growth: The Role of Labor Supply*, Cambridge, Mass.: Harvard University Press.

Kirk, D. (1946), *Europe's Population in the Interwar Years*, New York: Gordon and Breach.

Kirk, G. W. (1978), *The Promise of American Life: Social Mobility in a Nineteenth-Century Immigrant Community, Holland, Michigan, 1847–1894*, Philadelphia: American Philosophical Society.

Klein, H. S. (1983), "The Integration of Italian Immigrants into the United States and Argentina: A Comparative Analysis," *American Historical Review* 88: 306–29.

Krantz, O., and C.-A. Nilsson (1974), "Relative Income Levels in the Scandinavian Countries," *Economy and History* 17: 52–69.

Kravis, I., et al. (1978), "Real GDP Per Capita for More Than One Hundred Countries," *Economic Journal* 88: 215–42.

Krueger, A. (1978), *Liberalization Attempts and Consequences*, Cambridge: Ballinger.

Krugman, P. R. (1991), *Geography and Trade*, Cambridge, Mass.: MIT Press.

Krugman, P. R., and A. Venables (1995), "Globalization and the Inequality of Nations,"

NBER Working Paper No. 5098, Cambridge, Mass.: National Bureau of Economic Research.

Kuznets, S., ed. (1952), *Income and Wealth of the United States: Trends and Structure*, London: Bowes and Bowes.

——(1953), *Economic Change: Selected Essays in Business Cycles, National Income, and Economic Growth*, New York: Norton.

——(1955), "Economic Growth and Income Inequality," *American Economic Review* 45: 1–28.

Kuznets, S., and E. Rubin (1954), *Immigration and the Foreign Born*, NBER Occasional Paper 46, New York: National Bureau of Economic Research.

LaLonde, R. J., and R. H. Topel (1992), "The Assimilation of Immigrants in the US Labor Market," in G. J. Borjas and R. B. Freeman (eds.), *Immigration and the Workforce: Economic Consequences for the United States and Source Areas*, Chicago: University of Chicago Press, 67–92.

Landes, D. (1969), *The Unbound Prometheus*, Cambridge: Cambridge University Press.

Larsen, U. M. (1982), "A Quantitative Study of Emigration from Denmark to the United States, 1870–1913," *Scandinavian Economic History Review* 30: 101–28.

Lawrence, L., and M. Slaughter (1993), "International Trade and American Wages in the 1980s: Giant Sucking Sound or Small Hiccup?" *Brookings Papers on Economic Activity, Microeconomics* 2: 161–226.

Leamer, E. E. (1984), *Sources of International Comparative Advantage*, Cambridge, Mass.: MIT Press.

——(1995), "A Trade Economist's View of US Wages and Globalization," unpublished manuscript.

Lebergott, S. (1964), *Manpower and Economic Growth: The American Record Since 1800*, New York: McGraw-Hill.

Lee, E. S., A. R. Miller, et al. (1957), *Population Redistribution and Economic Growth, United States 1870–1950, Vol. 1, Methodological Considerations and Reference Tables*, Philadelphia: American Philosophical Society.

Leff, N. H. (1992), "Economic Development in Brazil, 1822–1913," First Boston Working Paper FB-92-02, Columbia University.

Lewis, W. A. (1954), "Economic Development with Unlimited Supplies of Labour," *Manchester School of Economic and Social Studies* 22: 139–91.

——(1978), *The Evolution of the International Economic Order*, Princeton, N.J.: Princeton University Press.

Lieberman, S. (1970), *The Industrialization of Norway 1800–1920*, Oslo: Engers Boktrykkeri.

Lindert, P. H. (1978), *Fertility and Scarcity in America*, Princeton, N.J.: Princeton University Press.

Livi-Bacci, M. (1961), *L'Immigrazione e l'Assimilazione degli Italiani negli Stati Uniti secondo le Statistiche Demografiche Americane*, Milan: Giuffre.

——(1977), *A History of Italian Fertility During the Last Two Centuries*, Princeton, N.J.: Princeton University Press.

——(1989), *A Concise History of World Population*, Cambridge, Mass.: Blackwell.

Ljungmark, L. (1992), "The Push- and Pull- Factors Behind the Swedish Emigration to America, Canada and Australia," in P. C. Emmer and M. Morner (eds.), *European Expansion and Migration*, Oxford: Berg, 79–103.

Lowell, B. L. (1987), *Scandinavian Exodus: Demography and Social Development of 19th Century Rural Communities*, Boulder, Col.: Westview Press.

MacDonald, J. S. (1963), "Agricultural Organisation, Migration and Labour Militancy in Rural Italy," *Economic History Review* 15: 61–75.

MacKinnon, M. (1987), "English Poor Law Policy and the Crusade Against Outrelief," *Journal of Economic History* 47: 603–26.

Mack-Smith, D. (1969), *Italy: A Modern History*, Ann Arbor, Mich.: Arno Press.

Maddison, A. (1982), *Phases of Capitalist Development*, New York: Oxford University Press.

——(1989), *The World Economy in the 20th Century*, Paris: OECD.

——(1991), *Dynamic Forces in Capitalist Development*, New York: Oxford University Press.

——(1993), "Standardized Estimates of Fixed Capital Stock: A Six Country Comparison," in R. Zoboli (ed.), *Essays on Innovation, Natural Resources and the International Economy*, Milan: Montedison, 3–27.

Magnussen, O., and G. Siqveland (1978), "Migration from Norway to the U.S.A. 1866–1914: The Use of Econometric Methods in Analyzing Historical Data," *Scandinavian Journal of Economics* 80: 34–52.

Mankiw, N. G., D. Romer, and D. N. Weil (1992), "A Contribution to the Empirics of Economic Growth," *Quarterly Journal of Economics* 107: 407–37.

Marshall, A. (1973), *The Import of Labour: The Case of the Netherlands*, Rotterdam: Rotterdam University Press.

Massey, D. S. (1988), "Economic Development and International Migration in Comparative Perspective," *Population and Development Review* 14: 383–413.

Massey, D. S., J. Arango, G. Hugo, A. Kouaouci, A. Pellegrino, and J. E. Taylor (1993), "Theories of International Migration: A Review and Appraisal," *Population and Development Review* 19: 431–66.

——(1994), "An Evaluation of International Migration Theory: The North American Case," *Population and Development Review* 20: 699–751.

Maurette, F., and E. Siewers (1937), "Immigration and Settlement in Brazil, Argentina and Uruguay: I," *International Labour Review* 32: 215–47.

McCloskey, D. N. (1970), "Did Victorian Britain Fail?" *Economic History Review*, 2nd series, 23: 446–59.

McDonald, J., and R. Schlomowitz (1990), "Mortality on Immigrant Voyages to Australia in the 19th Century," *Explorations in Economic History* 27: 84–113.

McGouldrick, P. F., and M. B. Tannen (1977), "Did American Manufacturers Discriminate Against Immigrants before 1914?" *Journal of Economic History* 37: 723–46.

McInnis, M. (1994), "Immigration and Emigration: Canada in the Late Nineteenth Century," in T. J. Hatton and J. G. Williamson (eds.), *Migration and the International Labor Market 1850–1939*, London: Routledge, 139–55.

Merrick, T. W., and D. H. Graham (1979), *Population and Economic Development in Brazil*, Baltimore, Md.: Johns Hopkins University Press.

Michigan Bureau of Labor and Industrial Statistics (1891), *8th Annual Report*, Lansing, Michigan.

Miller, K. A. (1985), *Emigrants and Exiles: Ireland and the Irish Exodus to North America*, New York: Oxford University Press.

——(1991), "Emigration as Exile: Cultural Hegemony in Post-Famine Ireland," in R. J. Vecoli and S. M. Sinke (eds.), *A Century of European Migrations 1830–1930*, Urbana: University of Illinois Press, 339–63.

Mitchell, B. R. (1980), *European Historical Statistics, 1750–1975*, 2nd ed., New York: Facts on File.

————(1983), *International Historical Statistics: The Americas and Australasia*, Detroit, Mich.: Gale Research.

————(1988), *British Historical Statistics*, Cambridge: Cambridge University Press.

————(1992), *International Historical Statistics: Europe 1750-1988*, 3rd ed., New York: Stockton Press.

Mitchell, B. R., and P. Deane (1962), *Abstract of British Historical Statistics*, Cambridge: Cambridge University Press.

Moe, T. (1970), *Demographic Developments and Economic Growth in Norway 1740-1940: An Econometric Study*, Ann Arbor, Mich.: University Microfilms.

Mokyr, J. (1980), "The Deadly Fungus: An Econometric Investigation into the Short-Term Demographic Impact of the Irish Famine," *Research in Population Economics* 2: 237-77.

————(1983), *Why Ireland Starved: A Quantitative and Analytical History of the Irish Economy, 1800-1850*, London: George Allen and Unwin.

Molinas, C., and L. Prados (1989), "Was Spain Different? Spanish Historical Backwardness Revisited," *Explorations in Economic History* 26: 385-402.

Moreda, V. P. (1987), "Spain's Demographic Modernization, 1800-1930," in N. Sanchez-Albornoz (ed.), *The Economic Modernization of Spain, 1830-1930*, New York: New York University Press, 13-41.

Mortara, G. (1913), "Numeri Indici dello Stato e Progresso Economico delle Regioni Italiane," *Giornale degli Economisti e Revista di Statistica* 47: 17-29.

Mulla, T. (1985), "The Economic Effects of Immigration," in N. Glazer (ed.), *Clamor at the Gates: The New American Immigration*, San Franscico: ICS Press.

Murphy, K. M., and F. Welch (1990), "Empirical Age-Earnings Profiles," *Journal of Labor Economics* 8: 202-29.

Neal, L. (1985), "Integration of International Capital Markets: Quantitative Evidence from the Eighteenth to Twentieth Centuries," *Journal of Economic History* 50: 219-26.

————(1990), *The Rise of Financial Capitalism: International Capital Markets in the Age of Reason*, Cambridge: Cambridge University Press.

Neal, L., and P. Uselding (1972), "Immigration: A Neglected Source of American Economic Growth: 1790-1912," *Oxford Economic Papers* 24: 68-88.

Nelli, H. S. (1983), *From Immigrants to Ethnics: The Italian Americans*, New York: Oxford University Press.

Nelson, R. R., and G. Wright (1992), "The Rise and Fall of American Technological Leadership," *Journal of Economic Literature* 30: 1931-64.

Norman, H. (1976), "The Causes of Emigration: An Attempt at Multivariate Analysis," in H. Rundblom and H. Norman (eds.), *From Sweden to America: A History of the Migration*, Minneapolis: University of Minnesota Press, 149-64.

Norstrom, T. (1988), "Swedish Emigrations to the United States Reconsidered," *European Sociological Review*, 4: 223-31.

North, D. C. (1958), "Ocean Freight Rates and Economic Development 1750-1913," *Journal of Economic History* 18: 538-55.

————(1960), "The United States Balance of Payments, 1790-1860," in *Trends in the American Economy in the Nineteenth Century*, Studies in Income and Wealth, Vol. 24, New York: National Bureau of Economic Research, 573-627.

Nugent, W. (1992), *Crossings: The Great Transatlantic Migrations, 1840-1914*, Bloomington: University of Indiana Press.

Nunes, A. B., E. Mata, and N. Valerio (1989), "Portuguese Economic Growth, 1833-1985," *Journal of European Economic History* 18: 292-95.

O'Brien P. K., and G. Toniolo (1991), "The Poverty of Italy and the Backwardness of its

Agriculture before 1914," in B. M. S. Campbell and M. Overton (eds.), *Land, Labour and Livestock: Historical Studies in European Agricultural Productivity*, Manchester: Manchester University Press, 385–409.

Obstfeld, M. (1994), "International Capital Mobility in the 1990s," International Finance Discussion Paper No. 472, Board of Governors of the Federal Reserve System.

O'Connell, P. (1993), "Puts and Calls on the Irish Sea: An Option Theory Model of Emigration," mimeo., Department of Economics, Harvard University.

Ó Gráda, C. (1975), "A Note on Nineteenth Century Emigration Statistics," *Population Studies* 29: 143–49.

———(1977), "Some Aspects of Nineteenth Century Irish Emigration," in L. M. Cullen and T. C. Smout (eds.), *Comparative Aspects of Scottish and Irish Social History, 1600–1900*, Edinburgh: John Donald, 65–73.

———(1980a), "Irish Emigration to the United States in the Nineteenth Century," in D. N. Doyle and O. D. Edwards (eds.), *America and Ireland 1776–1976*, Westport, Conn.: Greenwood Press, 93–103.

———(1980b), "Primogeniture and Ultimogeniture in Rural Ireland," *Journal of Interdisciplinary History* 10: 491–97.

———(1988), *Ireland Before and After the Famine: Explorations in Economic History, 1800–1925*, New York: Manchester University Press.

———(1994), *Ireland 1780–1939: A New Economic History*, Oxford: Oxford University Press.

Ó Gráda, C., and K. H. O'Rourke (1997), "Migration as Disaster Relief: Evidence from the Great Irish Famine," *European Review of Economic History* 1: 3–25.

O'Rourke, K. H. (1990), "Agricultural Change and Rural Depopulation: Ireland 1845–1876," Ph.D. dissertation, Harvard University.

———(1991), "Rural Depopulation in a Small Open Economy: Ireland 1856–1876," *Explorations in Economic History* 28: 409–32.

———(1992), "Why Ireland Emigrated: A Positive Theory of Factor Flows," *Oxford Economic Papers* 44: 322–41.

O'Rourke, K. H., A. M. Taylor, and J. G. Williamson (1996), "Factor Price Convergence in the Late 19th Century," *International Economic Review* 37: 499–530.

O'Rourke, K. H., and J. G. Williamson (1994), "Late 19th Century Anglo-American Factor Price Convergence: Were Heckscher and Ohlin Right?" *Journal of Economic History* 54: 892–916.

———(1995), "Open Economy Forces and Late 19th Century Swedish Catch-Up: A Quantitative Accounting," *Scandinavian Economic History Review* 43: 171–203.

———(1996), "Education, Globalization and Catch-Up: Scandinavia in the Swedish Mirror," *Scandinavian Economic History Review* 43: 287–309.

———(1997), "Around the European Periphery 1870–1913: Globalization, Schooling and Growth," *European Review of Economic History* 1: 153–90.

———(ongoing), *Globalization and History*.

O'Rourke, K. H., J. G. Williamson, and T. J. Hatton (1994), "Mass Migration, Commodity Market Integration and Real Wage Convergence: The Late-Nineteenth-Century Atlantic Economy," in T. J. Hatton and J. G. Williamson (eds.), *Migration and the International Labor Market, 1850–1939*, London: Routledge, 203–20.

Persson, K. G. (1993), "Introduction," in K. G. Persson (ed.), *The Economic Development of Denmark and Norway since 1870*, Aldershot, England.: Elgar.

Piore, M. J. (1979), *Birds of Passage: Migrant Labor and Industrial Societies*, Cambridge: Cambridge University Press.

Pollard, S. (1978), "Labour in Great Britain," in P. Mathias and M. M. Postan (eds.), *The Cambridge Economic History of Europe: Volume 7: The Industrial Economies: Capital, Labour, and Enterprise*, Part 1, Cambridge: Cambridge University Press, 97–179.

——(1981), *Peaceful Conquest: The Industrialization of Europe 1760–1970*, Oxford: Oxford University Press.

Pope, D. (1968), "Empire Migration to Canada, Australia and New Zealand, 1910–1929," *Australian Economic Papers* 7: 167–88.

——(1976), "The Push-Pull Model of Australian Migration," *Australian Economic History Review* 14: 144–52.

——(1981a), "Modelling the Peopling of Australia, 1900–1930," *Australian Economic Papers* 20: 258–81.

——(1981b), "Contours of Australian Immigration 1901–30," *Australian Economic History Review* 21: 29–52.

——(1985), "Some Factors Inhibiting Australian Immigration in the 1920s," *Australian Economic History Review* 25: 34–52.

Pope, D., and G. Withers (1993), "Do Migrants Rob Jobs? Lessons from Australian History, 1861–1991," *Journal of Economic History* 53: 719–42.

——(1994), "Wage Effects of Immigration in Late-Nineteenth-Century Australia," in T. J. Hatton and J. G. Williamson (eds.), *Migration and the International Labor Market, 1850–1939*, London: Routledge, 240–62.

Power, J. (1979), *Migrant Workers in Western Europe and the United States*, Oxford: Pergamon Press.

Prados de la Escosura, L., T. Sanchez, and J. Oliva (1993), "De Te Fabula Narratur? Growth, Structural Change and Convergence in Europe, 19th and 20th Centuries," Working Paper No. D-93009, Madrid: Ministerio de Economia y Hacienda.

Quah, D. (1993), "Galton's Fallacy and Tests of the Convergence Hypothesis," *Scandinavian Journal of Economics* 95: 427–43.

Quigley, J. M. (1972), "An Economic Model of Swedish Emigration," *Quarterly Journal of Economics* 86: 111–26.

Ramella, F. (1991), "Emigration from an Area of Intense Industrial Development: The Case of Northwestern Italy," in R. J. Vecoli and S. M. Sinke (eds.), *A Century of European Migrations, 1830–1930*, Urbana: University of Illinois Press, 261–74.

Rees, A. (1961), *Real Wages in Manufacturing 1900–1914*, Princeton, N.J.: National Bureau of Economic Research.

Richardson, H. W. (1972), "British Emigration and Overseas Investment, 1870–1914," *Economic History Review* 25: 99–113.

Richardson, J. D. (1995), "Income Inequality and Trade: How to Think, What to Conclude," *Journal of Economic Perspectives* 9: 33–55.

Riis, C., and T. Thonstad (1989), "A Counterfactual Study of Economic Impacts of Norwegian Emigration and Capital Imports," in I. Gordon and A. P. Thirlwall (eds.), *European Factor Mobility: Trends and Consequences*, London: Macmillan, 116–32.

Robbins, D. (1996), "Trade, Trade Liberalization and Inequality in Latin America and East Asia—Synthesis of Seven Countries," Harvard Institute for International Development, mimeo.

Rogers, R. (1985), *Guests Come To Stay: The Effects of European Labor Migration on Sending and Receiving Countries*, Boulder, Col.: Westview Press.

Romer, C. D. (1986a), "Spurious Volatility in Historical Unemployment Data," *Journal of Political Economy* 94: 1–37.

————(1986b), "New Estimates of Prewar Gross National Product and Unemployment," *Journal of Economic History* 46: 341–52.

————(1989), "The Prewar Business Cycle Reconsidered: New Estimates of Gross National Product, 1869–1908," *Journal of Political Economy* 97: 1–37.

Romer, P. (1986), "Increasing Returns and Long-Run Growth," *Journal of Political Economy* 94: 1002–37.

————(1989), "Capital Accumulation in the Theory of Long-Run Growth," in R. J. Barro (ed.), *Modern Business Cycle Theory*, Cambridge, Mass.: Harvard University Press, 51–127.

Rosenbloom, J. L. (1990), "One Market or Many? Labor Market Integration in Late Nineteenth Century United States," *Journal of Economic History* 50: 85–107.

————(1996), "Was There a National Labor Market at the End of the Century? New Evidence on Earnings in Manufacturing," *Journal of Economic History* 56: 626–56.

Rundblom, H., and H. Norman (eds.) (1976), *From Sweden to America: A History of the Migration*, Minneapolis: University of Minnesota Press.

Rutherford, T. (1988), *General Equilibrium Modelling with MPS/GE*, Department of Economics, University of Western Ontario, Canada.

Sachs, J. (1980), "The Changing Cyclical Behavior of Wages and Prices, 1890–1976," *American Economic Review* 70: 78–90.

Samuelson, P. A. (1948), "International Trade and the Equalisation of Factor Prices," *Economic Journal* 58: 163–84.

Sanchez-Alonso, B. (1995), *Las Causas de la Emigración Española, 1880–1930*, Madrid: Alianza Universidad.

Sandberg, L. G. (1979), "The Case of the Impoverished Sophisticate: Human Capital and Swedish Economic Growth Before World War I," *Journal of Economic History* 39: 225–41.

Schrier, A. (1958), *Ireland and the American Emigration, 1850–1900*, Minneapolis: University of Minnesota Press.

Scott, F. D. (1960), "The Study of the Effects of Emigration," *Scandinavian Economic History Review* 8: 161–74.

Semmingsen, I. (1960), "Norwegian Emigration in the Nineteenth Century," *Scandinavian Economic History Review* 8: 150–60.

————(1972), "Emigration from Scandinavia," *Scandinavian Economic History Review* 20: 45–60.

Shlakman, V. (1953), "Migration and Labor," (Review of *The Uprooted* by O. Handlin), *Journal of Economic History* 13: 241–44.

Shoven, J. B., and J. Whalley (1984), "Applied General Equilibrium Models of Taxation and International Trade: An Introduction and Survey," *Journal of Economic Literature* 22: 1007–51.

————(1992), *Applying General Equilibrium*, Cambridge: Cambridge University Press.

Shughart, W. F., R. D. Tollison, and M. S. Kimenyi (1986), "The Political Economy of Immigration Restrictions," *Yale Journal on Regulation* 4: 71–97.

Simon, M. (1967), "The Pattern of New British Portfolio Foreign Investment, 1865–1914," in J. H. Adler (ed.), *Capital Movements and Economic Development*, London: Macmillan, 33–70.

Simon, J. L. (1989), *The Economic Consequences of Immigration*, Cambridge, Mass.: Blackwell.

Sjaastad, L. (1962), "The Costs and Returns of Human Migration," *Journal of Political Economy* 70: 80–93.

Solow, R. (1957), "Technical Change and the Aggregate Production Function," *Review of Economics and Statistics* 39: 312–20.

Sori, E. (1979), *L'Emigrazione Italiana dall'Unita alla Seconda Guerra Mondiale*, Bologna: Il Mulino.

Straubhaar, T. (1988), *On the Economics of International Labor Migration*, Bern: Verlag Paul Haupt.

Summers, R., and A. Heston (1991), "The Penn World Table (Mark 5): An Expanded Set of International Comparisons, 1950–1988," *Quarterly Journal of Economics* 106: 327–68.

Sundstrom, W. A., and J. L. Rosenbloom (1993), "Occupational Differences in the Dispersion of Wages and Working Hours: Labor Market Integration in the United States, 1890–1913," *Journal of Economic History* 53: 379–408.

Surace, S. J. (1966), *Ideology, Economic Change and the Working Classes: The Case of Italy*, Berkeley: University of California Press.

Swierenga, R. P. (1976), "Dutch International Migration and Occupational Change: A Structural Analysis of Multinational Linked Files," in I. A. Glazier and L. de Rosa (eds.), *Migration Across Time and Nations*, New York: Holmes and Meier, 95–124.

———(1991), "Local Patterns of Dutch Migration to the United States in the Mid-Nineteenth Century," in R. J. Vecoli and S. M. Sinke (eds.), *A Century of European Migrations, 1830–1930*, Urbana: University of Illinois Press, 134–57.

Taylor, A. M. (1992a), "Argentine Economic Growth in Comparative Perspective," Ph.D. dissertation, Harvard University.

———(1992b), "External Dependence, Demographic Burdens and Argentine Economic Decline After the Belle Epoque," *Journal of Economic History* 52: 907–36.

———(1994), "Mass Migration to Distant Southern Shores: Argentina and Australia, 1870–1939," in T. J. Hatton and J. G. Williamson (eds.), *Migration and the International Labor Market, 1850–1939*, London: Routledge, 91–115.

———(1995), "Peopling the Pampa: On the Impact of Mass Imigration to the River Plate, 1870–1914," *NBER Historical Paper* No. 68, National Bureau of Economic Research, Cambridge, Mass.

Taylor, A. M., and J. G. Williamson (1994), "Capital Flows to the New World as an Intergenerational Transfer," *Journal of Political Economy* 102: 348–71.

———(1997), "Convergence in the Age of Mass Migration," *European Review of Economic History* 1: 27–63.

Temin, P. (1966), "Labor Scarcity and the Problem of American Industrial Efficiency in the 1850s," *Journal of Economic History* 26: 277–98.

Thernstrom, S. (1973), *The Other Bostonians: Poverty and Progress in the American Metropolis, 1880–1970*, Cambridge, Mass.: Harvard University Press.

Thistlethwaite, F. (1960), "Migration from Europe Overseas in the Nineteenth and Twentieth Centuries," reprinted in R. J. Vecoli and S. M. Sinke (eds.), *A Century of European Migrations, 1830–1930*, Urbana: University of Illinois Press (1991), 17–57.

Thomas, B. (1954), *Migration and Economic Growth*, Cambridge: Cambridge University Press.

———(1972), *Migration and Urban Development*, London: Methuen.

Thomas, D. S. (1941), *Social and Economic Aspects of Swedish Population Movements*, New York: Macmillan.

Thomas, M. (1987), "General Equilibrium Models and Research in Economic History," in A. Field (ed.), *The Future of Economic History*, Boston: Kluwer-Nijhoff, 121–183.

Thompson, W. S., and P. K. Whelpton (1933), *Population Trends in the United States*, New York, McGraw-Hill.

Timmer, A., and J. G. Williamson (1996), "Racism, Xenophobia or Markets? The Political Economy of Immigration Policy Prior to the Thirties," *NBER Working Paper* No. 5867. National Bureau of Economic Research, Cambridge, Mass. (December).

Todaro, M. P. (1969), "A Model of Labor Migration and Urban Unemployment in Less Developed Countries," *American Economic Review* 59: 138–48.

Tomaske, J. A. (1971), "The Determinants of Intercountry Differences in European Emigration, 1881–1900," *Journal of Economic History* 31: 840–53.

Turner, M. (1987), "Towards an Agricultural Price Index for Ireland 1850–1914," *Economic and Social Review* 18: 123–36.

——(1991), "Agricultural Output and Productivity in Post-Famine Ireland," in B. M. S. Campbell and M. Overton (eds.), *Land, Labour and Livestock: Historical Studies in European Agricultural Productivity*, Manchester: Manchester University Press, 410–38.

Tyrrell, I. (1991), "American Exceptionalism in an Age of International History," *American Historical Review* 96: 1031–55.

United States Immigration Commission (1911), *Reports*, 61st Congress, 3rd Session. Washington, D.C.: Government Printing Office.

United States Industrial Commission (1901), *Reports*, Vol. 15, 57th Congress, 1st Session. Washington, D.C.: Government Printing Office.

Urquhart, M. C. (1986), "New Estimates of Gross National Product, Canada, 1870–1926: Some Implications for Canadian Development," in S. L. Engerman and R. E. Gallman (eds.), *Long Term Factors in American Economic Growth*, Chicago: University of Chicago Press, 9–94.

Uselding, P. (1971), "Conjectural Estimates of Gross Human Capital Inflow to the American Economy," *Explorations in Economic History* 9: 49–61.

Vernon, J. R. (1994), "Unemployment Rates in Post-Bellum America: 1869–1899," *Journal of Macroeconomics* 16: 701–14.

Walker, M. (1964), *Germany and the Emigration, 1816–1885*, Cambridge, Mass.: Harvard University Press.

Weir, D. R. (1986), "The Reliability of Historical Macroeconomic Data for Comparing Cyclical Instability," *Journal of Economic History* 46: 353–65.

——(1992), "A Century of U.S. Unemployment, 1890–1990: Revised Estimates and Evidence for Stabilization," *Research in Economic History* 14: 301–46.

Wicksell, K. (1882), *Om utvandringen: Dess betydelse och orsaker*, Stockholm: Albert Bonniers Forlag.

Wilkinson, M. (1970), "European Migration to the United States: An Econometric Analysis of Aggregate Labor Supply and Demand," *Review of Economics and Statistics* 52: 272–9.

Williamson, J. G. (1964), *American Growth and the Balance of Payments, 1820–1913: A Study of the Long Swing*, Chapel Hill, N.C.: University of North Carolina Press.

——(1965), "Regional Inequality and the Process of National Development: A Description of the Process," *Economic Development and Cultural Change* 13: 3–84.

——(1974a), "Migration to the New World: Long Term Influences and Impact," *Explorations in Economic History* 11: 357–90.

——(1974b), *Late Nineteenth-Century American Development*, Cambridge: Cambridge University Press.

——(1980), "Unbalanced Growth, Inequality and Regional Development: Some Lessons from American History," in V. Arnold (ed.), *Alternatives to Confrontation: A National Policy Towards Regional Change*, Lexington, Mass.: D.C. Heath, 3–61.

——(1982), "Immigrant-Inequality Trade Offs in the Promised Land: Income Distribution and Absorptive Capacity Prior to the Quotas," in B. Chiswick (ed.), *The Gateway: U.S. Immigration Issues and Policies*, Washington, D.C.: American Enterprise Institute, 251–88.

——(1986), "The Impact of the Irish on British Labor Markets During the Industrial Revolution," *Journal of Economic History* 46: 693–720.

——(1988), "Migrant Selectivity, Urbanization, and Industrial Revolutions," *Population and Development Review* 14: 287–314.

——(1990), *Coping with City Growth During the British Industrial Revolution*, Cambridge: Cambridge University Press.

——(1991), *Inequality, Poverty, and History: The Kuznets Memorial Lectures*, Oxford: Basil Blackwell.

——(1994), "Economic Convergence: Placing Post-Famine Ireland in Comparative Perspective," *Irish Economic and Social History* 20: 1–24.

——(1995), "The Evolution of Global Labor Markets Since 1830: Background Evidence and Hypotheses," *Explorations in Economic History* 32: 141–96.

——(1996), "Globalization, Convergence and History," *Journal of Economic History* 56: 277–306.

——(1997), "Globalization and Inequality, Past and Present," *World Bank Research Observer* 12: 117–35.

Williamson, J. G., and P. H. Lindert (1980), *American Inequality: A Macroeconomic History*, New York: Academic Press.

Winter, J. M. (1985), *The Great War and the British People*, London: Macmillan.

Wolff, E. N. (1991), "Capital Formation and Productivity Convergence Over the Long Term," *American Economic Review* 81: 565–79.

Wood, A. (1994), *North-South Trade, Employment and Inequality: Changing Fortunes in a Skill-Driven World*, Oxford: Clarendon Press.

——(1995a), "How Trade Hurt Unskilled Workers," *Journal of Economic Perspectives* 9: 57–80.

——(1995b), "Does Trade Reduce Wage Inequality in Developing Countries?" mimeograph, Sussex, England: Institute of Development Studies.

Wright, G. (1986), *Old South, New South*, New York: Basic Books.

——(1990), "The Origins of American Industrial Success, 1879–1940," *American Economic Review* 80: 651–68.

Wrigley, E. A., and R. S. Schofield (1981), *The Population History of England: A Reconstruction*, Cambridge, Mass.: Harvard University Press.

Zamagni, V. (1978), *Industrializzazione e Squilibri Regionali in Italia*, Bologna: Il Mulino.

——(1993), *The Economic History of Italy 1860–1990*, Oxford: Clarendon Press.

Zelinsky, W. (1971), "The Hypothesis of the Mobility Transition," *Geographical Review* 61: 219–49.

Zevin, R. B. (1992), "Are World Financial Markets More Open? If So Why and With What Effects?" in T. Banuri and J. Schor (eds.), *Financial Openness and National Autonomy*, Oxford: Oxford University Press, 43–83.

Zunz, O. (1982), *The Changing Face of Inequality: Industrial Development and Immigrants in Detroit, 1880–1920*, Chicago: University of Chicago Press.

Index